# KNIGHTS OF THE GOLDEN CIRCLE

## CONFLICTING WORLDS

*New Dimensions of the American Civil War*

T. Michael Parrish, Series Editor

# KNIGHTS OF THE
# GOLDEN CIRCLE

## SECRET EMPIRE, SOUTHERN SECESSION, CIVIL WAR

### DAVID C. KEEHN

LOUISIANA STATE UNIVERSITY PRESS )(( BATON ROUGE

Published by Louisiana State University Press
Copyright © 2013 by David C. Keehn
All rights reserved
Manufactured in the United States of America
First printing

Designer: Barbara Neely Bourgoyne
Typefaces: Giza Condensed Display Rough, Alternate Gothic No. 2, and MillerText
Printer: McNaughton & Gunn, Inc.
Binder: Dekker Bookbinding

Library of Congress Cataloging-in-Publication Data
Keehn, David C.
  Knights of the Golden Circle : secret empire, southern secession, Civil War / David C. Keehn.
      p. cm.
Includes bibliographical references and index.
ISBN 978-0-8071-5004-7 (cloth : alk. paper) — ISBN 978-0-8071-5005-4 (pdf ) — ISBN
978-0-8071-5006-1 (epub) — ISBN 978-0-8071-5007-8 (mobi)  1.  Knights of the Golden
Circle—History. 2.  Secret societies—United States—History—19th century. 3.  Secession—
Southern States—History—19th century. 4.  Government, Resistance to—United States—
History—19th century. 5.  United States—History—Civil War, 1861–1865—Societies, etc.
6.  United States—History—Civil War, 1861–1865—Underground movements. I. Title.
  E458.8.K44 2013
  973.7'13—dc23
                                                                                2012027974

# CONTENTS

List of Illustrations ...................................................... vii

Prologue: The Shadowy Knights ....................................... 1

1. Powerful Antecedents ............................................ 6

2. Formal Organization .............................................. 17

3. The Drive for Mexico ............................................. 32

4. A Regional Coalition ............................................. 46

5. Transforming to Secession ..................................... 62

6. The Paramilitary's Core ......................................... 77

7. Seizure of Federal Forts and Arsenals ...................... 89

8. The Plot to Seize the District of Columbia ................. 100

9. Rustling Texas Out of the Union .............................. 113

10. Spreading Secession ............................................ 127

11. Call to Arms ...................................................... 140

12. The Struggle for Kentucky ..................................... 156

13. A Rejuvenated KGC? ............................................ 171

Epilogue ............................................................ 185

Acknowledgments ................................................. 191

Notes ............................................................... 193

Bibliography ....................................................... 261

Index ............................................................... 291

# ILLUSTRATIONS

Knights of the Golden Circle commission for Robert Harris Archer

Ben McCulloch

George W. L. Bickley

"Theory, Practice, Effect" engraving

John Wilkes Booth

Elkanah Bracken Greer

Paul Jones Semmes

Virginius Despeaux Groner

Cypriano Ferrandini

Group portrait of Richmond Grays at Harpers Ferry

Robert Charles Tyler

Louis T. Wigfall

Henry Alexander Wise

George Washington Chilton

*Illustrations follow page 112*

# THE SHADOWY KNIGHTS

S EVERAL STOCK ACTORS from Richmond's Dramatic Star Company joined a secret society that was spreading across the country during the summer of 1859. Called the Knights of the Golden Circle (KGC), it was dedicated to promoting southern rights and expanding American hegemony over the "Golden Circle" region that encompassed the Caribbean islands, Central America, and Mexico. Among the new recruits was a strikingly handsome twenty-year-old cast member from Maryland—John Wilkes Booth—whose now-deceased father was a theatrical icon. The Knights offered Booth, like other young men on the make, the chance for military adventure and foreign treasure wrapped up in the knightly mystique made popular by Sir Walter Scott. Growing up in Maryland, Booth had attended a military academy and been a member of the Know-Nothing Party. He relished involvement in secret societies as well as the chivalric code and military trappings.[1]

Young Booth (who, to assert his independence, went by the name "Wilkes") had been hired into the Richmond acting company of George Kunkel and John T. Ford in 1858 through the intervention of his well-known thespian brother Edwin. Wilkes had been welcomed into the upper echelons of Richmond society and basked in the gracious southern hospitality. By the summer of 1859, he was running around with similar high-spirited young men from the very best Richmond families, who were also enamored of chivalric mystique and military display. Many of them belonged to local militia units such as the prestigious Richmond Blues, whose members included Obadiah Jennings Wise, the rambunctious son of Virginia's then-sitting governor.[2]

Over the next few years, Wilkes Booth would rise to become a prominent leader in the Knights. He would draw on his KGC connections to obtain special access and favors that, among other things, enabled him to witness the hanging of the abolitionist zealot John Brown at Harpers Ferry. During the Civil War, he would rely on his knightly brothers for help in carrying out clandestine smuggling operations on behalf of the South. At the end of the war, he would seek their assistance in carrying out his audacious plan to remove the American president.

The Knights were a militant oath-bound secret society dedicated to promoting southern rights (including slavery) and extending American hegemony over the Golden Circle region. Membership was open to all southern men of good character as well as northern men who stood by the constitutional claims of the South. KGC recruiters told membership candidates, like Booth, that the society was dedicated to expansion southward and protecting constitutional liberties from the ravages of abolitionists and "Black Republicans." But the higher degrees of the society were pledged to a further secret proslavery and empire-building agenda that was not fully shared with the lower degrees.[3] By formulating their rituals around the real-world goals of Southern Hemisphere conquest and southern rights, the Knights were most like the revolutionary secret societies operating in Europe, such as "Young Italy" headed by Giuseppe Mazzini, which was dedicated to the reunification of Italy through insurrectionary action.[4]

Booth likely initially joined the First, or military, Degree, referred to as the "Knights of the Iron Hand." This included the rank-and-file of the KGC's army, which in 1859 was reported to number around seven thousand. The smaller Second Degree, known as the "Knights of the True Faith," was the commercial and financial division dedicated to raising funds and providing the Knights' army with logistical support including ammunition, horses, and other supplies. At the top of the hierarchy was the Third, or governing, Degree, known as the "Knights of the Columbian Star." This degree established laws, policies, and overall objectives for the KGC and then passed them down to lower-degree members, who had sworn an oath to obey. Much of the Third Degree's controversial ritual was kept oral, and its membership (which included loosely affiliated politicians) was not even disclosed to those in the lower two degrees.[5]

Knights in a given area were organized into a lodge called a "castle" that often met at a local meeting hall, barn, or warehouse such as those along the Richmond waterfront. A sentinel guarded the entrance to prevent unauthorized intrusion, and members were required to supply the password for entry. The regular castle meeting began with a prayer by the chaplain. The treasurer then collected dues, part of which was forwarded to the KGC's national headquarters. Following this, the captain entertained new business and gave a fifteen-minute pep talk, filled with pro-expansion and southern-rights rhetoric, to fire up the attendees. At the end of the meeting, the Knights of the military order engaged in drill, supervised by the captain or another drillmaster.[6]

Once qualified, prospective members like Booth and his actor friends were escorted into the castle's regular meeting and inducted through an oath-swearing ceremony led by the captain. This oath required the inductee to keep secret the Knights' codes, rituals, and undertakings; bear true allegiance to the Knights as a body and its superior officers; and extend the order and help put the KGC army in the field.[7] Once inducted, the new members received the KGC's signs, grips, and passwords, which allowed Knights to be known to each other.[8]

In some areas, a secret "Council of Thirteen" served as the governing board for the local castles. This included the top leaders of the lower two degrees and Third Degree political members.[9] The KGC in the United States was referred to in its rules as the "American Legion." The KGC's founder, George Bickley, claimed that there was a counterpart KGC organization in Mexico.[10]

As the secession crisis deepened, the structure and power center of the Knights shifted from Bickley to a decentralized network of KGC state regimental commanders. These were loosely coordinated by roving KGC emissaries and backed by affiliated southern editors and politicians. In late 1860, these state regimental commanders shifted the thrust of the Knights' efforts from colonization in the Southern Hemisphere to supporting the more radical southern governors in their drive toward secession. At this point, the Knights became the strong arm of secession in many areas by promoting disunion through public meetings and political action and by intimidating countervailing voices into silence. As Horace Greeley, the Republican owner/editor of the *New York Tribune,* later charged:

> Before the opening of 1861, a perfect reign of terror had been established throughout the Gulf States. A secret order, known as "Knights of the Golden Circle," or as "Knights of the Columbian Star," succeeding that known, six or seven years earlier, as the "Order of the Lone Star," having for its ostensible object the acquisition of Cuba, Mexico, and Central America, and the establishment of Slavery in the two latter, but really operating in the interest of Disunion, had spread its network of lodges, grips, passwords, and alluring mystery, all over the South, and had ramifications even in some of the cities of the adjoining Free States. Other clubs, more or less secret, were known as "The Precipitators," "Vigilante Committee," "Minute Men," and by kindred designations; but all of them were sworn to fidelity to "Southern Rights"; while their members were gradually prepared and ripened, wherever any ripening was needed, for the task of treason. Whoever ventured to condemn and repudiate Secession as the true and sovereign remedy for Southern wrongs, in any neighborhood where Slavery was dominant, was henceforth a marked man, to be stigmatized and hunted down as a "Lincolnite," "Submissionist," or "Abolitionist."[11]

During the early years of the Civil War, disaffected members of the KGC anonymously published widely circulated exposés that made a variety of sensational yet plausible claims. They charged that southern-rights members of the cabinet of Abraham Lincoln's predecessor, James Buchanan, were KGC members, including Vice President John Breckinridge and Secretary of War John Floyd. They said that the Knights were behind the 1860 splintering of the Democratic Party and that the secret society had helped precipitate a number of the southern and Border States into secession. They alleged that the Knights spearheaded a clandestine conspiracy to capture the federal forts and arsenals in the South, seize the nation's capital, and prevent the inauguration of a "Black Republican" president.[12] Later, the Knights were alleged to have orchestrated Lincoln's assassination and to have buried caches of gold so that the South could rise again.[13] This book will compare these allegations to the actual evidence as well as credible sources in order to explore their veracity.

Verifying claims regarding the Knights is sometimes difficult. They were, after all, a secret society, particularly at the upper level at which policy was established and where communications were generally oral. The KGC's front man, George Bickley, was known to exaggerate and fabricate, especially in his post-1862 accounts from prison. After May 1860, the Knights were decentralized and emerged as a loosely coordinated affiliation of state regimental commanders who did not always act uniformly. In addition, much documentation was destroyed when the Union government charged the KGC with treason and arrested their northern and Border State leaders during the Civil War.

Fortunately, sufficient primary-source material does still exist to piece together a credible account. The files at the National Archives, captured from Bickley, disclose the KGC's origins and intentions during the late 1859–late 1860 period when the secret society was more transparent. There are also many contemporaneous newspaper articles, diaries of some participants, and other firsthand accounts contained in Civil War–era archives across the country.

The sagas of the KGC's state regimental commanders also provide a good indicator as to what really happened. This book focuses on four of them who ultimately became Confederate generals or colonels: Texas's Elkanah Bracken Greer, Georgia's Paul Jones Semmes, Maryland's Robert Charles Tyler, and Virginius Despeaux Groner from the Old Dominion. These were military men of substance and drive—the backbone and sinew of the KGC. From these sources, it should be evident that the Knights were a much more powerful force and played more of a role in precipitating the Civil War than historians have heretofore recognized.

# 1

# POWERFUL ANTECEDENTS

T HE MYSTIC ORDER of the Knights of the Golden Circle was the brainchild of a multitalented doctor and editor living in Ohio named George W. L. Bickley. George had been born at Bickley Mills (Russell County) in southwest Virginia to a poor laboring family on July 18, 1823. When he was five, George's mother insisted that the family move to her home territory near Petersburg, Virginia, where George's father died of cholera a few years later. George's mother was left so destitute that a subscription had to be raised in Richmond for care of the family. George's gallivanting mother moved between Petersburg and Richmond, and shunted her young son off to relatives in southern Virginia. Here the emotionally neglected and unhappy George lived until he reached the age of twelve, when he ran away.

For the next ten years, George subsisted on the strength of his glib tongue and good looks while working at a series of odd jobs and then in a trading business at Geneva, Alabama (that was supplied out of New Orleans). In October 1846, George wrote a relative asking for forgiveness due to the "sircumstances [*sic*] I deceived you last Spring."[1] By 1847, George was living with relatives in Greencastle, Indiana, and attending the local college. He then moved to North Carolina, fathering a son there named Charles Simmons Bickley, whom he placed with relatives when his first wife died in 1850. At this point, George headed back to Russell County, Virginia, where he studied medicine under a local doctor and then opened his own office at the Union Hotel in Jeffersonville (now Tazewell).[2]

He is shown on the 1850 Russell County census as "G. W. L. Bickley (only one in family) 26 years old, male, Phrenologist, worth $400, native of Russell County, VA." At the time, phrenology—the study of contours of the skull as a predictor of human behavior—was popular and regarded by many as a true science although subject to abuse by con men.[3]

As a result of his unstable background, Bickley developed incurable habits of prevaricating and scheming. He also displayed a driving ambition, resourcefulness, and a determination to make a name for himself in wide-open nineteenth-century America. Somehow along the way, he picked up a credible knowledge of world history and a command of the English language that enabled him to become a prolific writer and a notable speaker.[4]

By 1851, the fast-talking Bickley made a considerable leap in status from a country doctor to professor at Cincinnati's Eclectic Medical Institute, a reform medical school started in the mid-1840s that focused on unconventional methods such as physical manipulation and herbal remedies. To obtain his faculty position, Bickley lied about his medical credentials, saying he had attended top medical schools in the East and on the European continent. His quick wit and brief experience as a country doctor allowed him to bluff his way as an accomplished phrenologist and as an authority on physiology and scientific botany.[5]

While at the Eclectic Institute, Bickley authored books on his medical specialties as well as several histories and a novel. He completed a *History of the Settlement and Indian Wars of Tazewell County, Virginia* that is relied on to this day. He finished a rustic novel set in a southwest Virginia cove, titled *Adalaska, Or, The Strange and Mysterious Family of the Cave of Genreva.*[6] Bickley also wrote copiously in his fields of pseudo-medicine, including an introductory lecture that traced the ancient and modern history of medical science with Eclecticism at its apex (he later penned a biography of the Eclectic Institute itself).[7] Students at the Eclectic Institute accused Bickley of being a "novelist" and unable to deliver an extemporaneous medical lecture. He nevertheless was a tireless worker, and claimed he dictated sixteen to twenty pages of foolscap an hour in writing a 209-page volume on physiological botany and a 2,700-page written course of lectures.[8]

Then, in early 1853, the ambitious Bickley freed himself from the mundane need to earn a living: he married Rachel Dodson, a wealthy widow and scion of Cincinnati's Kinney family of bankers. He soon took a leave of absence from the Eclectic Medical Institute and moved to Rachel's family farm near Portsmouth, Scioto County, in south central Ohio. Here Bickley pursued multifaceted interests including newspaper editing and local real estate development, as well as more far-flung ventures, reportedly including investing in coal mines in the Dominican Republic and exporting farm implements to Russia.[9] He also proposed the establishment of a "conservative daily newspaper" to Kentucky senator John Crittenden, to be owned and edited by prominent citizens from each of the thirty-one states in order to counter New York City's Republican papers (which Bickley believed were stirring up sectional animosities).[10]

In addition, Bickley also pursued several enterprises more directly tied to his formation of the Knights. Among these was the 1854 publication of a short-lived Manifest Destiny journal called *Bickley's West American Review,* which contained a variety of articles (mostly written by Bickley) on the arts, commerce, and politics. One early article titled "Inter-oceanic Railroad—Federal Capital" urged that the capital of the United States should be moved to the Ozarks because "the circle of our limits" will soon encompass "a part of the British possession, the West Indies, and Mexico."[11] In publishing his journal, Bickley likely came into contact with kindred "Young America" spirits such as John O'Sullivan and George Sanders, owners/editors of the *Democratic Review* that was published in New York City. Like the Young American wing of the Democratic Party, the *Democratic Review* preached that republicanism was the ultimate destiny of society and would lead to world peace through the extinction of monarchical despotism. Its editor, John O'Sullivan, had coined the phrase "Manifest Destiny" in 1845 to signify that the United States' expansion throughout the North American continent was inexorable and destined by Providence.[12]

Bickley also developed a fascination with secret societies that he felt contributed to the welfare and happiness of mankind as the source of immutable social and political laws. Secret societies flourished in nineteenth-century America since they allowed aspirants to temporarily escape from the monotony of their daily lives. Bickley formed a short-lived chapter (referred to as a "Circle") of a patriotic order based in Philadelphia called the "Brotherhood of the Union," which blended patriotic imagery with U.S. expansionism and social-betterment goals for the working class. Like the KGC after it, the Brotherhood of the Union was ruled by a supreme council, utilized a system of numbered codes to preserve secrecy, and was (at least in theory) to be divorced from political party strife.[13]

Like John Wilkes Booth, Bickley also joined a lodge of the Know-Nothings, a secret nativist movement that disparaged Catholics and immigrants, and utilized cryptic handshakes and codes. During the mid-1850s, the Know-Nothing movement transformed into the American Party, which nominated former U.S. chief executive Millard Fillmore for president in 1856. But it soon faded out as a national party when its northern and southern wings split over slavery.[14]

Another of Bickley's avocations was the formation of a drill company consisting of sixty young men whom he planned to equip with dazzling uniforms so that they could travel the globe and perform intricate military exhibitions. Such drill squads, usually connected with local militia units, were prevalent, especially in the South, and their competitions provided opportunities for military-minded men to get together and share their perspectives. Bickley's drill company provided him with a ready source of recruits that he shifted to the KGC when he established its first chapters in Scioto County and Cincinnati.[15]

But Bickley's entrepreneurial pastimes were suddenly interrupted in 1857, when his wealthy wife discovered that he had been secretly trying to convert her substantial assets to his own name. She got her banker brother to kick Bickley off their Scioto County farm. The pseudo-physician was forced to return to Cincinnati and resume teaching at the Eclectic Medical Institute.[16]

In 1858, Bickley become editor of the *Scientific Artisan,* the house journal for the American Patent Company, to promote inventions and the proper handling of patent cases. It was in the *Scientific Artisan's* offices that Bickley came up with the emblem for the Knights—a Maltese cross superimposed on the Lone Star—designed to be worn as a breast pin.[17] He also organized "The American Colonization and Steamship Company of 'I'

[Monterrey]" as a financial vehicle to raise capital for the KGC's planned ventures.[18] A coworker on the *Artisan* described Bickley as "an ignorant pretender, as restless and scheming as he was shallow, very vain of his person, exceedingly fond of military display, and constantly engaged either in devices to borrow money and crazy schemes of speculation."[19]

Bickley apparently got the message that he wasn't appreciated since he soon resigned from the *Artisan* and headed south. Here he reportedly worked with the "Southern Rights Associations" that had spread across the towns of the Deep South as well as North Carolina and Virginia in opposition to the various compromises over slavery during the 1850s. Through speeches, rallies, and by publishing tracts, these associations promoted states' rights, resisted further encroachments on slavery, and in some cases backed southern fire-eaters calling for separate state secession.[20] Bickley later alluded to the Knights' southern origins when he said it had been founded by southern men and was originally intended to advance the rights and interests of the southern states.[21] Bickley now devoted all his time to promoting the Knights as a vehicle to achieve his Manifest Destiny dream of southern empire and to selling KGC-related steamship bonds to wealthy planters.[22]

During his sojourn across the South, George was somehow able to convince the leaders of a preexisting southern society called the "Order of the Lone Star" (OLS) to merge with his Knights.[23] This had truly an exponential impact since the OLS already had more than fifteen thousand members in at least fifty chapters spread across ten southern states with large concentrations in Mississippi, Louisiana, Texas, and Alabama. It also had chapters in northern port cities including Baltimore and New York, where it operated out of Tammany Hall and the Empire Club. This merger with the OLS suddenly transformed Bickley's nascent KGC into a truly powerful force with far-flung members and prestige.[24]

To advance their expansionist agenda, the OLS and its members promoted a practice known as "filibustering"—the launching of a privately funded expedition to invade a neighboring country (with which the U.S. government was formally at peace). Although filibusterers often justified their expeditions as freeing the local inhabitants from tyrannical rule, the underlying purpose was generally to garner land and treasure for the participants.[25] The filibusters conducted in the 1840s and 1850s were usually headed by a well-known U.S. leader who had the capability to raise needed funds and recruit the idle young men who congregated in U.S. ports such as New Orleans and San Francisco.[26]

Cuban émigrés and southern expansionists had formed the OLS in September 1851 in the aftermath of Narciso López's disastrous filibustering invasion of Cuba at Bahia Honda.[27] López had launched his invasion with a band of 450 U.S.-based insurgents dedicated to freeing Cuba from Spanish rule. Upon reaching Cuba's northern coast, López and his men were surrounded and captured by Spanish-led troops after the expected indigenous support failed to show up. López as well as the expedition's artillery commander, William Crittenden (nephew of the noted U.S. senator from Kentucky), were executed. Indigenous supporters of the expedition from within Cuba were subsequently rounded up and arrested.[28]

As the López expedition proved, there were substantial risks to filibustering. One was in violating the U.S. Neutrality Act of 1818, which made it a felony to "prepare the means for any military expedition" from the jurisdiction of the United States against a country with which the United States was at peace.[29] Even more significant was the outcome experienced by López and his men—a hostile reception in the country or colony being invaded. Neighboring countries such as Cuba and Mexico made it a crime, punishable by death, to be involved in a foreign-based filibuster that reached their territory.[30]

To continue the mission of freeing Cuba from Spanish rule and eventually annexing it to the United States as a slaveholding territory, Cuban ex-patriots and southern adventurers formed the Order of the Lone Star in 1851 at the offices of the pro-expansionist *Lafayette (La.) True Delta* newspaper. John Henderson, a Mississippi cotton planter and U.S. senator, formulated the OLS ritual, and Pierre Soule, another U.S. senator from Louisiana, served as its president.[31]

The OLS, like its KGC successor, was organized in a hierarchical fashion with three degrees, including the military degree at the bottom and a fund-raising benevolent degree above that. At the apex was the political degree, with the goal of supporting U.S. political candidates who would advance the society's filibustering and proslavery objectives. A supreme council governed the group's overall policy.[32]

The OLS was structured so that once three divisions were formed in any state, a statewide general assembly was to be created. By the 1850s, the OLS was reputed to be a shadow organization within the Democratic Party, dedicated to expansionism and serving as a counterweight to the American, or Know-Nothing, Party.[33]

In Texas, the society was known as the "Order of the Lone Star of the West" and became very popular. John Salmon Ford, a noted Texas Ranger captain, legislator, and newspaper editor, founded the Austin chapter in 1853. Ford had moved from South Carolina to Texas in 1836, joining colonizing U.S. émigrés fighting to break away from Mexico. Ford practiced medicine until 1844 and then became one of Texas's leading advocates for annexation to the United States.[34] Ford described the OLS's secret initiation ceremony as highly ritualistic, with candidates passing through a succession of increasingly solemn steps incorporating cabalistic passwords. The final step was a dramatic conclusion that Ford said ended with something the initiate would never forget.[35] An observer of a Lone Star encampment at Richmond, Virginia, similarly described the initiation ceremony as a "magnificent spectacle" that pantomimed the López expedition.[36]

OLS members (in addition to many wealthy southerners) had reportedly helped bankroll the filibusters of noted adventurer William Walker to Mexico and Nicaragua. During 1855, the multitalented Walker, a onetime Tennessee physician and former newspaper editor, led an initial U.S. band of fifty-six "Immortals" to Nicaragua. They joined the internal León faction to conquer Nicaragua, install Walker as its president, and reinstitute slavery. Recruiters, such as Sam A. Lockridge in the Southwest and Walker's brother Norvell at Nashville, enticed a steady stream of further U.S. émigrés to go to Nicaragua. A number of Walker's lieutenants would become KGC members, including Lockridge, Chatham Roberdeau Wheat of New Orleans, and English freebooter Charles Frederick Henningsen. In Texas, OLS (and future KGC) fund-raiser Hugh McLeod helped raise and equip one thousand Rangers for Walker's missions.[37]

By 1853, the OLS's predominant leader was John Anthony Quitman. A Mississippi planter, former state governor, and noted Mexican War general, Quitman had led the U.S. Army division that stormed the gates of Mexico City in 1847, and he was recognized as a war hero. After the war, U.S. General Winfield Scott appointed Quitman to become military governor during the temporary U.S. occupation of Mexico. Quitman, who had supported the 1851 López invasion of Cuba, remained a leading expansionist, pushing for the United States to annex all of Mexico. He regarded the great bulk of the Mexicans as a "bastard and robber race, incapable of self-government, and fit only for servitude and military rule."[38]

Quitman was also a southern-rights zealot who had encouraged the formation of "Southern Rights Associations" across Mississippi. In 1852, he ran for vice president on the ticket of the short-lived Southern Rights Party.[39] Quitman's political stature and military connections enabled him to expand the normal universe of filibuster supporters to include not only clerks and workingmen, but also merchants, planters, and judges. This allowed him to spread the reach of the OLS to encompass all strata of southern society.[40]

In 1853, the Cuban junta of wealthy indigenous planters and U.S. émigrés (which was associated with the OLS) approached Quitman to lead a new filibustering expedition to free Cuba from Spanish rule. Quitman accepted the offered $1 million bonus and said he would be ready to move as soon as three thousand men and $220,000 in operational funding were raised. Extensive recruiting took place across the South, and those involved in preparations included many who would later show up in connection with the KGC, such as Thomas Hindman of Mississippi/Arkansas and Texans John Ford and Hugh McLeod.[41]

The scope of Quitman's plan for the Cuban filibuster was revealed in a letter to C. A. L. Lamar, a wealthy Georgia capitalist and slave trader from whom Quitman was seeking further financial support: "Our great enterprise has been planned with the advice and approval of some of the most distinguished military men of the country. It contemplates aiding a revolutionary movement in Cuba with from three to four thousand well armed and provided men embarked in swift and safe steamers."[42] Quitman sent confidential circular letters to OLS centers across the United States seeking recruits for the expedition and receiving many positive responses. These were soon leaked to the press, however, which embellished their contents by claiming that Quitman had already raised fifty thousand recruits, $1 million, twelve ships, and eighty-five thousand arms.[43] In response to the U.S. press accounts, the Spanish governor of Cuba threatened to defend the island by emancipating and arming Cuba's slaves. In the United States, this raised fears that southern slaves would revolt, seeking similar emancipation. Fear of spin-off insurrections further increased southern support for Quitman's expedition.[44]

But before Quitman could set off, the Pierce administration in Washington suddenly reversed its prior tacit approval for the expedition. During May 1854, President Franklin Pierce called pro-expansionist Democratic senators, including John Slidell (La.), James Murray Mason (Va.), and Stephen Arnold Douglas (Ill.) to a White House meeting. He advised them that he was about to issue a proclamation against filibustering, saying that the OLS's planned venture against Cuba contravened the letter and spirit of U.S.-Spanish treaties. Pierce's sudden reversal may have been partially spurred by the strident Spanish protests and unfavorable northern press stories. But the overriding cause was likely the northern outrage unleashed in May 1854 after Pierce signed the Kansas-Nebraska Act. This act overrode the Missouri Compromise line of 1820 and allowed slavery in territories north of the 36° 30' parallel.[45]

During early 1855, Quitman went to Washington and confronted President Pierce directly to protest the administration's reversal of support that was crippling OLS recruiting and fund-raising. Quitman came away convinced that Pierce was intransigent in his opposition, as the administration began seizing several of the vessels intended for the expedition. In April 1855, Quitman resigned as commander and in his public letter blamed the Pierce administration. The more than $500,000 in funds collected for the expedition were never returned to the donors and may have found their way into KGC coffers to help fund its planned Mexican expedition (which Texan John Ford and Kentuckian John T. Pickett had urged Quitman to undertake in conjunction with his Cuban venture).[46]

Following his withdrawal from the expedition, Quitman was elected to the U.S. Congress from Mississippi, where he remained a fervent advocate for southern rights and U.S. acquisition of Cuba, Mexico, and Nicaragua. Quitman constantly urged the repeal of the U.S. Neutrality Laws and supported renewed filibuster expeditions to the Golden Circle region until July 1858, when he met an untimely and suspicious death.[47] With Quitman gone, the OLS's dreams for southward expansion and empire would now be channeled through the successor order of the Knights of the Golden Circle, which incorporated ironclad oaths of secrecy to prevent the public exposure that had foiled Quitman's Cuban effort.

Meanwhile, the sectional chasm that had resulted from the Kansas-Nebraska Act only deepened since passage of the purported 1854 compromise. Northerners fervently resented the possibility of slavery extension in territories north of the Missouri Compromise line. This led to the 1856 ascendancy of the new Republican Party, dedicated to restricting slavery in the territories. Its leaders, such as the outraged Illinois lawyer Abraham Lincoln, feared a slaveholding conspiracy that would ultimately result in the removal of the U.S. prohibitions on the African slave trade.[48]

While most southerners had initially supported the 1854 compromise, they became increasingly disillusioned as northern state legislatures passed personal liberty laws to override constitutional protection for the return of escaped slaves. This disillusionment turned to anger as northern abolitionist societies sent emigrants to Kansas to sway the popular vote toward a free-soil outcome where slavery would be banned. Republican intransigence to further territorial expansion convinced many southerners that the only way to achieve their dream of southern empire would be to sever their ties with the federal Union.[49]

The earlier experience regarding the admission of Texas into the Union continued to fester with northerners. During the 1820s and 1830s, hordes of southerners from the United States had come to the sparse but fertile southwest region in response to Mexico's encouragement of colonization. But by 1835, the new settlers decided they wanted to have things their own way. They fought to break away from Mexico and establish an independent republic. Then, in 1845, they sought the security of the United States to deal with Indian and other threats on the Texas frontier, and applied for statehood. In the face of northern opposition, statehood for Texas was achieved through the sleight of hand of a congressional resolution during the waning days of the Tyler administration.[50] Texas provided a model for Bickley and the Knights, who felt that a similar pretense of colonization would allow them to achieve territorial expansion southward without the risks and stigma associated with a traditional filibuster.

In early 1859, Bickley shifted his focus from fund-raising in the southern heartland to the Baltimore/Washington area. This made sense for a number of reasons. Baltimore was a key commercial center whose merchants supplied the South and generally had prosouthern leanings. Castles of the KGC were already formed in Baltimore, and Bickley had established contacts.[51] The nearby District of Columbia was the home of the nation's political leaders, whom Bickley would need to cultivate in order to sell the KGC's colonization agenda. The District also had strong pro-South leanings as well as existing chapters of the Order of the Lone Star.[52] Therefore Bickley and the OLS's former leaders would now more formally organize the recently consolidated KGC order, establish its Washington, D.C., headquarters, and lay the formal groundwork for its initial field of endeavor—the barren but mineral-rich provinces of northern Mexico.

# 2

# FORMAL ORGANIZATION

A T LEAST ONE active castle of the Knights was operating in Baltimore by early 1859, when Bickley arrived. It existed in the south central neighborhood near St. Vincent's Church, where Wilkes Booth had grown up in a townhouse on Exeter Street. Among the castle's members were Samuel Street, a schoolmate of Booth, and the O'Laughlen brothers.[1] Michael O'Laughlen, a close friend of Booth, would later become one of the conspirators Booth enlisted in his Civil War plot to abduct the sitting president, Abraham Lincoln. It is likely that Booth became affiliated with this castle when he returned to Baltimore from his acting stint in Richmond.[2]

Robert Charles Tyler, the commander of the KGC's Maryland regiment, also joined the KGC in Baltimore in early 1859. Tyler, then working as a clerk, had been raised in Baltimore in a lower-class household. He had recently returned from Nicaragua, where he had served for the preceding three years as a first lieutenant of infantry for William Walker's filibustering expedition. During 1859, Tyler invested two thousand dollars of his own money in the Knights. In soliciting a potential KGC recruit from Boston, Tyler advised: "We all expect to be benefitted by being members, and if you enter the lists you will be rewarded according as your ability and zeal in the working for us may justify. In this organization, merit, not pride of family name or date of commission will have any influence whatever, it rests with the individual man himself to decide whether he reaps a rich reward or not."[3] KGC member Cypriano Ferrandini, the Baltimore barber and militia drillmaster who would lead the February 1861 plot to assassinate Lincoln, also appears to have joined the organization at this time.[4]

After arriving in Baltimore, Bickley employed his superb writing and editing abilities to produce an eight-page pro-expansionist newspaper titled the *American Cavalier: A Military Journal Devoted to the Extension of American Civilization*.[5] The first (and perhaps only) issue, dated May 28, 1859, is an eclectic array of articles on Manifest Destiny, definitions of "Fillibustero" and "Political Words," military tactics, as well as reports from correspondents in Cuba, Mexico, and other locations. In an article titled "What We Mean by American Civilization," the editor notes that it is "our duty to enlarge the area of its influence until the whole Continent shall be thus Americanized."

Downplaying Cuba as an expansion target, the paper indicates that another U.S. filibustering attempt was impossible there due to Spanish vigilance. It also notes that the "golden chance" to purchase that island from Spain by the Buchanan administration had slipped away due to "timid and unfriendly counsels" (as well as Republican and Spanish intransigence). It concludes: "There is no reason . . . that can be advanced for the acquisition of Cuba, which is not ten-fold more cogent for our exercising control over Mexico."[6]

The paper accordingly includes a May 8, 1859, letter from "76" [Bickley], who purports to be in Vera Cruz, the capital of Mexico's Liberal faction on its eastern seacoast. Bickley indicates that contrary to the popular belief that Mexico is a poor nation, it is a country rich in mineral and other wealth, but its corrupt rulers have continually robbed these from its people. He reports that in Mexico, there is an indigenous U.S. party as well as German and Swiss colonists who "really desire peace and good Government." Bickley notes that while the Liberal faction in Mexico, headed by Benito Juárez, hopes for assistance from the U.S. government, the U.S. Congress is unlikely to provide this directly and "would do well to let the job by contract [i.e., support the Knights' colonization drive]." He predicts that one of the two warring parties in Mexico's raging civil war will, "in desperation . . . invite private assistance from the Americans."

In an article titled "The Question of Mexican Interference," the editor [Bickley] tries to spur U.S. military men (such as Quitman's followers) into action:

> The fact is we want a fight, but how to get it is the question. The warhorse is saddled, but he has no rider; the cannon is charged, with no one to fire it.

While this is the case here, the Mexicans have just about finished the job of killing each other, and, as their strength will be inadequate to the completion of the job, they are imploring the Americans to come in, finish the work, quietly bury them and take their country in payment for the job. Who will be the executioner—who will put this man out of his misery?[7]

The advent of the *American Cavalier* was publicized in the District of Columbia and is noted in the diary of Edward Bates, a lawyer from Missouri who was then being touted as a Republican presidential candidate. Bates sarcastically mocks the "grandiloquently" of "Sir Knight (the Editor of the *Cavalier*)" in talking about the "prospect of universal expansion." He notes: "The paper, observe, is to be *military*—All this spread of 'American Civilization' is to be done by *martial law*. [President James] Buchanan wants to take *military* possession of Mexico; and [Illinois senator Stephen] Douglas wants a *seabound* Republic!"[8]

By mid-1859, the condition of Mexico and its 8 million inhabitants was dire and growing worse. The country was nearly bankrupt, with England and other foreign creditors demanding payment for preexisting loans. The Conservative Party, led by General Miguel Miramón, was backed by wealthy Mexicans and the Catholic clergy. They controlled the densely populated central portion of the country, including Mexico City, which constituted about nine-tenths of the land area with 65 percent of the population. The Liberal Party, headed by Benito Juárez, held the frontiers as well as the coasts and ports where custom revenues were collected. They had been driven out of Mexico City in 1858 and established their capital at Vera Cruz, an eastern seaport. The Liberals claimed authority under the Mexican constitution of 1857, and passed measures to break up the extensive property holdings of the Catholic Church and the wealthy aristocracy. The two sides were locked in a horrific struggle in which neither could gain the ascendancy. While the army of the Liberals suffered a series of reverses, new supporters continually appeared to replenish its ranks.[9]

The Liberal coalition, headed by the humble but tenacious Juárez, was an uneasy mix of shifting alliances and spheres of influence. Provincial governors, like strongman Santiago Vidaurri of northern Nuevo León Province, maintained personal militias and jealously guarded their power. Manuel Doblado, the governor of mineral-rich Guanajuato Province, had a militia of three thousand men. Many of these provincial governors were opportunists and had no compunction about deserting the Liberal coalition if the conditions were right. The coalition's leader, Juárez, was a fifty-one-year-old Zapata Indian from southern Mexico. Since he was operating outside his power base, Juárez tried to control the northern strongmen by playing one off against the other.[10]

U.S. filibusters had long been lusting after Mexico's four northern-tier provinces—Nuevo León, Coahuila, Chihuahua, and Sonora. These provinces were barren and sparsely populated, but Sonora, as well as Guanajuato Province to the immediate south, were rich in silver, gold, and other minerals.[11] In 1840, Texans had backed an attempt by Mexican Federalist Party leaders, including northern strongman Vidaurri, to declare independence from Mexico's central government and create an independent "Republic of the Rio Grande" to include the four provinces. This was nipped in the bud by Mexico's central army, but between 1849 and 1859, five separate U.S.-based filibuster expeditions had been launched to try to wrest portions of Mexico's northern provinces. Participants in each risked the outcome of the 1857 expedition into Sonora led by California state senator Henry Crabb. In Crabb's unfortunate case, the Mexican army captured and systematically executed him and his company of one thousand Californians.[12]

Bickley and the KGC sought to use the shaky position of the Liberals to advance their goal of expansion southward. Northern Mexican strongman Santiago Vidaurri was a committed KGC supporter and actively cooperated with its leaders. Manuel Doblado, second in command of the Liberal army and governor of Guanajuato Province, also had reportedly reached an understanding with the KGC's emissaries.[13] The KGC's 1859 *Degree Works* claims: "We have the invitation of four [Mexican] State Governors to come and shall receive their cooperation if only we take care of the people of those States." Bickley also claimed that he had reached an agreement with Liberal President Benito Juárez.[14]

By June 1859, the KGC's plans for Mexican intervention were being described in the U.S. press. The New York correspondent for the *San Francisco Daily Evening Bulletin* sarcastically notes that "the filibusters have got up a new dodge for raising the wind and filling their pockets with the products of other people's labor" by starting a new association called the "Knights of the Golden Circle." The correspondent indicates that the

KGC's headquarters appears to be in Baltimore and that the KGC proposes to raise a separate U.S. and Mexican legion of ten thousand men each to be headed by a Board of War. He observes that this looks like a scheme for putting money into the hands of the commander in chief by "playing on filibuster credibility."

The reporter also claims that he has been provided with a copy of the KGC's secret ritual for inducting new members, who are told they can resign but remain obligated to their vows of secrecy. He goes on to reveal portions of this initiation ritual, including that KGC candidates are informed that the object of the KGC is to "not only cultivate the martial pride of the people" but also "to render substantial aid to weak and oppressed nationalities." The referenced ritual text then continues: "We are soldiers whose objects are to conquer certain countries, and thereby spread over them the genial influences of our own institutions." At this point in the initiation, the KGC captain, after referring to the conquests of Rome, Great Britain, and Spain, is instructed to cajole the candidates: "Why should we not adopt a similar policy? See what California did for us—what Cuba will do for us. Every inch of territory is that much additional wealth. We threw out a colony in Mexico—it revolted and we won Texas, now one of the brightest stars in our empire. Now gentlemen, are you willing to be united with us?"[15]

Once the candidates indicate their assent, the captain is instructed to take them into the regular KGC meeting and to administer the oath requiring the inductees "to keep all secrets of the association, to stand by the flag of the legion, to obey orders and abide by the articles of war as promulgated by the commander in chief and his staff, and to march whithersoever ordered." The initiation then goes on to describe the 6,400 acres of land and seven dollars per month in specie and script that can be gained by participating in the Mexican expedition being organized after November 1859. It notes that large numbers have already enrolled, especially in the southwestern states, and "that Southern members of Congress and Federal office-holders are parties to the scheme, and that its existence is known to President Buchanan who regards the movement with favor."[16]

Charles Bickley, the reported nephew of the KGC general-in-chief, replies to the *Daily Evening Bulletin* correspondent's sarcastic remarks in a letter to the editor of June 15, 1859:

That such an organization [KGC] as to which you allude really exists in this country is doubtless true; but that it is, as you suspect, a "scheme of some designing persons to make money for themselves by playing upon filibuster credibility," is most emphatically denied.

The "K. G. C." is not a filibuster enterprise, but a spontaneous expression of public sentiment in regard to carrying out the Monroe doctrine.

The "K. G. C." embodies in its organization the wisest and best men of our country—men whose names are sufficient guaranty that whatever is undertaken by them will be faithfully and honorable [sic] carried out.[17]

George Bickley, as "Commander-in-Chief American Legion, K. G. C.," also replies on July 20 to some negative comments about the KGC that had appeared the week before in the *Baltimore Daily Exchange*. Bickley denies that the KGC intended to swindle parties through its issuance of stock and script, that the U.S. government had agreed to back the Knights' expansionist movements, and that the KGC intended to intervene uninvited in Mexico with three thousand volunteers. He asserts that the Knights are more than thirteen thousand strong and are "ready for any honorable work."[18]

In early August 1859, eighty to a hundred "military men and noted political leaders" attended a KGC conference held at the Greenbrier resort in White Sulphur Springs, Virginia.[19] This likely encompassed the first meeting of the Knights of the Columbian Star, the KGC's Third, or governing, Degree. The Greenbrier was packed at the time with more than 1,200 guests.[20] Separate accounts indicate that KGC leader Ben McCulloch, a noted U.S. marshal and Texas Ranger, planned to attend the KGC convention, and that then U.S. secretary of war John Floyd as well as District of Columbia KGC head L. Q. Washington were vacationing at the Virginia springs during the period of the convention.[21] Other contemporaneous Greenbrier vacationers include U.S. secretary of the interior Jacob Thompson; Governor Manning and Congressman Millard Bonham of South Carolina; Charles Conrad, a former Louisiana U.S. senator and Fillmore cabinet member; and noted Virginia fire-eater Edmund Ruffin.[22]

The Greenbrier was one of several elegant summer resorts in the mountains of western Virginia where wealthy southerners relaxed, socialized, and talked states'-rights politics. In fact, some of these mountain resorts staged elaborate jousting contests with costumed lords and ladies, feats of horsemanship, and displays of marksmanship. At one such event amid seven hundred spectators, twenty-eight "knights" entered the lists to try to spear a 1.5-inch-diameter ring while riding at full speed.[23] It may have been at such a jousting event that Bickley came up with the idea for the Knights.

The *Arkansas True Democrat* of September 7, 1859, contains a gossipy account of the KGC's Greenbrier convention by a reporter who claims to have stumbled upon it. The "curious reporter" says that the Greenbrier conclave had been preceded by a July 27, 1859, circular announcing a convention of southern men to be held the following week "to consider the steps necessary to render the political standing and material interest of the south more permanent." The circular says that "questions of vast national importance will be discussed" and expresses the hope "that every southern State will be represented here."[24]

At the beginning of the convention, the reporter eavesdrops on one of the plenary sessions addressed by "General Bickley, President of the American Legion, a secret southern military organization." The reporter says the session appears to be preliminary and "intended to sound the public feeling on acquiring more southern territory—Mexico was shown as a country in a state of anarchy, and likely to remain so until it was governed by Americans." The reporter also notes that "the relations of the north and south were examined, and a large amount of disunion feeling was expressed."[25]

In his speech to the gathering, Bickley claimed that he had a legion of thirteen thousand Knights, ready to march at short notice, and that the KGC army was "now strong enough to work out the destiny of the south against every opposition." Bickley told the attendees that they must rely on the regular delegates to arrange time and place [for the Mexican intervention] and that he is determined not to violate U.S. neutrality laws. Bickley asks the delegates to "sustain us at home while we do the work abroad—for we are going to fight a battle on other soil that must otherwise, in a few years, be fought at your own door." A further meeting was held in the evening, protected by a guard and a sentinel, and was "almost entirely composed of military men."[26]

Specific attendees that the reporter mentions include "Major [R. C.] Tillery and Colonel [William H.] Toler [from Arkansas]," who subscribed to some of the one-thousand-dollar KGC bonds being sold. William H.

Tolar had fought with the Little Rock Guards during the Mexican War. R. C. Tillery, from North Carolina, would later serve in the Civil War as a lieutenant with Colonel Turner Ashby's Second Tennessee Cavalry Regiment. Cypriano Ferrandini, the Baltimore barber who later headed an attempt to assassinate Lincoln in February 1861, also appears to have been in attendance, since his KGC captain's commission was signed by Bickley and dated August 8, 1859, at the tail end of the convention.[27]

The reporter says he was personally introduced to General Bickley, whom he describes as "about 35 years of age, 5 feet, 10 inches, with deep blue, sharp eyes, heavy beard, and looks as determined as man can." The reporter notes Bickley is erect and proud, but affable in conversation while measuring every word: "Few young men will talk with him five minutes without catching his enthusiasm."

According to the reporter, Bickley is thoroughly acquainted with the United States and Mexico, "but draws dismal pictures of Spanish American civilization . . . and argues strongly for the entire American control of the Gulf." The reporter suggests it is likely that President Juárez will look to the KGC for assistance, though, "if I am not mistaken, Bickley is looking only to the extension of negro slavery." He is "a disunionist in politics," the reporter writes, "and if he succeeds, will do much to bring about a disruption of the Union, though he says his movement alone will prevent it." With respect to the upcoming 1860 U.S. presidential election, Bickley said he was in favor of then Virginia governor Henry Wise, but if Wise were not the nominee, then he hoped Republican U.S. senator William H. Seward would be elected so that the South would have to separate. The reporter concludes: "I think [Bickley] a most dangerous man, and if he is not stopped, he will do the whole country an incalculable injury. . . . He is playing with the most dangerous passions of the southern people."[28]

Attendees of the Greenbrier convention undoubtedly approved the sixty-page booklet titled *Rules, Regulations and Principles of the American Legion of the K.G.C.* that was issued on September 12, 1859, "By Order of the Congress of the K. C. S. [Knights of the Columbian Star] and the General President" from "Headquarters, Washington City, D.C." This booklet appears to be a public document. It begins with a proclamation addressed to the KGC army and is signed by Bickley as "President of the American Legion," announcing with respect to Mexican intervention: "Soldiers—The time approaches when we must take the field." The proclamation then contemplates the KGC's audacious mission: "Let us think for a moment what we propose: the invasion of a nation by a new and vigorous race—the overthrow of old social systems, and the establishment of new ones—the disarming of a hostile faction and the erection of peace establishments— the overthrow of prejudice, and the indoctrination of the people with new ideas of peace and prosperity." Bickley, as "General-in-Chief," observes that he has borne "the brunt of public misapprehension" and nearly exhausted his personal fortune, but he concludes that their cause—an American empire stretching from Canada to Patagonia—will be worth it.[29]

The meticulously organized booklet then follows with twelve pages of "Laws of the American Legion, K. G. C. Military Department," the "K. G. C. Federal Constitution" (explaining how to set up a government for a mixed population); "Articles of War"; rules for organizing and working castles; a description of the American Colonization and Steamship Company of "1" [Monterrey]; military maxims; social, moral, and civil maxims; and political maxims. Bickley signed many of these as either "President" or "Commander in Chief" of the American Legion.[30]

The preamble to the "Laws of the . . . K. G. C. Military Department" indicates that they were enacted and promulgated by "the Executive and Legal Representatives of the Knights of the Golden Circle, in Congress here assembled [i.e., at the Greenbrier]." It states that "the American Legion, Knights of the Golden Circle" is to distinguish it from the "Legion K. G. C." in Mexico. Article 32 of the "Laws" provides:

> Article 32.—There shall be but three degrees in the ceremonial of this confederation. The first shall be purely military, and shall be given to every member of the Legion who is to bear arms. The second shall be moral, and shall be given only to non-commissioned officers, Lieutenants, and their superior officers. The third shall be political, and shall be given only to Majors and their superior officers.

This would indicate that the KGC's higher-degree members, while not necessarily expected to bear arms, are nevertheless officers.

The "Laws" further specify that the American Legion shall consist of four divisions, each of which is to be headed by a marshal responsible to the commander in chief, who could be superseded only by the unanimous request of the "Board of War" (i.e., the four marshals and eight brigadier generals). The "Laws" also detail the duties, pay, allowed horses and servants, and prescribed uniforms of the lower-ranking officers and departmental staff. Article 44 requires that for admission to the Knights, a candidate must be white, between the ages of twenty and fifty, of sound body and mind, and of good moral character. It further provides that candidates of the First Degree need to be "duly initiated and subscribed these laws," and pay a one-dollar initiation fee and five-cent monthly tax (which are increased for Third Degree members to a five-dollar fee and a fifty-cent monthly tax). Under Article 36, every member of the Legion, of whatever rank, is required to take an oath "to support and sustain the government established by the American Legion and its legal representatives" and to "obey the established laws of the Legion, the rules and regulations of their respective Castles, and all lawful orders delivered to them."

Article 37 declares that a member is "not [obligated] to do any thing which, in his judgment, would be contrary to the interest of the government of the United States," including violation of the U.S. neutrality laws. Article 38 makes clear, however, that every American citizen has "the unquestioned right to rebel against the existing government (as in the case of Texas)" and that "any nation has an undoubted right to invite Americans to colonize its territory, and there is no power in the federal government to prevent such emigration." It further asserts that "when a nation has lost its nationality—where society has given up its existence—then the territory so occupied is thrown open to adventurers from civilized nations, and may be seized by them for the purposes of Christian civilization."[31]

The *Rules* booklet also contains Bickley's General Order 52 to the KGC's "Soldiers." The general order describes members of the KGC legion as "mechanics, artisans, agriculturalists, and professional men, who are not mere adventurers, but good men whom any nation would be proud to own" and says it provides to them "a new field of enterprise" and "the open pathway to honor and fame." It calls for the Americanization of Mexico and notes that of the KGC's fifteen thousand members, more than two-thirds are expected to go along on the Mexican expedition. Provisioning and moving this ten-thousand-man legion is projected to require $3 million every ninety days. The order says that more than $2 million in capital had already been

26

subscribed through the American Colonization and Steamship Company, backed by 600,000 acres of Mexican land to be acquired. It urges every KGC member to become a subscriber of the capital stock of the company to "lessen the amount to be taken from other parties" (noting that General-in-Chief Bickley has furnished most of the working capital up to this point).[32] Each enlisted man who improves and occupies the land in Mexico is promised 640 acres with a sliding scale increasing by rank up to the commander in chief (Bickley), who is promised 3,200 acres.[33]

A coded, nonpublic *Degree Book* was published around this same time. It describes the missions and benefits of each of the KGC's three degrees, providing more revealing disclosures as to the KGC's intentions regarding the higher degrees.[34] The section concerning the "First or Company Degree of the 28 [Knights of the Iron Hand]" explains that the order has been established in seventeen states and is about fourteen thousand strong with about seven thousand then enrolled in the KGC's army. The First Degree oath is set forth as follows:

> Do you (calling each candidate by name) solemnly swear before God and these witnesses that you will keep sacred the signs, passwords and significations of the 28 [Knights of the Iron Hand] from all persons, save to members of the 28, except compelled to divulge the same in the due course of law in any Court of the United States, where you shall be required to testify to the same; that you will be true to your allegiance to the 28, and that you will defend them against all their enemies, on land or at sea. Do you swear to obey their laws, rules, and regulations, and to execute, if in your power, every lawful commission entrusted to you; that you will do all you can as an honorable man to promote the best interests of the 28; and that you will deal justly by every brother 28 as if he were your natural brother, so help you God! [*To this every candidate must answer "Yes" and kiss the Bible.*]

*The Degree Book* describes the KGC's object as "the entire and speedy conquest of 6 [Mexico], and the establishment of a separate and independent nation upon such basis as to render it subservient to the march of American Civilization." The KGC's planned movement is described as "DEFENSIVE COLONIZATION," for which it will need sixteen thousand men and at least $2 million. Once inducted, the candidate is provided with the signs, grips, and passwords, and requested to buy and wear the KGC's emblem.

It is noted that "These Signs &c are the same as are used by the 23 [apparently the KGC army in Mexico] which is now a powerful organization working in unison with us."

The ritual of the "Second, or Brigade Degree of the 28; or, the Degree of the 39 [Knights of the True Faith]" further discloses that once Mexico is Americanized, the other states of the Caribbean and Central America will be invited to join, "which will give us control of the Gulf." It notes that efforts are being made to purchase a steamer and to reconcile Mexican and U.S. authorities. Second Degree members are urged "to use every honorable means to raise capital and material." Members are to "always remember that this is a selfish organization, which looks to the pecuniary interests of its friends alone." The ritual optimistically predicts that "if we get fairly off this fall [1859], the next fall [1860] will witness us masters of 6 [Mexico] if not all of 21 [the Caribbean] and 49 [Central America]."

The ritual further discloses that, upon entry, members of the "Third or Division Degree of the 55, or, the Degree of the 50 [Knights of the Columbian Star]" become part of the KGC's "Army Council" with responsibility to establish a government in the invaded territories from among members of the First, Second, and Third Degrees. The Third Degree ritual declares:

> We aim at the establishment of a great Democratic monarchy—a Republican Empire, which shall vie in grandeur with the old Roman Empire, and which shall regenerate and vivify society in Spanish America. . . . We aim at the establishment of a government the fathers and founders of which shall be 50 [Knights of the Columbian Star]. To each of you we plainly say, the high places are for you; you have done more, and are expected to do more for the 55 [American Legion] than the 28 [First Degree Knights] or Company member 3, and you deserve more.[35]

This profession of a grand monarchical empire-building program and preferences for Third Degree members were not disclosed to lower-degree members or the public.

The KGC was not alone in the quest for a Central American empire. Southern fire-eaters backed by the OLS-affiliated "Southern Rights Associations" advanced similar goals. The fire-eaters argued that since Republican opposition prevented the addition of new slave territories through U.S. expansion, the South should secede and keep for itself the fortunes that could be obtained from exploiting Central America's agriculture and minerals.[36] In an 1858 speech, Robert Barnwell Rhett, the South Carolina fire-eater who would become known as the "father of secession," called for a slaveholding republic reaching from Virginia to Brazil, and told his audience that all of Mexico, Central America, and three-fourths of South America should be theirs by "civil conquest."[37] Albert Gallatin Brown, Mississippi's expansionist U.S. senator, similarly told his constituents: "I want Tamaulipas, Potosi, and one or two other Mexican states; and I want them all for the same reason; for the planting and spread of slavery."[38] In Virginia, the *Richmond Enquirer*, then controlled by the fire-eater Roger Pryor, called for the formation of a great southern confederacy to include an alliance with Cuba and Brazil. It said that this confederacy would rejuvenate southern manufactures, culture, and pride.[39]

At the southern commercial convention held at Montgomery in May 1858, William Lowndes Yancey, a fire-eating lawyer and editor who had previously worked with Quitman in launching the "Southern Rights Associations," made an impassioned speech calling for the reopening of the slave trade as one element toward southern nationalism. Yancey had earlier defended Walker's filibustering activities as "the cause of the South," and after his convention speech, he hosted a dinner party for Walker in his home.[40] The Montgomery convention resulted in demands for positive U.S. congressional protection for slavery in the territories (i.e., a federal slave code), even though this went well beyond the protections afforded in existing U.S. slave states. Yancey and Albert Gallatin Brown of Mississippi soon championed a positive slave code, and support spread to other prominent southern leaders such as Jefferson Davis and Henry Wise (both of whom had previously supported nonintervention by Congress on slavery). This sudden coalescing of fire-eaters around a slave-code proposal (that had no realistic chance of passing in Congress) led many to allege it was really a calculated attempt to break up the Democratic Party, cause the election of a Republican president, and propel the South out of the Union.[41]

Yancey and allied fire-eaters soon established a prosecession umbrella organization called the League of United Southerners to promote their southern-rights program. Yancey claimed that the league would save the Union by either guaranteeing southern rights or otherwise providing the vanguard for secession. In April 1858, Yancey wrote to his good friend and KGC sympathizer Louis T. Wigfall, who was then leading the states'-rights Democrats in Texas. In his letter, Yancey suggests they should consider uniting "the three Leagues into one massive League" to counter Buchanan's strict enforcement of the U.S. Neutrality Laws.[42] Yancey's nascent master league ended up suffering a reverse, however, when his June 1858 letter to James S. Slaughter found its way into the press. The letter reveals that Yancey urged, in connection with his league, that like our revolutionary fathers, we should "organize Committees of Safety all over the cotton States . . . [to] fire the Southern heart—instruct the Southern mind—give courage to each other, and at the proper moment, by one organized, concerted action, . . . precipitate the cotton States into a revolution."[43] This public exposure of revolutionary intent caused many of the other fire-eaters to back away and likely further convinced them of the need for a secret oath-bound society like the Knights of the Golden Circle.[44]

The plans for the KGC as well as southern secession were dramatically affected by an event that occurred at Harpers Ferry, Virginia, during October 1859. The abolitionist John Brown, backed by a cadre of twenty-two insurgents, assaulted and seized the federal armory on October 16 with plans to use the captured weapons to incite a slave uprising in Virginia and other southern states. Brown and his men succeeded in holding the armory building for a day, but they were then killed or captured in an assault by U.S. Marines under Colonel Robert E. Lee, whom Virginia governor Henry Alexander Wise had called in from Washington.[45]

On November 19, the actor John Wilkes Booth decided that he wanted to join in the action. He bolted from rehearsal at Richmond's Marshall Theatre and jumped on the special train sent by Governor Wise to take state militia from Richmond for the purpose of guarding the captured John Brown. To pursue his adventure, Booth donned the uniform of the Richmond Grays militia unit. He stayed in Harpers Ferry to witness the December 2, 1859, hanging of Brown, presided over by Governor Wise and attended by the Virginia fire-eaters Edmund Ruffin and Roger Pryor. An actor friend later indicated that it was Booth's KGC connections that had allowed him to board the train on which no civilians were allowed.

Upon his return to Richmond, Booth found the theater's managers had dismissed him, but his high-spirited friends from the militia (likely including those in the KGC) marched on the theater and successfully demanded

Booth's reinstatement.[46] At the time, Maryland KGC commander Robert C. Tyler claimed that "myself and many other K.G.C.'s were concerned in the capture of some of the Ward Beecher Sharp's carbines and lances of Old John Brown & Co."[47]

Instead of condemning him, many antislavery northerners described Brown as a martyr, and it was subsequently discovered that some northern abolitionists had financially underwritten his efforts.[48] Governor Wise expressed outrage over the northern sympathy for Brown, and used it to castigate all Republicans and abolitionists. He warned of a secret conspiracy of corrupted slaves led by abolitionists poised to unleash similar arsons, poisonings, and insurrections across Virginia and the southern states. Wise told Virginians that the abolitionists must be "met and crushed," that it was time to "organize and arm."[49] During the fall of 1859, George Bickley was in New York City trying to recruit a regiment for the KGC's Mexican venture. Bickley was spotted at Cooper's Institute in December 1859 in the company of Henry Clay Pate of Virginia, a noted pro-South militant who gave a speech entitled "John Brown in Kansas and Old Brown in Virginia."[50]

In late 1859 and 1860, the fears that resulted from the Harpers Ferry incident caused southerners to form vigilante committees to patrol and guard their neighborhoods against similar slave insurrections. It also resulted in the election of extreme states'-rights candidates to governorships and other elective positions and in southern intransigence to compromise. This was especially true in Texas, where Union sentiment declined precipitously, and the fire-eater and Knights' sympathizer Louis Wigfall was elected to the U.S. Senate in December 1859.[51]

The quest for a southern slaveholding empire was now firmly established, not only within the KGC, but also among sympathetic states'-rights and filibuster leaders. The army of the KGC, with support from its financial and political degrees, was gearing up to move into Mexico's northern provinces in cooperation with allied provincial governors. As Bickley had told his Knights in his General Order 52: "The time approaches when we must take the field." Could the Knights pull off their audacious plan for the colonization of northern Mexico, or would the growing U.S. sectional divide disrupt their efforts?

3

# THE DRIVE FOR MEXICO

NEARLY A QUARTER of President James Buchanan's December 1859 annual message to Congress focused on the deplorable and deteriorating conditions in neighboring Mexico. Buchanan noted that "Mexico ought to be rich and prosperous and powerful with . . . fertile soil and an incalculable store of mineral wealth," and asked whether the commercial nations of the world would give it up to "anarchy and ruin." Buchanan's address detailed a series of arrests, deprivations, and murders against the persons, property, and trade of U.S. citizens in Mexico and pointed out the numerous occasions that he and his ministers had called for the United States to do something. He blamed General Miguel Miramón's Conservative regime for these "barbarous" outrages and said there was little that the constitutional government of Benito Juárez could do since the Conservatives controlled Mexico's populous central regions. Buchanan proclaimed it was the "duty" of the United States as a neighboring state to restore peace and order for the benefit of the Mexican people.

Buchanan's message reiterated the request he had made the previous year for authorization to establish U.S. military posts across the Mexican line in Sonora and Chihuahua. But he now went much further, seeking authorization "to employ a sufficient military force to enter Mexico for the purpose of obtaining indemnity for the past and security for the future." Buchanan predicted that such a force would enable the constitutional government of Juárez to "soon reach the City of Mexico and extend its power over the whole Republic." Buchanan seemed to be playing into the KGC's hands in suggesting the use of volunteers who could be "early raised in [the United States] from among those who sympathize with the sufferings of our unfortunate fellow-citizens in Mexico."[1]

Buchanan's message was deemed so supportive to the KGC's objectives that a section of it was incorporated verbatim into the KGC's 1860 initiation ritual, which contained a portion where the KGC captain tells the initiates that "[the situation in Mexico] is horrible enough to mantle every American's cheek with a blush of shame." In the ritual, the captain is instructed to recite the words of Buchanan himself to the recruits:

> [Buchanan] says:—"outrages of the worst description are committed both upon persons and property. There is scarcely any form of injury which has not been suffered by our citizens in Mexico during the last few years. Peaceful American residents occupying rightful possessions have been suddenly expelled from the country in defiance of treaties, and by the mere force of arbitrary power. Vessels of the United States have been seized without law, and a Consular officer who protested against such outrages has been fined and imprisoned."

The KGC captain then laments: "And yet, in the face of such outrages, repeated over and over, the United States Government, with a population of nearly twenty-four millions had not the courage to stand up and shield her honor as a nation!" He concludes: "The K. G. C. would be an humble instrument to secure our citizens protection—no matter where they live."[2]

Elkanah Bracken Greer, the grand commander of the KGC's powerful Texas regiments, took away a different import from Buchanan's remarks. In a January 26, 1860, circular letter sent from New Orleans to "the K's. G. C. of Tennessee, Mississippi, Louisiana and Alabama," Greer notes that "the President, in his recent message, recommends to Congress the establishment of a protectorate over 6 [Mexico], so soon as Congress is organized." Greer says he believes that Congress will heartily concur in the president's recommendation and "then our [the KGC's] hands will be tied" for an independent intervention. Greer therefore urges the KGC to "make haste to take the initiative in our grand and glorious undertaking."

Greer issued his circular letter as "Commander-in-Chief, and President of the Texas Board of War." In it, he indicates that despite "the apparent lethargy upon the part of our Commander [Bickley]," two Texas KGC regiments are "ready to move immediately, and take possession of the [northern Mexican] States of Tamaulipas, Neuava Leon, Coahuila, and Chihuahua, and of them organize a Government . . . around which our valiant Knights will soon rally." But Greer says the Texas Knights need subsistence beyond the $500,000 already raised. Greer therefore asks his "Brother Knights" from the four indicated U.S. southern states to appoint delegates who would meet in New Orleans during March 1860 in order to discuss "matters of importance in connection with the enterprise." Greer promises that the expedition will not bring conflict with the U.S. government and, if provided with the necessary subsistence, the Texas regiments will succeed." He concludes: "The southern country, *its bone and sinew*, is ripe for the movement and will aid us."[3]

Greer, a ramrod-straight man of action, was a lawyer, railroad superintendent, plantation owner, and Democratic states'-rights activist from the KGC hotbed of Marshall, Texas. He had become involved with the KGC in 1858, when he assisted Bickley in establishing castles throughout Texas and Louisiana. He subsequently traveled around the country recruiting. Greer spent so much time in furtherance of the Knights' agenda that his in-laws accused him of neglecting his wife and three children. By 1859, he had assumed the lofty title of "Grand Commander" of the Texas KGC and was a noted power across Texas and the South.[4]

Greer had been born in 1825 at Paris, Tennessee. His family moved to Holly Springs, Mississippi, when he was eleven. At nineteen, Greer enlisted as a private in Jefferson Davis's First Mississippi Rifle Regiment at the beginning of the Mexican War, and subsequently rose to the rank of sergeant. Upon returning to Mississippi, Greer was elected major general of the Mississippi Militia and was responsible for organizing, drilling, and disciplining its soldiers. In 1848, he moved to a plantation owned by his new wife's family near Marshall, Texas, and soon became a lawyer and a prosperous planter in his own right.[5] Greer—a tall, lean redhead with an impetuous temper and an imperious manner—was "cool under fire" and a man of few words.[6]

Through his own family as well as his wife's, Greer had connections all over the South. His father, Captain James Greer, was a lawyer, planter, and legislator descended from a Virginia Revolutionary War officer. James Greer acquired land throughout Mississippi and sired seventeen children, many of whom became notable and spread across Tennessee, Mississippi, and Arkansas—three eventual strongholds of the KGC.[7]

In 1851, Elkanah married Anne Holcombe, the daughter of a prominent Marshall, Texas, family. Anne was the sister of Lucy Holcombe, the ex-fiancé of López's artillery commander, William Crittenden, who had been executed as a result of the failed 1851 Cuban filibuster. In 1855, Lucy published a historical novel titled *The Free Flag of Cuba*, dedicated to her friend U.S. General John Quitman, that portrayed López's 1851 filibuster to Cuba as a holy mission. Lucy later married Francis Pickens, the Civil War governor of South Carolina, and subsequently became known as "the Queen of the Confederacy."[8]

The second-in-command of the Texas KGC was George Washington Chilton, a state legislator and slave owner from Tyler, Texas, a town about sixty miles west of Marshall. Like Greer, Chilton also had important connections throughout the South. Most notable was his uncle, William Parish Chilton of Alabama, the law partner of William Yancey and an eventual leader in the Confederate Provisional Congress. George Chilton was a fierce-looking Tyler lawyer, Indian fighter, and KGC recruiter who would succeed Elkanah Greer in early 1861 as Texas "Grand Marshall." Chilton's son, who would subsequently become a U.S. senator for Texas, remembered his father as "mounted on a horse, dressed in some bright regalia, crossing the square, at Tyler, with a number of men composing the Knights of the Golden Circle."[9] From 1858 to 1861, George Chilton headed the KGC-affiliated Tyler Guards from Smith County.[10]

Hearing that the powerful Texas Knights were serious about moving into Mexico immediately, Bickley rushed to New Orleans to try to stall a precipitous move by the KGC from the four southern states. During the first week of February, Bickley promised Greer that he would move a KGC division from the east within four or five weeks to help with the Mexico intervention. Meanwhile, Greer told his brother-in-law that he had one thousand men enlisted in Texas and that "the Knights are eager to take up the line of march."[11]

Greer continued his independent course on February 20 by offering his "regiment of a thousand volunteers . . . ready to move at a moment's notice" to Texas governor Sam Houston, alleged to be a member of the Order of the Lone Star and a renowned Indian fighter and leader in Texas's 1835 fight for independence.[12] Houston was then considering his own grand plan to move into Mexico to establish a protectorate for "humanitarian purposes" that he said was distinguished from "filibustering." Houston claimed his protectorate would not only help the Mexican populace but also curb the Mexican bandits marauding into Texas, as well as slaves escaping from Texas into Mexico.[13] He replied to the offer of Greer's regiment, "We will see." Houston noted that he had applied to Washington for financial help for Mexican intervention since "the Legislature had adjourned without leaving me a dollar in the Treasury."[14]

In seeking federal military aid, Houston instructed his friend and confidant Ben McCulloch, then in Washington, to "see the President and Secretary of War." McCulloch was a Texas KGC and Ranger leader. Houston exuberantly told him, "There will be stirring times on the Rio Grande ere long." Houston sent a simultaneous February 13 letter to U.S. secretary of war John Floyd for the attention of President Buchanan. It complained about "the Indian troubles" and the "forays from Mexico on our Southern border" and noted Texas's "empty Treasury." The letter warned that as governor, Houston might be forced in self-defense "to not only repel the aggressions from Mexico, but also to adopt such measure as will prevent the recurrence of similar inroads upon our frontier." Houston concluded: "Texas can and will if appealed to, in thirty days, be able to muster in the field ten thousand men who are anxious, embarrassed as her finances are, to make reclamations upon Mexico. Can we hope for aid from the Federal Government?"[15]

In addition to the KGC regiments, Houston as Texas's governor also had at his disposal several regiments of the Texas Rangers, viewed as heirs to the chivalric knightly tradition, but who in reality fought Indians and bandits with brutal savagery.[16] Houston saw the Rangers, who were themselves loaded with KGC members, as the nucleus of the army that he would order into Mexico.[17] In addition to Ben McCulloch, old-time Ranger captains like Bart Sims, Jack Hayes, and James Callahan as well as then current Ranger captains like John R. Baylor, John Littleton, and Laurence Sullivan Ross were members of the Knights. John Salmon Ford, the Mexican War hero who commanded the Rangers, was one of the KGC's top Texas leaders.[18]

The account of James Pike describes the interaction between the Rangers and the KGC. Pike, a transplant to Texas via Ohio and Missouri, served in the Rangers from July 1859 until the spring of 1860, when his Ranger company was solicited by a KGC captain at Belknap, Texas. The KGC captain told Pike's unit that Governor Sam Houston intended to lead a force of twelve thousand Knights into Mexico to be funded by English capitalists for the purpose of annexing the northern Mexican states. Pike describes the pitch made by the KGC captain:

> The captain was a ready talker, and well calculated to seduce the unwary into his schemes; and nearly all the rangers were induced to become members of the order. . . . He was exceedingly lavish in his promises; to become a knight was to secure perpetual fame at once; and few of the rangers who joined but believed that the lowest position which would fall to their lot would be that of a field officer. "All promotions" [the captain said] "were to be made from the ranks" (an old story every soldier knows), and all the great estates in Mexico were to be confiscated to secure fortunes to the adventurers. Immense tracts of land were to be granted to members of the order; the mines in Sonora were to be parceled out; and every possessor to be made a Croesus at once.[19]

Contemporaneous news reports indicate that similar KGC emissaries were traversing other areas of Texas at the time, drumming up volunteers.[20]

In New Orleans, rumors flew that Sam Houston would lead a contingent of twelve thousand Knights into Mexico to boost his U.S. presidential ambitions and divert attention from the U.S. sectional controversy. KGC Captain Thomas Troup Gammage said he had helped initiate Houston into the Knights at this time so that Houston could head up the Mexican expedition.[21] Gammage predicted that "if [the Mexican bandit] Cortinas does make another raid . . . Governor Houston himself will lead an invading force, pledged to conquer and annex all of the country between the Rio Grande and the Sierra Nevada."[22] The Texas KGC leader and entrepreneur Albert Miller Lea and his brother Pryor even tried to interest U.S. Army Colonel Robert E. Lee in the Knights' annexation scheme. Lee had just arrived to assume command over the six thousand U.S. troops stationed along Texas's frontier. Albert Lee reported to Governor Houston that Colonel Lee "would not touch any thing that he would consider vulgar filibustering; but he is not without ambition, and *under the sanction of Govt.* he might be more than willing to aid you to pacificate [*sic*] Mexico."[23]

While Greer was tendering his regiment to Governor Houston, Bickley was apparently finalizing a treaty with Manuel Doblado, governor of the rich Mexican mining province of Guanajuato. The terms of the treaty were subsequently revealed in the secret 1860 ritual of the KGC's First Degree:

> Under a treaty closed with 3 (Manual [*sic*] Doblado, Governor of Guana-juato) on the 11th of February, 1860, we are invited to Colonize in 2 (Mexico) to enable the best people there to establish a permanent government. We agree to introduce a force of 15,000 men, armed, equipped, and provided, and to take the field under the command of 3 (Manual [*sic*] Doblado, Governor of Guanajuato), who agrees to furnish an equal number of men to be officered by the K. G. C.'s. To cover the original expenses of arming our forces, there is mortgaged to our Trustees the right to collect one half the annual revenues of 4 (Guanajuato) until we are paid the sum of $840,000. As a bonus there is also ceded to us 536,000 acres of land [each KGC immigrant to be ceded at least 610 acres]. To secure this there is mortgaged to us all the public property of 4 (Guanajuato) amounting in taxable value to $23,000,000. 3 (Manual [*sic*] Doblado, Governor of Guanajuato) is now there, making arrangements for our reception.[24]

Unlike the 1859 *Degree Book* or Greer's circular letter, the above passage makes no reference to the northern Mexican provinces of Tamaulipas, Nuevo León, Coahuila, Chihuahua, or Sonora. This was likely because northern Mexico's independent-minded strongman Santiago Vidaurri had defected from the Juárez Liberal coalition in September 1859 and had withdrawn his army from the field, in part due to fears of a filibustering invasion from Texas. Nor does the passage mention Liberal President Benito Juárez, since he and the majority of his cabinet had by now rejected the use of "ten thousand Yankee mercenaries." KGC leaders hoped Juárez would reconsider, since by February 1860, General Miguel Miramón's army had swept the Liberals from the field, and Juárez and his remaining ministers were under siege at Vera Cruz.[25]

Meanwhile, the U.S. Congress was considering the Treaty of Transit and Commerce negotiated by the Buchanan administration, which would provide the Juárez government with $4 million in desperately needed funds in return for specified U.S. transit rights in northern Mexico and Tehuantepec. Congressman Samuel Sullivan Cox, representing Bickley's former district near Cincinnati, pointed to the KGC-planned intervention as a reason to support the proposed treaty in a March 1860 speech to the U.S. House of Representatives:

> If our Government fails in its duty now [i.e., to approve the treaty], one thing will happen, and that is, the sudden apparition of Houston, with ten thousand Texans, in northern Mexico. Such movements are as irrepressible as fate. They may be even less responsible and more reckless than Houston's project. I know that such movements are now in process of organization. . . . They are led by the "Knights of the Golden Circle," whose mystic "K. G. C." has the magic of King Arthur's horn. . . . Proposals have been made to Juarez by these adventurous spirits . . . to place him in the capital and loan him $500,000, in consideration of the public lands to be granted in [northern Mexican provinces]. . . .The gentlemen in the country connected with these movements are men of military tact and approved courage. They profess to obey our neutrality laws; they will not infract them; but if they go into Mexico they will go as emigrants, on invitation, and carry the appliances of art, manufacture and agriculture.[26]

Cox concluded his extended remarks by waxing eloquent on behalf of U.S. Manifest Destiny and his favorite secret society: "The very stars in their courses are 'Knights of the Golden Circle' and illustrate the record of human advancement. They are the type of that territorial expansion from which this American continent cannot be exempted without annihilation. The finger of Providence points to our nation as the guiding star of this progress."[27] Alternatively, Republican U.S. senator James Rood Doolittle from Wisconsin charged that the drive to acquire "Cuba, Mexico, Central America, all tropical America" and the "reopening of the slave trade" represented "southern fanaticism" and "the solution of Walker and his filibusters: the solution of the slave propagandists, or of the Knights of the Golden Circle."[28]

Southern papers like the *Norfolk (Va.) Southern Argus* subsequently printed Congressman Cox's speech in full, noting that unless the disturbances on the Rio Grande were calmed, Governor Houston would soon intervene with ten thousand men, or "the Knights of the Golden Circle will, numbering forty thousand men, banded together with 'hooks of steel' . . . to be introduced upon the invitation of the Liberal Government at Vera

Cruz."[29] More than one hundred Knights, headed by a fife and drum, paraded in Norfolk, Virginia, to generate interest for upcoming meetings addressed by Norfolk's prominent citizens.[30] Virginius D. Groner, a lawyer who was active in the local militia, headed the Knights in Norfolk. Groner had recently returned from a stint with the Rangers in Texas and was now a leader in the KGC across Virginia.[31]

One thousand Knights—mostly young men from respectable families—were reported to be drilling in Baltimore, and 250 Knights were preparing at Memphis "for a foray into Sonora or an attack on Vera Cruz."[32] In New Orleans, 2,200 men were reported drilling, and a division of 2,500 was reported "armed and equipped" in Texas.[33] The *Yazoo Democrat* (Yazoo City, Miss.) proclaimed that the Knights were "*en rapport* with the Juarez Government" and said they were going as a military body "to occupy and annex Mexico *a la* Texas."[34] The *Dallas Herald* chimed in: "If Mr. Buchanan wants Mexico for the Juarez party, let him have it even with the assistance of the K. G. C.'s."[35] As of March 2, 1860, T. T. Gammage, captain of the Rusk County KGC castle in Texas, said that a departure date had been set, and he ordered his Rusk Knights to assemble on March 10 for movement to the rendezvous point.[36]

In mid-March 1860, the meeting of southern KGC leaders that Greer had called for in his circular letter took place at New Orleans. The KGC attendees included Greer, commander of the Texas division; Colonel Henry C. Young, commander of the First Tennessee Regiment; and Colonel Nathaniel J. Scott, commander of a KGC regiment in Alabama. Scott was a substantial merchant and plantation owner from Auburn, while Young was a Memphis lawyer who had been born in Alabama.[37] Bickley arrived for the meeting with KGC Colonel Temple and KGC surgeon Semple. New Orleans papers reported that the KGC leaders were maintaining hourly contact with hundreds of New Orleans citizens prepared to embark on the "noble work" of placing "the 'liberal' or Juarez party in the full and peaceful occupation of the City of Mexico, and thus prove to the world that Americans will never refuse to other struggling people the aid so opportunely rendered us by the French in 1777." But despite the favorable spin, Bickley was severely criticized at the meeting for failing to produce his promised KGC army division and the necessary additional funding for the expedition.[38]

This led Bickley, Colonel Nathaniel J. Scott, Major Henry C. Castellanos (a New Orleans criminal lawyer), and James Ross Howard (a New Orleans engineer) to immediately embark on a KGC fund-raising and recruiting drive through Alabama and Georgia.[39] They twice visited Montgomery, where more than two hundred KGC members were reported. Here KGC gentlemen from Virginia (likely including Groner) joined the group.[40] At Selma, the KGC speakers said their object was to throw eighteen thousand troops into Mexico. They claimed that some seventeen thousand men were already enrolled on the KGC's military list, more than $700,000 secured, and more than five thousand men were ready to cross the Rio Grande to enter into service of the Juárez government.[41]

In Georgia, Bickley gave several southern-rights lectures on March 20 at Atlanta's city hall, in which he said that one or more KGC regiments had already been tendered for Mexico from each of the other Cotton and Border States. He urged Georgia to "take with her sisters an equal share of the rich, glorious blessing by coming to the aid of an organization which embraces Southern Governors, Senators and Members of Congress." A resolution was passed that recognized the KGC as a movement to guarantee slavery, not only where it exists, but also its possible extension to the south.[42] Three of Atlanta's four newspapers supported the KGC, and Archibald Alexander Gaulding, the publisher/editor of the *Atlanta Intelligencer*, served as a KGC fund-raiser and speaker.[43] Bickley also spoke at Augusta the next evening on the need to acquire Cuba and Mexico for slavery expansion.[44] At Macon, the KGC speakers said their Mexican expedition would involve five thousand "picked men" and that the U.S. government was aware of its intention and would not interfere.[45]

Meanwhile, thousands of Knights from more than twenty different locations congregated around Gonzales on the Guadalupe River in south central Texas. Sizeable detachments arrived from the eastern port cities of Baltimore and New York, Norfolk and Petersburg in Virginia, with others coming from Arkansas, Kansas, and Nebraska. Major R. A. Crawford of Griffith led a regiment from Georgia.[46] A regiment of Texans arrived from Smith County under KGC leader George Chilton, with further Texas companies coming from Austin, Henderson, Rusk, San Antonio, and Sulphur Springs.[47] The *Gonzales Telegraph* reported that "a large army [of KGC] . . . well organized and equipped . . . are at this moment moving in scores to the rendezvous."[48] A sizeable number of Knights were reportedly preparing to embark from Baton Rouge, and 150 Knights were reported to have left on a schooner from New Orleans on the evening of March 29.[49]

By early April, a Brownsville, Texas, correspondent for the *New York Herald* indicated that many of the congregated Knights from Gonzales had reached Texas's southern border at the Rio Grande River: "This section of the country is filled up with members of this mysterious organization [KGC] . . . their fires are increased every night by new parties arriving during the day. . . . [F]rom this place to Goliad . . . there is a continuous caravan of them, coming in small parties, in large parties, on horseback and in wagons, armed and unarmed, with money and without it."[50] U.S. Army Major Samuel Heintzelman noted in his diary that there were almost two thousand Knights in Brownsville as of April 12. In addition, more than 780 Knights were reportedly assembled at New Orleans waiting for a steamship to take them to the Mexican border.[51]

But neither the U.S. Congress nor the Buchanan administration would approve federal funding for Sam Houston's proposed expedition. The U.S. Senate also refused to approve the negotiated Treaty of Transit and Commerce with Juárez, due to the growing U.S. sectional divide and concerns about mutual security entanglements. The Buchanan administration distinguished its objectives from the KGC's by noting that it advocated intervening in order to maintain, assist, and preserve Mexico as an independent republic, while the KGC proposed "to occupy and annex Mexico *a la* Texas."[52]

This lack of federal funding caused Texas governor Houston to reverse his pro-intervention stance. On March 21, he issued a proclamation ordering the Knights to disband. According to Ben McCulloch, who arrived in Gonzales in mid-March, a letter from Houston was posted on the wall of the city hall, saying the "group of citizens" gathering for the purpose of invading Mexico were "without authority from the government of the United States or the State of Texas." McCulloch wrote to Houston on April 6, pleading with him to reverse his position and assume command of the KGC expedition, but to no avail. The Knights and Texas Rangers gathering on Texas's southern border now hoped that Ranger Commander John Ford would lead the expedition.[53]

But the KGC's planned thrust into Mexico was suddenly threatened by dissension within its own ranks. Jefferson Davis's brother-in-law, Joseph Davis Howell, a noted New Orleans filibuster leader, hurled charges against Bickley as a charlatan and a fraud. A card signed by Howell and the directory publisher W. H. Rainey appeared in early April in the *New Orleans True Delta*, stating:

> Through representations [i.e., generous pay and land grants] made to us, which we believed and received in good faith, from an individual styling Himself GEN. BICKLEY, Commander-in-Chief of the K. G. C., we have been introduced [*sic*] to deceive between five and six hundred of our fellow citizens.
>
> For the purpose of vindicating ourselves to our friends, and to prevent others from all parts of the Union being deceived by this man, we pronounce him an IMPOSTER, for which we hold ourselves personally responsible.[54]

This was followed up by allegations of financial irregularities, alleging that Bickley had absconded with KGC initiation fees.[55] The six-foot, seven-inch Howell, the elder brother of Davis's wife, Varina, had served in Jeff Davis's First Mississippi Regiment during the Mexican War. In 1855, he had recruited a company of fifty men from New Orleans for General Quitman's aborted Cuban filibustering expedition. Afterward, he moved to California, where he reportedly served as a mercenary and then returned to New Orleans in 1857.[56]

At the time of Howell's charges, Bickley, as well as KGC Colonels Greer and Young and other Knight notables, were in New Orleans, likely meeting to decide how to raise further funds for the Mexican expedition.[57] Bickley quickly responded to the charges with his own card in the *New Orleans Evening Picayune* of April 5, saying he had called a meeting with the disaffected parties "and gave a full and fair explanation of my acts since the origin of the organization." Bickley asked the Knights to suspend judgment until "matters now forcibly held private can be made public."[58] Apparently his explanation wasn't satisfactory to the dissidents, since reports indicate that on April 7, the disaffected KGC of Louisiana and Alabama expelled Bickley and appointed Colonel Greenborough as commander in chief. The local KGC assets were placed under W. E. Starke, who the reports said would meet all obligations.[59] Starke was then a cotton broker in New Orleans, and he would later become a brigadier general in the Confederate army.[60]

Bickley subsequently defended himself by saying that members of the order interested in a "mere filibuster" had inappropriately pushed him "to precipitate matters without due preparation and prudence and without a proper observance of law."[61] He further explained that "it is a notorious fact, that the President of the K. G. C. has, on numerous occasions, been personated by other men, who have tried to make money out of the organization."[62] Bickley also said that KGC Major Henry Castellanos, the commandant of the KGC's Second Louisiana Regiment, had indicated that "the Creoles and French will stand by you. . . . You can depend on one regiment of twelve hundred men from New Orleans."[63] The *Atlanta Intelligencer,* published by the pro-KGC editor Alexander A. Gaulding, reported that Bickley had made a plausible defense of himself, and noted that "whatever the fate of General Bickley, we still have great faith in the Knights of the Golden Circle."[64]

While the New Orleans filibuster element may have been overeager, the most likely explanation for the dissidents' charges is that Bickley, as was his tendency, overpromised and then could not produce the needed funds, men, and invitation from Mexican authorities. Samuel A. Lockridge, a former Walker filibusterer and recruiter who was then considering an active part in the Knights' expedition, said as much. Lockridge indicated he had been led to believe that President Buchanan and his cabinet had their "heart and soul" in the cause. But when Lockridge asked to see "the money and everything pertaining to the expedition, . . . [he] found it was a humbug of the first order and that they had no means and never had the promise of assent by or from responsible parties." Despite this, Lockridge noted that "some of the first men in our country [are] in association of the K. G. C. and they are now forming under . . . a different basis in Texas and other states and may yet succeed in their objects."(Lockridge did subsequently join Greer's Texas KGC division.)[65]

Bickley's nephew Charles quickly came to his uncle's defense, stating that the schism was due to "rowdies, gamblers, and other disreputable elements" in New Orleans who didn't live up to the KGC's standard to "embrace only gentlemen of character and respectability."[66] Robert Tyler, commander of the KGC's First Maryland Regiment, similarly blamed the former Walker filibusterers for the ruckus and said that the "dissatisfaction [was an] attempt by William Walker, Sockridge [meaning Lockridge] and others in N. O. to break up our organization."[67] Despite the turmoil, Colonel Tyler addressed a large and enthusiastic KGC meeting at Norfolk at the beginning of May 1860.[68]

After unsuccessfully trying to defend himself before the New Orleans dissidents, Bickley, on advice of friends, left for Mobile, Alabama, to arrange a general and "final" KGC convention. Major James Ross Howard of Alabama (who would serve as the secretary for the Raleigh, Convention) assisted in making the arrangements. Born in Virginia, the ubiquitous Howard had been reared in Louisiana and educated as a civil engineer in Paris. He fought in the Mexican War, and during 1859–1860 turned up with the KGC in Alabama, Louisiana, and Maryland.[69] While preparing for the Raleigh Convention, Bickley called for an investigation of the allegations against him to be headed by Greer and Samuel J. Richardson from Marshall, Texas.[70]

The drive for Mexico had been imperiously demanded by Greer and his Texas Knights and was fueled by the desire of New Orleans's filibustering element for action. Given Greer's stature and persistence, Bickley probably had no other choice than to go along, despite realizing he had not raised the $2 million in funding needed to launch the expedition. When Joseph Howell and the New Orleans filibusterers discovered this, they blamed Bickley and lodged charges against him that halted pursuit of the venture. Would Bickley now be able to redeem himself, maintain leadership of the Knights, and reinitiate his drive for the Americanization of Mexico?

4

# A REGIONAL COALITION

A S A PRELUDE to the Raleigh convention, Bickley issued General Order No. 546 on April 6, 1860, from the headquarters of the KGC American Legion at Mobile, Alabama. Sent directly to KGC state commanders and appearing in southern newspapers, it ordered each KGC castle to assemble and elect delegates to a "final" KGC convention to begin on May 7 in Raleigh, North Carolina. It said that the purpose of the convention was to "elect a permanent Commander-in-Chief for the [KGC's] military department . . . [t]o elect a permanent financial chairman, and to thoroughly organize the monied department . . . [t]o elect a Permanent President of the third or governing department . . . and provide a board of advisement." It also indicated that the convention would enact a code that will "clear the organization of vicious characters" and "prepare an address to the people of the Southern States."[1]

Accompanying the general order was a "Circular Letter" to "Fellow Soldiers of the American Legion, K. G. C." in which Bickley melodramatically announces that upon the organization of the Raleigh convention, he will resign his positions as "de facto President of the Organization, and thereby the Commander of its Forces." In it, he makes a spirited defense of his past leadership in response to those who have tried "to break up our Organization, and turn it from the noble purposes for which it was organized, into a Fillibuster concern." Bickley states that the dissidents, "failing to get offices have become piqued and lost no chance to slander all connected with the Organization." He notes that "shafts of jealousy and misrepresentation" have been hurled not only at him, but also at the following KGC leaders:

46

At Col. R. C. Tyler of Md.; at Col. V. D. Groner, of Va.; at Major Tillery, of N.C.; at Lieut. Col. Tillery, of S.C.; at Major Kinney, of Ky.; at Col. H. C. Young, of Tenn.; at Major W. G. Iaeger, of Md.; at Col. R. A. Crawford, of Ga.; at Col. J. M. Wampler, of Va.; at Col. N. J. Scott, of Ala.; at Col. W. D. Robbins, of Miss.; at Major H. C. Castellanos, of La.; at Col. W. B. Temple, of Tenn.; at Gen. E. Greer, of Texas; at Major Larrentree, of Ark.; at Col. M. M. Black, of La.; at Major R. H. Archer, of Md.; and at nearly every leading member of the Organization.[2]

With respect to the KGC's planned Mexican intervention, Bickley affirms this is "our field of operations." He continues: "If President Juarez chooses to invite us to his country, or any Constitutional Governor of any Mexican State . . . as emigrants, it is our privilege to accept such invitation, and then if we are incorporated in the Constitutional army of Mexico, with the distinct understanding that we shall put the Government in possession of the capitol, then it is our right to make the best terms we can for this service." Bickley claims that the KGC's assurance not to violate the laws of the United States had prevented U.S. government interference despite the fact that for two years, the KGC has been drilling large bodies of men throughout the southern states in cities such as "Baltimore, Norfolk, Petersburg, Richmond, Lynchburg, Wilmington, Charleston, New Orleans, Memphis, St. Louis, Louisville, Atlanta and Vicksburg"—even "in Washington city, within earshot of the President's house."[3]

Bickley's circular letter then presents a unique breakdown of the strength of the Knights' army as of April 1860, as well as its state regimental commanders. Bickley first notes: "There is a Division of about 3,500 men in Texas and Arkansas under the charge of General Greer." This estimate was probably in the ballpark since in January 1860, Greer said he had two regiments of Texas Knights "ready to move immediately," and close to a thousand Knights were subsequently reported in Arkansas.[4] Bickley next states: "[There is] a Regiment of about 1200 men in Maryland in charge of Col. R. C. Tyler . . . a Regiment of about 1,000 men [in Virginia] in care of V. D. Groner; a Regiment in North Carolina of about 600 men in care of Maj. R. C. Tillery." These estimates were also likely fairly accurate since extensive KGC activity was reported in Maryland and Virginia, and Virginius Groner was known to have been instrumental in expanding the KGC into North Carolina.[5] Bickley also reports that there is "a full Regiment of 1,000 at Memphis, Tenn., commanded by Col. H. C. Young" (a Memphis lawyer who had been involved in the April 16, 1860, meeting in New Orleans) and "a regiment of 1,000 in Mississippi, commanded by Col. W. D. Robbins."[6]

The remainder of Bickley's estimate appears more speculative. He reports in his "Circular Letter":

> a regiment forming in South Carolina, by Lt. Col. S. H. Tillery; two Regiments forming in Georgia, one in charge of Col. R. A. Crawford, and the other at present unrepresented . . . a Regiment in detached companies in other parts of Tennessee, for which no appointments have been made; . . . and another forming in the State [Mississippi] for which no commission has been issued; two Regiments are forming in Alabama—the first commanded by a prominent citizen and an old soldier, and the second by Col. N. J. Scott; there is a regiment forming in Kentucky the commander of which has not been fixed upon, but will be tendered to Col. Ed. Marshall; there is a Regiment in New Orleans of 1000 men, the Colonel of which has resigned, and another forming for which no appointments have been made; and a Regiment in Northwest Louisiana, in charge of Col . M. M. Black.[7]

With respect to Alabama, Georgia, Kentucky, New Orleans, and South Carolina, the breakdown itself indicates these regiments are only "forming." It also admits that the prior colonel of the existing New Orleans regiment had resigned; given the dissension, the one in northwest Louisiana is also suspect.

Discounting the more speculative portion of Bickley's enumeration, the actual regiments in Texas/Arkansas, Maryland, Mississippi, Virginia, and Tennessee would together indicate a KGC army of 8,300 men. This is close to the 7,000 noted in the KGC's 1859 *Degree Book*. In general, the KGC military strength was concentrated in two power centers—the 3,500-man division in Texas/Arkansas under Greer, and the almost 3,000 Knights in Maryland/Virginia/North Carolina under Tyler/ Groner/Tillery. Bickley's enumeration mentions no KGC forces in Florida or for any western states, including Missouri and California, where substantial KGC membership would subsequently be reported.

Bickley's letter, in describing the three KGC departments, discloses that the "Second Department," which is purely financial, is "thus organized: A

Central Financial Bureau at New Orleans; State Central committees in each Southern State, and then in every important place sub-committees." Bickley concludes his "Circular Letter" by ordering each company of the KGC's American Legion to send one delegate to "Headquarters at Raleigh, N.C." with "full and discretionary powers," since they will not only be selecting new leaders, but also the date for departure to Mexico, as well as new ceremonials to sift the "rowdies" from the organization.[8]

A few weeks prior to the KGC's Raleigh gathering, the Democratic Party met in convention on April 23, 1860, at Charleston, South Carolina, to nominate their national candidates and adopt a party platform. While Stephen Douglas, the "Little Giant" from Illinois, was clearly the Democrat's front-runner for president, the convention decided to first obtain agreement on the party's platform. It required a two-thirds vote of authorized delegates for decision making.

Rhett and Yancey had previously worked out the strategy that the fire-eaters would employ at the Charleston Democratic Convention—they would present nonnegotiable demands for the right to hold slaves in all U.S. territories. If these were rejected, then the southern delegates should walk out and select their own candidates. If this demand for positive slavery protection caused the Republicans to win, then Rhett and Yancey proposed that southern governors should call for the election of delegates to state constitutional conventions and secede. Many saw the cooperative strategy of "Rhett, Yancey, & Company" as a conspiracy to destroy the Democratic Party and tear apart the Union.[9]

On the fifth day of the Charleston convention, William Avery of North Carolina made an impassioned speech, arguing that slave labor was crucial to the acquisition of new U.S. territories in Cuba, Mexico, Central America, and the Caribbean, which he noted was something all elements of the party desired. This was followed by a controlled ninety-minute address by Yancey, in which he unapologetically defended slavery and then warned the delegates that the South would insist on a plank in the platform guaranteeing slavery in the territories. The next day, the platform committee adopted this slave-code plank, but its action was then reversed on the floor by the full convention. To try to mollify the southerners, the convention decided to retain the ambiguous 1856 Democratic platform plank, which left the issue of slavery in the territories up to the Supreme Court.

After learning of the convention's reversal on the slave-code plank, six of the Gulf Coast state delegations immediately walked out and were soon followed by several others. The walkout was led by the Alabama delegation that included Yancey and his former aide Leroy Pope Walker. The Texas delegation, of which Elkanah Greer was a member, also joined in. Given the two-thirds voting requirement, the convention was unable to nominate front-runner Douglas and was forced to adjourn and try again at Baltimore in June 1860. The proceedings had generally played out in the way Yancey and Rhett had projected—the Democratic Party was split and would remain irrevocably divided.[10]

On April 27, just a week prior to the start of the Raleigh convention, the results of the report by Elkanah Greer and Sam Richardson on Bickley's alleged improprieties became known. KGC Major Richardson placed a card in the local Marshall, Texas, paper disclosing that when he and Greer arrived in New Orleans, they found things different than they expected. The card reported that "a few disaffected persons . . . had *worked themselves* into the Order for no other purpose than to attempt to break it up—[they] had been members less than a month, clamoring for departure and aspiring to position and to whom could not be confided the plans and movements—[they] assailed him [Bickley] through the press, and threatening [*sic*] to assault him on the streets." Richardson stated that after remaining a few days, it was evident nothing could be accomplished and that Bickley left New Orleans for Mobile, Alabama, where he was preparing an address and general order for the Raleigh, North Carolina, convention on May 7. In the card, Richardson also indicated that the order for the Raleigh convention arrived too late for the Texas castles to attend, but he felt confident that nothing would be done at Raleigh with which the Texas Knights would disagree. He called for cooperation among the enrolled KGC convention delegates and disclosed that the Mexican operation was being temporarily suspended due to lack of funds.[11] Meanwhile, the Knights along the Rio Grande began to disband, and a Brownsville correspondent reported on May 18 that no further activity would be undertaken "until fall, if ever."[12]

The KGC convention held at Raleigh, North Carolina, from May 7 to 10, was orchestrated to allow Bickley to save face, but there is no question that he was stripped of much of his authority. Bickley was allowed to keep his position as "President of the American Legion," which was now described as the KGC's political wing; he was no longer president of the KGC as a whole. Bickley was not reinstated as commander in chief of the Knights' army. The convention decentralized the KGC organization, vesting prime authority in each of the KGC's state regimental commanders. The state commanders were given the power to directly receive money, enact bylaws, and appoint their subordinates. The KGC's centralized staff was now assigned to assist the state commanders rather than Bickley.

The first and second days of the convention were nonpublic, but the proceedings of the third and fourth days were reported in the *Raleigh Press* and picked up by other KGC-affiliated newspapers. Colonel Robert C. Tyler, the former Walker filibusterer who commanded Maryland's 1,200-man regiment, chaired the convention. KGC Major J. Ross Howard, who had helped Bickley organize the convention at Mobile, Alabama, was appointed secretary.[13]

The published proceedings name twenty-three KGC members as among those who participated, primarily from the East and the Deep South. A companion newspaper article also generally mentions convention members "from Columbus and Atlanta, Ga.; Montgomery and Mobile, Ala; and from Mississippi."[14] As Richardson's April 27 card implies, there's no indication that Greer, Chilton, or any other Knights from Texas, Arkansas, or from west of the Mississippi River attended. Richardson's explanation that Bickley's April 6 order arrived too late seems contrived. The absence of the Texas/Arkansas Knights may reflect a predetermination on their part to retain independent control of the KGC's Southwestern Division and maintain their distance from Bickley and the Knights in the East (thus confirming Lockridge's observation that the KGC was forming on a different basis in Texas). There is also no indication that the disaffected Louisiana/Alabama faction under Colonels Greenborough and Starke attended.

At the beginning of the published proceedings, Bickley handed in his resignation as commander in chief of the military department, and it was accepted. A motion by Virginius Groner was adopted to defer naming the KGC's new commander in chief until the convening of the "last" military convention scheduled to meet in Atlanta, Georgia, on August 1, 1860. Paul J. Semmes of Columbus, Georgia, a thriving manufacturing center that had an active KGC castle, was unanimously appointed a brigadier general of the KGC order. Paul Semmes (a cousin of the noted Confederate Admiral Raphael Semmes) was a wealthy plantation owner and banker who was a brigadier general in the Georgia militia and served as captain of the Columbus Guards, a noted militia unit and drill squad. Semmes had studied military science at the University of Virginia, authored a book on drill and tactic, and served as advisor to the U.S. Military Academy on its Board of Visitation.[15] In addition to Semmes, Colonel F. W. Dillard, a local Columbus merchant and warehouseman, attended.[16]

Cleared of misfeasance by Greer and Richardson's prior report, Bickley was reelected to his office as president of the KGC's Third, or governing, Degree, retaining the title of "President of the American Legion." A series of resolutions were subsequently presented by the Maryland KGC and passed by the convention, thanking Bickley for his work in building "up our order to its present beautiful proportions" and approving "the calm and dignified course" pursued in responding to the "irresponsible and irregular faction in the city of New Orleans." Appreciation was also expressed "to Maj. Henry Castellanos for presenting the claims of the K. G. C.'s to the people of Louisiana, Alabama, and Georgia."[17]

At Bickley's request, a "Board of Advisement" was appointed to include the colonels of the KGC regiments, their superior officers, and the heads of several staff departments that were appointed. These staff officers included Jno. B. W. Dunbar, M.D. as surgeon general; Augustus McGibbony as police general; Reverend Isaac Spangler as chaplain general; G. Morris Wampler as engineer general; and Robert C. Tyler (already commander of the KGC's Maryland regiment) as quartermaster general. Nathaniel G. Scott, a prominent citizen of Auburn, Alabama, was elected paymaster general and made permanent chairman of the KGC's finance department.

The convention made clear that, in the future, KGC funds were to be deposited by N. J. Scott in suitable banks and transferred to him via KGC collectors and financial chairmen to be appointed for each state. A few months later, the names of six designated banks and the state financial chairmen, who were authorized to receive KGC funds, were published as follows:

Phillip D. Woodhouse, Col. V. D. Groner, Norfolk, Va., Col. Jno. L. Walker, Charles City C. H., Va.; A. J. McAlpin, Raleigh, N. C.; Col. Jas. E. Cureton,

Lancaster C. H., S. C.; Col. F. W. Dillard, Columbus, Ga.; Col. H. C. Young, Memphis, Tenn.; Major Charles Bickley, Knoxville, Tenn.; Major Wm. G. Jaeger, Baltimore, Md.; Col. Ben. M. Harney, Louisville, Ky.; Col. Jas. H. R. Taylor, Holly Springs, Miss.; Major H. C. Castellanos, New Orleans, La.; Wm. H. Judah, Esq., Pensacola, Fla.; Gen. E Greer and Major Sam. J. Richardson, Marshall Texas.[18]

This listing again indicates that the KGC's primary centers of power were Texas/Arkansas and Maryland/Virginia/North Carolina, with related centers in Georgia, Tennessee, Kentucky, Mississippi, and Louisiana.

The convention then authorized changes to the KGC's ceremonial (which Bickley said were intended to clear out vicious characters), including the oath and induction ritual for the KGC's First and Second Degrees. A committee consisting of Bickley, Groner, Tyler, and N. J. Scott was given authority by the convention to make such changes. It was noted that the ceremonial of the KGC's Third, or governing, Degree (reportedly largely in oral form) would remain unchanged. The convention also resolved to move the headquarters of the KGC to Knoxville, Tennessee, until November 1, 1860, at which point it would move to Monterrey, Mexico.

Nineteen KGC leaders were then designated as a committee to prepare an "Address to the People of the Southern States" in order to publicly explain the objects and aims of the KGC and to overcome the negative charges of secrecy.[19] In addition to those leaders noted above, members of the committee included "Capt. Ben. F. Lindsey . . . J. Gordon, Esq., . . . S. F. Vanchoate, Esq., . . . Maj. Jno. H. Steele [editor of the *Atlanta Daily Intelligencer*], C. H. Foster [editor of the *Murfreesboro (N. C.) Citizen*] . . . Col. J. A. Shinglee, and George Goldthwait [likely George Goldthwaite, a wealthy Montgomery, Alabama, lawyer]."[20]

The end result of the Raleigh convention was that the KGC was now a loose coalition of regional or state power centers, each headed by a KGC regimental commander (such as Greer and his powerful Southwestern Division) with independent authority to act. These were supported by a network of KGC-affiliated editors and allied local politicians and tied together through roving KGC emissaries such as Ben McCulloch and Virginius Groner. A number of eastern KGC leaders, such as Robert Tyler of the KGC's Maryland Regiment, continued to express faith in Bickley, but he had been stripped of most of his power. Given this, it is difficult to determine how much credence can be given to the explanation of Bickley and Reverend Isaac Spangler on the evening following the convention that the KGC's prime object was still the colonization of northern Mexico.[21]

Despite the KGC's announced collective approach, it appears that Bickley was the primary author of the Knights' twenty-nine-page *Address to the Citizens of the Southern States* released during the summer of 1860.[22] In the address, Bickley provides considerable background on the KGC, its three degrees, and its dues structure. He tries to place himself at the center of the KGC's formation by indicating that the KGC had been formed on July 4, 1854, in Lexington, Kentucky, "by five gentlemen who came together on a call made by Gen. George Bickley, the President of the American Legion, K. G. C." He notes that for this reason, a clause in the fourth article of the KGC obligations states: "I will never desert the order or its arms as long as five brothers can be found who remain true to its work." He also quotes the prayer from the Third Degree that "has only been given to a few persons." As of mid-1860, Bickley claims, the KGC "numbered 48,000 members, and its 14,000 man Army could be mustered to 100,000 if conditions require."[23]

The address describes the course of the escalating sectional crisis from the southern viewpoint, employing hot-button themes such as the threat of slave insurrections, the unfairness of the various congressional compromises to the South, the growing influence of northern abolitionists on southern children, and the growing animosity of northerners and Europeans to the "Divine Institution" causing eroding support for slavery in the Border States. It also provides an exposition on the distressful history of Mexico since its 1829 independence, explaining why its rich soil, minerals, and ecclesiastical wealth make it a desired and legitimate field for KGC operations. The address asserts that the "Americanization of Mexico" will develop the shipbuilding, manufacture, and mining of the South. While the address defends slavery, it states that the KGC in Mexico would "adopt the apprentice system of England, the old system of Brazil, and protect by law all Africans landed on our shores." It claims the Knights would not reinstate the slave trade, but it would protect slaves delivered by others.[24]

The address harmonizes the KGC's two objectives of building a southern empire and advancing states' rights by noting that the planned Mexico expedition could relieve the pressure for southern secession and provide an outlet for southern territorial expansion. It says this could lead to the creation of twenty-five new slave states and thus resuscitate the South's waning political power in the Union. In support, it notes that the KGC's Mexican expedition "would remove the coming struggle between the North and the South to the plains and valleys of Mexico. . . . [T]he mere announcement that the K.G.C. had crossed the Rio Grande, or landed at Vera Cruz with a force of ten or fifteen thousand men, would of itself be sufficient to divert the attention of the nation from the bitter sectional strifes [*sic*] that now threaten us with civil war."[25]

While presenting the KGC as a way to avoid civil war, Bickley makes it clear that the KGC is a "Southern association, and is for the *South first, and then the Union.*" He states that it would serve to protect the $2.4 billion of slave property in the South, and its [the KGC's] established domestic police system would serve as the nucleus of a southern army. In the event of secession, it would follow the lead of the southern governors.[26] The address concludes by summarizing the advantages of the KGC, noting that in addition to providing "peace and permanency to society in Mexico," it would keep Mexico "out of the hands of the Republican majority of the North." With respect to the secession crisis, the address also notes that the KGC would "cultivate the martial spirit" of the southern states so that "if one secedes all would go," and "it would provide a vanguard in the great army of the South, which must be, at no distant day, brought into the field."[27]

In conjunction with the KGC's *Address to the Citizens of the Southern States,* Bickley wrote a piece titled "An Open Letter to the Knights of the Golden Circle" that appeared in the *Richmond Whig* of July 17, 1860. Directing his letter to his "Fellow Soldiers," he dramatically notes at the outset: "Seated on my native soil, and amid the graves of my ancestors, I am penning this *open letter* for the great Southern Public as well as for you [the KGC]." He then reiterates many of the previously referenced southern-rights themes. Bickley says that Texas has already raised $489,000 for the KGC's expedition to Mexico, and appeals to other southern states to do as much, recognizing their direct financial interest in slaves worth $2.8 billion. After noting that KGC monies should now be sent to the listed KGC state financial chairmen, Bickley alludes to the KGC's recently decentralized organization: "Remember the K. G. C. do not follow me; they follow a policy which thus far, I have had the honor to direct."

Bickley then declares that "the K. G. C. must act *now*—at once, and with energy" and orders every KGC member belonging or desiring to belong to the military department "to repair to our camp at and near Fort Ewen, on the south bank of the Rio Nueces, and along the road on the ridge between Prita and Salado Creeks, in ENCINAL county, Texas, by the fifteenth day of September, 1860." He indicates that "the Rear Guard will remain in camp until October first." Bickley advises the Knights who volunteer to "bring your wagons, mules, oxen, horses, cattle, spades, axes, *'instruments'* [i.e., weapons], camp kettles, each two blankets, provision and all *material* useful to a Mexican emigrant. Above all let each man have twenty dollars or more in specie, as there will be an excellent opportunity to invest it profitably immediately upon crossing the Rio Grande." But he warns: "Under no circumstances must a K. G. C. cross the Rio Grande" prematurely since they must be invited in as emigrants by "our friends in Mexico" to avoid a violation of the U.S. neutrality and other laws. He indicates: "I have now announced the only time for moving ever intended except Nov'r 1st, 1859, and that was frustrated by the recognition of our friends' government in Mexico."

Bickley concludes his "Open Letter" to the Knights with a multifaceted appeal to "Young men of the South" ("we will show you a nobler field than the gaming table and the rumshop"); as well as to "Southern mothers and Southern sisters" ("send us the young and vigorous men—we will return them veterans covered with scars and glory"). He also invokes the memory of the Revolutionary and Mexican War patriots from the southern states:

VIRGINIANS:—Ye men of my blood—you whose fathers have been Presidents and Counselors in the nation . . . *as a Virginian* . . . I appeal to you . . . Maryland, have you no more Watsons? Has Kentucky no more Clays, McKees, and Marshalls? Has Arkansas no more Yells? Has South Carolina no more Butlers and Dickinsons? Texas no more Walkers and Hays? Mississippi no more Davises and M'Nulty's?—Tennessee no more Nelsons? Virginia no more Hamtramcks? North Carolina no more Paines? Georgia no more Jacksons and Calhouns? Alabama no more Withers and Coffees? Louisiana no more Walters and Markses? Has Missouri no more Eastons and Doniphans?[28]

Bickley's "Open Letter" wasn't always favorably received. The editor of the *Mobile (Ala.) Tribune* called it "bombastic moonshine" and lamented that "such people as the writer of this . . . bring ridicule and discredit upon the South."[29] The *Washington, D.C., Daily National Intelligencer* said Bickley's claim that the people of Texas are enthusiastic and have subscribed $800,000 in aid is "unmitigated bosh" and that Bickley was being denounced in various parts of the South as "a commander without men."[30] The *Louisville Democrat* editorialized that Bickley's letter shows that "the whole purpose [of the KGC] is political"—to break up the Democratic Party. Claiming that Yancey's Southern League was absorbed into the KGC, it alleges, "Mr. Yancey knows more about it than he chooses to tell, and so do others, no doubt."[31]

On August 8, 1860, the *North Carolina Standard* (Raleigh) and the *Charleston Mercury* carried KGC General Order No. 28, issued by Bickley's nephew Charles at San Antonio. This instructs the "Southwestern Division" of the KGC army to rendezvous on the south bank of the Rio Nueces in Encinal County, Texas, on September 15, 1860. It invites members from other KGC divisions, as well as other individuals "of Southern birth or entertaining sentiments favorable to the institutions of the South" to join in if they would report fully equipped as emigrants. The general order also solicits donations to support the movement and says that they may be deposited in any reliable southern bank to the order of "Col. Nat. J. Scott of Auburn, Alabama, Paymaster General of the KGC."[32] While having Bickley's nephew Charles issue the order does present a show of unity, it nevertheless appears that Greer's Southwestern Division, rather than Bickley or the KGC as a whole, was spearheading the renewed Mexican expedition.

There is no evidence that the August 1 KGC military convention in Atlanta called for by the Raleigh convention to elect a new KGC commander in chief actually took place (a subsequent publication of the Raleigh convention proceedings moves the scheduled date back to September 3, 1860).[33] This could mean that the KGC's state regimental commanders were able to maintain strict secrecy, but it is more likely that they decided to defer the KGC military convention until the course of the growing sectional crisis in the United States became more apparent. In the meantime, they relied on the KGC's roving emissaries such as Virginius Groner,

James Ross Howard, Ben McCulloch, and Bickley's nephew Charles to achieve coordination.

Bickley continued traveling and speaking across Virginia during the summer of 1860, accompanied by the KGC's chaplain, Reverend Dr. Isaac Spangler, as well as Reverend J. S. Clark. Speaking at Lynchburg, Bickley promised that the KGC flag would fly over Mexico City by January 1, 1861.[34] At Norfolk, Bickley claimed that the KGC had twenty-five thousand members in the United States, including two hundred from New York City, "and is apposite to a Legion in Mexico composed of the best and most patriotic men in that country."[35]

During mid-May 1860, the *Norfolk Southern Argus* said that if "a Black Republican President" is elected, "the glorious Southern legion [KGC] will take the initiative of rescuing the South from legalized wrong and oppression by guaranteeing the Southern States a peaceful withdrawal from a violated compact."[36] In July 1860, Major S. J. Richardson said that Bickley expected to be in Marshall, Texas, on or about August 20.[37] At the same time, northern newspapers noted in early August that "Gen. Bickley has been denounced in various parts of the South, and according to all accounts, he occupies the position of a commander without men."[38]

The scorching month of July was eventful in Texas, due to a fire that engulfed the town center of Dallas on July 8 and caused $400,000 in damage, including destruction of the offices of the southern-rights *Dallas Herald*. A few hours later, another fire ignited in the nearby town of Denton, resulting in a similar conflagration when twenty-five kegs of powder exploded. Copycat fires were soon reported in a variety of Texas locations, fueling rumors of a slave conspiracy. Vigilance committees were formed to ferret out the perpetuators. These committees often exacted forced confessions and summarily hung alleged participants. Under duress, slaves told tales of a conspiracy to commit arson, murder, and poisonings, masterminded by northern abolitionists. Fear and panic spread across the Lone Star State, and from there to the rest of the South.[39]

To make sure the alleged conspiracy received widespread attention, Charles Pryor, the editor of the *Dallas Herald* (whose offices had been destroyed in the fire) wrote letters detailing the presumed plot and its grisly consequences to other states'-rights newspapers across the South. Papers like the *Little Rock (Ark.) True Democrat* printed Pryor's reports verbatim on "the deep laid scheme of villainy to devastate the whole of northern Texas."[40] Since taking over the *Dallas Herald* in 1859, Pryor had used the newspaper to promote white supremacy. Originally a physician from Virginia, he frequently lauded the program of the militant Knights of the Golden Circle. For example, the *Dallas Herald* of February 29, 1860, had heralded the KGC's Mexican excursion by proclaiming: "Let those Texans range on the Mexican Frontier and infuse some of the Anglo-Saxon ideas of progressiveness into the stupid leaden souls of the people—and then the world will notice the change."[41] The KGC had a castle in Dallas, and Pryor was a KGC sympathizer and likely a member.[42] At least twenty Texas newspapers were similarly sympathetic to the Knights.[43]

Pryor's letters about the conspiracy caused widespread hysteria as Texans of all political persuasions became fearful for themselves and their families. Reports of new incidents of arson continued to circulate, particularly in towns like Marshall and Tyler that had active KGC castles. The harrowing phenomenon became known as the "Texas terror." Reference to the "incendiarism in Texas" was subsequently incorporated into the KGC's initiation ritual, and politicians supporting John Breckinridge for president frequently noted it. The panic helped the states'-rights Democratic ticket sweep the August 6 legislative elections in Texas. The opposition charged, on the other hand, that the states'-rights Democrats had created the hysteria for political purposes.[44]

While the KGC had been known to engage in burnings as acts of reprisal,[45] the more likely explanation for the original Dallas and Denton fires is the excessive summer heat that reached 110 degrees, coupled with the new phosphorus matches being introduced, which often prematurely ignited. Except for the initial two fires, most of the other incidents turned out to be hoaxes. But the resulting hysteria primed public support for the KGC's secret police force and surveillance system to strong-arm northerners and other suspicious characters.[46]

The paranoia soon spread to other states, as reports circulated of slave atrocities backed by northern abolitionists in Alabama, Arkansas, Georgia, Mississippi, South Carolina, and Virginia. A Mississippi planter informed his noted brother Joseph Holt (who was serving as postmaster general in Buchanan's cabinet) about an army of slave assassins numbering in the thousands who were preparing to act with poison, knives, and pistols furnished by northern emissaries.[47] Montgomery, Alabama, papers charged that the South was "infested" with hundreds of abolitionist agents ready to help enforce the rule of Lincoln, should he win the election.[48] *The Murfreesboro (N. C.) Citizen*, edited by Charles Henry Foster, used "the colossal Abolition conspiracy in Texas" as a rationale for commissioning new KGC castles to serve as minutemen in the event of a sectional crisis. Foster was a pro-expansionist editor who had helped Groner spread the Knights across North Carolina's upper-tier counties.[49]

During July, a New Orleans newspaper correspondent reported that Colonel John Ford and some of his officers had returned to the Brownsville, Texas, area. The correspondent speculated that this might mean a renewed KGC filibuster into Mexico could soon be getting under way. The *Harrison Flag* of August 10 observed, however, that conditions were not then propitious for a renewed Knights expedition, since a drought had ruined the grain crops and the Cortina War had depleted the cattle herds in the Rio Grande basin.[50]

Even more problematic were reports from New Orleans that Juárez's Liberal Party government at Vera Cruz (which had just undergone a cabinet shakeup) had now formally rejected the KGC's services.[51] In early August, the following note appeared in various U.S. newspapers dated July 3, 1860, from "The Consul General of the Republic of Mexico" stationed at New Orleans, who purported to speak on behalf of Mexican president Juárez: "It is true that this organization of the [Knights of the] Golden Circle, and other societies in the United States, have offered to the constitutional government their assistance in the civil war now raging in Mexico, but the President has constantly refused every aid of this nature. The rumors put in circulation by those who speak on behalf of the Golden Circle are false in every respect."[52] Beginning in August 1860, Juárez's Liberal Party army began to win victories on the battlefield as Manuel Doblado, with his ten-thousand-man force, rejoined the coalition. By the end of the year, the Liberals had driven General Miramón and his Conservative Party army back to Mexico City, from where Miramón subsequently fled to France. This led to Juárez's triumphal return to the capital on January 11, 1861, as the Liberal Party's government took control over virtually all of Mexico.[53]

Despite the apparent lack of Mexican support, Knights begin arriving in southern Texas during September. A series of KGC units were said to be passing through Corpus Christi on their way to Brownsville.[54] The *Norfolk Day Book* reported that large numbers of KGC, which it claimed had reached the formidable (and highly exaggerated) number of fifty thousand, were concentrating in Texas and "this nucleus is being surrounded by men from the various States." It continued:

> The first movement of the K. G. C.'s from Virginia will take place tomorrow from the little town of Hampton. One company under the "command of a competent officer and a worthy Virginia gentleman [i.e., Groner], will embark for Texas and will then inaugurate the exodus of the K. G. C.'s. That the object of this organization is to change the political and social principles of the country to which they go, there is little doubt, but they do not go unlawfully armed, at least from here; they profess to go as peaceful citizens and will revolutionize that unhappy country not by the fire and sword, but by settling in sufficient numbers within its borders, and changing and making wholesome laws, and seeing that they are enforced."[55]

As of September 9, forty-five additional Knights left Norfolk—twenty from Richmond—with further émigrés from Petersburg as well as Maryland and North Carolina.[56] On September 4, Bickley was reported leaving from Richmond for the Texas encampment, while the *New York Herald* of September 10, 1860, stated: "Colonel Groner has left for Texas via Richmond and Memphis where he expects to meet a large concourse of Knights of the Golden Circle."[57] The *Memphis Avalanche* said that several hundred KGC were in their city, which would became the center for operations, while two thousand under the command of Bickley and Greer were said to be "at present quartered on the Rio Grande, prepared at any moment to pour into Mexico and proceed to the capitol."[58]

Would this coalition of Knights from regional power centers hold together and would the indomitable Bickley be able to redeem himself? Would Juárez and his Liberal Party relent and invite the Knights to intervene? Would Greer's Southwestern Division finally be able to spearhead the Knights' expedition into northern Mexico and advance the South's dreams for a slaveholder's republic?

# 5

# TRANSFORMING TO SECESSION

ICKLEY HADN'T EVEN left for Texas on the scheduled rendezvous date of September 15, 1860, for the renewed expedition into northern Mexico. Instead, the KGC's front man was in southeastern Tennessee, appearing on platforms with KGC chaplain Reverend Isaac Spangler and Reverend J. S. Clark. In a speech at Cleveland, Tennessee, Spangler touted the KGC as a "powerful military organization, as a nucleus around which to hang such political considerations as will, if well managed, lead to the disenthrallment of the Cotton States from the oppressive majority of the Manufacturing and Commercial interests of the North." He claimed that the KGC order numbered "sixty-five thousand Southern men" and that several members of the Buchanan cabinet, as well as all except for three of the southern governors were members.[1] The KGC speakers also said the South should support the KGC as a domestic police force, and confidently predicted "*the Southern governors will have use for us within six months.*"

A writer reporting the Cleveland speech for the *Nashville Republican Banner* under the byline "Bradley" called the KGC's work a "treasonable conspiracy" and alleged that it was tied in with the southern fire-eaters promoting southern secession:

> They [the people of Tennessee] have heard much about GOV. WISE's letter of 1856 to the Southern Governors, W. L. Yancey's "Southern League," Yancey's letter to Mr. Slaughter, and Gov. R. J. Walker's letter of June 28, 1858 to President Buchanan in which he says: "*Cuba! Cuba!* (and Costo Rico [*sic*] if possible)." . . .

These Filibustering and revolutionary documents gotten up by men placed in high position by the people, indissolubly connect them with this K. G. C. Organization. The link between that, and the Yancey Southern League is so perfect, and well defined, that a fool cannot but observe it.

According to Bradley's account, Mr. A. Campbell, a resident of Cleveland, jumped onto the platform at the end of the "piratical discourse" by the "Reverend Filibusters" and denounced their aim as "revolution and ruin to the country." Campbell's denunciation reportedly excited so much indignation against Bickley and his entourage that personal violence was feared. Bradley concluded: "We hope these gentlemen will be shown up, and driven out of every community where they may attempt to preach their treason and establish their '*Castles*.'"[2]

In south Texas, the *Corpus Christi Ranchero* of September 22 reported with respect to the KGC's rendezvous: "It appears that they [the arriving Virginia and Maryland Knights] are bound to suffer disappointment, as they expected to meet a large force in Encinal county," but "there are no Knights in Encinal county, nor no one . . . concentrated at any point in this section."[3] This was followed up by a September 29 report that the scattered KGC members along the Mexican border were heading home. The *Ranchero* editor speculated: "There must be mismanagement on the part of the leaders, or else a concentration of forces would be better understood."[4] Bickley finally arrived in Galveston on October 11, indicating that he should have arrived on October 1 but had been "unavoidably detained."[5]

While some KGC members calculated that one thousand Knights had arrived in Texas, Bickley said that only four hundred to five hundred had reached the border and that prematurely crossing the Rio Grande into Mexico would invite disaster. To explain the deficiency, he cited the difficulty of transporting the requisite arms and provisions to the rendezvous point. He also alluded to the failure of General William Walker's filibustering expedition to Honduras, and the approaching presidential contest. Bickley proposed waiting a few weeks until the conditions were right.[6]

More telling, however, is Bickley's subsequent disclosure that "many of the prominent men in the organization believe that no attempt should be made until the first of December, at which time we may be more needed at home than abroad."[7] This indicates that Greer and other KGC regimental commanders had decided to defer the Mexican expedition to see whether the southern governors would need the Knights' help in dealing with the escalating secession crisis.

But the deferral of the Mexican expedition did not stop the ever-resourceful Bickley. He simply shifted his efforts to rejuvenating and expanding the more than twenty-five KGC castles that were spread across the rich agricultural counties of East Texas. With its growing plantation economy, fear of slave insurrection, and tradition of vigilantism, East Texas provided a fertile territory for the Knights' recruiting and organizing campaign.[8]

Bickley (described in some newspapers as one of the best speakers in the country) spent October and early November traveling from Galveston to Austin to Houston to Huntsville to Waco and back again, making speeches and visiting newspaper editors to better explain the KGC and its purposes. His brilliant but erratic nephew Charles, who headed the Charles Bickley Castle in San Antonio, accompanied him.[9] Virginius Groner, the KGC regional commander from Virginia, also assisted. Groner arranged a meeting for himself and Bickley with Texas governor Sam Houston. During the meeting, Houston renewed his threats to lead an army into Mexico if Spain made a hostile demonstration against Juárez and his Liberal Party at Vera Cruz.[10]

On October 17, Bickley was scheduled to speak in Austin, Texas's state capital. The town of Austin was fairly evenly divided between pro-South and Unionist adherents. Prior to Bickley's visit, KGC operatives distributed pamphlets and nailed placards throughout the town, notifying its 2,500 white citizens of a speech to be given by "KGC General George Bickley" at a local hall. The pamphlets warned that antislavery zealots and northern teachers and editors were indoctrinating Texas children, as well as the public, against the God-sanctioned institution of slavery. They said that the South must present "an unbroken front" to counteract these northern abolitionists who want to "re-enact the farce and folly of Jamaican Emancipation [where freed slaves outnumbered whites by twenty to one]." As the remedy for these ills, the pamphlets prescribed the KGC as an association like the Hudson's Bay and East India Companies: as these trading companies had won empires for Great Britain, so would the KGC for a southern confederacy. The pamphlets also reiterated Spangler's disunionist mantra from Tennessee: "The Knights of the Golden Circle constitute a powerful military organization as a nucleus around which to hang such political considerations as will, if well managed, lead to the disenthrallment of the cotton States from the oppressive majority of the manufacturing and commercial interests of the North."[11]

This prepublicity had the desired effect, and on October 17, Bickley addressed a sizeable Austin audience on the advantages of the KGC. To try to counteract the suspicions caused by its secrecy, Bickley read from the KGC's rules and its nonpublic First and Second Degree rituals. In describing the structure of the organization, Bickley noted that the First Degree of the KGC was the military division, composed of an army of sixteen thousand men with the mission to advance into foreign territories. A sizeable home guard in the United States served as its adjunct, to provide provisions and transportation. The Second Degree—the commercial division—was dedicated to raising funds and garnering favorable propaganda for KGC ventures. It contained many of the KGC's affiliated newspaper editors and moneymen. At the apex of the organization was the KGC's Third, or governing, Degree, known as the American Legion, of which Bickley remained president and where membership was based on influence rather than money. Bickley did not read from the Third Degree's nonpublic ritual since it was largely oral, and its membership was kept secret, even from the lower two KGC degrees.[12]

In his speech, Bickley denied that the KGC had a political objective. He said that in the ongoing presidential election campaign, the KGC could accept either the Democratic states'-rights candidate, John Breckinridge, who was the sitting vice president from Kentucky; or the northern Democratic candidate, U.S. senator Stephen Douglas of Illinois; or the Constitutional Union candidate, John Bell from Tennessee. But the KGC's political flexibility extended only so far. If Abraham Lincoln, the Republican candidate, were elected, Bickley predicted that "resistance would surely follow, and the 'K.G.C.' would become the rallying army for the Southern disunionist."[13]

Toward the end of his address, Bickley invited questions from the audience. Retired Texas judge George Washington Paschal rose to challenge him on several points. Paschal, a minor slaveholder and conservative Democrat, now served as editor of the *Austin Southern Intelligencer*.[14] He first challenged Bickley on the KGC's oath and asked whether the "allegiance which you swear rises above or [is] subordinated to the laws of the United States and of the respective States." In its 1860 oath, the KGC required an inductee to swear "allegiance to the K. G. C. and its lawful officers . . . and execute every commission entrusted to me [as well as] support the government established by my brothers in arms and their officers."[15] In defense of the demand for unquestioning fealty, Bickley read from the First Degree ritual that also required an inductee "to obey the laws of the United States and the States in which you live; that you will do no act of which an American citizen should be ashamed." He noted, however, that as citizens, KGC members had the right to judge the constitutionality of laws for themselves and act accordingly.

Pascal then asked whether "the Mexico which you may find in the District of Columbia, points to the contingency of the presidential election, and if the order stands ready to obey the Southern governors and to raise the standard of rebellion, if they are not satisfied with 'the presidential election.'" Bickley responded in the affirmative and said that the KGC would obey the directives of the southern governors. He claimed that Mississippi governor John Pettus, as well as other unnamed southern governors, were KGC members. To this Paschal (who was a confidant of Sam Houston) replied: "We elect governors to see that the laws are executed; not to inaugurate revolution. Much as I love the Governor of Texas, I declare that should he usurp the power of calling for soldiers to rend the constitution, laws, and lawful authority of the United States, I would denounce him as a traitor to his oath [noting, however, that Sam Houston would never do this]."

Paschal then focused on Bickley's frequent references to the KGC as a "Domestic Police System." He charged: "I have understood that it has been said the order acts as spies upon travelers, and even marks baggage, and that baggage has come marked to this city as suspicious. Is that so?" To this, Bickley simply replied: "It is." He declared that as to "baggage searching, the spotting of men &c . . . there ought to have been such an order thirty years ago. . . . [I]t was intended for the nutmeg men, the Yankee peddlers and other suspicious characters. Does anyone object to these sentiments and practices?"

Bickley's glib admission sent Paschal into a tirade. Paschal accused the KGC of being "a secret police agency—one which establishes a police above the law." He shouted that the KGC was an "institution of the order of Robespierre, which will plunge us into a sea of revolution worse than the bloodiest days of France. It cannot, it will not be tolerated. . . . It arrays itself with the misguided partizans [*sic*] who threaten to overthrow the government should they not elect their candidate! And it proposes, by secret means, to proscribe all who will not fall into their revolutionary purposes."[16]

The KGC was sensitive to charges of its secrecy, admitting in its 1860 ritual that "secrecy can be used for bad purposes by bad men." But it defended its secrecy as necessary to "select our men from the respectable walks of life . . . prevent the public from forcing us into political attitudes . . . be enabled to measure our actual strength, and to use the benefits that may accrue from our labors for the benefit of our own members."[17] Paschal's charges of vigilantism were timely in light of the local patrols that roamed East Texas and wreaked vengeance in response to reports of slave insurrections.[18]

In presenting the KGC as vigilance posses, Bickley and his KGC compatriots were capitalizing on the primordial instincts of fear and self-preservation fueled by Charles Pryor of the *Dallas Herald* and his allied KGC editors the preceding summer. These articles predicted that if Lincoln and the Republicans were elected, it would not only destroy the southern way of life but also threaten the personal security of all white southerners, who would now face the prospect of further slave insurrections and orchestrated attacks on white slaveholders. The articles raised the prospect that these uprisings could rival the horrendous August 1791 slave revolt in Saint-Domingue, where hundreds of thousands of avenging black slaves killed thousands of white planters and their families.[19]

As with Austin, large supportive crowds appeared at each of Bickley's stops on the East Texas recruiting campaign, and a record number of new Knights were enlisted for the cause. By the end of October, seven new castles and hundreds of new enlistees had been added to the eight thousand Knights existing in the Lone Star State.[20] Texans nervously awaited the result of the November 6 presidential election, but communications were rudimentary so it would take at least a week for the results to reach the Lone Star State. Even if Abraham Lincoln were elected, Democratic president James Buchanan would remain in office until March 4, 1861, due to the four-month interregnum period that existed at the time.

During the first week of November, Bickley headed to Marshall, Texas, one of the largest and richest towns in East Texas with about two thousand white residents. Marshall was the county seat of cotton-producing Harrison County, where almost 60 percent of the total fifteen thousand residents were slaves. Texas's fire-eating U.S. senator Louis T. Wigfall had established his law practice in Marshall. Wigfall, who publicly called for reopening the African slave trade and supported filibustering expeditions to Central America, was a KGC sympathizer and likely a member of its secret Third Degree political wing.[21] Marshall was also the home of Elkanah Greer, the KGC's Texas "Grand Marshall," and was a hotbed of proslavery and KGC sentiment. At Marshall, Bickley would meet up with key KGC leaders for a conclave to formulate strategy, in case Abraham Lincoln, the "Black Republican" candidate, won the election.[22]

Since the KGC conclave held at Marshall was secret, the full range of participants and agenda are not recorded, but it is known that Bickley and his nephew Charles were there. Since the conclave was held in Marshall, Elkanah Greer and KGC Major Sam Richardson were undoubtedly also in attendance. It is also likely that George Chilton from nearby Tyler, soon to become the new grand marshal for the KGC in Texas, attended the conclave.[23]

Virginius Groner, the thirty-three-year-old state commander of the KGC in Virginia, was also in attendance. Groner, a lawyer from Richmond, headed the powerful KGC castle at Norfolk and served as coordinator for the various Knights castles at Petersburg, Richmond, and other locations in Virginia and North Carolina.[24] Groner had left Richmond in early September 1860 with the expectation of meeting up with a large contingent of Knights in Texas. After traveling around the South and Southwest to gauge KGC sentiment (and likely the temperature of affiliated southern governors), Groner had linked up with Bickley in mid-October and joined in the Texas recruiting campaign.[25]

Like Greer, Groner had a military background. He had graduated from the Norfolk Military Academy in 1853 at the age of eighteen. Groner then worked for a few years as agent for an express company and was admitted to the bar after studying law with a private tutor. He organized a Norfolk military company known as the "Independent Grays," subsequently described as one of the "best military organizations on the seaboard," and was made a lieutenant colonel in the Virginia militia. Groner then got the travel bug and headed to Texas in 1859, at the invitation of its governor, Sam Houston. He tendered his services to a Texas Ranger company, headed by KGC member John Baylor, and fought Comanche Indians and Mexicans on the Texas frontier. After Groner's five-month stint in the Rangers, he returned home to eastern Virginia, where he became preoccupied with the KGC and helped spread new castles throughout Virginia and the tidewater area of North Carolina.[26]

Shortly before the Marshall conclave, Groner forwarded a letter to friends in Norfolk that subsequently appeared in the *Norfolk Southern Argus* on November 3, 1860. In the letter, Groner notes the delay of at least a few months in the KGC's Mexican expedition by explaining, "Until one has taken a practical part in the workings of this organization, he can have but little idea of the obstacles to be encountered." Groner continues: "Political objections arise, which have to be met and answered. What is called 'the conservative element' of the South would much prefer to see this work [intervention in Mexico] done by the Federal Government; but I assure you that prominent men of the K. G. C. are firmly convinced that it would be the worst thing that could happen for the South." Groner notes that he and Bickley had just had a conference with Texas governor Sam Houston, who had assured them that he would lead "the largest force of Texans and other volunteers, if Spain made a hostile demonstration against Vera Cruz."

Groner indicates that while the KGC is still focused on intervention into Mexico, "several Southern governors have requested that the movement be delayed until after [the election] shall have taken place. If Mr. Lincoln is elected, the K. G. C. will be held subject to the orders of the Southern governors." (Groner subsequently noted that "resistance is seriously contemplated" and "preparations are actually being made for that purpose.") If Lincoln is not elected, Groner says, the Knights can be "assured of large pecuniary assistance from several of the Southern States." He notes that Texas will "furnish three fourths of the vanguard going into Mexico," with Mississippi and Arkansas also tendering large bodies of men. Groner concludes: "If we are sustained by the press[,] we shall succeed, otherwise the result will be problematical, if not disastrous."[27]

During or shortly before the November 1860 conclave at Marshall, an informer said he had infiltrated a KGC "Council of War" in Texas. The informer passed along his intelligence to Colonel Joseph K. Mansfield, the U.S. Army's diligent inspector general, who was then touring Texas to inspect its U.S. military installations.[28] The informer reported that he had learned that John Floyd and Howell Cobb, the respective secretaries of war and of the treasury in the outgoing Buchanan administration, were KGC members. He also said that Jefferson Davis, then U.S. senator from Mississippi, as well as John Breckinridge, the sitting U.S. vice president from Kentucky who had run for president as the Democratic states'-rights candidate, were also members of the secret society.

According to the informer, this KGC "Council of War" had developed a plot "designed to seize Washington and inaugurate Breckinridge" as president. Presumably this would have to be done before March 4, 1861, when an incoming Republican administration was expected to take over. The informer also recounted that "in this Council of War, Orders were given to seize Navy-Yards, Forts, &c., while its members were yet Cabinet officers and Senators."[29]

Mansfield attached sufficient credibility to the report to transmit it up the army's chain of command, where it would eventually reach Salmon Chase, the incoming secretary of the treasury for the Lincoln administration. In his diary, Chase later reported the informer's revelations and indicated that the KGC was an organization to be reckoned with: "The Order of the K.G.C. ramified throughout the South. First offered services to Juarez, who refused them because too dangerous. They then plotted the invasion of Cuba, which failed. Then declared themselves Protectors of Southern Rights and levied a contribution upon all planters and slave-holders—some giving $5 and some $10, and some more or less. In this way they got large sums and commenced operations."[30] Mansfield undoubtedly also passed along the information to his superior, Winfield Scott, general-in-chief of the armies of the United States, who became convinced of a secret plot to seize the federal forts in the South as well as the District of Columbia before Lincoln's election.[31]

The formulation of this audacious KGC plot was undoubtedly what Texas congressman John Reagan disapproved of in his letter of November 1, 1860, responding to Oran M. Roberts, a Texas Supreme Court justice:

> Your reference to the Knights of the Golden Circle, and supposition that the organization may have in view some plan of action on behalf of

the South, and implied disapproval of any secret movement for such a purpose meets my unqualified approval. A secret movement, for such a purpose,
could not but prove disastrous in the extreme to the cause of the South. . . .
For any citizen or member of citizen's group as such to array themselves
against the federal government without the authority and protection of state
sovereignty, they would be rebels in law, and might be dealt with as such.[32]

Reagan, who would later become postmaster general for the Confederacy,
was a moderate who said he loved the Union but was concerned about
the reported slave insurrections and the South's self-preservation if the
Republicans were elected.[33] Justice Roberts, who would soon head Texas's
secession convention, was from Tyler, Texas, as was George Chilton, soon-
to-be-elected KGC Texas grand marshall, from whom Roberts likely received information as to the KGC's intended plan of action.[34]

The shift in the KGC's objectives from establishing a slaveholding empire in Mexico to supporting secession is reflected in Bickley's public remarks before and shortly after the Marshall conclave. Prior to that meeting,
Bickley referred to the planned Mexican incursion as the KGC's prime
objective, with assistance to the southern governors in merely hypotheti-
cal terms. In his letter of November 3 to the KGC, Bickley was still hoping
that "if no civil discord arises to demand our services at home, we shall
proceed at once to move the Texans to the scene of action."[35]

During his well-received public speeches at the Marshall courthouse
on November 9 and 10, Bickley still referred to the Mexican incursion
but now shifted his focus to the KGC as "a nucleus around which southern men could rally," proclaiming: "The 'wide awakes' of the North were
organized as was apparent to enforce Black Republican misrule upon the
South—to subjugate resisting Southern States. We require a counteract-
ing organization in the South. The K.G.C.'s numbered upwards of 115,000
men, 50,000 of whom could be concentrated at ten day's [sic] notice to
protect any Southern State struggling for its rights." Bickley also trum-
peted "the necessity of military organizations all over the South, so as to
keep down insurrection and to repel invasions."[36] By November 12, Bickley
proclaimed: "If I learn that Mr. Lincoln has been elected, no movement of
the KGC will be attempted until it is determined by the Southern States
whether they will submit or not."[37] The editor of Marshall's *Harrison Flag*,
who up until this point had been a KGC supporter, said that from Bickley's

November speeches, it appears that the secret society has shifted its objective from delivering Mexico from anarchy to the District of Columbia.[38]

This shift in emphasis is also consistent with changes that were made to the KGC's ritual around this same time. The 1859 First Degree ritual had been rather general, largely focused on the planned Mexican intervention, and devoid of any reference to a sectional conflict.[39] During 1860, the ritual was revised to read: "The first field of our operation is Mexico, but we hold it to be our duty to offer our services to any southern State to repel a northern army. We hope such a contingency may not occur."[40]

The ritual used in Texas beginning in late 1860/early 1861 had an even more sectional slant. It justified spreading southward into Mexico, Cuba, and Central America as necessary to beat the northern states to the spoils:

> The idea of expansion is as deep rooted in the minds of the people of the North as in the South. Cuba, Mexico, and Central America are much coveted by the North in order that free-soil States may be erected South of us. With her Homestead Bills, Emigrant Aid and Wide-Awake societies, she well knows that she can people rich Mexico, Cuba and fruitful Central America before *our* people could be able to settle up their business. . . . No greater calamity could befall the South than the planting of free-soil colonies in Northern Mexico, as that would be the first step of hemming us in and thereby cutting off the only outlet for our peculiar institutions. To build up a great and powerful empire, such as the world has never witnessed, it is only necessary for us to acquire lands which will yield coffee, dye-woods, gold and silver, tea and small grains. These lands are within our reach, and the K. G. C. would be the vanguard in their acquisition. We ask none but Southern men to assist us.[41]

"Ante-Room Work" was added to the ritual to qualify candidates for KGC membership. It now included a set of thirteen questions to prove an applicant's pro-South and proslavery disposition. The questions included the following:

9. If any attempt should be made to wrest from you your Constitutional rights would you defend them?

10. You know that there is a bitter sectional strife in this country—if it should ever result in war would you espouse the cause of the North or the South? . . .

12. Do you believe that negro slavery is right?

13. Will you defend the institution on any and all occasions from the assaults of abolitionists?

During the subsequent initiation ceremony, a First Degree applicant was ordered never to reveal anything that transpired at a castle meeting. He was also required to "solemnly swear before God, and in the presence of these witnesses, that [he] will bear true allegiance to the Knights of the Golden Circle as a body, and to the Superior Officers of the same [and] keep secret from all persons, except Knights of the Golden Circle, the signs, password, grip, token &c of the First Degree."[42]

The shift in emphasis was also incorporated into the ritual for the "Second or Financial Degree" in Texas. This new ritual required candidates to help resist the advance of abolitionism and to defend the rights of the people of the slave states against anarchy, insurrection, and massacre. The ritual contained a discourse on the historical development and justification for slavery and concluded:

> There is but one possible chance to maintain our independence and rights in the Union, viz: The acquisition of a sufficient quantity of territory in the south, to procure an equal representation in congress, by and through a system of defensive colonization. If the separations so long threatened between the north and south be carried out, then it will be the natural policy of the Southern Confederacy to foster any scheme which looks to the Americanization and Southernization of the Republic of Mexico.[43]

The "Third or Political Degree" ritual for a member of the "Knights of the Columbian Star" was also revised to provide that any candidate for this top degree had to be born in a slave state, or if born in a free state, be a Protestant and a slaveholder (or give evidence of character as a southern man). The ritual stipulated that the candidate also must pledge to use his best efforts to ferret out and report abolitionists and build up popular sentiment in his state for the expulsion of free Negroes.[44]

This shift to a predominant pro-South emphasis was not acceptable to a number of KGC members, who joined the organization largely because of its expansionist objectives. An unnamed "North Texan" from Sherman, writing to the *Louisville Journal* during January 1861, said he had previously been elected as a KGC captain and had assisted in the initiation of twenty KGC members, when the objective was the "peaceful 'Colonization of Mexico.'" But he said that in the fall of 1860, he had washed his hands of the "low-down, dirty concern, deserving the utter contempt of every true patriot and lover of our country." He complained that "Gen. Bickley . . . made his appearance in our State, and stumped a considerable portion of it. The purport of said speeches goes to prove that the real object of the association was the dismemberment of our Union, a treasonable effort to overthrow the Federal Government."[45] R. H. Williams, a proslavery English adventurer who had joined the KGC around San Antonio during October 1859, similarly claimed that while the KGC was ostensibly formed to protect southern rights, its real object was "to bring about Secession, and all its weight was thrown into that movement."[46]

The editor of the *Texas Republican*, in reporting Bickley's remarks, generally denounced secret organizations. He nevertheless agreed that "whenever the day of resistance comes, if come it must, there is not a Southern State that cannot send forth, armed and equipped, ten thousand men, who have been accustomed to the use of arms from their youth. These men will scarcely be missed from among us, and yet they will constitute an army of 150,000 men, who, in point of efficiency, intelligence, discipline, determined valor, intrepidity, and all the elements that constitute a valuable army, will be superior to any force that has even been sent to the field since the world began."[47]

Bickley echoed these themes in his November 12 report to the KGC's membership via the *Houston Telegraph*, noting, "If I learn that Mr. Lincoln has been elected, no movement of the K. G. C. will be attempted until it is determined by the Southern States whether they will submit or not." In such case, Bickley said: "I shall have to visit the east for material, and must therefore be absent from the State [Texas] for some weeks." If civil war ensues, Bickley said, "I believe it to be the duty of the members of this organization to lend their services to the Governors of their respective States." In a November 15 report, still from Marshall, Bickley exclaimed: "Thank God, the K. G. C. organization is now in the hands of the people of the South."[48] Bickley had apparently just learned that Lincoln had been elected president with slightly less than 40 percent of the popular vote—Breckinridge had swept Texas and the South, but he came in second in the national electoral vote count, and only received 60 percent of the popular votes of the regular Democratic candidate, Stephen Douglas.[49]

It appears Bickley left to go east around November 15, since his nephew Charles soon began filing the KGC's Texas reports. In a November 29 report, Charles Bickley replied to KGC Colonel John J. Cook of Montgomery that "General Bickley was at Marshall on the 10th," implying Bickley had left shortly thereafter. Charles advises Cook, "In case of a demand for troops on the part of the South, the services of the K. G. C. will be tendered."[50] This indicates that George Bickley may have been on his way to Montgomery, Alabama, which contained castles with at least two hundred members. By February 1861, Montgomery was designated as the KGC's headquarters.[51]

Elkanah Greer also spoke out boldly at a Marshall mass rally on November 16. For several years, Greer had been complaining about "the foul breath of Abolitionism" and "the diabolical imposition of the North on the free-born and liberty-loving Southerners." At the Marshall mass rally, under the waving flag of the Texas Lone Star Republic, Greer proclaimed "a more consummate piece of folly could not be committed than to wait for the North to inaugurate her withering, dishonoring, and diabolical policy." Advocating the South's immediate secession, Greer proclaimed: "The overt act [Lincoln's election] has been committed. Let the South speak now or forever hold her peace." At the end of his speech, Greer indicated he had tendered the services of one of the Southwestern Division's two KGC regiments to Francis Pickens (Greer's brother-in-law), who was soon to be elected South Carolina governor and who was now calling for South Carolina's immediate secession.[52]

The Texas KGC and South Carolina secessionists kept in communication through emissaries like Ben McCulloch, who, after meeting with South Carolina legislators in October, had penned a letter from Columbia informing an Austin newspaper editor that South Carolina would secede before the end of January 1861. In the same letter, he also urged Texans to take up the secession issue.[53] McCulloch kept in touch with the southern fire-eater Barnwell Rhett, whose *Charleston Mercury* noted on October 31: "The Texans are almost to a man for fight, if the Abolitionist LINCOLN should be elected, and they regard BICKLEY's forces as the most available nucleus for an army."[54]

In early December, the *Norfolk Day Book* reported that Colonel V. D. Groner had returned from his KGC coordinating mission to the South and the Southwest. It said that according to Groner, the KGC now had "one hundred twenty thousand members . . . each of whom is sworn to stand by the South. They are fully organized, constantly drilled, and can be brought into action, if necessary, in two weeks time." The article also reported that on his way back from Texas, Groner had stopped off at Mississippi, the home of Governor John Pettus, whom Bickley had identified as a KGC member.[55] Pettus had previously declared during his 1859 campaign for governor that he was for dissolution of the Union in the event of the election of a "Black Republican" president and would resign if the people would not sustain him in strong resistance. He saw secession as a matter of southern honor and accused northerners of "denouncing us as barbarians, pirates, and robbers, unfit associates for Christian or civilized men."[56]

On behalf of Bickley, Groner offered Pettus the services of soldiers from the KGC's army. Pettus thanked General Bickley for the offer but replied that he did not yet have authority to accept KGC soldiers. He noted, however, that the Mississippi state legislature would soon authorize him "to take such steps as are necessary for the defense of our rights," in which event he would avail himself of the KGC's offer.[57] In the interim, Pettus sent Groner on an errand to New York to supervise the purchase and shipment of a large quantity of arms for Mississippi, including rifles from the federal arsenal at Springfield, Massachusetts.[58]

The KGC's secession plot had now been laid and was being coordinated with the more radical southern governors. As Bickley promised, the KGC would soon become the nucleus for an army of volunteers, raised from across the South, that would help precipitate secession and attempt to seize the southern forts and the nation's capital at the District of Columbia. Charles Anderson, a Kentucky-born Unionist living near San Antonio, would subsequently charge that the KGC of Texas exercised "a decisive influence, in starting the great conspiracy" since "without [the movement of Texas] the Rebellion would have aborted in its earliest stage."[59]

# 6

# THE PARAMILITARY'S CORE

I N HIS NOVEMBER 10 speech at Marshall, Bickley described the KGC as "a nucleus around which Southern men could rally" and called for the formation of military organizations all over the South to keep down insurrections and repel [northern] invasions." In apparent response, a KGC captain at LaGrange subsequently urged his castle members: "Arouse the military spirit of your neighbor, organize them into companies, and teach them military tactics and science."[1] Knights often formed a secret inner core within the quasi-military organizations rising in the South and served as drillmasters for the new recruits. This allowed the Knights to quickly scale up their affiliated manpower and scope while sidestepping growing resistance to the KGC's secrecy.[2]

Charles H. Foster, the KGC editor of the *Murfreesboro (N.C.) Citizen*, revealed in August 1860 that an underlying purpose of the KGC in setting up home guards and vigilance committees was to establish "in every town and county in the Southern States, a sworn band of citizens, pledged under the sanctity of oath to defend our Constitutional rights and to espouse the cause of the South against the North in the event of a sectional collision." In urging the rapid expansion of KGC castles and affiliated sworn bands of citizens, Foster said that they "would be prepared to act at a moment's notice, though summoned from their bed at midnight, under known leaders and without confusion."[3] In doing so, he invoked the patriotic image of the minutemen from the 1776 American Revolution, when the best men of each militia unit were asked to stand ready at a moment's notice to execute the commands of the revolutionary Committees of Public Safety.[4] Foster's call presaged the rise of the most widespread of the new quasi-military movements during October and November 1860—the Minute Men—that enrolled more than two hundred thousand southerners.[5]

On October 7, 1860, the South Carolinians at Columbia revived and formalized the revolutionary concept in drafting the constitution for the "Minute Men for the Defense of Southern Rights," which called for the formation of volunteer infantry and cavalry companies across the Palmetto State. The Minute Men constitution warned that "the election of a 'Black Republican' President will be a virtual subversion of the constitution of the United States and . . . submission to such a result must end in the destruction of our property and the ruin of our land."[6] Organizers included the South Carolina fire-eater Barnwell Rhett, former governor James Adams, and Francis Pickens (Greer's brother-in-law), who had previously headed the Minute Men formed during South Carolina's 1833 nullification crisis. David R. Jones, a cousin of Jefferson Davis and a future Confederate general, was selected to lead the South Carolina Minute Men organization.[7]

The South Carolina Minute Men was open to any person who believed in the southern cause. All volunteers were asked to bring their own firearm and wear a blue cockade on the left side of their hats. They were required to "solemnly pledge, our LIVES, our FORTUNES, and our sacred HONOR, to sustain Southern Constitutional equality in the Union, or failing that, to establish our independence out of it."[8] In addition to drilling, the Minute Men formed vigilance committees in South Carolina's plantation districts to prevent slave insurrection and deal with suspected abolitionists. In the cities, the Minute Men led grand parades and torchlight processions to promote South Carolina's secession. They also supported the election of secessionist delegates to the South Carolina convention and intimidated Unionists. It was widely reported that an ancillary purpose of the organization was "to march at a minute's notice to Washington to prevent Lincoln's inauguration."[9]

Minute Men units soon spread across South Carolina. By the end of November 1860, eight thousand minutemen drilled in Columbia, and twenty-seven companies had been formed in South Carolina's Piedmont region. William Gilmore Simms called the movement "a perfect landsturm" and said there were twenty thousand minutemen armed in South Carolina with squads in every precinct.[10] One planter said he was cajoled into joining a Minute Men unit and claimed he was forced to participate in the hanging of six northern men and was aware of the hanging of hundreds more.[11] Similar companies of Minute Men formed in towns and cities across Alabama, Arkansas, Georgia, and Mississippi. Like their South Carolina counterparts, they formed vigilance committees that harassed Unionists and held parades and rallies supporting secession.[12]

In eastern Virginia, thousands of minutemen joined companies formed in response to the October 25 call of former governor Henry Wise (an OLS/KGC sympathizer), who was referred to locally as "the gallant Knight of Virginia."[13] The KGC leader Virginius Groner (likely taking some credit for affiliated minutemen) reported that the Knights "now numbered 120,000 members who are fully organized, constantly drilled, and can be brought into action if necessary in two weeks time." Groner informed Mississippi governor John Pettus, "Every day new volunteer companies are being formed and our State is being put in a complete state of defense."[14]

A good example of the KGC's behind-the-scenes role in organizing the rising quasi-military groups is the formation of the Minute Men of Atlanta (Fulton County) Georgia. KGC members Alexander Wallace, an insurance company agent and prominent secessionist, and Alexander Gaulding, the editor of the *Atlanta Intelligencer*, had chaired Bickley's March 1860 fund-raising appearances in Atlanta. They, as well as Dr. J. K. Alexander, had been appointed to the KGC's seven-man committee to collect contributions and report to the KGC's State Central Committee.[15] Now, in November 1860, Gaulding called to order the organizational meeting of the Fulton County Minute Men, which was chaired by Dr. J. K. Alexander (both men served on the organizing committee). Alexander Wallace, now captain of the Atlanta Grays, at whose armory the meeting was held, gave a spirited southern-rights speech to the more than one hundred men who showed up for the meeting. A resolution was passed endorsing "any action that the sovereign state of Georgia may take in asserting her independence." Soon more than four hundred joined the new Atlanta Minute Men chapter.[16]

The Atlanta Grays' connection also demonstrates the KGC's affiliation with the voluntary military clubs that existed in the South, which often attracted men from the upper classes who enjoyed military drill and display. The number and size of these independent clubs increased substantially after John Brown's October 1859 raid at Harpers Ferry. As the secession crisis deepened, the military preparations of these voluntary clubs became more intense, and their purpose was redirected to actively promoting secession.[17]

In towns where the KGC had castles, the military clubs were often affiliated with the castle and assumed responsibility for military drill of KGC members. In San Antonio, the KGC castles sponsored several affiliated militia units, including the Alamo Guards and San Antonio Guards, which supervised military drill for castle members. Similarly, at Galveston, the Knights' castle was affiliated with the Galveston City Guards that merged with the Lone Star Rifles in 1857 to become the Galveston Artillery Company, charged with protecting the city's harbor.[18] In Dallas, KGC leader John Good organized and was elected captain of the Dallas Light Artillery in March 1859, which contained many of Dallas's prominent citizens.[19] As a former KGC member noted: "Every castle is, in truth a regular military company. . . . thousands of castles have been drilling two or three times per week, for several years."[20]

Like Atlanta Grays Captain Alexander Wallace, a number of KGC military commanders served as the head of an affiliated military club or militia unit. KGC Colonel Virginius Groner headed the Norfolk Grays, which at one point was described as "the best military unit on the seaboard."[21] George Chilton, soon to become the KGC's Texas grand marshall, headed the "Tyler Guards."[22]

In Harford County, Maryland (the familial home of John Wilkes Booth), Robert Harris Archer had organized a private militia company called the Spesutia Rangers in March 1860, serving as its initial captain. The forty-year-old Archer had fought in the Seminole and Mexican Wars, then returned to work on his family's Harford County plantation (but taking time off to travel in Mexico and the South). According to Archer's KGC commission as "Colonel" and "Staff Quartermaster," Archer joined the Knights in December 1859 in New York. By November 1860, Archer had assumed a much broader role, recruiting young men from the five counties in Maryland's Second Congressional District for a new private regiment to be offered to the governor of South Carolina, "if he, in the crisis through which that State is about to pass, require their services."[23]

In Georgia, KGC Brigadier General Paul J. Semmes had served as the captain of the Columbus Guards, which was filled with fifty "gentlemen of education and high social standing." It was similarly described as "one of the oldest, if not the best drilled volunteer corps at the South."[24] By October 1860, after being appointed a brigadier general in the KGC, Semmes was in the process of forming a brigade in a new organization called the "Southern Guard." It was purposely formed outside the regular Georgia militia system so that it could be called into service in states other than Georgia.[25]

On November 12, Georgia held a military convention at Milledgeville involving military clubs and militia units from across the state. Georgia's fiery prosecession governor, Joseph Brown, addressed the assembled militia members, affirming each state's right to secede and proclaiming that the duty of the other southern states was to support South Carolina. If the federal government tried to prevent secession, Brown threatened to resist and to hang two federal soldiers for every Georgian who should be executed for treason.[26] After approving resolutions for Georgia to obtain armaments and equipment (to put it on a war footing), the convention voted two to one in favor of Georgia's immediate secession.[27]

A number of known or suspected KGC leaders were in Milledgeville around this time, including Gideon Pillow, the adjutant general of Tennessee's voluntary forces. One of the key players at the military convention was KGC Brigadier General Paul Semmes, who had recently accused the northern government of robbing the South of $105 million per year and urged: "Let a united South rally and strike down this God-forsaken Union with robbers, fanatics, incendiaries, assassins, infidels. Southrons arise! Buckle on your armor; trust in God and strike for independence." At the end of November, Semmes was appointed by Georgia's Governor Brown as a special agent to obtain arms and munitions pursuant to the $1 million appropriation provided by the state legislature. Semmes soon headed to New York City to arrange the purchases.[28]

The KGC leader and arms salesman Ben McCulloch was also in Milledgeville around the time of the convention. Shortly following it, McCulloch warned Texas governor Sam Houston that "if the South submitted to Mr. Lincoln's rule, there will be insurrection in some of the States. . . .

Then upon the election of Mr. Lincoln's successor (another Black Republican,) the South will march an army to Washington city to resist the inauguration."[29] By November 25, McCulloch was in Columbia, South Carolina, from where he wrote his brother Henry that "the strong party" in South Carolina will obtain a unanimous vote in its convention for secession by December 20 and will "at once sieze [*sic*] the Forts and U.S. arsenals." McCulloch urged that "the eight cotton states [should] go out as soon as possible" and that Texas should join them "so that she will not be behind every southern State that makes cotton."[30]

In addition to involvement in the Minute Men movement, the KGC was also at the center of the paramilitary conversion of the Breckinridge and Lane Clubs that took place in the latter part of 1860. John Breckinridge, the states'-rights candidate for president, was accused of being a disunionist due to his radical states'-rights supporters and his equivocal denials during the campaign. In 1860, most extreme states'-rights men, including Robert Rhett, Louis Wigfall, and William Yancey, supported Breckinridge, in part due to a speech that Breckinridge had made in December 1859, proclaiming that if the Republicans were elected, "resistance in some form is inevitable."[31] Breckinridge was also rumored to have worn KGC emblematic jewelry while serving as vice president in Washington, and was publicly charged with being a member of the Knights by notable politicians, including Kentucky's U.S. senator John Crittenden.[32]

During the late summer of 1860, the notorious fire-eater William Yancey decided to embark on a campaign tour on behalf of Breckinridge's candidacy after receiving invitations from various Breckinridge and Lane Clubs. This tour encompassed twenty major addresses over a seven-week period in towns across the South, the Border States, and the North. Yancey said he was undertaking the grueling campaign tour because he was angry at being described by northern papers as the architect of disunion; he wanted to show the North that he didn't have horns. Others alleged, however, that Yancey's underlying purpose was to gauge Border State sentiment for secession and ramp up the militancy of the Breckinridge and Lane Clubs.[33]

Yancey, a medium-sized man with a melodious voice, was the most spellbinding and fearless orator in the South. He began his campaign swing with a speech in Memphis on August 14, in which he said that if the Republicans were elected, he hoped "some great Washington [will] arise who will scourge them from the temple of freedom, even if he is called a traitor, an agitator or a rebel." He then proceeded to Knoxville, Tennessee, where he exchanged verbal threats with the pro-Unionist newspaper editor William Ganaway ("Parson") Brownlow.[34] After stopping at the home of Secretary of War John Floyd in Abingdon, Virginia, Yancey moved on to Richmond and Staunton. At the District of Columbia, he spent five days in mysterious meetings with states'-rights politicians and researching government documents. During a speech from his hotel's balcony, Yancey warned that the Republican Wide-Awakes were arming and training to force northern rule upon the South. He also described the glory that would attend an independent southern republic where southern port cities would become dynamos of commerce, eclipsing those of the North.[35]

Yancey then moved on to Maryland's Eastern Shore, where former governor Enoch Louis Lowe escorted him. He made appearances in Annapolis and Baltimore. After canvassing Maryland, Yancey moved on to address a meeting of the Breckinridge Democrats at Wilmington, which was followed by a public procession of two thousand stretching for one and a half miles. He then crossed the Mason-Dixon Line to speak in New York City, where he made a major address defending slavery and castigating the alleged abolitionist plots by northern ministers in Texas. Yancey next ventured to Boston, the heart of abolitionism, where he vigorously defended slavery, contending that "no laboring people on the face of the earth are so happy, so uniformly well fed and clothed and provided for, in sickness and in health, as the slaves of the South."[36]

After journeying west to a number of northern-tier cities, Yancey swung back south through Kentucky during mid-October with major addresses at Lexington and Louisville, and whistle-stops in smaller towns along the way. George Prentice in his *Louisville Journal* subsequently charged that Yancey, during his swing through Kentucky, had "made the establishment of the Order of the Knights of the Golden Circle a part of his special business if not his chief business." More specifically, Prentice said that Yancey spoke at Lebanon in central Kentucky's Marion County "and remained there a day, organized a lodge, or branch, or whatever else, the name may be."[37]

On September 2, 1860, the *Louisville Daily Democrat* had published the KGC's "Address to the Southern People," incorporating the public summary of its May 1860 Raleigh, North Carolina, convention. The editors noted that the pamphlet shows the KGC's "whole purpose is political. . . . While its members belong to open political parties, their acts are controlled by secret obligations." It further alleged that "the first great object to be accomplished was to break [up the Union]" and that "Mr. Yancey knows more about it than he chooses to tell."[38] Yancey, while admitting he had been solicited by the Knights, subsequently denied that he was a member or was engaged in establishing castles of the KGC.[39]

Yancey's tour culminated on October 29 in New Orleans, where he spoke to a crowd of thirty thousand people, the largest public attendance for a speech in the city's history. The growing militancy of the Breckinridge and Lane Clubs was now evident, as related paramilitary units joined in the lengthy procession that escorted Yancey to the podium. In his speech, Yancey advocated resistance if the Lincoln administration sent more incendiaries like John Brown and similar abolitionist agitators. He proclaimed that all citizens had a reserved right of secession, as well as the right to resist (for the purpose of self-preservation) from a government that endeavors to crush them. Confirming the intelligence-gathering purposes of his tour, Yancey said his trip convinced him that the Border States would never permit a hostile army to cross them to try to coerce the states of the Deep South.[40]

Yancey's militarizing efforts undoubtedly played a role in the metamorphosis of the Breckinridge and Lane Clubs of Baltimore and Washington, D.C., into the National Volunteers during late 1860. In Baltimore, the National Volunteers was formed following a huge October 22 meeting of Breckinridge and Lane boosters, where a canvas was displayed proclaiming, "Maryland must and will be true to the South." At the meeting, a new paramilitary organization was announced, to be called "the National Democratic Volunteers" and to consist of twenty-four companies under "Chief Marshall William Byrne."[41]

During early November, the Volunteers organized a large torchlight parade in Baltimore in which five thousand participated. Byrne, bedecked with a blue sash, led the entourage mounted on a fine horse. After the election, the National Volunteers, who wore red ribbons on their coats and met near Barnum's Hotel on Fayette Street, expanded their membership and drilling. They would soon become the focus of the drive to prevent the inauguration of the "Black Republican" Lincoln and to also prevent northern troops from moving through Baltimore to reach the District of Columbia.[42]

Byrne was a prosperous Baltimore businessman who served as a principal Breckinridge delegate. He was subsequently chosen to officially carry Maryland's pro-Breckinridge vote to the District of Columbia. Here he met with Vice President Breckinridge as well as former governor Enoch Lowe and others who were attempting to force Maryland's governor, Thomas Hicks, to call a sovereignty convention to consider its secession.[43] Byrne, like other members of the secret committee at the core of the National Volunteers, was a Knight of the Golden Circle. Also serving on this secret committee were KGC Cypriano Ferrandini; William H. Turner, a clerk of the county court; and Otis Hilliard, a soldier of fortune who had recently returned from the South and was also likely to be a Knight.[44] Hilliard would later reveal that National Volunteer leaders who were forced to testify before the congressional investigating committee in Washington had been ordered not to divulge the secrets, nature, or objects of their organization.[45]

The KGC paramilitary leaders in Baltimore, such as Byrne and Ferrandini, met secretly at the Eutaw House, a six-story hotel at the corner of Baltimore and Eutaw Streets. The KGC's Third Degree political leader was John V. L. McMahon, a fiery attorney who represented Baltimore's up-and-coming merchant community. The impetuous McMahon, who suffered from partial blindness and ill-health, lived in retirement at the Eutaw House. His rooms were frequently the locus of political intrigue.[46]

The National Volunteers of Washington, D.C., then numbered around three hundred and similarly grew out of the local Breckinridge and Lane Clubs. Charles Henry Winder, a prominent pro-South Washington attorney, prepared the National Volunteers' constitution (that likely also applied to Baltimore, New York, and other locations where the National Volunteers had chapters).[47] After holding several preliminary meetings in September and October, the Washington club took one hundred men to march with their Baltimore compatriots in the massive torchlight parade on behalf of the Breckinridge and Lane ticket.[48]

Dr. Cornelius Boyle, a successful medical doctor and substantial property owner, was the senior officer, captain, and president of Washington's National Volunteers' council of five. Boyle had started in the drug business and then graduated from Columbia College in medicine. His patients and friends encompassed Washington's Democratic political elite, including Breckinridge, Stephen Douglas, and James Buchanan. As a long-standing resident of the District of Columbia, Boyle's sentiments were allied with Maryland. He predicted that four-fifths of the citizens of the District of Columbia would side with Maryland rather than the federal government if Virginia and Maryland seceded.[49] Dr. A. Y. P. Garnett, another noted District of Columbia physician (soon to become personal physician for Jefferson Davis), was also a National Volunteers leader and would subsequently be elected surgeon of the Washington, D.C., chapter. Garnett would feed intelligence to his father-in-law, Virginia's former governor Henry Wise, on the defensive position of the District that could be used by Wise in formulating an attack on the capital.[50]

As in Baltimore, leaders of the KGC in Washington also held key positions in the National Volunteers. National Volunteers president Cornelius Boyle spoke about a "secret Southern association" known as the Knights of the Golden Circle that met at Temperance Hall and was composed of some of the "first men in town."[51] Littleton Quinton [L. Q.] Washington, the political head of Washington's Knights, was a key leader in its National Volunteers. In 1860, L. Q. worked as a Washington newspaper correspondent and political operative for Virginia senator Robert M. T. Hunter, who was then considered a possible compromise candidate for president. L. Q. had previously served as clerk for President John Tyler and was active in Democratic states'-rights politics.[52]

After Yancey's appearance at Wilmington, the Breckinridge and Lane Clubs in Delaware became more militant. Thomas F. Bayard, the son of Delaware's U.S. senator and a Wilmington lawyer, was a leader of the Breckinridge Democrats who channeled funds to Delaware's southern counties to resist the Republican's efforts to try to elect Lincoln (Breckinridge carried Delaware). By January 1861, Bayard had enlisted sixty former members of Wilmington's Breckinridge and Lane Club in forming a company called "the Delaware Guards, that soon possessed the best arms in the state." Similar prosecession militia units sprang up in Delaware's middle- and southern-tier towns, and Bayard, acting as his father's agent, channeled weapons to some of them. Both Thomas Bayard and his senator father were alleged to be members of the Knights of the Golden Circle.[53]

Abraham Lincoln, the president-elect, was aware of the growing southern militancy. On October 20, 1860, Lincoln's friend Major David Hunter wrote to inform him that during a visit to Virginia, he had received a report that a number of young men had bound themselves, "by oaths most solemn," to assassinate Lincoln if he were elected.[54] KGC castles and companies of Minute Men that were active throughout Virginia could have been the source of the threat. Lincoln was concerned enough to ask Hunter to keep him appraised of southern plots against the government.[55]

During November, Joshua Speed from Louisville, Lincoln's closest friend, provided similar warnings. In a congratulatory letter written soon after the election, Speed told Lincoln that, with respect to preserving the Union, Lincoln would have to "deal with the combustible material lying around you without setting fire to the edifice." He then noted in passing, "I can not but tremble for you."[56] Speed's reference to "combustible material" is eerily similar to R. H. Wilson's description of the KGC "Boys" in Texas during the election campaign, whom he called "Southern inflammable material gathered together, only waiting for a spark to set the blaze."[57]

Due to his great concern, Speed subsequently met with Lincoln on November 22 in Chicago to confidentially "impart some information as to men and public sentiment here." It's likely that Speed filled Lincoln in on the machinations of the KGC, which had five castles in Louisville.[58] It is also likely that Speed, who had been a Douglas supporter, advised Lincoln of the "Little Giant's" belief in an ongoing southern conspiracy to dismember the Union, as well as the rapid rise of southern paramilitary organizations and threats to prevent Lincoln's inauguration.[59]

Douglas, himself a committed expansionist, said that southern fire-eaters had orchestrated the schism at Charleston as a pretext for their bold plan to create a powerful new slaveholding empire around the Gulf of Mexico, stretching from Cuba through Mexico into Central America. He predicted that the supporters of Democratic states'-rights candidate John Breckinridge would win the fifteen Cotton and Border States, as well as California and Oregon, and throw the election into the U.S. House of Representatives, which would declare Breckinridge the rightful president. Breckinridge would then use the authority of his Democratic administration to control the U.S. departments and ministries including the U.S. Army and relations with foreign countries.[60] Based on information from his well-placed operatives, Douglas became so convinced of a southern conspiracy to break up the Union that he took the unprecedented step of campaigning personally throughout the southern and Border States during September and October.[61]

Thus, by the end of 1860, the KGC had significantly expanded and inserted its members into the core of the paramilitary organizations rising in the South and Border States such as the Minute Men and National Volunteers. Private military clubs and militia units had also been marshaled in support of secession, and Knights' leaders were well represented at related military conventions. Fears of slave insurrections and attempted coercion by the North gripped the South and aroused southern hearts and minds. Conditions were now ripe for the KGC to implement its plot laid out at the Marshall conclave—seize federal forts in the South as well as the District of Columbia and prevent the "Black Republican" Abraham Lincoln from taking office.

# 7

# SEIZURE OF FEDERAL FORTS
# AND ARSENALS

T HE U.S. ARMY informer who had infiltrated the KGC's November
1860 Council of War reported that "orders were given to seize Navy-
Yards, Forts &c, while KGC members were still Cabinet officers and
Senators." Soon afterward, several seizures of federal forts in the South by
paramilitary insurgents occurred that were likely related to the KGC. The
army informer also referenced Secretary of War John Floyd and Secretary
of the Treasury Howell Cobb as KGC members, as well as Vice President
John Breckinridge.[1] Expositions of the KGC produced during the Civil War
similarly charged that a year before Lincoln's election, John Floyd had
secured "large sums from the U.S. Treasury" and established "plans for
securing arms from the U.S. Arsenals and for possessing all the southern
fortresses."[2] Both Cobb and Floyd did embrace secession during November
1860, and although Cobb resigned in December, Floyd remained in office.
His actions thereafter are highly suspicious.[3]

At this time, a string of thirty federal forts stretched along the coastline
of the United States, the majority of which were in the South. Construction
of these forts had begun after the War of 1812, for the purpose of protecting
the coastal states from a seaward assault—not to defend against a land-
based raid from domestic insurgents. In addition, numerous interior forts
and barracks, as well as six federal arsenals, existed in the southern states.
The land for most of these federal installations had been donated by individual states. As southern states moved toward secession, fire-eaters were

demanding that the forts and arsenals be returned to the individual states in which they were located.[4]

The fifty-two-year-old Floyd had served as a three-term U.S. congressman and then governor of Virginia in the early 1850s, where his tenure was tainted by a banking scandal and financial irregularities. He was a strong proponent of states' rights, as well as U.S. expansionism, and had been present at the Greenbrier (White Sulphur Springs, Virginia) during the period of the KGC's August 1859 convention. Floyd was appointed secretary of war in 1856 through the recommendation of Henry Wise, who had been Buchanan's initial choice. Floyd saw himself as a bold man of action who should not be bothered with administrative details. He now headed the War Department, with eight bureaus and ninety-three employees that supervised the extensive supply network and finances of the U.S. Army.[5]

As early as 1859, Floyd's War Department was supplying the six Cotton States with a disproportionate share of the federal arms that were provided to support state militias. By the end of 1860, all the states that would eventually secede had received their full quota of federal arms for 1861. Floyd approved South Carolina's request for its full 1861 allocation only ten days before the state began its secession convention.[6] Rifles and muskets were also transferred to federal arsenals in the South, where they would be available for subsequent seizure.[7] In addition, Floyd approved government sales of obsolete federal arms to secessionist sympathizers that were suspiciously channeled through intermediaries.[8] By January 1861, southern newspapers were bragging that 290,000 stands of arms had been acquired through the takeover of federal arsenals, with 417,000 further arms purchased by the Cotton States, noting that the total could increase to a million once Texas and the Border States joined the Confederacy.[9]

Floyd was also accused of filling key federal military positions with pro-South officers. In the spring of 1860, he appointed Colonel William W. Loring, a North Carolinian (and reputed KGC member), to become commander of the U.S. Army's Department of New Mexico.[10] In November 1860, Floyd appointed Brigadier General Albert Sidney Johnston, a native Kentuckian who had relocated to Texas to head the U.S. Army's merged Department of the Pacific, headquartered at San Francisco. Johnston, a close friend of Jefferson Davis, sympathized with his adopted Texas, where he had served as its first army commander and maintained extensive land holdings.[11] Floyd also appointed Brigadier General David Twiggs, a native Georgian and states'-rights sympathizer, to assume command of the huge Department of Texas, with almost one-third of the U.S. Army's manpower.[12] Louisiana native Major P. G. T. Beauregard was also appointed as superintendent of West Point despite Beauregard's secessionist proclivities. During his month-long tenure, Beauregard advised southern cadets as to when they should leave the academy to join the Confederate army (and was also accused of forming castles of the KGC).[13]

On his way to New York, Beauregard likely tied in with KGC Brigadier General Paul J. Semmes, who had been appointed by Georgia's Governor Brown as special purchasing agent to acquire arms and munitions for Georgia with the $1 million appropriation recently approved by the Georgia legislature. U.S. Army Colonel William J. Hardee, the prior commandant of West Point, assisted Semmes in this effort. During December 1860, Semmes and Hardee set up shop at New York's Fifth Avenue Hotel and finalized contracts with northern manufacturers such as Colt, Parrott, Veile, E. I. du Pont, as well as for six Columbiads from the U.S. government's Fort Pitt Foundry. On the way north, they had stopped off at Washington, D.C., and obtained advice and assistance from personnel in Floyd's War Department on military-related purchasing.[14]

In addition to approving disproportionate arms sales and appointments of southern officers, Floyd became increasingly erratic in his behavior after November 1860, supporting suspicions of his disloyalty and alleged KGC connections. During the first part of November, Floyd met directly with a number of ardent secessionists, including Francis Pickens, who was soon to become governor of South Carolina. By early December, Floyd announced to the press that he believed the secession of the Cotton States was inevitable.[15]

At the end of October 1860, Winfield Scott, the seventy-four-year-old general-in-chief of the U.S. Army, tried to alert President James Buchanan to the likely plots against federal installations as reported by the army informer. In his "Views Suggested by the Imminent Danger . . . ," Scott warned that "from a knowledge of our Southern population, it is my solemn conviction that there is some danger of an early act of rashness preliminary to secession viz., the seizure of some or all of [nine designated federal forts in the southern states including Forts Moultrie and Sumter at Charleston harbor and Fort Monroe at Hampton Roads, Virginia]." Scott noted that these forts had insufficient garrisons and recommended that "all these works should be immediately so garrisoned as to make any attempt to take any of them by surprise or *coup de main* ridiculous."[16]

Scott was able to circumvent his prickly superior, Secretary of War John Floyd (who despised Scott and often pocketed his recommendations), and present his "Views" directly to President Buchanan. A wily diplomat from Pennsylvania, the sixty-nine-year-old Buchanan had obtained his 1856 nomination by catering to southern interests and had subsequently appointed three southerners to his cabinet. Like Floyd, the southern cabinet officers predicted a disastrous reaction if U.S. troops suddenly appeared in the South to reinforce the federal forts. At his meeting with President Buchanan, Scott indicated that he presently had only five companies available to provide reinforcements. This made it easy for Buchanan, who was trying to head off the secession movement in the South, to dismiss Scott's suggestions as impractical and speculative.[17]

Buchanan did have concerns, however, about the security of the forts, particularly those in the harbor at Charleston, South Carolina. After Lincoln's November 6 election, Buchanan repeatedly reviewed the security of the federal forts with his cabinet, which was evenly divided between northern hard-liners and southern appeasers. Secretary of War Floyd strongly opposed sending reinforcements to Charleston, telling an associate that he would sooner cut off his hand. At this point, Buchanan generally accepted the views of the southern cabinet members, hoping to stave off the growing southern militancy.[18]

In his annual message to Congress of December 3, 1860, Buchanan claimed that the federal forts were "property of the United States" and "had been purchased for a fair equivalent, by the consent of the legislature of the State." He said that if an attempt were made to seize the forts, "the responsibility for consequences would rightfully rest upon the heads of the assailants." Buchanan also said that the secession of any state was equivalent to revolution and was not justified on the basis of Lincoln's election. He, nevertheless, seemed to countenance secession by noting that if the northern states refused to repeal their obnoxious personal liberty laws, which impeded southerners from reclaiming their slave property, then the injured southern states, after pursuing all constitutional means, "would be justified in revolutionary resistance to the government of the Union." And he undercut any threat of federal retaliation by conceding that the United States government lacked authority under the constitution to militarily coerce any seceding state.[19]

On December 12, General Scott arrived in Washington to again urge reinforcement of the forts, and he now detailed a larger complement of army companies that he could assign for this purpose. Since Secretary Floyd continued to disagree, a December 15 interview was arranged for Scott to present his recommendations directly to President Buchanan. With respect to the Charleston harbor forts, Buchanan still felt he did not want to send in reinforcements, but instead intended to await the final action of South Carolina's convention and the arrival of South Carolina commissioners in Washington to try to negotiate the issues. Buchanan hoped to prevent South Carolina's likely secession from spilling over to the other southern states. He felt that these other states would condemn any aggressive action by South Carolina against the forts in Charleston harbor.[20]

In the midst of the turmoil precipitated by South Carolina's December 20 secession, Floyd found himself at the center of several major scandals. Charges against him alleged that he was surreptitiously channeling 124 heavy guns to several southern forts still under construction. The huge guns, called Columbiads, had been initially ordered in October and were manufactured at Pittsburgh's Allegheny Arsenal. On December 20, Floyd gave highly unusual verbal instructions to the U.S. Army ordinance officer to have the guns loaded on the ship *Silver War* and sent to Ship Island, Mississippi, and Galveston, Texas, for which they had not originally been intended. Upon learning that the Columbiads were being loaded at the dock, a committee of outraged Pittsburgh citizens sent a telegram to President Buchanan on Christmas Day complaining that "an order has issued from the War Department to transfer all the effective munitions of war from the arsenal in this city to Southern forts."[21] A northern newspaper lamented: "The Columbiads are the largest and most destructive species of ordinance known to our service. At a time when Mississippi, Louisiana, and Texas are preparing to make war upon the Union, an order is issued by Floyd to transport these guns into the midst of the avowed enemies of the country. The people of Pittsburgh met, protested against the criminal act, and asked the war department to countermand the order."[22] Buchanan did quickly countermand the order, while the *Montgomery Advertiser* later applauded Floyd for trying to transfer the guns to the Confederate cause.[23]

With respect to financial matters, an Interior Department employee named Godard Bailey, who was a relative of Floyd's wife and whom Floyd had recommended, had transferred $870,000 from the Indian Trust Fund to a defense contractor on the basis of drafts that Floyd had previously endorsed. When Buchanan found out about it on December 22, he became outraged, since he had previously told Floyd to stop issuing the drafts. This, coupled with the irate telegram from the Pittsburgh citizens over the Floyd-authorized Columbiad shipments, convinced Buchanan that it was time to ask Floyd to resign. Not wanting to confront Floyd directly, Buchanan sent Floyd's cousin, Vice President John Breckinridge, to break the bad news. Floyd initially agreed to resign but then became irate and said he needed to protect his honor. He vacillated for nearly a week, during which time he continued to show up for cabinet meetings and serve as the secretary of war.[24]

Then, during the night of December 25, Major Robert Anderson secretly moved his federal garrison at Fort Moultrie to the more defensible Fort Sumter in the middle of Charleston's harbor. This decision was made by Anderson himself in order to protect his men from the increasingly belligerent Charleston mobs. It stunned Floyd, who was brought the news by none other than U.S. senator Louis Wigfall from Texas.[25] Buchanan was equally blindsided and convened a series of contentious cabinet meetings during which Floyd was surprised to learn that he had previously signed a memorandum giving Anderson authority to use his "sound military discretion" to protect his garrison.

After his northern cabinet members threatened to resign, Buchanan decided to back Anderson's move to Fort Sumter. In the interim, the newly installed governor of South Carolina, Francis Pickens, had ordered the seizure of Moultrie and the other federal forts, arsenal, and customhouse at Charleston. To save face, Floyd alleged that Buchanan had gone back on his pledge to the South to preserve the status quo and used this as the reason for finally submitting his resignation on December 29. Joseph Holt, a hard-hitting Unionist from Kentucky (who had been serving as postmaster general) was chosen to replace Floyd as secretary of war.[26]

By early January 1861, Floyd was in Richmond helping to organize the radical elements in favor of secession. He admitted that he had supplied arms to the South in anticipation of armed rebellion, and, at a banquet held in his honor, flaunted his double-dealing while serving as Buchanan's secretary of war.[27] After he left office, Floyd was indicted on multiple charges, but by then it was too late. The *New York Tribune*, assuming that Floyd had resigned of his own volition, subsequently noted that "the conspirators were thunderstruck at this *faux pas* of Floyd."[28]

Floyd's resignation triggered a series of incidents involving the federal forts in the South. On January 2, Louis Wigfall telegraphed Congressman Milledge Bonham at Charleston: "Holt succeeds Floyd. It means war. Cut off supplies from Anderson and take Sumter as soon as possible."[29] Wigfall had earlier coauthored the "Southern Manifesto" for the establishment of a Southern Confederacy joined in by thirty other southern congressmen. At the Willard Hotel in Washington, Wigfall was allegedly overheard boasting of the extent and power of the KGC to such an extent that members of the legislative cabal had to tell him to keep quiet.[30] During late December 1860 and January 1861, seizures occurred at more than twenty federal forts and arsenals. Most of these seizures were made after the state in which the installation was located had seceded. But several of the seizures were carried out before state secession by irregular bands of insurgents who claimed to be acting on their own authority.[31]

In Virginia, Henry Wise's mouthpiece, the *Richmond Enquirer* (edited by his son Obadiah Jennings Wise), openly advocated seizure of the federal forts in Virginia and Maryland, as well as government installations in the District of Columbia. On December 17, the *Enquirer* said:

> Let the first convention then, be held between Maryland and Virginia, and, these two states agreeing, let them provide sufficient force to seize the city of Washington, and, if coercion is to be attempted, let it begin by subjugating the States of Maryland and Virginia. Thus practical and efficient fighting in the Union will prevent the power of the Union from falling into the hands of our enemies. We hope Virginia will depute her commissioners to Maryland first, and providing for the seizure of Washington city, Forts

McHenry, Washington, and Old Point, Harpers Ferry and Gosport navy yard, present these two States in the attitude of rebels, *inviting coercion.* This was the way Patrick Henry brought about the revolution and this is the best use that Virginia can make commissioners of any kind.[32]

Wise advocated the approach of "fighting within the Union," arguing that the country belonged to those who had kept the proslavery and states'-rights covenants of the U.S. Constitution, not to those who had broken them. He urged southerners to remain in the Union and fight for their constitutional rights as well as their proportional rights to the federal treasury, military installations, and territories. Wise argued that the southern states had ceded the land for the forts and arsenals to the federal government, and the government therefore had the right to reclaim them with force if necessary.[33]

The *Richmond Enquirer* editorial didn't mention Fortress Monroe in the harbor off Norfolk, probably because it was already under surveillance, and KGC leader Virginius Groner was actively planning its seizure. At the time, Groner was serving as a keynote speaker at prosecession meetings alongside other Virginia firebrands such as John Tyler Jr., the son of former president John Tyler.[34] On December 17, Governor Pickens of South Carolina sent Lieutenant Colonel John Green to Virginia in order to obtain intelligence on Fortress Monroe. This is the same fort from which President Buchanan would launch the ill-fated *Star of the West* mission on January 6, 1861, to try to relieve Anderson's besieged garrison. Green worked with Charles Norris, the head of the Norfolk Minute Men (and a future Confederate intelligence officer). Together they recruited spies at Fortress Monroe and the Gosport Navy Yard and forwarded reports to South Carolina governor Pickens.[35]

Later in December, Groner spearheaded a group of volunteers who were prepared to seize the then lightly garrisoned Fortress Monroe in Norfolk's harbor. Groner, together with Virginia's Adjutant General Richardson, approached Virginia governor John Letcher with a letter from Henry Wise advocating the seizure. Letcher later confirmed: "As far back as January 8, [1861], I consulted with a gentleman [i.e., Groner] whose position enabled him to know the strength of [Fortress Monroe] and whose experience in military matters enabled him to form an opinion as to the number of men that would be required to capture it."[36] Letcher undercut the seizure plan, however, by demanding that the insurgents first seek approval from other Virginia officials. Groner felt that this would lead to leaks and alert federal authorities. Wise was also infuriated, which may have led him to consider launching a coup to take over the Virginia state government in April 1861.[37]

In Wilmington, North Carolina, an anomalous group called the Cape Fear Minute Men held a series of prosecession meetings in mid-December 1860. The platform stage for the meeting was decorated with the OLS insignia—a large Lone Star of white on a red background—and prominent Wilmington merchants gave spirited speeches advocating "uncompromising disunion."[38] Then reports came from Washington that a federal revenue cutter was on its way to garrison two unmanned federal installations, Forts Johnson and Caswell, located within a few miles of each other about thirty miles downstream on the Cape Fear River. William S. Ash, a prominent railroad president and Democratic politician, approached North Carolina's newly installed states'-rights governor, John Willis Ellis, on January 1, 1861, seeking permission to seize the two federal forts. Despite urgings from South Carolina, Ellis refused, contending he had no authority to authorize such an act.[39]

The Cape Fear Minute Men, led by the Wilmington dry-cleaning merchant John J. Hedrick, decided to proceed anyway. The Smithville Guards, from a town close to the forts, joined them. Stephen Decatur Thurston, a Smithville physician, was later careful to point out that the Guards "did not as a company occupy this fort [Johnson] but that members of said company did as citizens."[40]

At 4:00 a.m. on January 9, a band of about twenty insurgents arrived by steamboat and surrounded Fort Johnson, a barracks-like fort situated on a six-acre bluff overlooking the river. The raiding party knocked at the door of the fort's sole caretaker, a sergeant, and asked him to give up the keys to the fort's magazine, containing its arms and ammunition. The sergeant initially threatened to protect the ordinance stores with his life, but he eventually gave them the keys. Fifteen men were left to guard Fort Johnson, while the remainder proceeded to nearby federal Fort Caswell, a bastioned masonry structure controlling the entrance to the Cape Fear River. There the men carried out a similar seizure.[41]

After learning about the occupation of the two forts, Governor Ellis quickly told the acting head of North Carolina's militia to go to Smithville and order Captain Thurston to restore the forts to the possession of the United States. Thurston and Hedrick complied, withdrawing their men and turning the forts back to their federal army caretakers on January 14. Ellis then sent a letter to President Buchanan notifying him of his withdrawal order. He explained that the takeover was precipitated by discredited reports that federal troops were on the way to garrison the forts, and he asked Buchanan whether "the U.S. forts in this State will be garrisoned with federal troops during your Administration" (to which Buchanan responded "no").[42] At the same time, Buchanan allowed his secretary of interior, Jacob Thompson (later to become the spymaster for the Confederacy in Canada), to visit North Carolina as a commissioner on behalf of Thompson's home state of Mississippi. Thompson urged Ellis to adopt "efficient measures for the common defense and safety of the south."[43]

A few days later, Ellis separately covered his bases with Georgia's fiery governor, Joseph Brown, who, in early January 1861, had ordered the seizure of Fort Pulaski at Savannah and then urged the other Cotton State governors to seize federal forts within their jurisdictions.[44] Ellis explained to Brown that the North Carolina forts were generally indefensible, and he did not believe the federal government had a present intent to garrison them. Ellis also said that a peremptory takeover of the forts would have an injurious effect on the cause of southern rights in North Carolina, where the immediate secessionists and "those disposed to give Lincoln a trial" were locked in a struggle in the legislature.[45]

A band of insurgents similarly seized the partially completed federal fort at Ship Island in Mississippi. This was one of the forts to which Secretary of War Floyd had suspiciously ordered the Columbiad shipments that had been halted by the outcry from Pittsburgh's citizens. Mississippi's KGC-affiliated governor, John Pettus, was concerned about the establishment of a new federal fort on Ship Island. Pettus feared the federal government would use the fort to restrict commerce and land troops once Mississippi passed its secession ordinance (which its convention did on January 9, 1861).[46]

Before noon on January 13, an armed party of men landed on Ship Island, telling the federal overseer that they were acting on their own responsibility and that they came to take possession of the works under construction. A second group arrived in the afternoon, hoisted a flag, and left ten men on the island, who occupied a vacant engineering building. This second group appears to be the one referred to in the January 16 *New Orleans Daily True Delta*, which reported that "Ship Island, Miss., some twelve miles from Biloxi, was taken possession on Sunday [January 13] night by Capt. Howard and about fifty men from Biloxi" (the Howard referred to may have been the ubiquitous KGC Major James Ross Howard, who was from Louisiana).[47] On the morning of January 20, a third body of armed insurgents arrived and took forcible possession of the fort, causing the army lieutenant overseeing the crew to finally cease construction and cede possession of the island.[48]

Thus, as plotted at the KGC's Marshall conclave, a number of federal forts and arsenals in the South were seized in early 1861 by irregular bands of insurgents before the respective states had seceded. As in Virginia, where Groner and Wise were involved, the KGC was known to be active in North Carolina, as well as Mississippi, where Governor Pettus was a recognized KGC sympathizer. Such insurgent actions co-opted strategic federal defensive positions and captured a sizeable quantity of weapons and ammunition for the nascent Confederacy. Weapons were also transferred directly to the seceding states through the machinations of John Floyd, Buchanan's outgoing secretary of war. But would the KGC succeed in capturing the nation's capital—the District of Columbia—that had also been targeted in the KGC's Council of War order?

8

# THE PLOT TO SEIZE
# THE DISTRICT OF COLUMBIA

T HE U.S. ARMY informer who infiltrated the Knights' Texas conclave
around November 1860 had reported that a plot "was designed to
seize Washington and inaugurate Breckinridge."[1] As the Knights'
mission shifted to supporting the southern governors, KGC leaders cryptically noted: "The Knights of the Golden Circle may find its Mexico in the
District of Columbia."[2] The District of Columbia had been the headquarters of the Knights through 1859 and most of 1860. Bickley, in his circular
letter of April 1860 to the KGC's American Legion, boasted that Knights
"have been constantly and openly drilled [i]n Washington city, within
hearing of the President's house," and he referenced two separate KGC
Regiments of at least one thousand men each, in Maryland and Virginia.[3]

Of the seventy-five thousand residents who lived in the District of Columbia in 1861, one-third of them leaned toward the South. Within the
District (which included Washington City, Georgetown, and a rural enclave) sat the ten-square-mile government tract that had been donated
by the State of Maryland in 1788. More than 75 percent of the District's
population had roots in surrounding Maryland and Virginia, so the federal enclave had a decidedly pro-South character. Federal activities were
largely clustered in the string of buildings extending along 1.2 miles of
Pennsylvania Avenue, from the U.S. Capitol to Executive Square, where
the Executive Mansion, Navy and War Departments, and massive U.S.
Treasury Building were located. In this confined area, a handful of federal

cabinet officers supervised a bevy of often southern-leaning clerks and secretaries.[4]

During the fall 1860 election campaign, Stephen Douglas—the presidential candidate of the northern wing of the Democratic Party—had warned that "a widespread and intricate conspiracy existed in the South" that threatened to take over the U.S. government through an internal coup d'état as early as November or December 1860. Douglas feared that a combination of anti-Lincoln southerners and westerners would try to take over the U.S. government and name John Breckinridge as de facto president with Buchanan's backing. The South and West would then sanction the Breckinridge-led government and seek recognition from the U.S. Army and foreign powers.[5]

In support of Douglas's warning, General-in-Chief Winfield Scott received a flurry of letters in late 1860 warning of a planned attempt to seize the District of Columbia and prevent Lincoln's inauguration. Letters were forwarded from St. Louis, Chicago, Cincinnati, Pittsburgh, New York, Philadelphia, and Baltimore. A letter from Nashville, Tennessee, warned: "A secret society exists through all the southern States, bound together by solemn obligation to prevent it [Lincoln's inauguration] at all hazards, even to the extent of causing his assassination before taking office." The letter further charged that several members of Congress and other "men high in public life" were in on the conspiracy.[6] Scott's new boss, Secretary of War Joseph Holt, also believed in the conspiracy's existence based on "information, some of which was of a most clandestine character [likely referring to the U.S. Army informer] that reached the Government from many parts of the country."[7]

Another letter reported that "vast numbers of men, say 400 or 500" were infiltrating the capital with arms concealed in their baggage, to be accommodated in the homes of the disaffected. It said that southern-leaning government clerks stood ready to render assistance at the appointed time and were bribing military companies to offer support. The letter added that when summoned, companies of Minute Men would rush in from Virginia and Maryland, take over the government's public buildings and archives, cut the telegraph wires, kidnap doughface President James Buchanan, and leave the District of Columbia isolated. Then John Breckinridge or Jefferson Davis would be appointed president of a new pro-

South republic, and prominent men not cooperating would be arrested or put to death.[8]

Lincoln's close friend and supporter Joseph Medill, the managing editor of the *Chicago Tribune,* sent the president-elect a confidential note on December 26 that further highlighted these threats: "The evidence of my ears and eyes are forcing me to believe that the secessionists are seriously contemplating resistance to your inauguration in this Capitol. There is certainly a secret organization in this city numbering several hundred members having that purpose in view—sworn armed men, and branches or lodges affiliated with them in design, extend south to Richmond, Raliegh [*sic*] & Charleston." Medill indicated that they would first need to control Baltimore, but "if things go thus for the next 60 days as they have for the last 30, [Baltimore] will be under the complete control of Disunion vigilance committees and a reign of terror will domineer over that city." He further warned: "It is the intention of the dis-unionists, if they get Baltimore on their side, to prevent you reaching this city [Washington] by force, and with the aid of the lodges here and in Virginia and South to 'clean out' the Republicans here, take psssession [*sic*] of the capital and proclaim the Southern Confederacy."[9]

As Medill indicates, one difficulty with reclaiming the District of Columbia was the fact that it was surrounded by the state of Maryland on three sides and by the Potomac River and Virginia to the south. Since Maryland had ceded the land for the District of Columbia in 1788, Maryland's secession was first necessary in order to make a legal claim for the District's reversion. But Maryland was itself surrounded by states remaining in the Union. Unless and until Virginia seceded, it would be difficult for Maryland to go it alone. For this reason, secession leaders decided to make Maryland their base of operations and precipitate its secession in conjunction with their plan for reclaiming the District.[10]

Maryland's moderate governor, Thomas Holliday Hicks, had been advised of the takeover plot by credible sources and included a passage in his January 3, 1861, "Address to the People of Maryland" warning that:

> Secession leaders in Washington have resolved that the border States, and especially Maryland, shall be precipitated into secession with the cotton States before the 4th of March. They have resolved to seize the federal

Capitol and the public archives, so that they may be in a position to be acknowledged by foreign governments as the "United States," and the assent of Maryland is necessary, as the District of Columbia would revert to her in case of dissolution of the Union. . . . The plan contemplates forcible opposition to Mr. Lincoln's inauguration, and consequently civil war upon Maryland soil, and a transfer of its horrors from the States which are to provoke it.[11]

Secessionists exerted tremendous pressure on Hicks to call a convention in order to take Maryland out of the Union. On Christmas Eve of 1860, Hicks was visited by a local states'-rights delegation that threatened his personal safety if he continued to refuse to call the Maryland legislature into session. Former Maryland governor Enoch Lowe, a secessionist leader, confirmed that a meeting was held in Washington City during December to discuss how to pressure Hicks into calling a convention. Lowe said that the participants included the Breckinridge electors for the state of Maryland, a group that was headed by William Byrne, the leader of Baltimore's KGC and National Volunteers.[12]

U.S. Supreme Court Justice John Campbell from Alabama, who was serving as a mediator between Lincoln's cabinet appointees and the three Confederate commissioners, was also convinced that a KGC-led raid on Washington was in the works. During late 1860/early 1861, Campbell advised Thomas Ewing, a Peace Conference delegate from Ohio, that the District's public offices were about to be captured by "a combined movement of the clerks within and the Knights of the Golden Circle, who held chapter on 4½ Street, without." Ewing said he had advised General-in-Chief Scott about the threatened seizure but was informed that Secretary Floyd had denied Scott's request to bring in military reinforcements. This left an inadequate force of District militia and only thirty-five marines to defend the capital.[13]

The warning letters, congressional caucuses, and rise of independent military organizations soon led to newspaper reports about the plot to seize the District. One of the most widely circulated was the account in the *National Intelligencer* of January 11, 1861, titled "The Disunion Programme." It was published under the byline of "Eaton," who was reputed to be Lemuel D. Evans, a former Texas congressman. Evans had previously been an organizer for General Quitman's aborted 1854 Cuban expedition, but he was now a vocal opponent of Texas's secession.[14]

Eaton charges that senators from seven southern states met in Washington "to assume to themselves the political power of the South, and to control all political and military operations for the present." He then repeats the gist of the southern senators' resolutions that secession should be carried out as soon as possible and that a convention to establish a Confederacy should be held in Montgomery, Alabama, before February 15. But Eaton further alleges that during the meeting, the senators agreed to instruct their states to "complete the plan of seizing forts, arsenals and custom-houses." He says the caucus also resolved to "dragoon" the legislatures of the Border States into seceding, with an appeal to the people of Maryland to follow "the same revolutionary steps which promise a conflict with the State and Federal Governments in Texas." According to Eaton, the plotters had taken control of all avenues of information in the South, including the telegraph, the press, and the postmasters, and they confidently relied on defections from the U.S. Army and Navy. With respect to the District of Columbia, Eaton says that the southern congressmen had deliberately conceived a conspiracy for the overthrow of the government through "the military organizations, the dangerous secret order, the 'Knights of the Golden Circle,' 'Committees of Safety,' Southern Leagues, and other agencies at their command."[15]

The respected Texas judge George Paschal, who had confronted Bickley at the October 1860 KGC meeting in Austin, similarly warned a friend in Washington City that the South was virtually in arms and moving northward with the objective of seizing the capital. He said that the Texas KGC leader Ben McCulloch would lead the assault. Rumors separately circulated that Ben McCulloch was encamped in northern Virginia with a force of five hundred Texas Rangers who would sweep into Washington and prevent Lincoln's March 4 inauguration.[16]

The Texas senator (and KGC sympathizer) Louis Wigfall, who spearheaded the January 5 caucus of southern senators calling for the formation of an independent southern confederacy, remained in the U.S. Senate until late February 1861. His purpose was to spy for his native South Carolina and prevent the Buchanan administration from responding to the secession crisis. Wigfall also helped convert the Breckinridge and Lane Clubs in Baltimore and Washington City into paramilitary organizations that could assist in a takeover.[17]

The militancy of the District's National Volunteers further increased following a meeting on January 10, 1861, attended by several hundred at Harmony Hall in Washington City. At the meeting, resolutions were passed advocating the secession of the District. A committee headed by Dr. Cornelius Boyle and the KGC chief L. Q. Washington had drafted the resolutions, and both men delivered speeches in favor of adopting them. The preamble to the resolutions proclaimed that if Virginia and Maryland were to secede, the City of Washington should be allowed to go with them and "would naturally be the seat of government for a new confederacy." The resolutions then provocatively declared "that we will stand by and defend the south" and that "in event of the withdrawal of Maryland and Virginia from the Union, [we will act] in such manner as shall best secure ourselves and those States from the evils of a foreign and hostile government [i.e., the United States] within and near their borders."[18]

By January 1861, a variety of independent military companies were organized and drilling in the District of Columbia, Maryland, and Virginia for the purpose of aiding in the seizure of the District and the prevention of Lincoln's inauguration. These companies included the National Volunteers as well as the National Rifles, a company of more than one hundred young men from the District and Baltimore under Captain Francis Schaeffer. Before Floyd's resignation, the National Rifles had been issued a large supply of federal ammunition and rifles, as well as two mountain howitzers that were not standard issue for an infantry company. The National Rifles planned to participate, along with the National Volunteers, in seizing the District's federal installations including the massive U.S. Treasury Department Building that had been designated by federal authorities as their bastion for defense.[19]

Colonel Charles Stone, an ex-army officer who was appointed by General-in-Chief Scott as the new inspector general for the District of Columbia, soon got wind of the National Rifles' and National Volunteers' plans for seizing the federal installations. Stone said that assertions were made at the Washington meeting of the National Volunteers indicating that there were "1500 men who could be depended on to take the city," and that they had been promised arms from Virginia's former governor, Henry Wise, through his son-in-law, Dr. Alexander Y. P. Garnett. Stone quickly assigned detectives who infiltrated the District's existing militia companies and set about organizing new, loyal ones.[20]

When National Rifles' Captain Schaeffer stopped by Stone's office to obtain his previously granted commission as a major, Stone insisted that Schaeffer first take a loyalty oath, which Schaeffer refused to do. Stone then stripped Schaeffer of all rank, which resulted in Schaeffer's resignation as well as that of the prosecession members of his National Rifles company. Dr. Boyle of the National Volunteers also stopped in to request federal arms. In reply, Stone insisted on a muster roll containing the names of the one hundred–plus members of the District's Volunteers. Dr. Boyle came back and presented it, but Stone refused to provide the weapons and kept the muster roll for further investigation. Boyle's National Volunteers company soon dispersed and left for Alexandria, Virginia, where Boyle was commissioned as a major in the Virginia Volunteers during late April 1861.[21] The KGC's plot for the seizure of the District's federal installations had been foiled by Stone's decisive action.

Meanwhile, President-elect Lincoln continued to receive death threats while at his home in Springfield, Illinois. An example is the January 18, 1861, letter from R. A. Hunt, a purported "friend" from Lynchburg, Virginia. Hunt warned Lincoln that he had overheard several persons vowing, "If you ever did take the President Chair that they would go to Washington City expressly to kill you." A secessionist paper in the KGC hotbed of Atlanta confidently predicted, "The South will never permit Abraham Lincoln to be inaugurated President of the United States, this is a settled and a sealed fact."[22] Judge Handy, a commissioner sent by Mississippi, told Maryland's Governor Hicks that "Mr. Lincoln and Mr. Hamlin would never be installed into office," and Jacob Thompson, Buchanan's pro-South secretary of the interior, confided that southern-rights advocates had talked about overriding Lincoln's election by either Congress's refusal to count the Electoral College votes or by organizing a force to prevent his inauguration.[23] Secretary of War Joseph Holt believed that such "solemn utterances" by "men in high political position" could not be regarded as "empty bluster."[24]

Similar reported threats, which included destruction of the rail lines serving Baltimore and Washington, were soon brought to the attention of Samuel Morse Felton, the president of the Philadelphia, Wilmington, and Baltimore Railroad (PWBRR). Felton became convinced from his own sources "that there was an extensive and organized conspiracy through the South" to capture Washington, "destroy all avenues of communication," and prevent Lincoln's inauguration. Felton retained the noted Chicago detective agency headed by Allan Pinkerton, a former sheriff who was originally from Scotland. On February 3, 1861, Pinkerton and four agents arrived in Maryland with the mission to unearth and trail suspected conspirators. Unbeknownst to Felton and Pinkerton, General-in-Chief Scott and Senator William Seward separately enlisted the help of New York City police superintendent John Kennedy, who also dispatched detectives to Baltimore to delve into the threats.[25]

The reports of threats also resulted in the appointment of a select committee of five U.S. congressmen to "inquire whether any secret organization hostile to the Government of the United States exists in the District of Columbia; and if so, whether any official or employe of the city of Washington, or any employes or officers of the Federal government, in the executive or judicial departments, are members thereof." William Howard, a Republican congressman from Michigan, chaired the select committee, which was comprised of two Republicans and three Democrats. Committee member Lawrence O'Bryan Branch, a states'-rights Democrat from North Carolina (who would soon leave Congress to join the Confederate army), did his best to impede Howard's investigation and railed against General-in-Chief Scott's ongoing buildup of federal troops around Washington.[26]

Beginning on January 29, the select committee heard testimony from twenty-four witnesses over a two-week period, including General-in-Chief Winfield Scott, Maryland governor Thomas Hicks, former Maryland governor Enoch Lowe, and various municipal and military officials. Also called to testify were several parties who would turn out to be actually involved in the conspiracy such as KGC Captain Cypriano Ferrandini, the Italian barber known to be handy with a stiletto, and Otis K. Hilliard, a twenty-eight-year-old New York native and soldier of fortune who, for the last two years, had been traveling throughout the South.[27] Hilliard testified that sixty companies of the National Volunteers were drilling in Baltimore. Ferrandini said their purpose was to prevent northern militia or volunteer companies from passing through Maryland and coercing the South. Hilliard would later admit to Pinkerton's agent that the conspirators had sworn a solemn oath not to divulge "the object nor the nature of our organization" to the committee.[28]

The committee's final February 15 report (not joined in by Lawrence Branch) says that the two weeks of testimony showed disaffected persons, at least informally, consulted on "resistance to the counting of the ballots, to the inauguration of Lincoln, the seizure of the Capitol and the District of Columbia." It notes, however, that if any such plots were entertained by an organization, it "seems to have been rendered contingent upon the secession of Maryland, Virginia, or both." The report ambiguously concludes that while political clubs in the District as well as Maryland have assumed the character of military organizations, "there is no proof that they intend to attack the Capitol or the District, unless the surrender should be demanded by a State to which they possess a higher degree of allegiance."[29]

On February 11, Abraham Lincoln left his hometown of Springfield, Illinois, on a twelve-day whistle-stop train excursion. Planned by Lincoln's handlers, the trip was to traverse the intervening northern states and then end up in the District of Columbia before Lincoln's March 4 inauguration. At the Springfield train station, Lincoln wistfully told his longtime friends: "I now leave, not knowing when, or whether ever, I may return, with a task before me greater than that which rested upon Washington."[30]

Before embarking, Lincoln had told his Republican allies in Congress to resist Kentucky senator John Crittenden's compromise proposal regarding slavery extension, in part because it contained an "after acquired clause" that would permit slave ownership in any new territories acquired south of the former Missouri Compromise line. He wrote Congressman Elihu B. Washburne that compromise on slavery extension will "immediately [recommence] filibustering." He similarly told his incoming secretary of state, William Seward, that such a compromise would "put us again on the high road to a slave empire," and informed Buchanan's emissary that it would lead to constant demands by the South for territorial acquisition of Mexico, the Caribbean, and Central America.[31]

Lincoln's first overnight stop was at Indianapolis, where massive crowds, headed by Indiana's Republican governor, Oliver Morton, greeted him. In Lincoln's speech at the downtown Bates Hotel, he drew the distinction that he would soon use in his inaugural address between "coercion"—such as "the marching of an army into South Carolina without the consent of her people"—and noncoercive "responses of the Government to state secession such as holding or retaking its own forts or collecting duties on foreign imports." While the heavily Republican crowd cheered his position, Kentucky's prosouthern *Louisville Courier* said Lincoln's remarks foreshadowed civil war and the triumph of the radical wing of the Republican Party.[32]

Meanwhile, the Pinkerton operative Charles D. C. Williams issued a February 12 report from Baltimore saying he had learned of a vile conspiracy by which the participants were proposing to "blow up the Capitol on the day the Votes were counted [February 13], and then blow up the Customs House and Post Office" [in Baltimore]. His contact told him that a group was meeting secretly every night at the Eutaw House, which was headed by "a d—d white-headed son of a b—, a Lawyer, named Mc—, [i.e., Maryland KGC leader John V. L. McMahon] who goes to Washington every day to bring news back to the conclave."[33]

Back on Lincoln's whistle-stop tour, the train next appeared in Cincinnati—the second overnight stop on his journey—where George Bickley had established the first KGC castles. From the balcony of the Cincinnati's Burnett House, Lincoln made an appeal to the Border State Kentuckians in the audience, promising "to leave you alone, and in no way interfere with your institution."[34] Before leaving Cincinnati on February 13, Lincoln's primary handler, Norman Judd, received a visit from one of Pinkerton's agents warning of trouble in Baltimore. For the time being, Judd decided not to pass the information on to Lincoln.[35] As Lincoln's train prepared to leave Cincinnati, a railway attendant spotted a small carpetbag under Lincoln's seat in the president's car. Upon opening it, he discovered a grenade, set to explode within fifteen minutes, with a force sufficient to kill everyone in the car. The bag was carefully removed and the grenade disposed of; the perpetrator was never identified.[36]

As the February 13 Electoral College vote count approached, rumors continued to percolate that a mob would rush the Senate Chamber, and that Ben McCulloch was preparing to swoop in with his Texans to install Breckinridge as president. Washington's hotel rooms were filled with out-of-towners—Louis Wigfall said this was in order to "have our friends on the ground in case of an emergency."[37] Given his knowledge of the KGC's clandestine plot as well as intelligence garnered from the National Volunteers' meetings, General-in-Chief Scott gave a great deal of credence to these threats. He dispatched seven companies of regular U.S. Army troops from Fort Monroe and other nearby locations, with twenty-four pieces of artillery. With Scott's troops guarding the Capitol as well as other government buildings, the vote count—supervised by Vice President John Breckinridge—went off without a hitch. For Scott's preparedness, southerners, such as Virginia congressman Daniel De Janette, castigated him as drawing his sword against his native state of Virginia.[38]

While all this was taking place, Lincoln continued on his rail tour to nine other northern cities. While the president-elect was speaking at New York's statehouse on February 18, John Wilkes Booth was appearing in the *Apostate* at Albany's downtown Gayety Theatre. The Gayety's management had recently reprimanded Booth for his disloyal prosecession outbursts, perhaps fueled by Lincoln's concurrent visit or Mayor Fernando Wood's proposal for the secession of New York City. Since appearing in Columbus, Georgia, and Montgomery, Alabama, in the fall of 1860 (both cities had active KGC castles), Booth had become "very strongly Southern." While in Montgomery, Booth likely heard William Yancey's prosecession speech on October 23, 1860. Upon returning to Philadelphia, Booth drafted his own speech calling on northerners to accommodate slavery and southern rights.[39]

In the meantime, Pinkerton ingratiated himself with the Baltimore stockbroker James Luckett, who had been elected as a commissioner to the informal prosecession convention that was to take place in Baltimore on February 18. Luckett said he received regular reports from Cypriano Ferrandini about a "secret organization" that "was powerful enough to bid defiance to Lincoln and his Abolitionist Crew" and would prevent northern troops from passing through Maryland to the capital. Luckett further confided to Pinkerton on February 15 that Captain Ferrandini was leading the group that planned to assassinate Lincoln (although Louis Wigfall later said that the KGC leader William Byrne served as the overall captain).[40]

On the evening of February 15, Luckett introduced Pinkerton to Ferrandini, who claimed during their conversation that murder was justifiable to save the rights of the southern people. Captain William H. H. Turner, a clerk of the Baltimore Circuit Court, was also present and accompanied Ferrandini to the secret meeting. The fifteen or so plotters at the meeting drew straws to see who would be the one to plunge the knife into the hated "Black Republican" president-elect. Pinkerton's agent in Harford County said that he had learned there were "One Thousand men well organized" in Baltimore, ready to back them up. The Perryville militiamen that Pinkerton's detective befriended included Captain Keen, who was a member of the Spesutia Rangers reporting to KGC Colonel Robert H. Archer.[41]

Allan Pinkerton, who had infiltrated the ring of conspirators, suspected that Baltimore's police commissioner, George Marshall Kane, was involved, due to his observed familiarity with "rabid Secessionates." Pinkerton had overheard Kane at Barnum's Hotel implying that he would not provide the Lincoln party with a police escort and that the Baltimore police would not interfere with the conspirators.[42] Kane had been a grain and grocery merchant who ran for chief of police as a reform candidate. He also served as a colonel of the Baltimore City Guard, the same militia unit in which Ferrandini served as a captain.[43] In June 1861, Kane would be arrested and locked up by Union military authorities for his "notoriously deep sympathy with the rebels." At the time of his arrest, an arsenal of weapons was discovered.[44]

Once Lincoln's whistle-stop excursion reached Philadelphia, he was informed by two separate sources that a verified plot to assassinate him was being planned by a band of conspirators linked to the Knights of the Golden Circle. On Thursday night, February 21, Pinkerton finally met with Lincoln and told him that a militant group of fifteen to fifty men, led by extremists such as Ferrandini, planned to overpower his carriage as it passed through Baltimore and assassinate him. Pinkerton said that dedicated paramilitary groups outside Baltimore would simultaneously blow up the railroad bridges and cut off communication. Pinkerton strongly recommended that Lincoln secretly head to Washington City according to the alternative itinerary that Samuel Felton, the president of the Philadelphia, Wilmington, and Baltimore Railroad, had worked out .[45]

Later that night, Frederick Seward, the son of Lincoln's designated secretary of state, handed the president-elect messages from Seward's father and General-in-Chief Scott. These messages warned that about fifteen thousand men were organized to prevent Lincoln's passage through Baltimore and that arrangements had been made to blow up the railroad on which he was traveling. Scott had received his information from the New

York police detectives dispatched by Commissioner Kennedy, a source separate from Pinkerton. Scott was so concerned about the plot that he was ready to send U.S. troops to Baltimore if Lincoln didn't change his plans. After hearing this corroborating report, Lincoln reluctantly agreed to Felton's clandestine itinerary, although he insisted on keeping his commitments in Harrisburg.[46]

On Friday, February 22, Lincoln spoke to Pennsylvania's legislature in Harrisburg, but the reception planned for that evening was called off. The telegraph lines from Harrisburg to Baltimore were temporarily disconnected, and Lincoln sped back to Philadelphia in a special one-car train. There, Lincoln donned an old overcoat and soft felt hat and boarded the last sleeping car of the PWBRR's night train to Baltimore accompanied only by his heavily armed bodyguard, Ward Hill Lamon, and Pinkerton. Lincoln's sleeping car was pulled into Baltimore's Camden Station at 3:30 a.m., Saturday morning, February 23, without incident. Lincoln then boarded the B&O train and arrived at the Washington station at 6:00 a.m. When southern newspapers found out about Lincoln's subterfuge, they lambasted him for being a coward.[47]

The KGC's plot to assassinate Lincoln was subverted by Lincoln's clandestine passage through Baltimore. The plot to seize the District of Columbia was similarly foiled by General Scott's timely military buildup, coupled with the inability of Virginians and Marylanders to push through secession. But the KGC would continue to try to strike an audacious blow on behalf of the South. Events were quickly coming to a head in Texas, where the KGC was spearheading the drive for secession and the capitulation of the 2,500-man U.S. Army stationed along the Texas and western frontier.

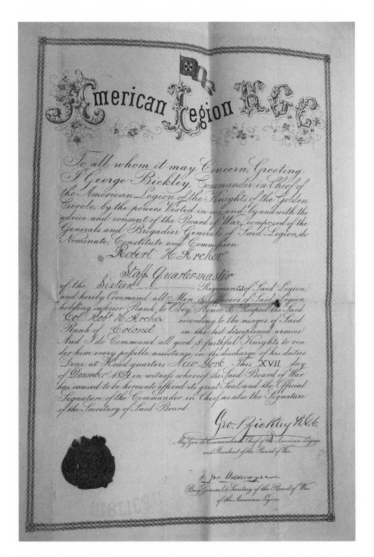

*Archer (Robert Harris) KGC commission:* Knights' colonel and militia leader from Harford County, Maryland, who recruited Marylanders for South Carolina in early 1861. Served under brother, who was a brigadier general, during the Civil War. On April 24, 1865, Archer was captured in a rowboat on the Potomac possibly intending to assist in John Wilkes Booth's escape. Courtesy of the Historical Society of Hartford County, Inc., 143 N. Main St., Bel Air, MD, 21014.

Ben McCulloch. Noted Texas Ranger and U.S. marshal who served as KGC emissary. Headed the 1,100-man KGC Army that forced the capitulation of the 2,500 U.S. Army soldiers stationed along the Texas frontier in February 1861. Later became a Confederate brigadier general.

George W. L. Bickley. Founder and general-in-chief of the Knights until stripped of control over the KGC Army at the society's May 1860 convention. Continued as head of KGC's political arm and subsequently served as KGC recruiter in Texas and Kentucky. Courtesy of Special Collections, Fine Arts Library, Harvard University.

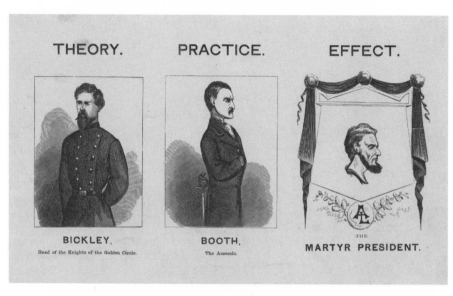

THEORY.  PRACTICE.  EFFECT.

BICKLEY.
Head of the Knights of the Golden Circle.

BOOTH,
The Assassin.

THE
MARTYR PRESIDENT.

Engraving from 1865 alleging KGC was behind Lincoln assassination. George Bickley, as the head of the Knights, is labeled "Theory," John Wilkes Booth, with a dagger behind his back, is labeled "Practice," and Abraham Lincoln is shown as "Martyr President."

John Wilkes Booth. After joining the KGC in Richmond around 1859, subsequently became Knights' leader relying on members to assist in smuggling activities during the Civil War. A curious number of Knights were connected with 1865 plots to abduct Lincoln.

Elkanah Bracken Greer. Powerful grand marshall of Knights' regiments in Texas and Arkansas. Pushed for Mexican intervention and tendered two KGC regiments to South Carolina. Served as colonel of the Confederacy's Third Texas Cavalry with many KGC recruits. Courtesy Smith County Historical Society.

Paul Jones Semmes. Militia leader from Columbus, Georgia, who was appointed KGC brigadier general at the May 1860 convention in Raleigh. Commissioned by Georgia's governor to purchase arms, then commanded Second Georgia Infantry. Courtesy of the House Divided Project at Dickinson College.

Virginius Despeaux Groner. Militia leader and former Texas Ranger who headed KGC in Virginia. Spearheaded the aborted January 1861 plot to seize Fortress Monroe and then became one of first commissioned Confederate officers, rising to colonel of the 61st Virginia Infantry Regiment. Courtesy The Library of Virginia.

Cypriano Ferrandini. Baltimore barber who served as militia drillmaster and captain in the Knights. Reputedly head of cabal that planned to assassinate Lincoln as the president passed through Baltimore in February 1861.

Richmond Grays at Harpers Ferry. Members of Richmond Grays militia company went to
Harpers Ferry in November 1859 to insure execution of radical abolitionist John Brown.
John Wilkes Booth (possibly at top right of photograph) tagged along. Courtesy Virginia
Historical Society.

Robert Charles Tyler. Former Walker filibusterer who became KGC regimental commander in Baltimore. Enlisted in 15th Tennessee Infantry at the beginning of Civil War and rose to brigadier general. Described as "one of the bravest men I ever saw." Courtesy Virginia Historical Society.

Louis T. Wigfall. Knights sympathizer who became U.S. senator from Texas. Recruited Marylanders for South Carolina and accepted initial surrender of Fort Sumter. Commanded Texas Brigade and became member of Confederate Congress.

Henry Alexander Wise. Former Virginia governor and KGC sympathizer who participated with Virginius Groner in a plot to seize Fortress Monroe. He subsequently headed the southern rights faction in Virginia's convention and helped precipitate Virginia's secession in April 1861.

George Washington Chilton. Headed the Texas Knights after February 1861. As member of Texas secession convention, he demanded that Sam Houston resign. Recruited KGC for Confederate Army, then served under Elkanah Greer in the Third Texas Cavalry and later in Duff's Partisan Rangers. Courtesy DeGolyer Library, Southern Methodist University, Dallas, Texas, Ag2088.0005.

# 9

# RUSTLING TEXAS OUT OF THE UNION

A CORE GROUP OF committed secessionists convened in the Austin office of Attorney General George Flournoy in late November 1860 to come up with a way to precipitate Texas's secession from the Union. John S. Ford, a KGC colonel and Texas Ranger commander, was one of the ringleaders. Ford had recently arrived in Austin, and he immediately began agitating and speaking out boldly in favor of secession. Oran Milo Roberts, a politically active Texas Supreme Court justice, also assumed a key role at the meeting. Roberts was from Tyler, the home of soon-to-be KGC grand marshall George Chilton, who was likely involved behind the scenes.[1] This core group proceeded to issue a citizens' call (on its own authority) for the early January selection of delegates to a state constitutional convention for the consideration of Texas's secession. The convention would be held in Austin on January 28.[2]

In support of the call, KGC member Thomas Green, a Texas Supreme Court clerk, helped the core group to rapidly organize a meeting at the Travis County Courthouse, attended by more than two hundred secession sympathizers. The call was simultaneously sent to Waco, Houston, and other Texas cities, where it was published by southern-rights newspapers, and similar meetings were held to endorse the proposed extralegal program. The call appeared in the *Austin State Gazette* on December 8, signed by seventy-two citizens.[3] According to the Unionist Charles Anderson, a majority of the signers of the call were clerks in Austin, and all were Knights of the Golden Circle.[4]

Knights had played a key role in the events leading up to the call. The KGC leader Ben McCulloch, who was meeting with members of the South Carolina legislature in October 1860, had written his Texas southern-rights contacts, urging the convening of a convention. McCulloch said that if Governor Houston won't convene a convention, "there ought to be a primary meeting in every [Texas] county of the state calling for a convention."[5] From Washington City, KGC sympathizer Senator Louis Wigfall similarly wrote that "all hope of compromise was exhausted" and urged Texans to secede.[6]

The estimated eight thousand Knights in Texas played an equally instrumental role in applying the political pressure and strong-arm tactics needed to precipitate Texas's secession. KGC operatives orchestrated many of the mass prosecession meetings and torchlight parades held throughout Texas during late November and early December. In Austin, John Ford spoke fervently from platforms draped with the Lone Star flag and helped break up meetings called by Unionists.[7] In Tyler, Knights George Chilton and John C. Robertson, a Harvard-trained lawyer, engaged in similar prosecession agitation, while the KGC leader John A. Wilcox led a meeting orchestrated by the Knights at San Antonio.[8] In Galveston, Congressman Guy Bryan churned out propaganda that urged Texans in other areas to select a slate of delegates. Judge Roberts embarked on a related trip across East Texas in support of the secessionists' program.[9] U.S. Army Major John Sprague, who was then serving in the Lone Star State, said that the "display of force, and the harmony and secrecy" provided by Texas's eight thousand Knights "hold in subjugation the sentiment and conduct of the entire population of the State."[10]

The call recommended the election (to take place on January 8, 1861) of two delegates from each Texas county or district. The call suggested that the chief justice of each county should order the election. Failing that, it recommended that the county commissioners or a committee of five citizens order the election.[11] Despite the call's recommended procedures, many delegates were both nominated and selected at public meetings such as those held in the KGC hotbeds of Harrison and Gonzales Counties. In Galveston, three delegates were officially nominated at a mid-December public meeting, where secession leaders intimidated Unionists by patting their revolvers and warning that there would be no abolitionist speeches allowed.[12]

A number of counties held elections in advance of the specified January 8 date. James Newcomb, the pro-Union editor of the *Alamo Express*, reported that where the local justices failed to call an election, the polls were opened by the KGC. Newcomb said that the people looked upon the informal and illegal election as a "farce" and that many Unionists simply didn't vote. Nevertheless, delegates were selected in some fashion in 92 of Texas's 122 counties.[13]

Despite KGC intimidation, Texas's sixty-eight-year-old governor, Sam Houston, tried to stem the prosecession tide by calling the Texas legislature into secession. In December, the aged warhorse again took to the stump and made a series of pro-Unionist speeches at various Texas cities. When Houston showed up at Galveston, his friends urged him not to speak, for fear of his personal safety. Instead, Houston boldly appeared on the balcony of the Tremont House and, with his deep basso voice, solemnly warned his listeners:

> You may, after the sacrifice of countless millions of treasure and hundreds of thousands of precious lives, as a bare possibility, win Southern independence; if God be not against you; but I doubt it. I tell you that . . . the North is determined to preserve this Union. They are not a fiery, impulsive people as you are, for they live in colder climates. But when they begin to move in a given direction, where great interests are involved, . . . they move with the steady momentum and perseverance of a mighty avalanche; and what I fear is, they will overwhelm the South with ignoble defeat.[14]

On December 17, Houston partially acceded to the prosecession juggernaut and issued a call for the Texas legislature to convene in special session on January 21, 1861. He still hoped to waylay the convention, however, by gaining support for a general convention of southern states to demand their rights *within* the Union.[15]

In the January 8 vote for convention delegates, KGC leader George Chilton was selected by Smith County. John Ford was selected to represent Cameron County (which encompassed Brownsville, along the Mexican border), even though Ford didn't officially reside there.[16] At least 11 of the 177 delegates elected to the secession convention were known or suspected members of the Knights of the Golden Circle. In addition, a number of further delegates were KGC sympathizers and a majority of delegates (93, or 53 percent) came from counties where the KGC was known to have active castles.[17]

When the Texas legislature convened on January 21, Sam Houston urged its support for a general convention of southern states to demand their rights within the Union. But many of the legislators had been elected in 1859, and were of the radical southern-rights variety, as compared to Houston, who had run on an independent "Opposition" ticket. KGC sympathizer M. D. K [Marion Dekalb] Taylor was Speaker of the Texas House of Representatives, and sixty Knights reportedly served in the Texas legislature.[18] The Texas legislature quickly squelched Houston's plan for a general southern convention and validated the extralegal selection of delegates for the Texas secession convention. The legislature did accept one Houston suggestion, however: that the people of Texas should, through a popular referendum, have the right to ratify or reject any convention action to separate Texas from the Union.[19]

Houston also sent a confidential messenger to warn seventy-year-old General David Twiggs about the possibility of a mob attack to seize the U.S. Army's substantial equipment and government stores held at its western headquarters in San Antonio. Twiggs had arrived in Texas on December 1, 1860, to command the 2,500-man military Department of Texas. Given Twiggs's strong sympathies toward his native state of Georgia, he was suspected by Unionists of being in league with Texas's secessionists. Unionists also believed that the "Buffalo Hunt," organized near San Antonio in December 1860 by Texas Ranger Captain and KGC member John Baylor was merely a pretense for Baylor's one-thousand-man force to try to capture the U.S. Army's arms, munitions, and equipment. Houston asked General Twiggs whether he wanted to turn the U.S. government property at San Antonio over to the State of Texas for safekeeping. Twiggs declined, saying he was without instruction from Washington as to what he should do.[20]

While a KGC connection is apparent for 11 of the 177 delegates to the January 28 secession convention, it is probable that other delegates were members or sympathizers with the secret society.[21] As a committed core of secession proponents, the Knights would play a significant role in the outcome of the convention as well as its appointed "Committee of Public Safety." The convention was primarily composed of lawyers (40 percent) and farmers/planters (35 percent), although most of the older and wealthiest planters were not directly involved. More than 90 percent of the delegates had been born in the South, and almost 72 percent owned slaves.[22]

From the KGC's standpoint, one of the key occurrences was the convention's first official act—the election of Texas Supreme Court judge Oran Roberts, from Tyler, as the president of the convention. Roberts, the brother-in-law of soon-to-be KGC grand marshall George Chilton, had been one of the earliest and most fervent prosecession advocates. John Ford was instrumental in the selection of Roberts, who then reciprocated by selecting Ford to the convention's all-powerful "Committee of Public Safety."[23]

The direction of the convention was clear on its second day, when the Brazoria County delegate, John Wharton, offered a resolution to declare Texas's independence from the United States, with the details to be worked out later. Texas attorney general George Flournoy immediately moved for a vote, and without debate, the convention voted 152 to 6 in favor of secession. John McQueen of South Carolina and General John Sanford of Georgia soon arrived as commissioners for their respective states to urge Texas's secession; both subsequently addressed the convention and complimented the convention on its quick, enlightened action.[24]

On the third day, Convention president Roberts appointed fifteen members to the Committee of Public Safety, which would emerge as one of the most powerful entities in the history of Texas. In addition to John Ford and John Robertson, other KGC-affiliated members appointed to the committee included Phillip Nolan Luckett, a surgeon who had served in the Texas Rangers under Ford, and John A. Wilcox, who had previously been a Mexican War colonel and U.S. congressman.[25]

On January 30, Thomas Jefferson Chambers, the chairman of the "Committee of Federal Relations," submitted the secession ordinance proposed by his committee to the convention. The proposed ordinance asserted that the federal Union was merely a compact between the states, and claimed that the power of the federal government was now being used as "a weapon with which to strike down the interests and prosperity of the Southern people." It therefore proclaimed that "all powers delegated by Texas to the federal government are revoked and resumed" and that Texas is now "a separate sovereign state."[26]

A serious debate did erupt over the issue of whether to submit the convention's decision on secession to a popular vote (included as "Section 2" of the proposed ordinance). This consumed most of the convention's secret sessions of January 30 and 31. On the evening of January 31, a letter arrived from Governor Sam Houston with the veiled threat that "when the voice of the people of Texas has been declared through the ballot box, no citizen will be more ready to yield obedience . . . than myself." Houston's cajoling, plus the likelihood of eventual disclosure of the vote, broke the back of those opposing a popular referendum. The motion to strike section 2 of the ordinance was defeated 145 to 29.[27]

The convention's final public vote on the secession ordinance took place on February 1. Judge Roberts invited members of the state legislature, prominent local citizens, and the heads of the various state departments to attend. He also wanted Governor Houston to be present in order to give the convention's extralegal action a further cloak of legitimacy. Houston had previously brushed off overtures to consult on the convention's deliberations, but this time Roberts sent a delegation of Houston's friends, who left the governor with little alternative except to attend.[28]

Upon arriving at the State Capitol on February 1, Houston was greeted with thunderous applause and seated at the right hand of Convention president Roberts. The delegates were then asked to declare their votes one by one. Thomas Hughes of Williamson County, a longtime Houston supporter, was the first to shout "No." When his turn came, James Throckmorton, the leader of the small antisecession minority from north Texas called out: "Mr. President, in view of the responsibility in the presence of God and my country—and unawed by the spirit of revolution around me, I vote no." His declaration was greeted by hisses from the crowded gallery. Throckmorton then rose and replied, "Mr. President, when the rabble hiss, well may patriots tremble." Only six other delegates showed themselves willing to incur the wrath of the hall, and the ordinance was approved by a vote of 166 to 8. Sam Houston left the assemblage with a dour face but said nothing that would show his real intentions.[29]

The convention then proceeded with implementation actions. It specified the voting procedures for the February 23 public referendum—a simple "For [or] Against Secession." Although the popular referendum had not yet occurred, the convention selected a seven-man delegation, including the firebrand Louis Wigfall, to represent Texas at the Provisional Confederate Congress being held at Montgomery. The convention also promulgated a statement titled "Declaration of the Causes Which Impel the State of Texas to Secede from the Federal Union," drafted by a committee of five that included the KGC leader John A. Wilcox. The declaration blamed Texas's secession on the North's challenge to white supremacy, its fomenting of sedition and servile insurrections, the impoverishment of the South through biased legislation, and the election of a sectional president pledged to continue these wrongs to the ruin of the slaveholding South. The declaration also demanded that the Texas legislature surrender its authority and recognize the convention's "supreme and sovereign power." The legislature refused to cede its authority, but it did pass an act that legitimized the outcome of the convention and affirmed the convention's decision to submit the secession ordinance to the people.[30]

Before it adjourned, the convention, in secret session, authorized the Committee of Public Safety to continue, and granted it the extraordinary power to seize any federal property within the state of Texas. The committee sent a delegation to visit Governor Sam Houston and to try to involve him in its plans. Houston replied that, given his oath to the Constitution of the United States, he could not agree to seize federal property while Texas remained in the Union.[31]

As the campaign for the public referendum got under way, Texas Unionists finally spoke out and published their own "Address to the People of Texas." They blamed South Carolina for the Texas convention's "revolutionary movement," warned that Texas's secession convention would eventually take over all the functions of government, and predicted that Texas's secession would result in higher taxes and drive Texas's slaves to border regions. The "Address" was signed on February 6 by a group of twenty-four that included James Throckmorton and I. [Isaiah] A. Paschal, the brother of former Texas judge George Paschal. A few days later, Throckmorton and a few others spoke publicly at Buass Hall in Austin, denouncing the convention "for its usurpation of powers—its establishment of a Committee of espionage, styled Safety—its secret sessions, its midnight plottings, its attempting to establish in our midst and to carry out the Reign of Terror, inaugurated in parts of Texas by Vigilance Committees."[32]

Judge Roberts prepared his own address making the case for secession,

KNIGHTS OF THE GOLDEN CIRCLE

while Sam Houston generally remained silent in order to leave the decision up to the people. Houston did note that he believed the convention had exceeded its authority in sending delegates to the Confederacy. He believed that if Texas were to secede, it should resume its prior status as an independent republic.[33]

But then, the Committee of Public Safety learned that U.S. Colonel Charles Waite, an ardent Unionist, had been ordered to replace General Twiggs as the commander of the U.S. Army's Department of Texas in San Antonio. Waite, who was commanding U.S. troops at Camp Verde in Texas, had written Twiggs on February 12, recommending that Waite consolidate his men with those in San Antonio. Waite had heard that Texas state authorities intended to force the U.S. Army to leave and would strip the departing troops of their arms. He warned that this "would lead to the most disastrous consequences" since his men would resist.[34]

General Twiggs recognized the dilemma he was facing. If he abandoned federal property, he would be branded a traitor and could be court-martialed. But if he didn't, he would face Texas state forces, with whom he was in sympathy, especially now that Twiggs's native Georgia had seceded. Twiggs had written a series of letters to General-in-Chief Winfield Scott asking to be relieved of his command. He told Scott that he would not fire on Texas citizens and pleaded for instructions as to what he should do when Texas secedes. The only guidance Twiggs received was in Scott's letter of December 28, 1860, telling Twiggs to protect government property without waging war or acting offensively. Meanwhile, Newcomb's *Alamo Express* accused Twiggs of being in league with the KGC and conspiring to hand Texas over to the secessionists.[35]

Pursuant to the convention's resolution, the Committee of Public Safety selected a subcommittee of three, including reputed KGC member Philip Luckett, to go to San Antonio and negotiate with Twiggs for the surrender of the federal forts and property. By this time, news had arrived that federal forts and arsenals were being seized throughout the Cotton States. The Texas convention had secretly instructed the Committee of Public Safety to avoid wounding the pride of Twiggs and his men, but to remind Twiggs that federal troops had been stationed in Texas to provide protection and not for the subjugation of its people. On February 3, the committee also appointed KGC leader Ben McCulloch, noted Texas Ranger and

U.S. marshall for East Texas, to raise a body of volunteers in case a display of force became necessary.[36]

The negotiations between General Twiggs and the subcommittee of three commenced on February 6. Twiggs generally indicated that upon Texas's final secession, he would surrender the federal property but not his command or weapons. During the subsequent daily negotiations, Twiggs assured the subcommittee that he was in favor of southern rights and that he did not want to bring on a civil war. Twiggs orally offered to march the federal forces out of Texas, but when the subcommittee asked him to put this in writing, he refused. He said they would have to wait until March 4, when Texas was expected to finally approve secession. On February 15, in discussing the detailed terms for surrender, the U.S. Army negotiators suddenly informed the subcommittee that later in the day, Colonel Waite was replacing General Twiggs and that they would have to hold off on further negotiations until receiving Colonel Waite's instructions.[37]

That night, Ben McCulloch assembled a force of approximately four hundred volunteers at Saluda Creek, just five miles north of San Antonio. Most of the men came from the seven local castles of the KGC and styled themselves "McCulloch's Army of the Knights of the Golden Circle." These included the castles at New Branfels and Seguin to the east of San Antonio, Pleasanton to the south, and Castroville to the west.[38] McCulloch headed toward San Antonio, ordering his men to dismount and march the last three miles, so as not to disturb the sleeping 160-man U.S. army garrison at the Alamo. For identification, each of McCulloch's men wore a red states'-rights insignia sewed on their otherwise diverse coats or shirts. According to R. H. Williams, a Knight who was there, the two companies of U.S. troops could have easily defended with artillery, since McCulloch's men had none. Instead, McCulloch's advancing force didn't even encounter a picket guard and were able to occupy a commanding position on the flat roofs of the surrounding houses.[39]

When McCulloch's KGC "Army" reached town before sunrise on February 16, they were joined by men from at least two of San Antonio's four KGC castles—the Charles Bickley Castle, under former Walker filibuster Trevanion Teel, and a castle headed by Major W. J. Clarke. Several KGC-affiliated militia units, the Alamo Rifles and the San Antonio Guard under Colonel John A. Wilcox, joined them. Inside help was provided by Knight

W. M. Edgar, a clerk in the U.S. Army's Quartermaster Department (and head of the Alamo City Guards), who had withdrawn the sentries from the U.S. government stores.[40] McCulloch's force was soon further supplemented by Knights arriving from eight more distant counties (Gonzales, Guadalupe, Caldwell, Atasosa, Comal, Medina, DeWitt, and Fayette), accompanied by a bevy of local dignitaries. Altogether, 1,100 Texas volunteers participated in the San Antonio occupation, and it is estimated that four-fifths of them were KGC members.[41]

By 7:00 a.m. on February 16, the U.S. flag was hauled down, and the Lone Star was raised to cheers and hurrahs. Mrs. Caroline Darrow, who witnessed the scene, said that early in the morning, General Twiggs himself came down to the plaza, where he was immediately surrounded by secessionists demanding the government property. Twiggs met with McCulloch and went through an initial show of refusal. But after being given six hours to reconsider, Twiggs surrendered all the U.S. posts and stores in Texas. The KGC units then assumed guard over the captured quartermaster departments, the federal arsenal and ordinance stores, the clothing depot, and the commissary. Altogether, these had an estimated value of $1,229,500.[42]

Earlier that afternoon, an unsuspecting U.S. Army Colonel Robert E. Lee, who had been assigned to the Department of Texas several months before, rode into San Antonio. Lee was shocked to see the town occupied by McCulloch's men with their red insignias. McCulloch's men told Lee of Twiggs's surrender and then said he was a prisoner of war. McCulloch tried to convince Lee to join the Confederacy, but Lee, who opposed secession, said he owed his allegiance to the United States. A few weeks later, Lee was allowed to head to Washington, where he faced an anguished decision. General-in-Chief Scott offered Lee command of the United States Army, but Lee instead decided to resign his commission in favor of his native state of Virginia.[43]

By the end of the day on February 16, the final surrender terms for the U.S. Army had been agreed upon. Colonel Waite arrived that afternoon, but it was too late for him to do anything about it. The two federal companies and light batteries of artillery were then allowed to march out of San Antonio to a camp beyond the city. James Newcomb said that as the federal troops left, San Antonio's Unionists "cheered the troops all along the streets and many followed them to the head of the San Pedro, where they encamped. After this scene, our city settled down into a solemn gloom."[44]

On February 18, Twiggs issued General Order No. 5, directing all thirty-seven companies of regular U.S. Army troops in Texas to evacuate their posts and retreat to the Texas coast with their arms and equipment. Despite ordering the forcible takeover of Twiggs's command, the Texas convention's subcommittee of three recognized that the federal troops in Texas had been there to provide frontier protection to its citizens and that "they are our friends." The 2,681 federal troops then in Texas constituted nearly 20 percent of the U.S. Army. The total value of the military property transferred at San Antonio and the twenty-one forts along the one-thousand-mile frontier, was estimated at around $3 million.[45] Within a few hours after issuing his order, Twiggs left for New Orleans, where he was soon commissioned as a major general in the Confederate army. Upon receiving the news of the surrender, the *Dallas Herald* exulted, "Hurrah for the noble band of K'sGC who in the hour of need, prooved [*sic*] themselves so prompt in striking for the rights of the South!"[46]

Efforts were made to convince the U.S. Army officers, and particularly the native southerners, to defect with their evacuating troops to the Confederacy. Only six of the federal officers under Twiggs did so. In his report a few days after the takeover, Ben McCulloch expressed his disappointment to U.S. senator Louis Wigfall and U.S. congressman John Reagan that few U.S. officers would defect, even though many of the southerners said they would resign rather than serve under Lincoln. McCulloch disagreed with Twiggs's order allowing the evacuating U.S. troops to keep their arms, and he urged that "if Virginia secedes, to go at once to her and get, if possible, those Morse guns that are at Harpers Ferry."[47]

After the takeover, the Public Safety Commission divided Texas into three military districts. The colonel heading each district was a leader of the KGC. Ben McCulloch assumed command of Texas state units for the middle district, his brother Henry McCulloch for the northwest district, and John Ford for the Rio Grande district. Each then proceeded to lead their respective units (containing and/or supplemented by KGC volunteers) in forcing the surrender and reoccupation of the U.S. government's twenty-one far-flung outposts on the Texas frontier. Again, KGC volunteers were prevalent among the Texas forces, with KGC Captain John Wilcox and his Alamo Rifles playing a leading role.[48]

The KGC held their state convention in San Antonio on February 22, 1861, in the aftermath of the U.S. Army's capitulation. The day before, the local KGC castles had taken out an ad in the *San Antonio Herald*, holding up George Newcomb and his *Alamo Express* to "the contempt and execration of all true southern men."[49] At the KGC convention, George Chilton was elected "Grand Marshall of the Texas Division," with Elkanah Greer now becoming "General of the Eastern Texas Brigade." John Ford was elected general for the Texas KGC's middle brigade and John Wilcox for its western brigade. James Vance, from a prominent San Antonio banking and hotel family, was elected treasurer, while V. W. Thompson, the editor of the *La Grange States Right Democrat*, was appointed as the KGC's state printer. The Texas KGC, with eight thousand Knights, was said to be in a flourishing condition and containing "the best and brightest of Southern soldiers."[50]

Perhaps fearing a backlash from Houston's supporters, the KGC conventioneers were warned to prepare for impending danger. The convention pledged its resources to the State of Texas in the event of turmoil. The convention also entertained a resolution to warn foreign countries, like Britain and France, that the Knights regarded Mexico as their personal province and to stay out.[51] The *Daily Ledger and Texan* reported that the Knights had divined Governor Houston's intention to use federal forces to put down the rebellion, but the risk of a collision had been averted by the Committee of Public Safety's decision to avail itself of the KGC.[52]

The KGC also played a role in obtaining the prosecession majority of 76 percent in the popular referendum of February 23. In a number of counties, the KGC castles paraded through the streets en masse and voted as a group. In Waxahachie (Ellis County, south of Dallas), where Knights voted en masse, 203 voters favored secession out of a total of 259. In Bexar County (containing San Antonio), reports circulated that the KGC was policing polling places. James Newcomb alleged that many of the reported secessionist majorities in the counties were inaccurate. By this point, however, the Unionists were already facing defeat, and it is doubtful they could have done anything to turn the tide of the reported 46,153 to 14,747 vote in favor of Texas's secession.[53]

At the resumed secession convention on March 4, Judge Roberts triumphantly announced: "Texas is now a free and independent state." Knight John Wilcox moved that the secession convention confirm the previously selected seven-member delegation that included Louis Wigfall and John Reagan to represent Texas at the Provisional Confederate Congress in Montgomery. Knight Samuel A. Lockridge went along to Montgomery so he could relay communications back to the Texas Provisional Congress in Austin.[54]

On March 14, KGC grand marshall George Chilton, on behalf of the Texas convention, visited Governor Sam Houston at the governor's mansion and insisted that Houston take an oath of allegiance to the Confederacy. Telling Chilton that he would reply the next day, Houston appeared on March 14 in the Texas House of Representatives and said that he did not acknowledge the authority of the convention and refused to take their required oath of office. Knights Thomas Cook and William Montgomery were then assigned to keep an eye on Houston.[55]

Over the preceding weekend, Houston and his friends, including James Throckmorton and George Pascal, had deliberated as to what Houston should do. Houston informed them that the recently inaugurated Union president, Abraham Lincoln, had sent a letter offering Houston command of seventy thousand troops to resist Texas's secession. But Houston feared a further lack of public support if coercion were applied. Both Throckmorton and Pascal agreed with Houston that he should not try to resist. On March 18, the convention voted to elevate Ed Clark to the position of governor and ordered Houston to move out of the executive mansion.[56]

The record shows that the KGC, through its "good old boys" network, played a significant role in the secession of Texas as well as the capitulation of the western U.S. Army. By applying coordinated local pressure through intimidation and militant action, the KGC was able to force the convening of Texas's extralegal secession convention, influence Texas's legislative representatives to provide a cloak of legitimacy for the convention's actions, and orchestrate the seizure of the federal forts and property in Texas. The San Antonio editor James Newcomb called the KGC a "powerful instru-

ment in the hands of the conspirators" and concluded: "Through this organization the first secession convention was effected, the first armed rebels
under Ben McCulloch were members of this order; it furnished the vigilance hanging committees, and to them belong the credit of the murders
and the arsons committed during the secession times."[57]

The KGC had rustled Texas out of the Union, and the U.S. Army out of
the Lone Star State. Using Texas as a model, the KGC was now ready to
spread its reach across Arkansas and Indian Territory, as well as to California and Oregon, where it would push for an independent Pacific republic.
It would also spearhead the drive for secession in the pivotal Border State
of Virginia, whose participation was essential to the nascent Confederate
nation.

# 10

# SPREADING SECESSION

FTER PRECIPITATING THE secession of Texas and the seizure of its U.S. Army installations, the KGC tried to spread secession westward to Arkansas, Indian Territory, and the recently created Pacific coast states of California and Oregon. Arkansas had an 1860 population of 435,000 (of which 110,000 were slaves). KGC castles with more than six hundred members existed at Little Rock, the state capital, while other castles were reported in the southern plantation counties around Camden. Bickley had previously visited Napoleon, then Arkansas's second-largest city, about seventy miles south of Helena on the Mississippi River, where KGC castles also likely existed.[1] The Arkansas KGC battalion, commanded by Little Rock sign painter Augustus Larrantree, was part of the 3,500-man Texas/Arkansas Knights division under Elkanah Greer, who had close relatives living at DeValls Bluff, Arkansas.[2]

The apparent political head of the Arkansas Knights was U.S. congressman Thomas Hindman, a transplant from Mississippi who had served in the Second Mississippi Rifles during the Mexican War. After moving to Helena in 1854, Hindman recruited for General John Quitman's aborted 1854 Cuban filibustering expedition, became leader of the eastern Arkansas Democrats, and purchased newspapers in Helena and Little Rock that frequently ran articles promoting the KGC. Hindman was a zealous advocate for reinstituting the African slave trade, for expanding slavery into Mexico and Central America, and for southern secession. During his 1859–61 tenure as a U.S. congressman, he established a national reputation as one of the South's more virulent firebrands and was also one of the founders of the Minute Men organization in Arkansas.[3]

With Hindman's backing, Arkansas voters elected Henry Rector as governor in August 1860 over the candidate backed by the state's political machine. Rector, initially a moderate, became an ardent secession advocate following Lincoln's November 1860 election. After being subjected to aggressive southern-rights pressure, the Arkansas legislature passed a bill in mid-January 1861 calling for the people to vote on February 18 as to whether they wanted to call a convention to consider secession.[4]

In the interim, an early February attempt was orchestrated for the takeover of the lightly garrisoned U.S. Army arsenal at Little Rock.[5] Leading the effort were militia units from Helena (directed from Washington by Hindman) who were joined through a network (likely involving the Knights) of eclectic insurgents from Arkansas's southern plantation counties.[6] Governor Rector tried to pose as a neutral in negotiating the terms of surrender with the arsenal's federal commander, but upon the capitulation, Rector accompanied the two thousand insurgents to the arsenal grounds and made a jubilant speech.[7] The strong-arm tactics backfired, however, as conservative citizens from northern and central Arkansas now saw Governor Rector as a Hindman-directed zealot and registered a 27,412 to 17,927 vote against secession on February 18. Arkansas wouldn't finally secede until May 6, 1861, nearly three months later.[8]

The KGC was also active in the 5-million-acre Indian Territory to the west of Arkansas, where KGC Indian agents such as Robert Cowart of Georgia and Douglas Cooper of Mississippi (who would return in mid-1861 as a Confederate colonel) had helped spread the secret society among the mixed-blood Native Americans. Knights were especially prevalent among the mixed-blood Cherokees, who owned more than 3,500 slaves in 1860. Full-blooded Cherokees generally opposed African slavery and formed their own secret society—the Keetowahs—to promote the traditional Cherokee ways.[9]

The Confederate government formed a Bureau of Indian Affairs in March 1861 and sent newly appointed Brigadier General (and KGC leader) Ben McCulloch and lawyer Albert Pike to recruit the five civilized Indian tribes as allies. Arkansas governor Rector and his emissaries also tried to convince John Ross, chief of the twenty-three thousand Cherokees, to side with the new Confederate government. Pike and McCulloch offered the Ross-led Cherokees extremely generous terms if they would join the Confederate cause.[10]

The Confederates simultaneously courted the mixed-blood faction, constituting about one-third of the Cherokees, by offering them weapons and protection if they would actively support the Confederate government. The mixed-blood faction was led by Stand Watie, an educated lawyer and businessman who was trying to undercut Ross and take control of the Cherokee nation. A serious guerilla war developed between the Watie and Keetowah factions that threatened to split the Cherokee nation in two. Such a division had already occurred among the Creeks, whose predominant pro-South faction joined the Confederacy in early March, while a splinter group supported Ross and his Cherokees in resisting southern pressure.[11]

The wily Ross did everything possible to remain neutral. By the fall of 1861, however, with Union forces withdrawing from the area and Watie nipping at his heels, Ross was finally forced to give tacit support to the Confederacy. This thwarted the attempts by Watie's KGC faction to take control of the Cherokee Nation. In the meantime, Stand Watie was commissioned as a Confederate colonel. He was subsequently regaled as a hero for the mixed-blood Cherokees' role in the Confederate victory at the August 1861 Battle of Wilson's Creek in Missouri.[12]

The KGC also spread to the Pacific coast, including the recently created states of California and Oregon, where one-third of the population was of southern origin. In northern California, the KGC was especially active in agricultural regions such as Maryville, north of Sacramento (where mixed-blood Cherokee John Rollin Ridge served as an editor and KGC recruiter), and Tulare, south of Fresno, where the mayor, sheriff, and other local officials were reportedly Knights. In southern California, the KGC was active in El Monte (established by a company of Texans), as well as Los Angeles and the San Bernardino Valley.[13] In 1861, San Francisco's Unionists estimated "that there are upward of 16,000 'Knights of the Golden Circle' in this State, and that they are still organizing even in the most loyal districts."[14]

The reputed leader of the Knights in California was William Gwin, California's first U.S. senator.[15] Gwin had formerly been a Tennessee medical doctor and then a New Orleans customs official. He moved to California in 1849 and became instantly wealthy when a gold mine was discovered on his property. He used his wealth to promote the "Chivalry wing" of the state Democratic Party that placed many of its adherents in key state and local offices. While senator, Gwin pushed for U.S. expansion to mineral-rich areas such as Mexico. In early 1861, he predicted that the secession of the South was a foregone conclusion and that the Far West would follow, forming a separate Pacific republic.[16] Other prominent leaders of the KGC and its Third Degree, called the Knights of the Columbian Star, included Beriah Brown, the editor of the *San Francisco Press;* C. L. Weller, a San Francisco politician; and John Bigler, California's 1852–56 governor.[17]

The drive to form an independent Pacific republic had been going on for some time, but became more active once the southern Confederacy came into being. States'-rights leaders in southern Oregon—known as "Dixie of the Northwest"—had joined with Gwinn and the Californians in pushing for a separate republic. Many of rural southern Oregon's settlers had come from the South, and southerners also predominated in its various mining camps. At the beginning of the war, Oregon's governor and congressmen were states'-rights Democrats, as well as Joseph Lane, who served as the vice-presidential running mate for John Breckinridge. Ten castles of the KGC reportedly existed in southern Oregon, with a membership of 2,500 out of a total state population of fifty-two thousand.[18]

During early 1861, wealthy members of an oath-bound secret society of southern sympathizers met in San Francisco to formulate a plot to seize the U.S. military installations and force the establishment of an independent Pacific republic. Each was asked to raise substantial funds in order to organize a fighting force of approximately eight hundred from among the local "ex-veterans of the Mexican war, ex-filibusters, ex-Indian fighters, all eager to engage in any undertaking that promised adventure and profit."[19] The KGC and its Third Degree Knights of the Columbian Star were the predominant pro-South secret societies in San Francisco at this time, and commentators attribute the secret plot to them.[20]

The conspirators' plan was to launch a night attack to seize the lightly defended San Francisco federal military installations, including Fort Point, Fort Alcatraz, Mare Island, and the arsenal at Benicia. They would then move to seize the arsenal of the California militia in San Francisco. One of the conspirators reported: "With this abounding military equipment, we proposed to organize an army of Southern sympathizers, sufficient in number to beat down any armed resistance." This army would then force California to declare its independence from the Union and establish a Pacific republic.[21]

The conspirators hoped to secretly recruit to the plot members of the U.S. Army's Sixth Regiment, headquartered in San Francisco.[22] They also hoped to enlist Albert Sidney Johnston, the newly arrived commander of the U.S. Army's Sixth Regiment. Johnston was a native Kentuckian who helped lead the fight for Texas's independence; he was a close friend of Jefferson Davis, who described him as one of the most capable officers in the U.S. Army.[23] At an introductory meeting in mid-January 1861, Johnston reportedly short-circuited any talk of the seizure plot, however, by indicating at the outset: "I . . . will defend the property of the United States with every resource at my command."[24]

After taking office, the Lincoln administration became concerned about Johnston's loyalty and sent General Edwin Sumner, a tough U.S. cavalry officer originally from Massachusetts, to take command of the Pacific Department. Sumner arrived in San Francisco on April 24. He quickly shored up California's defenses by removing the federal arms around San Francisco to the now well-guarded Alcatraz Island, brought in troops from posts in Oregon and Washington State, and sent a strong detachment of soldiers to Los Angeles.[25] The drive to create a separate Pacific republic had been thwarted by General Sumner's quick reaction and Johnston's apparent unwillingness to betray his command.[26] The supersecret Knights of the Columbian Star would continued to operate on the Pacific Coast during the Civil War.[27]

On the East Coast, the KGC was instrumental in the push for secession and seizure of military installations in pivotal Virginia, where KGC castles extended from the central cities of Richmond and Petersburg, to Norfolk, Southampton, and other towns along Virginia's southern border. On December 24, 1860, Virginius Groner, who commanded a regiment of one thousand "Military Knights," accompanied General John Tyler (former president John Tyler's son) in delivering prosecession speeches at a huge rally held at the estate of Henry Wise near Norfolk. During January 1861, Groner, in conjunction with former governor Henry Wise and his Minute Men, had been prepared to seize Fort Monroe in the Norfolk harbor. Their plan had been stymied by the cautiousness of Virginia's moderate governor, John Letcher. But Groner, Wise, and the Knights were now ready to help precipitate Virginia's secession.[28]

Surprisingly, the February 4, 1861, vote by Virginians for the selection of delegates to their convention resulted in an overall victory for the Unionists. Only 30 of the 152 delegates elected advocated immediate secession. Western Virginians were generally against immediate secession, while most of those willing to consider secession came from Virginia's eastern Tidewater and central Piedmont regions.[29]

Leading the committed secessionist minority was Virginia's eccentric former governor Henry Wise, who represented the Norfolk area at the convention. Described by his friends as the "knightly champion of Southern Rights," Wise remained angry at Governor Letcher for refusing to authorize the takeover of Fort Monroe in January, and urged a change in Virginia law so that he could replace Letcher as governor. Wise's hotheaded son Obadiah Jennings ("O. J.") Wise was editor of the pro-South *Richmond Enquirer* and had recently been elected a captain in the Richmond Light Infantry Blues militia unit.[30]

Die-hard Unionists like John S. Carlisle and Robert Y. Conrad opposed the secessionists. Carlisle was a lawyer from Clarksburg in far-western Virginia who led the convention's Unionist caucus. Conrad was a businessman and lawyer from Winchester in Virginia's Piedmont region, who would serve as the chairman of the convention's Committee on Federal Relations. Despite western Virginia's opposition, a fellow Unionist predicted in early 1861 that the "never tiring wire-worker and tricksters" in the convention's secessionist caucus will appoint "vigilance committees and minute-men" in each district, to work openly and secretly as spies and "use all means, whether fair or foul, to inflame the public mind, to excite and arouse the worst and most depraved portion of the population . . . to drag Virginia into revolution whether her people are willing or not."[31]

From the convening of the convention on February 13 to the submission of its Federal Relations Committee's initial report on March 9, the Unionists were able to constrain the secessionist drive by Wise and his minority caucus.[32] Virginians hoped that a compromise could be worked out at the Washington Peace Conference, called by their state and attended by representatives of twenty-four of the remaining thirty-four northern and Border States. But Congress rejected the Peace Conference's report on February 27, in part due to Republican intransigence. This caused former president John Tyler, who had served as the Peace Conference's chairman, to swing over to the secessionist cause. Tyler, a close friend of Henry Wise, thereafter spoke out in favor of secession as the only way to retain white supremacy and southern hopes for future territorial expansion in Cuba and the Caribbean.[33]

In early March, District of Columbia KGC leader L. Q. Washington advised Confederate secretary of war Leroy Walker that the Virginia convention would not pass an ordinance of secession unless collision or war ensued. L. Q. had a direct pipeline to the states'-rights caucus of the Virginia convention through its leader Lewis E. Harvie, from Amelia County, who was L. Q.'s close friend.[34] During mid-March, L. Q. advised Walker that Virginia seemed to be moving toward disunion and noted that Virginians were holding prosecession meetings all over the Old Dominion. He further predicted that once Virginia had seceded, the other Border States would soon follow and the "Yankee Government" would desert Washington in three or four days.[35]

The firebrand senator Louis Wigfall also continued his intelligence-gathering activities on behalf of the Confederacy, but now expanded his repertoire to include recruiting soldiers for the southern cause. In February, Wigfall had received permission from his friend Jefferson Davis to establish a recruiting station in Baltimore and to recruit a regiment for the Confederacy. By March, Wigfall was drawing Confederate funds for this purpose, channeled through W. T. Walker & Co., a large Maryland liquor distributor owned and operated by its secessionist namesake.[36] On March 15, Wigfall spoke to a Baltimore gathering of National Volunteers and other "friends of the South" who came to serenade him. He said that he regretted that "Maryland, Virginia, North Carolina, Tennessee and Kentucky had not joined their sister States of the South," but assured his admirers that "the separation was final."[37]

By the end of March, Wigfall had recruited sixty-four Marylanders, who were sent to General Beauregard in Charleston. Wigfall continued to meet with leading Maryland secessionists, including KGC political head John V. McMahon, and reported to Walker that his Maryland contacts would consider precipitating Maryland's secession on their own if Walker would send them the necessary arms.[38] In conjunction with KGC Colonel Robert H. Archer's recruiting in Harford and the other counties north of Baltimore, Wigfall would supply hundreds of Marylanders to add to the out-of-state units helping Confederate General Beauregard man the Charleston defenses.[39]

In addition to spying and recruiting, Wigfall also spent part of March assisting the ubiquitous KGC operative Ben McCulloch in purchasing arms for the South. On March 9, the Texas legislature appointed McCulloch as its agent to arrange the purchase of one thousand Morse and Colt rifles, before the Union government closed off the pipeline of munitions. After stopping off at Mobile and Montgomery, Alabama, McCulloch headed for Richmond in mid-March to make arrangements for the arms purchases. During the last weeks of March, McCulloch met with Wigfall on several occasions in Washington and in Alexandria, Virginia.[40]

Rumors spread throughout the North that McCulloch's visit involved motives other than arms purchases. McCulloch was reported to have visited the home of U.S. senator William Gwin, who represented California and was said to be the leader of its Knights. Stories also circulated that McCulloch was encamped in northern Virginia with five hundred Texas Rangers who were preparing to kidnap and murder President Lincoln. Attorney General Edwin McMasters Stanton subsequently reported, "Ben McCulloch has been here [in Washington] on a scouting expedition and he carefully examined all the barracks and military posts in the city and said that he expected to be in possession of the city before long."[41]

Throughout March, the secessionists in Virginia's convention redoubled their efforts, with Henry Wise asserting, "We must train the popular mind and heart."[42] Prosecession mobs arrived in Richmond from the KGC hotbeds of Petersburg and Lynchburg and roamed the streets at night. At a March 15 mass meeting, three hundred Petersburg rowdies arrived, carrying the Confederate flag as well as a petition signed by 1,700 citizens, and demanded immediate secession.[43] Similar petitions emanated from public meetings held across Virginia, which were read verbatim by secessionist leaders in the convention. By now all three Richmond papers were advocating secession. Unionist John Carlisle accused Wise's *Richmond Enquirer* of engineering a scheme to drive Virginia out of the Union.[44]

This constant barrage was having an impact on the convention's conditional Unionist delegates, who had indicated they would oppose any attempt by federal authorities to coerce the seceding states and whose opinions could be changed depending on developments. By the end of March, approximately 20 more delegates had joined with the original group of 30 unconditional secessionists to comprise a voting bloc of 50 out of the 122 delegates.[45] In addition, Virginia's southern-rights leaders had reportedly infiltrated and gained control of Richmond's secession mobs and militia companies. Unionist leaders Carlisle and Conrad spent three or four hours each night drilling their colleagues, to steel them against the arguments and intimidation of the secessionist forces. Conrad privately wrote his wife that "bands of men are arming and organizing in this city, ready for revolution, and determined to begin it upon the least opportunity."[46] O. J. Wise was courting western Virginia delegates who were wavering, and he told one delegate that if they didn't vote for an ordinance of secession, they would be driven from the hall at the point of a bayonet.[47]

During the latter part of March, Henry Wise, together with eight other secessionist advocates (including several members of the Virginia convention and legislature), sent out a confidential circular letter (subsequently leaked to the press) to several hundred "reliable" southern-rights supporters. The letter requested the supporters' presence in Richmond during the week of April 15, "to consult with the friends of Southern rights as to the course which Virginia should pursue in the present emergency." The letter requested them to report to a specified contact and "bring with you or send a full delegation of true and reliable men from your county; and if convenient, aid the same object in the surrounding counties."[48] William H. Edwards, who was present in Richmond when these "delegations" arrived, described the members as "long-haired, wild-eyed strangers, many of them said to be Knights of the Golden Circle."[49]

At about this same time, Henry Wise (backed by his son O. J. Wise and his company of Richmond Blues) developed an audacious plot to take over the Virginia state government. The plot called for secretly kidnapping and carrying off Governor Letcher as well as Unionist leaders of the convention, such as Conrad and Carlisle. If, after thirty hours, a majority of the convention still refused to vote for secession, the remaining Unionists would be arrested and the secession of Virginia declared as a voluntary act. Harpers Ferry and the Norfolk Navy Yard would then be seized. Virginia's prosecession lieutenant governor, Robert Montague, as well as David Chalmers, who was soon to become president of the southern-rights conclave, were also reportedly involved in the plot.[50]

Meanwhile, the pressure on the dwindling Unionist-Centrist majority in the Virginia convention intensified, and the threats against the Unionist delegates became more direct. Robert Carlisle was ridiculed on the street and threatened with hanging by a mob that surrounded his boarding-house. Within the convention, the various factions agreed on April 8 to appoint a commission of three—a Unionist, a moderate, and a secessionist—to meet with President Lincoln and determine whether he intended to reinforce the southern forts.[51]

Then, on April 13, word arrived that South Carolina's bombardment of Fort Sumter had begun. O. J. Wise and Virginia attorney general J. Randolph Tucker led a Richmond celebration, bringing cannon and firing a 100-gun salute at the State Capitol.[52] South Carolina governor Francis Pickens telegraphed Governor Letcher on April 14: "The war is commenced, and we will triumph or perish. . . . Please let me know what Virginia will do."[53]

President Lincoln issued his proclamation on April 15, calling for 75,000 troops to suppress the insurrection in the seceding states, of which Virginia's allocation was 2,340 men. Governor Letcher, like many of the Border State governors, responded forcefully that Virginia would provide no troops to subjugate the South. Letcher added, "You have chosen to inaugurate Civil War."[54] The Virginia secessionists were ecstatic since the Old Dominion would now have to decide whether or not to secede. The three-member committee that had met with Lincoln on April 13 returned and reported that the president, while disclaiming any intention for the use of offensive force, had reiterated his policy to "hold, occupy, and defend" the southern forts. This caused even the committee's Unionist delegate to conclude that there was no hope of an amicable arrangement with the Lincoln administration.[55]

On April 14, a group of 250 (likely including Knights who had arrived in Richmond in response to Wise's circular letter) vowed to break up the Virginia convention by force the next day. Marshall Ambler, a prosecession delegate from Louisa County, told the "precipitators" that the convention was on the verge of voting for secession and they should hold off trying to take over by force. Henry Wise also appeared on the portico and solemnly pledged that the ordinance would be passed within forty-eight hours, and this consoled the mob for the time being.[56]

On April 16, the regular Virginia convention met and voted to go into secret session. Then William Ballard Preston of Montgomery County presented an ordinance for Virginia's secession and moved for the vote. John Scott of Fauquier County offered a counterresolution providing for a vote by the people on the fourth Thursday in May. The vote would offer the alternatives of immediate secession or consultation with the other slave-holding states. The convention's Unionists, who saw their numbers rapidly dwindling, charged they were being gagged by the opposition and warned that western Virginia would never secede.[57]

Several hundred delegates convened for the southern-rights conclave on the morning of April 16 at Metropolitan Hall, about a block from the regular convention meeting. The doorkeeper of the conclave stood with a drawn sword to make sure only invited states'-rights proponents attended. David Chalmers of Halifax County served as the conclave's president; many of the attendees were from Virginia's old-line families. At the meeting, O. J. Wise delivered an electrifying speech advocating immediate action. Near the end of the day, William Parker arrived from Henry Wise's Norfolk district and informed the conclave that, with the acquiescence of Governor Letcher, he had blocked the channel of the James River in order to box in the federal ships and naval stores located at the Gosport Naval Yard. At the end of the day, the southern-rights conclave decided to adjourn in order to give the regular convention one more day to pass the ordinance of secession.[58]

On April 16, Henry Wise ran into his southern-rights compatriot John Imboden on the street in Richmond. Imboden, a lawyer and state representative from Staunton, was the captain of a militia artillery company; he would later become a noted Confederate raider and brigadier general. Wise asked Imboden to bring together a group of militia officers who would be willing to join in a plan to capture the federal arsenal at Harpers Ferry. Six officers attended the meeting that evening, including Turner Ashby, who headed a militia company from Fauquier County, and Alfred

Barbour, the superintendent of the Harpers Ferry arsenal, who now sympathized with the secessionists. Governor Letcher refused to provide state authority for the contemplated action, so Wise drew up the seizure order.[59]

After the meeting, Turner Ashby left for Fauquier to rouse his Black-Horse Cavalry, while Imboden went to Staunton to rally his artillery company. Around this time, Wise received a telegram from Washington's National Volunteer leader, Dr. Alexander Y. P. Garnett (Wise's son-in-law) indicating that a one-thousand-man Massachusetts regiment had been ordered to Harpers Ferry. Wise also received a dispatch from William Parker at Norfolk asking: "The powder magazine here [at Gosport] can be taken and the Yankee vessels can be captured and sunk so as to obstruct the harbor. Shall we do it?" Wise wrote "yes" on the telegram and sent it back to Parker.[60]

Both the regular convention and southern-rights conclave met at their appointed time on April 17. The southern-rights conclave spent the morning debating the subject of a new political organization for Virginia, but then someone announced that the regular convention was taking a vote. A member shouted: "We will give them another chance to save themselves. But it is the last!"[61] Over in the regular convention, Henry Wise rose from his seat at a predetermined signal, drew out a large horse pistol, and launched into a moving diatribe that brought former president John Tyler to tears. One commentator said: "The speaker was supernaturally excited. . . . His hair stood off from his head, as if charged with electricity."[62] On the basis of a telegram he received from Captain Imboden that morning, Wise told the convention that while he was speaking and by his orders, Harpers Ferry was being taken by patriotic volunteer revolutionists. When Unionist William Baldwin asked who they were, Wise replied that some of them were from Augusta, in Baldwin's own district.[63]

Then Wise followed up by announcing that the federal naval yard at Norfolk was being similarly seized. While Carlisle and other Unionist delegates protested the action, Wise and several secessionist delegates went to Governor Letcher, who now authorized the seizures, but rejected Wise's further request for Virginia troops to seize the District of Columbia. Wise's dramatic announcement of already initiated paramilitary action had the desired effect—the convention immediately passed the ordinance of secession by a vote of 88 to 55.[64]

Over in the southern-rights conclave, Lieutenant Governor Montague informed the attendees that the ordinance of secession had finally been passed. Soon Henry Wise and former president John Tyler appeared and amid a chorus of cheers were escorted arm in arm to the platform. Tyler made a fifteen-minute speech, describing Virginia's secession as the culmination of its quests for liberty and independence, and lamenting the blindness that had prevented Virginia from seizing the District of Columbia. He concluded by leading the delegates in the collective chant, "Independence or Death."[65]

Subject to the pro forma popular vote that took place on May 23, the secession of Virginia, with its substantial manufacturing and manpower base, had been achieved through extralegal pressure of the type employed in Texas and with the KGC's apparent participation.[66] A few months later, a committee of San Francisco businessmen wrote to Secretary of War Cameron expressing concern about the sixteen thousand Knights in California: "We need only appeal to the examples furnished by . . . Virginia to show that the efforts of a comparatively small number of audacious and unscrupulous men are sufficient to precipitate an unwilling population into disunion."[67]

11

# CALL TO ARMS

O N APRIL 10, Confederate secretary of war Leroy Pope Walker forwarded his fateful order to General Beauregard, a former OLS
sympathizer, authorizing the bombardment of Fort Sumter in
Charleston harbor: "You will at once demand its evacuation and if this is
refused[,] proceed, in such manner as you may determine, to reduce it."[1]
Walker's April 10 telegram, which initiated the Civil War, was transmitted by none other than KGC Colonel Virginius Groner, then serving as a
captain on Walker's staff in the Confederate War Department. Groner had
traveled to Montgomery in March to join the Confederate service after de-
clining an offer by Governor John Pettus to become Mississippi's adjutant
general. Shortly after arriving in Montgomery, Groner visited Jefferson
Davis and was appointed to Walker's staff, with the duty of organizing the
volunteers arriving from throughout the South. Groner became the fifth
military appointment to the new Confederate government enlisting under
the auspices of Mississippi, since Virginia did not officially secede until
after its May 23 popular vote.[2]

After reports were received of the shelling on Fort Sumter, a jubilant
celebration took place on the evening of April 12 in the Montgomery town
square. Secretary of War Walker made a rousing speech predicting that
Fort Sumter would fall the next day and that the Confederate flag would
fly over Washington City within three months. George Chilton, the KGC's
recently appointed grand marshal for Texas, was also on the platform, and
at the end of Walker's speech, he led the crowd in repeated huzzas. Chilton was then being considered for the position of Confederate postmaster

general, likely through the influence of his uncle, William Parrish Chilton, a prominent member of the Confederate Provisional Congress.[3] Groner and Chilton were just two of the many Knight leaders who played a key early role in supporting the Confederate war effort and in ramping up a southern army from nothing to more than two hundred thousand men in about five months.[4]

Secretary of War Walker had issued an April 8 message asking the governors of each of the seceded states to drill and equip three thousand volunteers and "hold them in instant readiness to meet any requisition from this Department." Jefferson Davis decided to increase Walker's requested troop allocations to five thousand on April 16 in order to build a Confederate army of fifty thousand. This was in response to Abraham Lincoln's April 15 proclamation that called on northern and Border State governors to provide seventy-five thousand militia to put down the southern insurrection.[5]

In support of Walker's call, a tripartite order dated April 17, 1861, was sent out from Montgomery to the Knights of the Golden Circle throughout the South. As the *Charleston Mercury* had previously indicated: "BICKLEY's forces [are] the most available nuclus [*sic*] for an army."[6] The first part of the KGC's tripartite order was from George Chilton as grand marshall of the Texas Division. It assumed "the threatened invasion of Texas by Lincoln's abolition horde" and said that the Confederate army was inadequate to provide protection at the "many points exposed to attack from the enemy." Chilton ordered the captains of each KGC castle in Texas to meet him at Galveston on May 1, 1861, with their complete muster rolls: "Each Castle will hold itself in readiness for immediate orders." Higher-level KGC field officers were also asked to attend.[7]

KGC Major Augustus Larrantree, commander of the Arkansas Battalion, issued another part of the order, which was more constrained since Arkansas had not yet seceded. Larrantree ordered "all Companies of the K. G. C.'s in the State of Arkansas [to] hold themselves in readiness for further orders" and requested newspapers in Arkansas to copy. At the time, the KGC was reported to have about six hundred members in Little Rock as well as castles in Camden and other locations.

George Bickley, as "President of the K. G. C.'s American Legion," issued a separate part to the order, stating: "The K. G. C.'s in Kentucky, Virginia,

North Carolina, South Carolina, Georgia, Alabama, Tennessee, Missouri, Arkansas, Louisiana, and Florida will pay attention. Maryland has her hands full. Let no member of the Order now flinch."[8] Since Bickley no longer had authority over the KGC army, his appeal was necessarily limited to asking the non-Texas KGC members to "pay attention."

Reports indicate that Bickley was in northern Kentucky during early April, around the time of issuance of the KGC's order, where he threatened to plant a battery on the hill in Covington and bombard Cincinnati if the North attempted coercion assuming Kentucky seceded.[9] Bickley also wrote Jefferson Davis from Louisville on April 4, tendering thirty thousand troops to stop Mexican General Pedro de Ampudia's rumored invasion of Texas. Shortly after Bickley's letter, Colonel Earl Van Dorn returned to Montgomery from Texas and reported that the rumors of an impending invasion by Mexican General Ampudia were not true.[10] At the time, the KGC's Southwestern Division was apparently still lusting after northern Mexico's provinces. Doctor E. L. Billings of Vicksburg, Mississippi, a KGC emissary, was on his way to Mexico City to try to procure from the Mexican Congress the right to build a railway across northern Mexico as a ruse to bring in five thousand armed men and occupy Chihuahua and Sonora.[11]

The reference to Maryland having "her hands full" in Bickley's order refers to the revolutionary fervor unleashed in Baltimore as a result of Virginia's announced secession. Baltimore's leading secessionists, including KGC political head J. V. L. McMahon, held a meeting on the evening of April 17 to organize armed resistance to the expected passage of Union troops through the city.[12] The day before, Police Marshall George Kane had written to the PW&BRR Company's agent seeking "an explicit understanding" regarding the reports that troops from New York would be transported through Baltimore "to make war upon the South." The agent immediately passed the message along to PW&BRR president Samuel M. Felton, noting: "It is rumored that the marshal has issued orders to his force not to permit any forces to pass through the city."[13]

On April 18, the National Volunteers, headed by KGC member William Byrne, held a large rally attended by seven hundred, with many vowing to stop northern troops from passing through Baltimore.[14] Emissaries also arrived from Charlestown with word of Virginia's secession. They sought guarantees from the Baltimore & Ohio Railroad's management that fed-

eral troops would not be transported through Virginia nor arms and munitions moved from the Harpers Ferry arsenal (implying that otherwise, the
great railroad bridge over the Potomac at Harpers Ferry would be blown
up).[15] Henry Wise and the plotters enlisted to take the Harpers Ferry arsenal were planning to transport the weapons seized to arm the Baltimore
secessionists and launch an attack on the capital. This was foiled, however, by the retreating Union garrison, which set the Harpers Ferry armory
building on fire, destroying its fifteen thousand stands of arms.[16]

The Baltimore secessionists' outrage came to a head on the morning of
April 19, when a train arrived carrying seven hundred troops of the Sixth
Massachusetts Volunteer Regiment plus seven companies of unarmed
Pennsylvania volunteers. A crowd of more than five hundred locals pelted
the northern troops with rocks, bottles, and in some cases pistol shots, as
the soldiers marched the two-and-a-half miles from Baltimore's President
Street to its Camden Street train station. In response, some of the northern
soldiers fired back, and at least four rioting civilians were killed and more
than three dozen wounded. The Baltimore police under Marshall Kane
eventually arrived and formed a wedge between the frenzied crowd and the
marching soldiers, who reached the Camden Street Station at 1:00 p.m.
and took off for Washington.[17] Later that day, Kane sent an inflammatory
call to Bradley Johnson, a pro-South militia leader in Frederick who had
offered to supply troops, stating: "Streets red with Maryland blood; send
expresses over the mountains of Maryland and Virginia for the riflemen
to come without delay. Fresh hordes will be down on us tomorrow. We
will fight them and whip them or die." Baltimore's mayor would later try
to explain away Kane's unauthorized act of summoning volunteers from
across Maryland and Virginia by saying, "he got carried away by the frenzy
of the hour."[18]

On the afternoon of April 19, an immense public meeting convened on
Monument Square at which Baltimore leaders, including Mayor Brown
and Governor Hicks, called on the Lincoln administration to stop sending
troops through Maryland. Pro-South supporters began organizing into
military companies, and the Board of Police enrolled volunteers to serve
under the command of Colonel Isaac R. Trimble (later to become a Confederate brigadier general), who sent his adjutant on a secret mission to
Virginia to acquire further weapons.[19] That evening, mobs roamed the

streets, and Baltimore was in the hands of the secessionists. Allegations were subsequently made that the KGC was behind the Baltimore mobs.[20] City leaders then made the decision to burn the railroad bridges and telegraph lines north of the city. Baltimore's police, militia, and independent militia, under the direction of Marshall Kane, carried out the bridge-burning directive that same night.[21]

The crisis didn't begin to abate until April 22, when federal authorities agreed to bypass Baltimore and ordered the 2,400 northern troops encamped at Cockeysville, just north of Baltimore, to return to Harrisburg, Pennsylvania. Pro-South Marylanders continued to stream in, and George Steuart, a West Pointer who had resigned his western U.S. Army commission, organized the First Light Division of Maryland Volunteers, for which Steuart was appointed its major general. With Jefferson Davis's support, Steuart's division received some arms from Virginia and, on April 25, moved two regiments to Annapolis Junction. The regiments had to retreat, however, after unexpectedly encountering Massachusetts regiments under General Benjamin Franklin Butler, who had arrived in Maryland on April 20, rebuilt the rail lines to Washington, and established camp at Relay, where several rail lines intersected.[22] Butler's aide de camp at Relay said he learned from several sources that a thousand "Baltimore Roughs . . . a portion [of which] were Knights of the Golden Circle" planned to attack the Union camp and kill soldiers.[23]

In the midst of the turmoil, KGC member John Wilkes Booth arrived in Baltimore during the last week of April, after his Albany appearance was cut short when a jealous actress stuck a knife into his neck. He soon moved into a boardinghouse on High Street, near his old neighborhood, and shared a room with his actor friend William A. Howell. Booth spent his time visiting local saloons and participating in the heated diatribes of southern sympathizers as recruiting continued for the Confederate army (with young men being offered one hundred dollars in gold to join up). Booth and Howell flirted with a plan to raise their own company. Booth was to recruit in his native Harford County, where he was reportedly a member of a local militia unit, and take the men to Richmond, where he would be commissioned as a lieutenant. During May 1861, Booth stole through the Union picket line to travel to Harford County and alert local militia leader Herman Stump of his impending arrest.[24] In deference to his mother and his acting career, however, Booth decided not to become a Confederate officer. He realized he could nevertheless help the South through his wealth and affiliation with the Knights.[25]

On the evening of May 13, General Ben Butler, on his own authority, slipped into Baltimore with a thousand federal soldiers and occupied Federal Hill overlooking the city. Butler quickly confiscated caches of weapons and ammunition, and arrested southern sympathizers, such as noted industrialist Ross Winans. Butler then issued a proclamation ordering local militia leaders and arms manufacturers to report to him. His order also prohibited displaying the Confederate flag as well as the assembling of armed bodies of men.[26]

As the federal crackdown expanded, Booth's hatred for Union authorities was undoubtedly fueled by the June 27 arrest of the Baltimore police commissioners, including Police Marshall George Kane. Upon hearing of the arrest, Booth flew into a rage and shouted: "I know George Kane well, he is my friend and the man who could drag him from the bosom of his family for no crime whatever but a mere suspicion . . . deserves a dog's death."[27] Meanwhile, Baltimore's southern adherents, such as Booth's childhood chums Sam Arnold and Michael O'Laughlen (a KGC member), headed south to Virginia, where they were mustered into Confederate service.[28]

James Ross Howard, the secretary of the KGC's April 1860 Raleigh convention, was elected captain of one of the proposed companies of Maryland volunteers in Richmond. Howard later served as major of the Eleventh Alabama Cavalry and colonel of the Third Confederate Cavalry.[29] KGC Colonel Robert Harris Archer of Havre de Grace also went south to Virginia around this time. By October 1861, Archer (whose brother was a Confederate brigadier general) was serving as lieutenant colonel of Virginia's Fifty-Fifth Infantry Regiment.[30]

By late 1860, the commander of Maryland's First KGC Regiment—Robert Charles Tyler—had already left for his native state of Tennessee. He set about raising a company of recruits, capitalizing on his KGC and prior Walker filibuster connections. On April 15, Tyler took his men to Jackson, Tennessee, where they enlisted in the Fifteenth Tennessee Infantry Regiment, which was composed mostly of companies from western Tennessee, but also included a privately raised company from Kentucky and southern Illinois. Tennessee's adjutant general, Gideon Pillow, a wealthy owner of plantations in Arkansas and Tennessee, had organized the Fifteenth Tennessee Infantry shortly after May 6, when Tennessee declared its independence and entered into a military league with the Confederacy. Tyler was soon appointed "Regimental Quartermaster."[31]

Tyler's contacts and quiet competence soon catapulted him to higher command and eventually the rank of brigadier general. A fellow officer described Tyler as "a stout, robust Tennesseean" who was "one of the bravest men I ever saw."[32] By October 1861, Tyler had risen from private to commander of the Fifteenth Tennessee Infantry Regiment, leapfrogging his company commander. Serving under Tyler as lieutenant colonel of the Fifteenth Tennessee was James H. R. Taylor, an editor from Holly Springs who had served as the KGC's designated fund-raising contact for Mississippi.[33]

By September 1861, Tennessee KGC commmander H. C. Young was serving as assistant adjutant general on the staff of Confederate Brigadier General William Henry Carroll, who was attempting to deal with Unionist sympathizers and bridge burners in east Tennessee. Young advocated mercy for four hundred Union sympathizers, who were picked up and sent off as Confederate prisoners of war. By 1864, Young was serving as acting assistant inspector-general in the cavalry brigade of Confederate Major General Nathan Bedford Forrest.[34]

KGC leaders in Georgia also played prominent roles in organizing recruits for the nascent Confederate army. After his stint as Georgia's quartermaster general, Paul Semmes was picked as one of three Georgia militia leaders to enroll its more than two hundred organized military companies into the First Division of Georgia Volunteers. Semmes enrolled the Second Brigade from his west central Georgia territory and ordered them to report to Columbus for training. At the outbreak of the war, Semmes was commissioned colonel of the Second Georgia Infantry Regiment that he took to the front in Virginia. In the spring of 1862, he was promoted to brigadier general of the Confederate army.[35]

During April 1861, Atlanta KGC leaders R. J. Cowart and Alexander Gaulding also assisted in recruiting volunteers for the Confederate Army, with Gaulding offering free rail transportation to recruits on his Western & Atlantic Railroad.[36] In May, Confederate authorities appointed KGC member and former Indian agent Douglas Cooper, from Atlanta, to raise a regiment among the western Indians. Cooper was soon commissioned colonel of the First Choctaw and Chickasaw Mounted Rifles.[37] Wealthy merchant Frank W. Dillard, a KGC compatriot of Semmes, was appointed assistant quartermaster in August. Dillard made Columbus a center for the manufacturing of uniforms for the Confederate army. Another KGC colonel—R. A. Crawford of Griffin, Georgia—fought throughout the war with the Georgia First Infantry Regiment Regulars, which had been recruited from Atlanta and Brunswick.[38]

Initially, the Confederate War Department refused to accept troops from states that had not yet seceded. Arkansas governor Henry Rector got around this by devising the subterfuge of having T. B. Flournoy, a militia colonel, "privately" raise a regiment that was then armed and equipped from the Little Rock arsenal.[39] A similar subterfuge was worked out in Kentucky. In early April, Blanton Duncan, a wealthy Louisville lawyer and political operative, began to organize a regiment from Louisville and other areas of the commonwealth (which Bickley would later imply included more than five hundred Knights). Kentucky's governor, Beriah Magoffin, secretly allowed the Confederates to recruit unhampered, and willingly served as an intermediary by forwarding Confederate Secretary of War Walker's telegrams on to Duncan.[40] In late April, Duncan's regiment was tendered to the Confederacy as part of the Louisiana contingent, and sent to join the Confederate forces at Harpers Ferry.[41]

Such subterfuge was no longer necessary after April 22, when Confederate secretary of war Walker called for an additional twelve thousand troops and included the Border States of Kentucky, Arkansas, North Carolina, and Tennessee in his call. Most came forward with the promise of a regiment. North Carolina governor John Ellis promised to have ten thousand volunteers in the field in a few days. Militia commander Gideon Pillow, backed by Tennessee governor Isham Harris, responded that Tennessee could furnish ten thousand men in three weeks.[42]

Many of the newly arriving soldiers did not have rifles, and the Confederacy's available supply of around 159,000 weapons was not sufficient to provide arms to all the new recruits. This led the Confederate Congress to enact legislation in early May that limited the acceptance of troops to those willing to enlist for three years or the duration of the war. While initially unpopular with recruits who had signed up for twelve months, the three-year term made sense from the standpoint of efficiently allocating the available supply of weapons and equipment, and preparing for a more long-term engagement.[43]

On May 1, 1861, Bickley issued a further order as "K. G. C., President of American Legion" that appeared in the *Memphis Daily Appeal* of May 7. Like the April 17 call, it advised Texas and Arkansas castles in the KGC's Texas Division to report to "Gen. Geo. W. Chilton, Marshall of the Division at Tyler, Texas, or to Col. Charles A. Russell, acting adjutant general, at Helena, Karnes county, Texas." The Texas/Arkansas KGC members were "to respond fully and promptly to the call of Generals Chilton, Ford, Wilcox and Green, and stand on the defensive until our national troubles are ended."[44] "Wilcox" was John A. Wilcox, who was the leader of the KGC's Western Texas Brigade, and subsequently became a Confederate congressman. "Green" was Thomas Green, who had served with the Texas Rangers and Walker's Nicaraguan filibusterers, and who, as a Texas Supreme Court clerk, had helped initiate its secession. Green subsequently recruited the Texas Fifth Cavalry and was commissioned a colonel (later a brigadier general) in the Confederate army.[45]

In his May 7 order, Bickley ordered other KGC castle commandants to forward their muster roles of military companies to the KGC's general headquarters, now relocated at Louisville, Kentucky (likely because this is where Bickley was situated). Each castle commandant was to take immediate steps to complete its military organization that "shall consist of one captain, one first lieutenant, two second lieutenants, four sergeants, four corporals, two musicians, and ninety privates." General, field, and staff officers of the American Legion were similarly ordered to report by letter (indicating that Bickley had lost track of the KGC's military command structure). He nevertheless claimed that due to his successful recruiting drive in Kentucky, he had added 1,483 members to the KGC order, "534 of whom have been sent to the army of the Confederate States." Altogether, Bickley claimed that the KGC "has now 17,643 men in the field, and has no hesitation in saying that the number can be duplicated if necessity requires."[46]

In Texas, George Chilton recruited at least two prewar military units, while KGC Colonel Charles Russell organized three Texas military companies in addition to the local Helena Guards. After the KGC's May 1 muster at Galveston, KGC castles formed independent military companies with names like the "Texas Hunters" (from Harrison County) and the "Ed Clark Invincibles" (from Smith County). Many of these companies would enlist en masse in Texas for Confederate service.[47]

KGC soldiers comprised a substantial portion of the Texas frontier regiments that the Confederate War Department had authorized Ben McCulloch to raise in April. Ben, who was holding out for a higher command, passed the authorization on to his brother Henry, who was then commissioned as its colonel. Henry McCulloch's regiment encompassed Texas's First as well as its Second Texas Mounted Rifles, commanded by KGC Colonel John Rip Ford. Included in the Second Texas Mounted Rifles were the W. P. Lane Rangers from Marshall, for which KGC member Sam Richardson was elected captain. The W. P. Lane Rangers were sworn into state service on April 19. They headed off to San Antonio, where they were sworn into Confederate service on May 23, becoming Company "F" of the Second Regiment Texas Cavalry, which was also commanded by John Ford. During May 1861, KGC castles in the Galveston area and around San Antonio assisted newly installed Confederate commander Earl Van Dorn in forcing the surrender of the federal troops at Indianola and other frontier garrisons that had not yet been evacuated by Union authorities.[48]

Probably the greatest concentration of Texas Knights was in the Third Texas Cavalry, under Elkanah Greer, who was authorized to raise a Confederate regiment in May (and commissioned as colonel in early July). Greer ordered the KGC-affiliated units in East Texas to muster at Dallas. Here they consolidated into the ten companies of the Third Texas Cavalry Regiment, which were sworn into Confederate service on June 13, 1861. Initially lacking proper weapons, the men brought shotguns, any kind of rifles, and huge knives from home. George Chilton served as a major of the regiment, and KGC member John Good of Dallas served as its artillery commander. The regiment was assigned to the command of Ben McCulloch (who had been appointed on May 11 as the first civilian brigadier general in the Provisional Confederate Army with authority over Indian Territory).[49]

KGC units in Arkansas similarly responded to Greer's call to enlist in the nascent Confederate army. Shortly after April 17, the local KGC castle at Camden formed the Camden Knights of the Golden Circle, under Captain William L. Crenshaw, which became Company C of the First Arkansas

Infantry. A second KGC unit was subsequently formed under Captain John L. Logan and outfitted with the same red shirts and black pants worn by Knights in Texas and Georgia.[50] In eastern Arkansas, Thomas Hindman, who had resigned from the U.S. Congress, set out to recruit a regiment, at his own expense, that included the Yell Rifles and Phillips Guard from Helena as well as the Jefferson Guards, Napoleon Grays, and Monroe Blues. The ten recruited companies were organized into the First Arkansas Volunteer Infantry by early May, and they elected Patrick Cleburne as colonel (Hindman was commissioned in June as colonel of the Second Arkansas Infantry).[51]

While Bickley was trying to segregate KGC volunteers into separate units under his control, it appears that KGC soldiers in Texas and Arkansas were swearing their full allegiance to their state governors and Confederate authorities.[52] This is evidenced by the "Address" that KGC regional recruiter Charles Arden Russell forwarded to the Texas Knights in May 1861. While Russell encouraged them "to establish the working machinery of the Order until our Castles shall arise like monuments all over the land," he nevertheless spoke of their broader duty to serve the South:

> I have been told that such an organization as ours would become an evil in that hour when our country needed the service of her sons in battle. That petty jealousies and a spirit of party monopoly would prevent us from taking part in active warfare, unless we could be called into service as a body with our own officers and organization. . . . I am satisfied that the result will disprove the assertion. We have taught no such practice. I admonish you to go forth wherever your country may call singly or in companies, as circumstances may require.

Russell said the Knights claimed "only a desire to serve our country," and he urged the Texas Knights to "arouse the military spirit of your neighbors, organize them into companies and teach them military tactics and science. Carry out the recommendations of our Governor in his late proclamation, until every able-bodied Texan shall be enrolled as a citizen soldier for the defense of our State."[53]

In late April, KGC sympathizer Louis Wigfall arrived in Montgomery to take up his seat as Texas's representative in the Confederacy's Provisional Congress. Wigfall had been in his native South Carolina since early April, serving as a voluntary aide to Confederate General Pierre Beauregard. On April 13, Wigfall commandeered a small boat and rowed out through the shrapnel to the beleaguered Fort Sumter in Charleston harbor. He offered terms of surrender, which U.S. Major Robert Anderson accepted. General Beauregard had not authorized Wigfall's mission, but Confederate authorities subsequently decided they could accept the terms that Wigfall proposed. Wigfall was now touting himself as the man who had forced the surrender of Fort Sumter, and he was given a hero's welcome when he arrived in Montgomery.[54]

Due to his newfound fame, Wigfall was courted by Jefferson Davis and other Confederate officials. Wigfall had helped make Jefferson Davis the first president of the Confederacy by gaining support for him from other fire-eaters, such as Robert Barnwell Rhett. He had also helped convince Davis to name Alabama lawyer L. P. Walker as the Confederacy's first secretary of war. Wigfall and Davis saw each other frequently and expressed mutual admiration for each other, and Davis consulted Wigfall in filling military appointments. At the end of May, as the Confederate government was getting ready to move to Richmond, Davis convinced Wigfall to serve on his personal staff.[55]

Given his substantial influence, Wigfall was besieged by Texans and others seeking Confederate military commissions, for which fifty thousand requests had already been submitted. William J. Clarke, the head of one of San Antonio's KGC castles, had journeyed to Montgomery in late April but wrote home that Secretary of War Walker was still delaying higher appointments in the regular army. Nevertheless, Clarke reported, "Mr. Wigfall . . . seems to feel a warm interest in me, [and] pressed [Walker] so hard last night that he said he would appoint me a Captain if I would go recruiting." Clarke held out, however, and was subsequently appointed in July as colonel of the Fourteenth Regiment, North Carolina Volunteers.[56]

Another petitioner was KGC leader Ben McCulloch. McCulloch had already asked Confederate secretary of war Walker to let him raise a regiment from Texas, but Walker deferred, saying the Confederacy was not yet ready to receive them.[57] Jefferson Davis, as a West Pointer, veteran of the Mexican War, and a former U.S. secretary of war, had reservations about the rough-and-tumble tactics of the Texas Rangers as well as former filibusterers. Davis preferred West Point–trained officers for high Confederate commands and tried to get as many as possible. One of the thousands of military applicants in Montgomery during mid-March noted, "First place in line for appointments was going to Military Academy graduates."[58] But on May 11, Davis did appoint McCulloch as the Confederacy's first civilian brigadier general, with authority over the Indian Territory. Davis had been impressed by McCulloch's daring during the Mexican War, and Wigfall undoubtedly bent the president's ear on McCulloch's behalf.[59]

On May 5, Sir William Russell, a roving correspondent for the *Times* (London) arrived in the Confederate capital of Montgomery, where he was feted by Confederate authorities urgently seeking recognition from England. During his May visit, Russell met with Davis, Walker, Attorney General Benjamin, and General Beauregard, who was then visiting Montgomery. Wigfall became Russell's constant companion and made every effort to convince him of the merits of the Confederate cause. Wigfall presented the South to Russell as a rustic society with rice, sugar, tobacco, and cotton that could provide unlimited trading opportunities for a mercantile power like England.[60]

During his visit, Russell stayed at one of Montgomery's three hotels, which were packed with congressmen, military men, and speculators, all trying to get an appointment with the embryonic Confederate government. Here Russell was forced to share accommodations with five gentlemen in a room with only three beds. Russell noted on May 5 that among the hotel's guests were "many filibusters, such as Henningsen, Pickett, Tochman, and Wheat." In connection with the filibusterers, Russell said, "I hear a good deal about the association called the Knights of the Golden Circle, a Protestant association for securing the Gulf provinces and states, including . . . them in the Southern Confederacy, and creating them into an independent government."[61] Russell also likely heard about the Knights from Wigfall, McCulloch, Greer, and other KGC leaders then in Montgomery.

General Charles F. Henningsen, one of the four filibusterers that Russell mentioned, had been born in England, served as commander of artillery for Walker's 1856–57 Nicaragua campaign as well as in subsequent filibusters, including revolutionary intrigue in Mexico. Henningsen, who had recently married a rich Georgia widow, was well past his prime. Davis put off responding to Henningsen's entreaties for a command, leaving it to Henningsen's old friend Henry Wise to call him into service in June.[62]

Colonel John T. Pickett, another of the filibusterers Russell mentioned (and whom he described as "a striking looking man . . . with a knightly appearance and demeanor which brings to mind the men of the sixteenth century") had participated in López's and Quitman's aborted Cuban expeditions. From 1853 to 1861, Pickett was the U.S. consul to the Juárez regime at Vera Cruz. He had recently served as the Confederacy's peace commissioner to Washington and would soon be appointed by Davis as commissioner to Mexico.[63]

The other two hotel mates mentioned by Russell were in Montgomery looking for authority to raise regiments in New Orleans, a hotbed of filibustering. Gasper Tochman, who had been exiled from Poland after participating in its 1830 uprising against the Russian empire, was now promoting the organization of a Polish brigade. He was authorized by Jefferson Davis to raise two regiments of Poles (which ultimately included other foreign nationals).[64] Roberdeau Wheat, recognized as a KGC member, was a thirty-five–year-old lawyer who had been a soldier of fortune in Cuba, Mexico, Nicaragua, and more recently, Italy. Wheat had raised a battalion (First Special Battalion, Louisiana Infantry) that included the Tiger Rifles from the back alleys and jails of New Orleans, and the Walker Guards, a company largely composed of ex-Walker filibusterers. On May 25, Louisiana governor Thomas Overton Moore issued Wheat a commission as a major. Wheat was mustered into Confederate service a few weeks later and left for Virginia.[65]

During May, Jefferson Davis also responded favorably to former governor Henry Wise's request for an "independent partisan command" by authorizing Wise to raise an expeditionary force to preserve the allegiance of the Kanawha Valley in western Virginia. Davis knew that Wise was lacking in military training, but he could not afford to offend the popular former governor, who had a sizeable following of Virginia militants. Wise immediately accepted Davis's offer and was soon made a brigadier general in the Provisional Army of the Confederate States. Despite ongoing illness, Wise approached the task of raising and supplying his expeditionary force with gusto. He issued proclamations and newspaper articles seeking recruits, made speeches at county courthouses in lower Virginia, and contacted friends—including ex-filibusterers and Knights. The hodgepodge battalion that became known as "Wise's Legion" was formed by June and soon consisted of 2,800 partisan rangers, including many former Nicaraguan filibusterers and "snake-hunters" from the West, with ex-Walker artillery commander Charles Henningsen serving as second-in-command.[66]

Wigfall was commissioned as a Confederate colonel during August 1861 and given command of the First Texas Infantry while still trying to maintain his positions in the Confederate Congress and as an aide to Davis. The First Texas Infantry included the KGC-affiliated companies of Alfred and Edwin Hobby from Refugio County, Texas. They, as well as the Lone Star Rifles from Galveston (under Knight William Redman), would became part of John Bell Hood's Eighth Texas Infantry Regiment formed in 1862.[67] KGC and former Walker filibusterers also filled the ranks of Ross's Texas Brigade, formed in 1862, which included Greer's Third Texas Cavalry.[68] William Edgar's Alamo Knights became the First Texas Light Artillery that served in New Mexico and in Arkansas and Louisiana. KGC Trevanion Teel from San Antonio also organized a light artillery company that fought in the New Mexico campaign.[69]

Altogether, forty-five of the fifty-five identified Texas KGC captains enlisted in Confederate military service. Of these, 42 percent were commissioned as Confederate captains or higher, with George Chilton, Alfred Hobby, John B. Jones, Sam Lockridge, and Trevanion Teel reaching the rank of major; James Duff, Thomas Lubbock, William Redwood, and John S. Ford reaching the rank of colonel; and Ben and Hugh McCulloch, Elkanah Greer, and Thomas Green reaching the rank of general. In addition to the officer corps, Knights likely also comprised a respectable proportion of the 24,448 Texans who volunteered for Confederate military service during the first year of the war.[70]

Thus the KGC played a significant role in the formation of the armies supporting the South, helping them ramp up from nothing to around two hundred thousand men by October 1861. While Davis had reservations about non–West Pointers, he nevertheless appointed McCulloch and Wise as brigadier generals in the Provisional Army of the Confederate States, with commands that they could fill with KGC compatriots, such as Greer and Henningsen. Their preexisting KGC network helped them find committed subordinate officers and recruits who had prior training in military drill and weaponry.[71]

Unlike Bickley, who hoped to maintain KGC-segregated units, Knights state commanders such as Greer, Groner, McCulloch, Semmes, and Tyler gave their primary allegiance to the Confederate government once they were commissioned. While the KGC state commanders were busy training their raw Confederate recruits, Bickley shifted his efforts to the strategic Border State of Kentucky, with its central location, significant manpower, and industrial resources. Would he be able to fire up its Knights and help local secessionists wrest Kentucky from the Union in order to add its substantial resources and manpower to the Confederate cause?

12

# THE STRUGGLE FOR KENTUCKY

A S THE KGC state commanders concentrated on training their raw
Confederate army recruits, George Bickley directed his efforts to
expanding the Knights in the pivotal Border State of Kentucky.
Both the Confederacy and the Union were courting Kentucky, given its
strategic position, abundant manpower, and industrial resources.[1] Bickley
reported in May 1861 that since the first of February, he had "been laboring in Kentucky—principally in the city of Louisville—and has added to
the order 1483 members, 534 of whom have been sent to the army of the
Confederate States" (presumably as part of Blanton Duncan's regiment).[2]
Kentucky had strong filibustering roots established by Quitman, Pickett,
and others, and was where Bickley claimed the KGC had been founded.

After repeated sparring, Kentucky's evenly matched Southern Rights
and Union Democratic Parties worked out a standstill agreement declar-
ing Kentucky neutral with respect to the impending Civil War during May
1861. Kentucky governor Beriah Magoffin issued a related Neutrality Proclamation on May 20. Despite his pro-South leanings and alleged KGC connections,[3] Governor Magoffin had little interest in forcing Kentucky into
a position that was not supported by her citizens. He also felt that further
steps toward secession should be deferred until suitable weapons could be
supplied to Kentucky's substantial State Guard, then consisting of sixty-
one companies.[4]

Governor Magoffin convinced southern-leaning banks to loan the
state eighty thousand dollars and dispatched his agents to procure arms.
Among the agents was Luke Blackburn, a wealthy Louisville physician,

who showed up in New Orleans promising that if the Confederates would supply them arms, Kentuckians would march right out of the Union with the guns on their shoulders.[5]

Meanwhile, Bickley canvassed Kentucky's south central tobacco-growing region, establishing new castles and instigating intimidation. Bickley was reported to have told a well-known Unionist in Simpson County that the man would have to leave or "pull a limb." The KGC's alleged goal was reportedly to force every man in a given town into their way of thinking or else force them into silence.[6]

During late May, meetings were held in each of Kentucky's ten congressional districts to nominate candidates for the June 20 special election necessitated by President Lincoln's convening of a July 4 special session of the U.S. Congress. Kentucky's Southern Rights Party, which had been formed in March to consolidate the various pro-South factions, held a convention at Russellville (in south central Kentucky) during May 1861. Bickley appeared and made a fiery speech in favor of Kentucky's secession, arguing that its true interests were with the South. He said that the KGC was ready to assist any southern governor to plant the southern flag on the northern side of the Ohio River, and he exhibited a letter asking Tennessee governor Isham Harris to support such a move. Bickley predicted that if Kentuckians were allowed to show their true sentiments at the polls, they would vote for secession by a large margin. But Bickley reportedly said that even if the secessionists constituted a respectable minority, he would raise men in Tennessee to come to their assistance.[7]

In response to Bickley's speech, George Prentice, the editor of the pro-Union *Louisville Journal*, asked: "What do the people of Kentucky think when the Chief of a secret and oath bound order, which he boasts, is numbered in the country by hundreds of thousands and in our State by tens of thousands, goes through the land proclaiming publicly such plans and intention? . . . Why is not this strolling General arrested and tried for treason?"[8]

At about this time, the Louisville aunt of Joseph Holt, Buchanan's secretary of war, wrote Holt that his nephew John had recently joined a Kentucky KGC castle and that one of its secret oaths was to "shoot all the influential men in the Cabinet . . . until they get them all destroyed." (An informer subsequently testified that the second part of the KGC oath used at Marion, Ohio, required the applicant to swear: "I will not rest or sleep until Abraham Lincoln, now President, shall be removed out of the Presidential Chair, and I will wade in blood up to my knees, as soon as Jefferson Davis sees proper to march with his army to take the City of Washington and the White House ").[9] A letter was also circulated from Garrett Davis and other central Kentucky Unionists warning that the Knights intended to make a demonstration against the U.S. Army barracks in Newport, Kentucky (just south of Cincinnati), as a prelude to forcing Kentucky out of the Union.[10]

On May 24, the heads of the five Louisville KGC castles issued a secret circular, convening a general statewide convention to be held in Louisville on June 3. Among the castle leaders were J. M. Foree and J. H. Watson (later a surgeon with the First Tennessee Regiment), who were both later revealed to also be members of the KGC's secret Third Degree. The stated purpose of the convention was for "a thorough reorganization of [the] order." All of Kentucky's castles were urged to send as many Knights as possible "as the growth and success of our order in future depends greatly on the numbers and appearances on that occasion." Attendees were asked to "be very cautious that outsiders do not find out what we are doing." Cincinnati papers accused the convention of having treasonable objectives, but the proceedings were not otherwise reported.[11]

Toward the end of May, the Kentucky legislature also focused its attention on the Knights. In reaction to a Kentucky House resolution seeking an investigation of the Lincoln administration's efforts to infiltrate arms into Kentucky, Unionist Nat Wolfe of Louisville introduced an amendment seeking a report on the KGC including the names of its officers, whether members of the Kentucky legislature were involved, and what obligations its members were required to take in opposition to the United States government. The resolution also sought secret correspondence between Governor Magoffin and Confederate authorities or seceded states as to the furnishing of troops or the secession of Kentucky. Wolfe's investigating committee quickly issued hundreds of subpoenas to high government officials, the head of the Southern Rights Party's executive committee, and the *Louisville Courier*'s editor. But the legislature adjourned on May 24 and did not provide funds or authority for Wolfe's committee to continue its investigation.[12]

In reaction to Representative Wolfe's resolution, George Bickley himself, as president of the KGC's American Legion, published "An Open Letter to the Kentucky Legislature" in the pro-South *Louisville Courier* of May 30, in which he states: "Mr. Wolfe and a few of his intimate friends who have bargained away the honor and independence of Kentucky to the *usurping tyrant, Abe Lincoln,* have placed themselves in a most ridiculous position by instituting a legal crusade against an institution [the KGC] . . . which was always ready to publish for the world the information they profess to desire." Bickley writes that to save the legislature any trouble, he has forwarded Governor Magoffin "a full and complete set of our *Degree Works* (retaining only the unwritten portion of the same)," and he includes in his "Open Letter" the obligations of the KGC's First and Second Degrees.

Bickley further claims that the KGC has "nearly eight thousand in the State, distributed through every county, and the organization is growing in favor and importance; and the work will be pushed with the utmost vigor until the tri-colored flag of the Confederate States floats in triumph from the dome of the capitol in Frankfort." He threatens that if Kentucky "should be tied to the Northern Confederacy," the KGC will "invite and carry from the State ten thousand families of Kentucky's best citizens, and plant them on the broad and fertile prairies of the noble State of Texas, where the K. G. C. in that State, will meet them with open arms and warm hearts." While disclaiming a direct connection with the Confederacy, Bickley says that the KGC membership "sympathizes deeply with the struggling people of the South . . . and hold themselves in readiness . . . to lend the helping hand in the critical hour." He also notes that one regiment [presumably Blanton Duncan's] has already left Kentucky and others will soon follow."[13]

The *Journal* of June 5 reiterated Bickley's claim that since February 1, 1861, he had sent 535 men from Kentucky to the Confederate army and that further regiments were being formed, subject to the orders of Kentucky's governor. In the article, Prentice ominously warns, "Such fellow-citizens of Kentucky are the purposes, and such the agencies of the conspirators in the midst of us."[14] The *Frankfort (Ky.) Commonwealth* of June 4 published a similarly hard-hitting article titled "The Treasonable Plot Confessed." It exhorts: "Arouse Kentuckians, and place your heels upon an organization which boldly and defiantly announces its purpose to take from the dome of the State Capitol the glorious star spangled banner, and place in its stead the 'tri-colored flag of the Confederate States.' We tell these valiant Knights that when they dare come to the capital for such purpose, every Union man, woman and child in Franklin county will welcome them 'with bloody hands to hospitable graves.'"[15]

The Knights of the Golden Circle were especially active in the "Jackson Purchase" region, consisting of the eight far-western counties of Kentucky beyond the Tennessee River, referred to by Unionists as "the infected district" because of the strong pro-South sentiment. In late May, Bickley was in Christian and surrounding counties "drilling his men, depositing large sums of money, and secretly scattering circulars of all kinds."[16] The *New York Herald* reported that in the Jackson Purchase, "scarcely is there a town, village or school district that has not its KGC 'castle' and scarcely a family that has not one or more members pinioned in its fatal embrace."[17] Vigilance committees intimidated Unionists throughout the Purchase region. At Paducah, White Fowler's KGC "Committee of Thirteen" operated with impunity in driving out Unionists and, for a time, taking over some local government functions for the area. During late May, secessionists gave serious consideration to splitting off the Jackson Purchase from Kentucky and forming a military alliance with Confederate Tennessee, but this was deferred, pending further developments.[18]

To counterbalance the secessionists' machinations, Lincoln and his allies began to secretly supply arms to the Kentucky Unionists in May 1861. William "Bull" Nelson, a U.S. Navy commander stationed at the Washington Naval Yard, returned to his native Kentucky to coordinate the distribution through Lincoln's close friend Joshua Speed. Together Speed and Nelson secretly enlisted six prominent loyalists in Frankfort and organized a "Union Defense Committee" to oversee the initial shipment of five thousand "Lincoln guns" that were augmented with further shipments. Kentucky's legislature also passed the Militia Act, leading to the establishment of a Military Board that made sure Kentucky's state weapons were evenly allocated between the pro-South State Guards and the pro-Union Home Guard units being established in each county.[19] In addition, a powerful patriotic letter was widely circulated from Joseph Holt to Joshua Speed, claiming that secession was being precipitated by a few score of self-serving men, and invoking the words of Henry Clay: "I owe a supreme allegiance to the General Government, and to my State a subordinate one."[20]

The end result was that once Kentucky's polls closed on June 20, the Union Democrats captured nine out of the ten congressional seats, achieving a popular majority of 54,700 (82,145 out of the approximately 120,000 ballots cast). The only exception was the far-western Jackson Purchase district, where Southern Rights Party candidate Henry Burnett won convincingly. U.S. Navy Commander Bull Nelson subsequently wrote to Joshua Speed: "I am told that 'your [Holt's] letter' and 'my guns' did the business."[21] The stage was now set for the even more significant Kentucky legislative elections of August 5.

Meanwhile, despite Kentucky's proclaimed neutrality, Union and Confederate recruiting continued unabated. During May and June, several regiments of Kentuckians were recruited for Union training camps that had been established across the Ohio River (at Camp Clay near Cincinnati and at Camp Holt in Jefferson County, Indiana, across from Louisville). The head of Louisville's Home Guard, Lovell Rousseau, was commissioned as a Union brigadier general, and appointed commander of Camp Holt. Major Robert Anderson, following his heroic defense of Fort Sumter, was promoted to brigadier general and reassigned to Cincinnati to raise as many regiments of Union volunteers from Kentucky and West Virginia as possible.[22]

On behalf of the South, Jefferson Davis appointed several Mexican War veterans to raise Kentucky regiments. He authorized Colonel Temple Withers, a native Kentuckian then living in Mississippi, to recruit up to twenty-six companies. Colonels Lloyd Tilghman from Paducah and Robert P. Trabue, a native of Columbia then living in Natchez, Mississippi, were each authorized to raise a regiment for Confederate service. In early July, a Confederate recruiting camp—named Camp Boone—was established about eight miles south of the Kentucky line near Guthrie. By mid-July, several thousand Kentucky volunteers arrived at Camp Boone, including the nucleus of Withers's Second Kentucky Regiment and 1,800 men from western Kentucky, which would form the nucleus of Lloyd Tilghman's Third Kentucky Regiment.[23] A July 12 letter to the *Louisville Journal* alleged that the Kentucky companies arriving were "mostly K. G. C.'s."[24]

Not to be outdone, Bickley began recruiting his own Independent Corps of KGC Voltigeurs—a term used by Napoleon in the French Infantry for the handpicked company of irregular rifleman within each regiment. As "President" of the KGC's American Legion, Bickley issued a circular from Clarkesville, Tennessee, on June 29, 1861, headed "Volunteers Wanted":

> Desiring to organize a Voltigeur Corps of Kentuckians, I hereby issue the following proposition: I will accept every company that shall be tendered to me at Clarkesville, Tenn., on or before the 25th day of July, 1861. This force will act as an Independent Corps, to be employed on the borders, and will receive the following pay. . . . If necessary, this force, which is already accepted, will be used in any locality where the enemy may be found. All companies will report to me at this place on or before the 25th day of July next, at which time I shall form a Camp of Instruction, to be under a competent and experienced corps of Instructors.

Bickley concluded his circular by noting: "It is extremely desirable and important to organize the State of Kentucky before the August elections, and to accomplish this[,] every precinct in each county of the State should have one or more castles."[25] Bickley reported in the *Clarkesville Chronicle* of August 2 that [KGC] "Capt. Sloan, Capt. Robertson, Capt. Bristoe and Capt. Duvall arrived on Saturday, [July] 27" (presumably to begin instructing Bickley's independent Voltigeur Corps recruits).[26] At the end of July, Bickley also said that Tennessee governor Isham Harris had authorized him and Colonel John. D. Morris to raise twenty-six companies from the counties southwest of the Green River. He also noted that he had supplied troops to almost every one of the regiments now reporting to Camp Boone.[27]

KGC recruiting also took place at the Kentucky State Guard's militia encampments. On August 1, Bull Nelson reported to Joseph Holt in Washington on the State Guard encampments held in June and July: "Governor Magoffin's camps at Muldraugh Hill and Cynthiana were openly recruiting reserves for the confederate army. I saw myself the secession flag displayed on two different days by companions coming from the camp. Cheering for Jeff Davis all the time. I am told that the K. G. C.'s held their chapters there and swore in as many as they could seduce."[28] The *Louisville Journal* reported that the State Guard encampment at Muldraugh's Hill, near Lincoln's boyhood home south of Elizabeth, was so strongly pro-South that it was doubted whether any Union man would come there. The *Journal* also subsequently reported that at a State Guard muster in Louisville, Knights paraded with the Guard and were provided weapons. Many Unionists believed that the State Guard was just waiting for an order from Governor Magoffin to carry out a coup d'état that would take Kentucky out of the Union. Such reports led to the Kentucky Military Board's issuing an order in mid-July for the State Guard to turn in their arms, and the Board's refusal to appropriate any further money for State Guard encampments.[29]

In the interim, George Prentice, the flamboyant editor of the *Louisville Journal,* published a hard-hitting exposé of the KGC on July 18, 1861. In it, Prentice calls the Knights "an intensely disunion concern. Its members bear the same relation to other disunionists that regular soldiers do to the militia." Prentice says that he has all the secret documents of the order before him (likely received from KGC Third Degree turncoat A. A. Urban). He defiantly proceeds to reveal the Knights' secret rituals, recognizing that "hundreds of members of the Order have sworn dreadful oaths that they would kill any . . . editor or printer who should be guilty of publishing their mysteries."[30]

Prentice's revelations are unique in that they disclose the ritual of the KGC's Third, or governing, Degree. In the ritual, the inductee swears an oath of absolute secrecy and promises to report to the KGC leaders on abolitionists, Roman Catholic ministers, and northern teachers, and do all in his power to put down insurrections that those suspect individuals might foster. The ritual then proceeds to an unabashed declaration that when the KGC intervenes in Mexico, it will "sustain the effort to reduce the 88 (Peon System) to 89 (Perpetual Slavery)" and to divide the newly created slaves proportionately among the members of the KGC's three degrees. Third Degree members are given a preference for high office in establishing the government in Mexico. The ritual provides that a "Limited Monarchy" should be recognized as the best form of government until the civil, political, financial, and religious reconstruction of Mexico has been completed (with eventual annexation of Mexico to the United States as a slave state).[31]

In his related *Journal* article, Prentice lambastes the KGC's prohibition of Roman Catholics and foreign-born citizens as members, its declaration in favor of "Limited Monarchy," and the preference given to the Third Degree for offices in Mexico over the First and Second Degrees. He asks whether any man of respectable standing would "have the audacity to avow himself [a Knight], and proclaims, "If public opinion has not utterly lost it virtue, it will speedily sweep this miserable Order off the face of the earth." Prentice concludes by alleging that the Knights of the Golden Circle "is now and has all along been the central arm of the secession party of Kentucky."[32]

A few weeks later, on August 12, Prentice published the names of eleven Third Degree KGC members in Louisville, which included "Reverend G. W. Robertson, bookstore keeper," as well as "J. W. Foree," and "J. H. Watson," who had been previously referenced as Louisville castle heads. Prentice said that the KGC had, at one time, three thousand members in Louisville, but this number had recently decreased to four or five hundred members, since many had gone south. He claimed that his July 7 exposé, "which was published everywhere except in the South," dealt a deathblow to the Knights.[33] "Col Ben M. Harney," who had previously been a López filibuster and in July 1860 had been listed as the KGC fund-raising contact for Kentucky, is no longer shown as a Louisville KGC leader. Harney, the nephew of U.S. Army General Ben John Harney, joined the Ninth Kentucky Cavalry on the Union side in 1862.[34]

The strident newspaper exposés were matched by the growing intensity of the July political campaign for the Kentucky legislature. The Southern Rights Party waged a vigorous campaign, recognizing that the August 5 vote would be crucial. Free barbecues were held across Kentucky at which states'-rights luminaries, such as former governor James Morehead, James Clay, and Humphrey Marshall, spoke on behalf of the local party candidates. The pro-South *Louisville Courier* warned that if a majority of Lincoln men were elected to the legislature, a conspiratorial plan would be set in motion to march northern troops across the state to Tennessee and abrogate Kentucky's neutrality. The *Courier* also contended that the *Journal's* exposés on the Knights of the Golden Circle were really a smokescreen to cover up the Unionists' own clandestine military organizations.[35]

The Unionists similarly waged an active campaign. Joseph Holt returned to Kentucky for a series of hard-hitting pro-Union speeches, heralded not only in Kentucky, but also across the nation. Holt's most widely circulated speech, given at Louisville's Masonic Hall on July 13, was titled "The Fallacy of Neutrality." In it, Holt asks Kentuckians why they "would even consider standing aside and watching the best government in the world destroyed?" He denounces Governor Magoffin for refusing to respond to President Lincoln's request for volunteers and calls Senator John Breckinridge "a lever in the hands of the conspirators." Holt vividly raises the specter of Kentucky's desolation, if it were to secede, by recounting "the confiscations and spoliations" in Virginia and Tennessee. He concludes by begging his fellow Kentuckians to hold fast so that the blood of the Union would "not be found on the skirts of Kentucky."[36]

The results of the August 5 election gave the Union Democrats a clear majority in both Kentucky houses, which was sufficient to overcome the governor's veto. After hearing the tally, Kentucky congressman Charles Wickliffe exuberantly announced to the U.S. House of Representatives in Washington: "The news from Kentucky is to the effect that she is wholly for the Union; that as she was one of the first to come in, she will be one of the last to leave it."[37] The *Louisville Journal* heralded the result as a mandate for the Union and said that the Southern Rights Party should "abandon all thought of further resistance and quietly acquiesce in what the people have spoken and done." On the other hand, the Southern Rightists said the close vote in many precincts showed a mounting southern sentiment and that things might have gone the other way if those Kentuckians who had already gone south were included.[38]

In reaction to the election setback, Kentucky's Southern Rights Party organized a series of peace meetings throughout the commonwealth, hoping to unite both Unionists and Southern Rightists behind the cause of neutrality. At a Louisville meeting, "Peace Rights" speakers called on Kentuckians to wear white rosettes and fly peace flags from their homes and vehicles. A white flag was soon flown at Reverend G. W. Robinson's bookstore in Louisville, where a castle of the Knights of the Golden Circle regularly met. On August 20, the *Journal* sarcastically asked "whether [Robinson] and the rest of the Knights mean to invade Mexico with white flags over their heads, white rosettes upon their bosoms, and white ribbons in their button-holes."[39]

These peace meetings were soon followed by neutrality picnics at which Southern Rights Party notables, such as Senator John Breckinridge, James

Clay, and on occasion Governor Magoffin, spoke to the assembled participants. Brigadier General William "Bull" Nelson and his men soon decided
to put an end to these "anti-Lincoln picnics." After warning Governor
Magoffin not to attend, Nelson's men showed up at a September 5 picnic
in Owens County, where they intended to arrest John Breckinridge. But
Breckinridge had gotten word of his impending arrest and led the exodus
of many of the Southern Rights Party leaders toward eastern Kentucky
and then to Richmond.[40] In Richmond, Breckinridge accepted a Confederate commission as a brigadier general. He returned to Bowling Green,
Kentucky, in November to serve in the Confederate army in central Kentucky commanded by former State Guard commander Simon Buckner,
who was now also a Confederate brigadier general.[41]

In the interim, on September 3, Gideon Pillow, with seventeen thousand Confederate troops, invaded western Kentucky. This prompted a
counterinvasion from Cairo, Illinois, by Union General Ulysses Grant, who
took and held Paducah.[42] The *New York Herald* subsequently reported that
Grant had captured documents from the KGC castle at Paducah allegedly
showing that Breckinridge, Pillow, and Governors Harris and Magoffin
were members of the KGC, and that two members of Buchanan's cabinet
had furnished information helpful to the South.[43]

In mid-September, the Kentucky legislature took a strong Unionist position and ordered the Confederate (but not the Union) troops to with-
draw. After initially ordering a Confederate withdrawal, Jefferson Davis
eventually authorized Pillow to remain in Kentucky on the basis of "military necessity."[44] The Confederates would soon occupy the lower third of
Kentucky, but the state was now safely in the hands of the Unionists, as
tens of thousands of federal troops poured in. They would drive out the
Confederates by late 1861—the struggle for Kentucky was essentially over.

Bickley's efforts to establish an Independent Voltigeur Corps had apparently come to naught. He said that he received an August 2 order to report
to Nashville, where he learned from Confederate officials that he would be
expected to present his corps as a body, which he felt was impossible to do.
Bickley accordingly gave notice that he would "take no steps outside of the
State except on the order of President Davis, or Secretary of War, L. Pope
Walker." He lamented: "I have impoverished myself in this cause, and only
ask to be treated fairly. I have furnished to the southern army over 38,000

men who are now in active service." He contended he had not received "good faith" treatment "from the superiors in authority." But despite this, Bickley said: "Yet no one of us will desert the cause of the South. We will never desert our principles."[45] Like the other pro-South champions, Bickley exited Kentucky in September 1861 to avoid his probable arrest.

After fleeing Kentucky, Bickley returned to his native southwest Virginia, where he attempted to raise a battalion of light dragoons. He sought Governor John Letcher's support to obtain supplies for them in early 1862. But it appears that Bickley's further effort to establish an independent command in Virginia also ended in failure.[46]

During the first half of 1863, Bickley served as a surgeon in General Braxton Bragg's Army of Tennessee. He drew his pay from the Twenty-Ninth North Carolina Regiment, which was composed largely of men from the western mountains around Asheville.[47] It was in mid-December 1862, in Bristol, Tennessee, that "Geo. W. Bickley, M.D." penned his abbreviated biography, taking credit, in his typical flamboyant fashion, for initiating the Civil War: "I was thrown on the world penniless and friendless; yet with great energy I educated myself and rose to eminence in the profession of medicine. I have written many books, and vast quantities [of] minor essays on all conceivable subjects. I have built up practical secession and inaugurated the greatest war of modern times."[48]

As Bickley fled and the KGC state commanders and soldiers left to join the Confederate army, the KGC castles in the South became less active. In August 1861, Dr. Frederick G. Weiselberg formed the last known KGC castle in Texas, at Castroville. After this, the Knights' prestige began to fade, as the hardships of war became a reality and Texans placed much of the blame for secession on the Knights.[49] During late May 1861, the *Daily Ledger and Texan* (edited by KGC member Hugh McLeod) confirmed that the Knights had become "a much abused organization" due to the secrecy enveloping its operations.[50] While recognizing that the KGC played a pivotal role in Texas's secession, San Antonio Unionist editor James Newcomb wrote that "after secession was consummated [the KGC] were suppressed by the very persons who had used them; either fearing or loathing them as they would an assassin accomplice."[51] Castles in other southern states became similarly dormant as the KGC's former leaders devoted themselves to the Confederate cause.[52]

For a time, the KGC castles in Border States like Kentucky remained active, refocusing their mission on encouraging Union desertions and resisting the draft. In late 1861–62, KGC castles were reported to be spreading across the southern counties of Ohio, Illinois, Iowa, as well as Indiana, where the order was estimated to have attracted fifteen thousand members.[53] Increasingly, though, newspaper accounts regarding the KGC were coupled with reports on the arrest of their leaders, as Unionist authorities cracked down on the allegedly treasonous organization.[54]

In August 1862, a federal grand jury in Indiana found the KGC had spread across the Midwest and found its activities treasonous; more than sixty Knights were indicted for resisting payment of federal taxes and preventing enlistments in the federal armies.[55] Union General Henry Beebee Carrington treated the KGC in Indiana as a public enemy, and newspaper accounts said that this would result in its annihilation. This constant barrage of investigations and arrests did sap the strength of the KGC in the Midwest.[56]

During June 1863, Bickley engaged in a suspicious series of maneuvers that were likely related to the cavalry raid launched at the same time across northern Kentucky, Indiana, and Ohio by Confederate Brigadier General John Hunt Morgan. General Braxton Bragg, under whom Bickley was serving, had ordered Morgan's raid into Kentucky in order to divert the Union Army of the Ohio from eastern Tennessee. Morgan and 2,500 handpicked Confederate cavalrymen set off from Sparta, Tennessee, in early June. For the next forty-six days, they traveled one thousand miles across Tennessee, Kentucky, Indiana, and Ohio, disrupting Union communications and spreading fear and havoc throughout the Midwest.[57]

One of the purposes of Morgan's raid was to enlist the Knights and other disaffected elements in the Midwest to rise up against the northern war effort. General Bragg had previously issued a proclamation to the people of the Midwest urging them to join in the cause of the South. Morgan assigned one of his officers to establish contact with the Democratic states'-rights and peace-oriented groups (known as "Copperheads"), which reportedly had ninety-two thousand members. KGC lodges in Indiana were claiming they had the support of Knights in Kentucky and Tennessee who would help them "raise the standard of revolt" in an upcoming raid by Morgan.[58] Southern sympathizers did converge on Indianapolis on May 20, 1863, with plans to seize the weapons and ammunition at the state arsenal and use them to free and arm the Confederate war prisoners confined at nearby Camp Morton. Union authorities learned of the plot, however, and relieved the sympathizers of five hundred loaded rifles and pistols, after which the insurgents departed without incident.[59]

The Union soldiers trailing Morgan initially failed to catch up and capture his raiders, which Indiana newspapers said was due to the food, horses, and information provided by the Knights of the Golden Circle.[60] Morgan's men were eventually surrounded and captured, and Morgan himself was taken prisoner in eastern Ohio on July 26. He was incarcerated at the Ohio State Penitentiary in Columbus (a residence that he would soon share with Bickley).[61]

In his suspicious quest to go north, Bickley first applied for authority to pass through Union lines so that he could return to his purported home in Cincinnati, Ohio. He was then sent to the headquarters of Union General William Starke Rosencrans at Tullahoma, Tennessee, for questioning. Here he denied that he was "the famous General Bickley," but instead said he was the nephew of the KGC's founder. Bickley was then paroled and ordered to report to General Ambrose Everett Burnside in Cincinnati, but Union authorities assigned a detective to tail Bickley on his journey. When Bickley arrived in Louisville, he left the train and headed to the nearby suburb of New Albany, Indiana, apparently to establish contacts with KGC castles in the area.[62]

The detective trailing Bickley arrested him in New Albany on July 17, 1863, confiscating the trunks and possessions belonging to Bickley and his female traveling companion. Among their possessions were KGC paraphernalia, pamphlets, and a strange white powder that was determined to be part opium. Letters were also found that confirmed Bickley was in fact the head of the KGC. Nothing directly tied Bickley with Morgan's June–July 1863 raid, although the press and Union authorities generally assumed this was the case. After his arrest, Bickley was taken to Louisville, where he was placed in solitary confinement; local witnesses confirmed that he was, indeed, the head of the Knights.[63]

Bickley's capture was widely reported in the press and helped to spread the rumors that KGC subversive agents were still operating widely in the Border States and the North. In August 1863, Bickley was secretly transferred to the state prison in Columbus, then to Fort Lafayette in the harbor of New York City. During his two-year incarceration, Bickley forwarded a series of appeals for his release to national and state officials, including one to Abraham Lincoln, in which he offered to instruct KGC members to support Lincoln in the upcoming 1864 election. Bickley was not granted a civil or military trial or even a hearing since the Lincoln administration considered him dangerous.[64] Did Bickley's arrest, as well as that of many of the other KGC leaders, spell the end of the secret society? Or did the KGC become rejuvenated, continue its resistance to the Union war effort, and assist in John Wilkes Booth's assassination of sitting president Abraham Lincoln?

# 13

# A REJUVENATED KGC?

A s BICKLEY LANGUISHED in prison and the KGC became increasingly dormant, another secret society called the Order of American Knights (OAK) was spreading across the midwestern and Border States. Phineas Wright, a quixotic St. Louis lawyer, had developed the OAK's high-sounding "declaration of principles," and he appointed himself "Supreme Grand Commander." The first OAK temple meeting was held in St. Louis during February 1863, with the St. Louis chapter expanding to more than one thousand members by the end of the year. Wright traveled to Illinois and Indiana, establishing further chapters and appointing a "Grand Commander" for each involved state. Former Missouri governor Sterling Price, now a Confederate major general, backed the society's formation to help unite southern sympathizers in support of his planned invasion of Missouri. Price reportedly became the "Supreme Commander" of the OAK's southern section.[1]

Like the KGC, the OAK was organized in a series of three degrees, with the secret mission of the organization revealed only to the inner circle of the highest degree. The OAK's publicly professed purpose, disclosed to lower-degree members, was to protect states'-rights principles and constitutional liberties and fight against the Lincoln administration's related wartime edicts, such as the suspension of habeas corpus and the Emancipation Proclamation. The OAK's alleged secret mission was to undermine U.S. military authority, aid the southern Confederacy, promote insurrection, and create a separate northwestern confederacy in the states stretching from Ohio to Minnesota.

Local OAK temples were organized by township, county, and state, and headed at the national level by a "Supreme Council." A grand commander was appointed for each involved state, which was divided into military districts, each headed by an OAK major general. The OAK's rituals incorporated signs, passwords, and an oath of secrecy that mandated obedience to the grand commander's orders and required the defense of the society's principles "with . . . sword and life." Each local temple was expected to arm and drill, and a system of secret police, mail carriers, and smugglers was initiated.[2]

Felix Stiger, a Union spy who infiltrated the OAK, said that its Indiana leaders told him that the OAK was a reorganization of the KGC.[3] William Stinson, a former KGC member who was also serving as a spy for Union authorities, said the OAK was formed at Confederate Major General Sterling Price's request because the KGC had become unsafe since its rituals and secrets had been exposed and so many questionable characters were being initiated.[4] It appears that over time, many of the KGC castles in the Midwest and Mid-Atlantic states shifted their affiliation to the OAK. Several OAK leaders, such as Indiana lawyer Lambdin Purdy Milligan, are known to have been KGC members.[5] But in reality, the OAK was a separate organization with different principles, rituals, and, in most cases, leadership.

Newspapers throughout the country also associated the OAK with the KGC, alleging that the OAK was "being erected on the ruins of the Knights of the Golden Circle."[6] In April 1863, reports circulated throughout the country about the arrest of four alleged Knights of the Golden Circle (more likely OAK) in Reading, Pennsylvania, for resistance to the draft and allegedly organizing a rescue of prisoners.[7] In August 1863, Cincinnati's Republican papers reported that the KGC (rather than the OAK) was intending to import fifty thousand members from neighboring states in order to elect Clement Vallandigham as governor of Ohio.[8] Such reports caused widespread concern among northerners, who suspected a KGC operative was lurking behind every tree.[9] Before the Battle of Gettysburg in July 1863, scam artists sold paper tickets purportedly related to the KGC to local farmers, The scammers told the farmers that the tickets would protect them from Lee's invading Confederates (who knew nothing about the ruse). Similarly, the New York City draft riots of July 1863 were blamed on the KGC.[10]

The Lincoln administration and its army minions did everything possible to associate the new secret societies with the KGC, in order to smear them with the negative notoriety that the southern Knights had by now achieved. For example, despite the fact that the widely circulated October 1864 report by Judge Advocate General Joseph Holt concentrated solely on the Order of American Knights and Sons of Liberty, it began by stating that these Midwest secret societies were originally known "more widely as the 'Knights of the Golden Circle,' . . . being little other than an extension among the disloyal and disaffected at the North of the association with the latter name, which had existed for some time at the South, and from which it derived all the chief features of its organization."[11] Democratic newspapers responded to the smear campaign by charging that the attempt to associate the KGC with disaffected Democratic groups in the North was really "a delusion . . . that has been purposely created by the Republican press."[12]

The OAK's membership significantly expanded after February 1864, when a group of peace Democrats (called "Copperheads," after the snake, by the Republican press) met in New York City and decided that an auxiliary to the Democratic Party would be useful in their fight to prevent Union General McClellan from obtaining the Democrat's 1864 presidential nomination. They changed the name of the OAK to the "Sons of Liberty" and gave the reconstituted organization a more overtly political objective. Phineas Wright was removed from leadership, and Ohio politician Clement Laird Vallandigham, who had been banished by Lincoln and was then living in Canada, became the northern head of the merged society.[13]

During early 1864, Confederate authorities decided to marshal the secret societies rising in the North and Border States to try to influence the fall 1864 presidential elections and counter the South's deteriorating military and home-front situation.[14] Jefferson Davis accordingly sent Captain Thomas H. Hines, from Morgan's command, to meet with northern and Border State society leaders to gauge their pro-South sentiment and their ability to help in releasing the more than twenty-six thousand Confederate soldiers then languishing in northern prison camps.[15] During March 1864, Joseph Tucker, a Missouri fire-eater and newspaper editor, provided a confidential statement to Davis regarding the OAK and its acts of sabotage against Union military installations, factories, and transport facilities, in-

173

cluding steamboats on the Mississippi. In his report, Tucker bragged that the order "is the most perfect and the most secret the world has known. Out of 490,000 [members], only two individuals have ever shown a disposition to betray the secrets of the order; and these two men disappeared mysteriously."[16]

During April, Davis appointed two Confederate commissioners—Jacob Thompson of Mississippi, a former U.S. congressman and secretary of interior in the Buchanan administration, and Clement Clay, a former U.S. senator from Alabama—to move to Canada to interface with the northern secret societies and peace advocates. Confederate secretary of state Judah Benjamin candidly described the commissioner's mission as "secret service in the hope of aiding in disruption between the Eastern and Western States in the approaching election at the North" and "to purchase some of the principal presses in the Northwest." The commissioners were provided with $1 million to carry out this mission, which included rear-guard actions to release Confederate prisoners.[17]

Clay, Thompson, and University of Virginia law professor James Holcombe (who was already in Canada on a Confederate mission) began meeting with the various northern and midwestern secret societies and peace parties in April. Among others, Holcombe met with C. L. Weller, an outspoken San Francisco Copperhead politician who served as the chairman of California's state Democratic Committee as well as lieutenant governor of its Knights of the Columbian Star (KCS). As the supersecret Third Degree of the KGC, the KCS had its own internal hierarchical set of degrees (the 33rd, 57th, etc.). Meetings of the KCS were infrequent, and initiates were limited to candidates well known to current members.

Doctor Fox of San Francisco, one of the most active KCS members, claimed that the KCS had twenty-four thousand members in California, which, "together with the Knights of the Golden Circle and the men they control could reach 50,000." At this point, the KCS's mission was to resist Lincoln's election with all possible means, including force of arms. Money collected by the KCS was sent back to the East, likely to aid in the subversive activities of the KGC and its affiliates.[18]

But predominantly, the Canadian commissioners concentrated on establishing a coordinated plan of action with the leaders of the reformulated OAK, now known as the Sons of Liberty (SOL). Various meetings

were held with SOL leaders from Indiana, Illinois, and Ohio, each reportedly representing more than fifty thousand members, as well as Kentucky
and Missouri, where the SOL lodges were increasing. In April 1864, Canadian commissioner Jacob Thompson met with the SOL's northern leader,
Clement Vallandigham, at a large SOL conclave held at Windsor, Canada.
Vallandigham was a former Ohio congressman who had been exiled for
his outspoken states'-rights and antiwar views. Thompson pushed Vallandigham and the other SOL leaders to work for the establishment of
a separate confederacy in the Northwest. They deferred, but did allow
Thompson to channel funds to the SOL's "Grand Lecturer," James Barrett
of St. Louis, for the purchase of arms.[19]

Thompson again met with representatives of the SOL in July 1864,
and together they formulated a plan for instigating simultaneous uprisings in Chicago, Rock Island, and Springfield, Illinois, to be coupled with
takeovers of the nearby Union prison camps that collectively held more
than twelve thousand Confederate soldiers. The plan was to time the uprisings with the opening of the Democrats' national convention in Chicago. Related uprisings were also planned for Indiana and Ohio as well
as Kentucky and Missouri, to be aided by the movement of Confederate
regiments. Ben Wood, the editor of the pro-South *New York Daily News*,
agreed to supply arms and offered to foment a diversionary riot in New
York City. Once the uprisings were in motion, attempts would also be
made to take over midwestern state governments, establish a Northwest
confederacy, and sue for peace. In conformance with this plan, the Confederate secret service infiltrated sixty-two agents from Canada to Illinois,
and SOL insurgents streamed into Chicago from across the Midwest.[20]

But before the August 29 uprising in Chicago could take place, federal
authorities (tipped off by informers) arrested several of the SOL's state
leaders, including Judge Joshua Fry Bullitt of Kentucky. Thousands of federal soldiers had been brought into Illinois to reinforce the Union prison
camps. Despite this, other SOL leaders still hoped to proceed, but they
then learned that Indiana grand master Harrison H. Dodd, who was ready
to march to Chicago with five thousand SOL supporters, had also been
arrested. On the eve of the convention, Captain Hines tried to rally the
remaining SOL insurgents to join with the Confederates in an assault on
Camp Douglas, but the SOL leaders balked. Hines accordingly recognized

that there was no hope of carrying out the uprisings and related prisoner releases, so most of the Confederates reluctantly returned to Canada. More than one hundred of the SOL insurgents were subsequently arrested.[21]

Local SOL leaders did assist Confederate saboteurs in the attempted burning of New York City hotels in early November 1864. The plot was only marginally successful, however, since the perpetuators utilized bottles containing recently developed "Greek Fire" (a solution of phosphorus in bisulfide of carbon) that failed to maintain combustion.[22] Union General Ben Butler arrived with ten thousand federal soldiers and arrested many of the participants. SOL leaders refused to carry out the further uprisings and conflagrations planned for the November 8 presidential election. By this time, Confederate authorities realized that federal agents had infiltrated the SOL and that the organization lacked the wherewithal to follow through on coordinated subversive actions.[23]

John Wilkes Booth also met with the Confederacy's Canadian agents (perhaps as a KGC representative) during a ten-day stay in Montreal, October 18–28, 1864. At the time, Booth was active in financing the smuggling of quinine and other essential drugs to the Confederacy, for which he drew on his KGC connections.[24] Eight months prior to the Montreal meeting, Booth had spent several days in Cincinnati with H. C. Young, the Memphis lawyer who headed the KGC's Tennessee regiment (and was then serving on the staff of a brigade in Nathan Bedford Forrest's Cavalry Department). After the meeting, Booth tied in with the Knights at Memphis on his journey to New Orleans.[25] In mid-August 1864, Booth had been in Baltimore, where he enlisted his boyhood chums and ex-Confederate soldiers Samuel Bland Arnold and Michael O'Laughlen Jr. (a KGC member) in his audacious plot to kidnap President Lincoln. It therefore is likely that Booth's abduction plot was discussed during his October 1864 meetings with the Confederate secret service in Montreal, and may account for the three hundred dollars in gold provided to Booth during his visit.[26]

While in Canada, Booth is known to have spent time with two southern zealots. One was George Sanders, a native Kentuckian who had been a leading spirit in the Democrats' Young America movement during the mid-1850s. Sanders advocated the use of assassination to end autocratic tyranny and achieve political ends. He had reportedly threatened to apply the "theory of the dagger" (derived from Italian revolutionary Giuseppe

Mazzini) to the hated "Black Republican" president in the event of Lincoln's reelection.[27] The other zealot was Patrick Charles Martin, a former Baltimore liquor dealer described as "an uncompromising rebel," who had been in Canada for several years after being released from arrest in Baltimore. In Canada, Martin operated as a blockade-runner and Confederate abettor. Booth gave Martin his theatrical wardrobe to be shipped to a southern port, while Martin provided Booth with the name of Dr. William Queen from southern Maryland. In a few weeks, Queen would introduce Booth to Dr. Samuel Mudd, who would later aid in Booth's post-assassination escape.[28]

The kidnapping plot that Booth and his cohorts were working on involved capturing Lincoln on one of his unescorted trips to the Old Soldier's Home, or a nearby location in northeast Washington City, and then absconding with the Union president to Richmond, the Confederate capital. Lincoln could then be used as a bargaining chip to extract concessions on behalf of the South, including the release of the twenty-six thousand Confederate soldiers held in northern prison camps. After enlisting Sam Arnold and Michael O'Laughlen in the abduction plot, Booth left Baltimore in August 1864 to wrap up his acting and financial affairs so he could devote his full time to its implementation.[29]

At around this same time, a number of similar attempts to kidnap Union political officials and generals were carried out or planned by Confederate operatives. Northern Virginia partisans operating under Confederate Colonel John Singleton Mosby had actually captured Union General Edwin Henry Stoughton at Fairfax Courthouse, Virginia, in 1863, and were formulating further plans in mid-1864 to kidnap General Phillip Sheridan and Maryland governor Augustus Bradford.[30] In March 1864, the *New York Daily Tribune* revealed details of a plan proposed to the Confederate War Department to kidnap Lincoln. It also said a subscription had been raised from wealthy citizens of Richmond for Lincoln's abduction or assassination. A similar plot to capture Lincoln, to be led by the KGC and prominent men from Baltimore (allegedly involving nine thousand secretly organized men), was also reported around July 1864.[31]

During early 1865, Booth enlisted further southern sympathizers as conspirators. These included John Harrison Surratt, a Confederate spy and messenger; the hulking Lewis Thorton Powell, recently a partisan in

Mosby's Raiders; David Edgar Herold, a Washington drugstore clerk who knew the southern Maryland countryside; and George Andreas Atzerodt, a Port Tobacco carriage maker who doubled as a boatsman. Indications are that many more were involved.

Thomas A. Jones, the Confederate's chief signal officer north of the Potomac, said that he became aware of a big scheme to abduct President Lincoln during December 1864 and make him a hostage, so that the Confederacy could dictate terms to end the war. Jones said that in addition to Booth and John Surratt, "quite a number of persons were involved." He mentioned the use of men dressed in federal uniform to escort Lincoln's carriage out of Washington and relays of fast horses held in readiness all along the route to Richmond.[32] Fellow conspirator Davy Herold said that Booth had told him there were "35 others in Washington [involved in the abduction plot], and four that ought to have joined me" as well as "five men [who signed a pledge and] ought to have met [Booth]." Samuel Chester, an actor friend whom Booth had solicited, said Booth told him the capture plot extended to not only Lincoln but also "the heads of the Government at Washington." Chester said that Booth told him that "there is an immense party connected with it" (which Chester took to mean fifty to one hundred) and that they were "sworn together by a solemn oath that the man that betrays them they will hunt down through life."[33]

On March 17, Booth's core group rode out to abduct Lincoln on his way back from attending a play for wounded soldiers, held at Campbell's Hospital near the Old Soldier's Home in northeast Washington. Their specific action plan was to overpower Lincoln's carriage, handcuff the president and his driver, and make a mad dash through southern Maryland, where they would cross the Potomac and proceed with their captive to Richmond. On the morning of March 17, the conspirators assembled at a nearby restaurant but found that Lincoln had decided to remain in Washington to attend an impromptu military ceremony. The conspirators were forced to abort their plan and returned to Washington in disgust. Thereafter, Booth, along with several other conspirators, made several mysterious trips to the OAK/SOL hotbed of New York City.[34]

From this point on, the abduction plan became increasingly impractical as the Union army placed Richmond under siege. On April 3, 1865, the Confederate government was forced to flee Richmond to seek refuge farther south. This caused Booth to revise his plan from abduction to assassination. On the evening of April 14, 1865, Booth, backed by a number of the core group of conspirators, fired a bullet into the head of Abraham Lincoln while the president attended a performance of *Our American Cousins* at Ford's Theatre in Washington. At the same time, Louis Powell viciously stabbed Secretary of State William Seward at his residence.[35]

In the month following Lincoln's April 14, 1865, assassination, Union authorities undertook a massive dragnet, bringing in and/or taking statements from hundreds of suspects, including Bickley at his prison cell at Fort Warren.[36] A surprising number of these witnesses referenced the old Knights of the Golden Circle as being involved with plots against Lincoln. For example, Charles Cowlen, a Confederate conscript who resided in Richmond after 1863, stated that he had heard frequent references to plans to assassinate the U.S. president and cabinet officers as part of a broader plot to overthrow the U.S. government: "While I believe that the organization known as the K. G. C. was the active working party, they were controlled and ordered by the officials of the Rebel Govt."[37]

Henry Burnett, the special judge advocate appointed by the Union government to marshal the massive evidence developed for the Lincoln assassination trial, saw evidence of a rejuvenated KGC. In a May 2, 1865, memo, Burnett states: "Soon after the commencement of the Rebellion, the secret order, known as the 'Knights of the Golden Circle' throughout the Western and border states, ceased to meet or show any signs of vitality." Burnett further states that in late 1862 and early 1863, "the order had been rechristened under the name of 'American Knights' and grown to formidable proportions" in the North, although he notes that federal authorities had thwarted its attempt to establish a northwestern confederacy. But at the end of his memo, Burnett observes that more recently, men of "a perverted nature" have been seen drifting up from the South: "I find the footprints of this old Order of the Knights of the Golden Circle crossing my path in all directions, probably brought here from the South."[38]

Before the war, castles of the KGC were active in Baltimore, Richmond, and the District of Columbia and were known to have interacted with each other. Was the KGC as an organization rejuvenated in 1865, and could it have been behind Booth's plots to abduct and then assassinate Lincoln and his cabinet?

As indicated, Michael O'Laughlen confessed to having belonged to the KGC, and his older brother William was also identified as having been a KGC member before the war. William O'Laughlen, described as a large, rough-looking man with sandy whiskers, was seen in Washington a few weeks before the assassination, looking for letters at the boardinghouse that Michael had recently vacated.[39] Samuel Street, a former Confederate soldier who now served as a sergeant in the Union army outside Washington, stated that he had joined the KGC with William O'Laughlen during the late 1850s. Street knew Wilkes Booth from their old Exeter Street neighborhood and had been a college mate of the future actor. In the weeks prior to the assassination, Street obtained four passes to go to Washington on frivolous pretexts (running into Booth and O'Laughlen several times). On the night of the assassination, he allegedly passed suspicious characters through the Union lines and spoke of "something going to happen that night."[40] Could Street have been one of the men in federal uniform that Thomas Jones said would escort the conspirators out of Washington?

The fact that other conspirators did not, like O'Laughlen, admit to belonging to the KGC, does not mean they did not. As indicated, the KGC's higher degrees prohibited members from telling outsiders about involvement upon threat of pain or death. Samuel Arnold later denied being a member of the KGC, but he admitted that Booth had administered an oath of secrecy to him and the other conspirators. Arnold had three brothers who could have been KGC members; like Sam, they had grown up in Booth's old Baltimore neighborhood and had joined the Confederate army.[41] Co-conspirator Edman Spangler, a long-standing Booth devotee who shared his pro-South sentiments, had also lived in the old Exeter Street neighborhood where a Baltimore castle of the KGC met.[42]

Lewis Powell claimed he first met Booth in Richmond at the beginning of the war and was mesmerized by the actor's grace and charm. Perhaps Booth convinced Powell to join the Richmond KGC at that time.[43] Powell spent January through March 1865 in Baltimore, residing at Joseph Branson's boardinghouse and frequenting David Preston Parr's china shop, where Powell established ongoing contacts with Confederate courier and conspirator John Harrison Surratt Jr. Shortly after being arrested as a Confederate spy during March 1865, Powell left Baltimore. On the eve of his hanging, Powell confessed that the owner/operator of the Baltimore boardinghouse (Joseph Branson) was in on the abduction plot and that Powell had, for months before the assassination, worked in the Confederate secret service journeying back and forth between Richmond and Washington in conference with prominent men. Powell also revealed that leading men of Richmond were intensely interested in the abduction plot for which Booth was the key player.[44]

In a letter dated May 14, 1865, to the War Department, an anonymous correspondent from Baltimore alleges that several conspirators had familial connections to the KGC. The letter states that "the elder Herold" was a Knight and also "Surratt."[45] Since David Herold had only sisters, the "elder Herold" likely refers to his father—Adam Herold—who was an employee of the Washington Navy Yard, a member of various fraternal organizations, and who owned several buildings in his native Baltimore and Washington City.[46] "Surratt" may refer to John Surratt's father, a known southern sympathizer who died in August 1862. It also may refer to John Surratt's older brother, Isaac, who lived in Baltimore and went to Texas shortly before Lincoln's election, reportedly to show his disdain for the incoming Republican administration. In Texas, Isaac served as a mail courier and then joined the Confederate army in 1862, where he served (alongside George Chilton) in Duff's Partisan Rangers (Thirty-Third Texas Cavalry), rising to the rank of sergeant.[47] At the end of the war, Union Major General Frederick Steele reported that Isaac was "a desperate character" who was returning to Washington for the purpose of assassinating President Johnson (although Isaac's subsequent conduct didn't confirm this).[48]

With respect to KGC involvement by Booth's theater friends, Samuel Chester said that in addition to Booth, several members of the Richmond acting company joined the "secret organization" in 1858 or 1859. Chester specifically mentioned Louis Carland, who in 1865 was the wardrobe man at Ford's Theatre. Carland was there on the night of Lincoln's assassination and later admitted to having talked with Booth only an hour before. After the assassination, Carland reportedly hid in his house for three days out of fear of being apprehended. A few weeks before, Carland had stirred up "some damned Yankee officers" by expressing pro-South sentiments and saying he "wished the damned Yankees were all killed." He had earlier met with Booth along with a group of men at the Waverly House that included "Tom Burns of Baltimore, MD" (possibly KGC head James Byrnes).[49]

Like Carland, Edman ("Ned") Spangler, a carpenter and sceneshifter at the theater and longtime Booth confidant, was there on the night of the assassination. A witness said he overheard Spangler offering Booth any assistance he needed and wishing "that the damn old son of bitch will be killed here tonight." An assistant sceneshifter also testified that after Booth fled, Spangler slapped him on the back of his hand and said, "Don't say which way he went."[50] Other witnesses said that James Lamb, the scene painter at Ford's, had frequently used derogatory language against Lincoln and, on one occasion, had said he ought to be killed.[51] A number of the other Ford's Theatre staff also displayed strong pro-South sympathies, came under suspicion, and were arrested. These included Ford's head carpenter, James Gifford; its property man, James Maddox; as well as Henry Clay Ford, brother of the theater owner, who was a confidant of Booth and had alerted him that Lincoln would be attending the theater on the night of the assassination.[52]

Several of Booth's other actor friends could also have been among those who joined the KGC in Richmond, including Samuel Knapp Chester, who told government investigators about Booth's and Carland's involvement in the Richmond secret society. Chester further said that Booth told him that "he had broached the abduction affair to several other actor friends," including John Matthews, who supposedly also refused to become involved. Matthews was the actor to whom Booth gave a letter for the *National Intelligencer,* which explained why Booth was committing the assassination (which Matthews subsequently destroyed). A mutual friend testified that Matthews "is knowing of all Booth's proceedings."[53] Booth also was rooming with his long-standing actor friend John McCullough at the National Hotel in the weeks leading up to the assassination. Given Booth's loose lips regarding the abduction plot, it seems likely that McCullough would have become aware that something was going on. McCullough had earlier made derogatory statements regarding Lincoln and said that he "should be put out of the way."[54]

Around the time of the assassination, there were a number of Knights in northern Virginia who were likely intending to be involved in aiding

Booth's escape. Davy Herold said Booth indicated that at the time they crossed to Virginia, there were five men who had signed a letter pledging to meet him.[55] Maryland KGC leader Robert H. Archer, together with Virginian John Tayloe VI (who claimed to be with Mosby's Raiders), were captured on April 24 in a rowboat on the Potomac River off Nanjemoy Creek. This was around the time that Booth and Herold were expected to be crossing the Potomac River into Virginia. Both Archer and Tayloe had previously served in the Confederate army, but asserted that they had been paroled and were operating as private citizens at the time of their capture.[56] Upon reaching Virginia, Booth told Dr. Richard Stewart [Stuart], "we are Marylanders and want to go to [John] Mosby." At the time, the Confederate partisan ranger unit under John Mosby did have men in northern Virginia near the point where Booth was expected to be escaping.[57]

Booth also told a Confederate Signal Corps officer that he was trying to reach the Orange County Courthouse, which was near the Confederate camp at Gordonsville, Virginia, commanded by Cornelius Boyle, formerly the head of the District's National Volunteers and a likely member of its KGC.[58] Boyle, a noted Washington medical doctor, was now provost marshal for northern Virginia and had commanded the Gordonsville camp since 1862. He was heavily involved in Confederate undercover operations, serving as an essential link for the Confederate Signal Corps as well as for the "secret line" of Confederate agents who passed messages between Richmond and Washington.[59]

Boyle's apparent relationship to the Lincoln assassination plot is also indicated by counterpart letters sent from "Senior" of New York on April 10, 1865, to "Geo. Surratt (care of the Surratt Boarding House in Washington)," as well as "Jno. Surratt, and Dr. Cornelius Boyle," stating, "Your [sic] are to attempt the murder of Secretary Seward while I am to attempt for the life of Mr. Chase and if we succeed in getting away we are all bound for Canada."[60] "Senior" was the title used by the Order of American Knights for its presiding officer at meetings, and there were reportedly sixty thousand members of OAK/SOL in New York City.[61] In addressing "Geo. Surratt," the correspondent may have meant conspirator George Atzerodt, who was staying at the Surratt boardinghouse in early April.[62] Atzerodt, in his subsequently disclosed confession, said that Booth told him of a plan by "a party in New York who would get the prest. [president] certain" by mining the Executive Mansion (for which Thomas F. Harney, a sergeant in the Confederate Torpedo Bureau, had led an aborted attempt backed by the Confederate government in early April). Booth and his associates had reportedly met with members of a separate action team emanating from New York who were recognizable by a secret sign when they were in Washington. Atzerodt said that Booth had urged his own action team to move quickly before the New York team could carry out the deed.[63]

Booth may have also tied in with George Kane, the 1861 chief of the Baltimore police, whom Booth said he knew well. Pinkerton alleged that Kane was aware of Ferrandini's February 1861 assassination plot and indicated he wouldn't intervene.[64] Kane had been imprisoned from June 1861 to November 1862 by Union authorities. He then migrated to Canada, where he joined the Confederate secret service, with the rank of colonel, and became actively involved in planning raids to liberate the Confederate prisoners.[65] During February 1864, Kane returned to Richmond to serve as its liaison with the Canadian secret service. He convinced Jefferson Davis to establish a separate Maryland Line in the Confederate army and asked to be allowed to organize a secret service corps.[66]

There is no doubt that a number of the conspirators and allies who assisted Booth had ties to the KGC during its 1859–61 heyday. It remains unknown whether the KGC castles around Washington City remained active during the Civil War and whether the KGC was involved in the assassination on an organizational basis (once the KGC was declared a treasonous organization by Union authorities, its activities and members went underground and the paper trail largely ends). Alternatively, Booth may have enlisted his former KGC compatriots as individuals since he knew they were pro-South, detested Lincoln, and would abide by an oath to keep a secret. It is known, however, that the KGC had orchestrated the February 1861 assassination attempt led by Ferrandini (who was still around in 1865), continued its threats to assassinate the northern president and his cabinet (which was incorporated in the KGC's oath), and was still active as an organization in California, Oregon, and other locations (where it largely operated under the name of the Knights of the Columbian Star).[67] Given this and the number of Knights (or former Knights) associated with the 1865 assassination, it is possible that future revelations may show organized KGC involvement.

# EPILOGUE

WHILE IT IS possible that cells of the KGC continued around Washington City, it does not appear that the KGC's prewar state regimental commanders were in a position to help orchestrate Booth's 1864–65 abduction/assassination plots against President Lincoln. Ben McCulloch, the first KGC leader to be appointed to the Confederate provisional army as a brigadier general, had been mortally wounded at the July 1862 Battle of Pea Ridge/Elkhorn Tavern, Arkansas. Paul Semmes, Georgia's KGC regimental commander, had been killed in July 1863 leading the Confederate assault on Little Round Top during the Battle of Gettysburg.[1]

Maryland's former KGC commander, now Confederate Brigadier General Robert Tyler, was recuperating from the loss of a leg at West Point, Georgia, in early 1865. On April 16, West Point came under attack, and Tyler led a contingent of "old men and boy volunteers" in defense of the town. Union sharpshooters cut Tyler down as he was peering over a defensive wall of the earthworks.[2] James H. R. Taylor, a KGC leader from Mississippi who had served as a lieutenant colonel under Tyler in the Fifteenth Tennessee Regiment, was threatened with a court-martial in November 1861 and resigned from Confederate service shortly thereafter.[3]

Virginius Groner, the KGC's Virginia regimental commander, was at Appomattox Courthouse on April 9, witnessing Lee's surrender with the remnants of his Sixty-First Virginia Infantry Regiment. Groner had been appointed colonel of Virginia's Sixty-First Regiment on October 1, 1862, and except for a short period when recuperating from wounds, led it through the bloody campaign of the Wilderness and Lee's failed defense of Richmond.[4]

Elkanah Greer, the KGC's former Texas grand marshall, was at Marshall, Texas, in April 1865, serving as the commander of the Reserve Corp of Texas as well as for the Conscription Bureau for the Confederate army's Trans-Mississippi Department.[5] George Chilton, who succeeded Greer as the KGC's Texas grand marshall, resigned his commission in the irregular Duff's Partisan Rangers that operated on the Texas frontier during late 1864, and returned to Tyler to edit the *Confederate Journal*.[6]

Tennessee's KGC commander, H. C. Young, had written Stanton from Cincinnati on April 20, 1865, offering details to assist in the identification of the body of John Wilkes Booth, whom Young said he had "known well . . . for several years." Perhaps Young was afraid he would come under suspicion and was trying to exonerate himself from Booth's heinous act. After the war, Young served as the passenger agent on railroads at Cleveland, Pittsburgh, and other cities.[7]

James Ross Howard, from Alabama/Louisiana, had served as a colonel of Alabama's Third Confederate Cavalry and was severely wounded at the September 1862 Battle of Stones River. He resigned from field duty in March 1863 and served out the war as a judge for the military court in Major General Joseph Wheeler's cavalry corps of the Confederate army of Tennessee.[8] Louisiana's KGC commander Henry Castellanos joined the Confederacy's Twelfth Battalion Heavy Artillery in 1862, and fought in Virginia, Alabama, and Mississippi, but was discharged in 1863 due to a hospitalization. After the war, Castellanos became a respected member of New Orleans's legal fraternity and penned hundreds of vignettes on city life that were collected in the book *New Orleans As It Was*.[9]

Languishing as a prisoner at Fort Warren, George Bickley's mental and physical health continued to deteriorate, and he increasingly engaged in flights of fantasy.[10] During 1865, he tried to present the KGC as simply a prewar colonization society. In a March 1865 letter published in the *New York Times*, Bickley contended that the KGC had been solely dedicated to helping establish a constitutional government in Mexico. Bickley said that French royalist Louis Napoleon's 1864 establishment of a "Latin Monarchy" in Mexico had now subverted the KGC's goal. In his letter, Bickley claimed that the total membership of the KGC as of July 1, 1862, was 486,398 in the United States and 42,000 in Mexico.[11]

Bickley's March letter was followed by an even more curious "Circular Letter and Order" published in the *New York Times* on July 11, 1865, in which he claimed that the KGC was not in favor of filibustering, slavery, or secession. He said that the KGC had been established in every state of the South, except South Carolina, and in seven-eighths of the northern states. Accompanying the letter, Bickley issued a "General Order" indicating that operations of the KGC had been suspended during the Civil War and would remain suspended until July 1, 1870. His "General Order" released the members of the Military Department from their allegiance to the KGC and said that in order to preserve an unbiased history, "statements in reference to the occurrences of the war and American Society between the first day of January, 1858, and the first day of June, 1865" could be forwarded to the KGC's assigned depository, Mr. Charles Templeton at Halifax, Nova Scotia.[12]

Bickley was finally released from Fort Warren on October 14, 1865. He signed an oath of amnesty without any charges ever having been filed against him. Bickley lived the remaining two years of his life in relative obscurity, although one account says he tried to cash in on his secret society notoriety by launching a lecture tour in England. Bickley died in Baltimore in early October 1867, and was buried at Green Mount Cemetery, in the same Weaver family vault that would temporarily house the body of John Wilkes Booth.[13]

As Bickley's comments imply, to understand the historical significance of the KGC, it must be viewed during two separate periods. The first is the 1859–mid-1860 period, when the KGC's primary goal was expansion into the Southern Hemisphere. During this period, Bickley was in control and the KGC operated largely on a centralized basis. The second is the mid-1860–1861 period, when the KGC's state regimental commanders like Greer, Groner, Semmes, and Tyler were in control and the Knights' second objective—promotion of southern rights and support for the southern governors—became paramount. During this period, the KGC operated on a decentralized basis in regional power centers loosely tied together through KGC coordinators. Bickley, who had been stripped of authority at the May

1860 Raleigh convention, was essentially a man without an army and was forced to follow the KGC's regimental commanders' directions.

During both periods, the KGC possessed several features that distinguished it from the plethora of secret societies operating in antebellum America.[14] Unlike secret societies that sought mystical otherworldly knowledge, the Knights pursued a real-world agenda of Southern Hemisphere expansion and promotion of southern rights. The KGC's secret knowledge was a practical program of Manifest Destiny expansion incorporated by true believers in the here and now. Furthermore, the Knights focused on military drill and training in preparation for militant action. This was an outgrowth of its Order of the Lone Star (OLS) forebear and was useful whether the goal was southward expansion or promoting secession. Its OLS background also enabled the Knights to involve all strata of southern society in a hierarchical structure where top leaders could pass down controversial goals and commands to KGC foot soldiers in oathbound secrecy. Given these features, the Knights most resembled the revolutionary secret societies then operating in Europe such as Mazzini's "Young Italy" or the Fenian (Irish) brotherhood.[15]

The KGC was not successful in achieving its primary goal from the earlier 1859–mid-1860 period of Mexican colonization, largely because the American Civil War intervened. In early 1861, elements of the KGC still hoped to pursue Mexican colonization with support from the Confederacy.[16] Confederate secretary of state Robert Toombs wanted to establish an alliance with Mexico and sent Colonel John Pickett to try to achieve diplomatic recognition. These overtures had to be constrained, however, since the Confederate government did not want to lessen its chance for a much more significant alliance with France, which also had its eyes on the Mexican prize. The French did intervene in Mexico, occupying Mexico City by June 1863, chasing out Juárez's Liberal government, and reinstalling the Conservatives, who invited Austrian archduke Ferdinand Maximilian to assume the Mexican throne. If the U.S. sectional crisis hadn't intervened, one wonders whether Juárez and the Liberals would have changed their mind and invited the Knights to establish a Mexican colony as a counterbalance against French intervention.[17]

It is during the mid-1860–1861 period—when the Knights shifted its paramount goal to supporting the southern governors—that the KGC achieved its greatest successes. The Knights provided a multistate network of state and local militia leaders that helped coordinate the drive for secession. In states like Texas and Virginia, the Knights became the strong arm of secession, employing extralegal measures to force secession and intimidate Unionists. It also served as a militant base to initiate bold actions such as the takeover of federal forts in the South. Knights who were not in favor of disunion (like the "North Texan") dropped or were forced out. The success of the KGC's program in helping to achieve secession unfortunately showed that a clandestine militant group of oath-bound zealots could get their way by influencing public opinion and silencing dissenters.[18] This undoubtedly led to the formation of similar hierarchical militant groups after the Civil War such as the Ku Klux Klan.[19]

The Knights' secrecy ultimately became a double-edged sword, however. It initially served to shroud the more controversial militant and pro-slavery aspects of the KGC's program and prevent the type of press and public disclosures that had undermined Quitman's 1854 Cuban expedition. But the KGC's oath and secrecy eventually inhibited recruiting and forced the Knights to operate as the core of more transparent front organizations such as the Minute Men and National Volunteers. Its secrecy also served as the point of attack by its opponents such as Judge George Paschal and James Newcomb in Texas, George Prentice in Kentucky, as well as Lincoln administration hard-liners, like Joseph Holt, and the Union Leagues.

It is clear, given its multistate operations and the stature of its regimental commanders, that the KGC was a more powerful and extensive organization than historians have generally assumed.[20] While much has been uncovered, it is likely that some things remain unknown due to the loss or destruction of records during the Civil War. We know that the Knights held state conventions in Kentucky and Texas, but were similar conventions held in other states where the KGC existed? Probably. Did the Knights' state regimental commanders ever hold a further meeting in late 1860 or early 1861? Possibly. And then there are the legends that the Knights buried gold throughout the South so it could rise again and that it assisted with and/or benefited from the robberies of Frank and Jesse James and their gang.[21] Doubtful.

The key points regarding the KGC are known, however, and are truly significant. In early 1861, the Knights formed a powerful militant force that helped wrest a number of key southern states, like Texas and Virginia, from the Union. They then contributed leaders and manpower to the nascent Confederate army that enabled it to ramp up from nothing to two hundred thousand men by September 1861. As Bickley claimed, the Knights "built up practical secession and inaugurated the greatest war in history."

# ACKNOWLEDGMENTS

I N WRITING A research-intensive multistate book of this nature, I had to rely on assistance from archives, historical societies, and public and university libraries across the country, and I am most appreciative to the many staff people who went out their way to provide help. The "Primary Sources" section of the bibliography (coupled with the photographic credits) references more than twenty such institutions from Georgia, Maryland, Massachusetts, Mississippi, Virginia, Washington D.C., Oregon, and Texas. I would particularly like to express my appreciation to Laurie Verge and Sandra Walia of the Surratt Society for their help, which went well beyond the call of duty. Other helpful institutions not referenced in the bibliography include the Filson Society of Louisville, Kentucky, the Kentucky History Center (and particularly Stuart Sanders), Central and Murray State Universities, the Norfolk, Virginia, Public Library, and the Universities of Kentucky, North Carolina, Tennessee, and Virginia.

In addition to out-of-state institutions, I must also thank those closer to my home in eastern Pennsylvania, including the Allentown Public Library (and especially their interlibrary loan specialist, Diana DeFanti), Cedar Crest College, Desales University, Kutztown University, Lafayette College (especially archivist Diane Shaw), Lehigh University, Muhlenberg College, as well as my alma mater, Gettysburg College, and the U.S. Army Military Institute at Carlisle. They have an astounding collection of historical resources, and their staffs have been universally willing to help me. In this regard, I must specially note Dr. Daniel J. Wilson from Muhlenberg College, who was willing to read an early draft of the manuscript and convinced me to focus on the Knights in the first place. Bob Locke, Attorney Malcolm Gross, and Joe Garrera, Director of the Lehigh Valley Heritage Museum, furnished helpful comments and support along the way.

I also wish to thank those at LSU Press. These include Dr. T. Michael Parrish from Baylor University, who encouraged me to proceed with a book on the KGC and provided useful articles, editing, and primary-source material during the four years it took to finish. My second reader, Dr. Robert E. May, provided perceptive suggestions and corrections. And my editor, Rand Dodson, was always there with helpful and timely responses. In addition, I'd like to recognize those historians who blazed the trail—Ollinger Crenshaw and Roy Sylvan Dunn, for their seminal journal articles; and William H. Bell and Linda S. Hudson, whose diligent work in digging out information on the powerful Texas Knights convinced me to take a closer look at other areas of the country.

Finally, there are those special people who were willing to pitch in and help out with research in various locations. These include my boyhood friend Glenn Rambo, who helped out during our many research trips; Chris Lyons from Carrollton, Texas, who traveled all over the Lone Star State to dig out hard-to-find items; and Jim Chrismer, a historian and independent researcher from Harford County, Maryland. Of course, I can't forget my two daughters: Alison helped with research around Boston and edited the final manuscript, and Molly helped with research in Kentucky and Massachusetts. While in Kentucky, we benefited from the gracious hospitality of our relatives Jim and Louise Miller. Last and foremost is my cherished wife, Sally, who not only put up with me during this lengthy process, but also provided ongoing help and encouragement.

# NOTES

## PROLOGUE: THE SHADOWY KNIGHTS

1. William C. Edwards and Edward Steers Jr., eds., *The Lincoln Assassination: The Evidence* (Urbana: University of Illinois Press, 2009), 347: statement of Samuel Knapp Chester; ibid., 1391–92: statement of George Wren. This volume reproduces and systematizes the U.S. government's Lincoln assassination evidence file located in the National Archives and Records Administration, Records of the Office of the Judge Advocate General (Army), together with the assassination trial proceedings, which have been photographed onto sixteen reels of microfilm designated Microcopy No. 599. It will hereafter be cited as *Lincoln Assassination Evidence*. John Rhodehamel and Louis Taper, eds., *"Right or Wrong, God Judge Me": The Writings of John Wilkes Booth* (Urbana: University of Illinois Press, 1997), 45–46; Nora Titone, *My Thoughts Be Bloody: The Bitter Rivalry between Edwin and John Wilkes Booth That Led to an American Tragedy* (New York: Free Press, 2010), 142–43.

2. Titone, *My Thoughts Be Bloody*, 178–83; Stanley Kimmel, *The Mad Booths of Maryland* (Indianapolis: Bobbs-Merrill, 1940), 151–55; Angela Smythe, "Has He Been Hiding in Plain Sight? John Wilkes Booth and the Richmond Grays," May 10, 2010, 16–17, 31 n. 9, www .morningfourstars.com/JWB/Hiding_In_Plain_Sight/.

3. Ollinger Crenshaw "The Knights of the Golden Circle: The Career of George Bickley," *American Historical Review* 47, no. 1 (October 1941): 30–35.

4. Alan Axelrod, *The International Encyclopedia of Secret Societies and Fraternal Orders* (New York: Facts on File, 1997), vii–xiii, 270; Mark A. Lause, *A Secret Society History of the Civil War* (Urbana: University of Illinois Press, 2011), 11.

5. Walter H. Bell, "Knights of the Golden Circle: Its Organization and Activities in Texas Prior to the Civil War" (master's thesis, Texas College of Arts and Industry, 1965), 207–17; "The Order of the Knights of the Golden Circle—Important Revelation," *Louisville Journal*, July 18, 1861; J. W. Pomphrey, *A True Disclosure and Exposition of the Knights of the Golden Circle* (Cincinnati: printed for the author, 1801).

6. *K. G. C. First, or Military Degree*, Castroville, Texas, Castle (San Antonio: Herald Steam Press, ca. 1860; Bell, "Knights of the Golden Circle," 135–39, reproducing "By-Laws of the San

Antonio Castle, K. G. C"; "Rules for the Castle," in *Rules, Regulations, and Principles of the K. G. C.,* issued by Order of the Congress of the K. C. S. and the General President, Head-Quarters, Washington City, D.C. (New York: Benj. Urner, Printer), 39, in Bickley Papers, National Archives, Judge Advocate General Office, Washington, D.C., Record Group 153 (hereafter cited as "Bickley Papers, National Archives").

7. *Degree Book: First or Company Degree of 28,* Bickley Papers, National Archives; *K. G. C. First, Degree.*

8. Robert C. Tyler letter, April 6, 1860, in *K. G. C.: A Full Exposition of the Southern Traitors, the Knights of the Golden Circle: Their Startling Schemes Frustrated* (Boston: E. H. Bullard, 1861[?]), 2.

9. Berry Craig, "The Jackson Purchase of Kentucky in the Secession Crisis of 1860–1861" (master's thesis, Murray State University, 1973), 77; *Louisville Journal,* August 12 and 20, 1861.

10. *Rules, Regulations and Principles of the K. G. C.,* 9, Bickley Papers, National Archives; *Columbus (Ohio) Crisis,* December 30, 1863; Bell, "Knights of the Golden Circle," 11–12, citing Bickley's Statement of Fact in *Crisis,* August 1, 1863.

11. Horace Greeley, *American Conflict: A History of the Great Rebellion* (Hartford: O. D. Case, 1865), 1: 350, 492–93; 2: 18–19. Focusing on minor discrepancies and partisan affiliations, historian Frank Klement attempts to discredit the secret society and conspiracy findings of Greeley and multiple generations of historians and observers (including direct participants) as myths. With respect to the KGC, a southern society, Klement was generally looking in the wrong place (the Midwest rather than the South or Border States) at the wrong time (during rather than before the Civil War) (see Frank L. Klement, *Dark Lanterns: Secret Political Societies, Conspiracies, and Treason Trials in the Civil War* [Baton Rouge: Louisiana State University Press, 1984], 12–33, 234–44).

12. *An Authentic Exposition of the "K. G. C." "Knights of the Golden Circle": or, A History of Secession from 1834 to 1861 by a Member of the Order* (Indianapolis: C. O. Perrine, 1861), 34–43; A. Sanford, *Treason Unmasked: An Exposition of the Origins, Objects and Principles of the Knights of the Golden Circle* (Albion, N.Y.: John Marsh, 1863), 6–9, 17–27; *Narrative of Edmund Wright: His Adventures and Escape from the Knights of the Golden Circle* (Cincinnati: J. R. Hawley, 1864), 54–58.

13. Warren Getler and Bob Brewer, *Shadow of the Sentinel: One Man's Quest to Find the Hidden Treasure of the Confederacy* (New York: Simon and Schuster, 1993), 67–80.

## CHAPTER ONE: POWERFUL ANTECEDENTS

1. James Hagy, "George Washington Lafayette Bickley: The Early Years," *Historical and Biographical Sketches of Southwest Virginia,* Publication 6 of Historical Society of Southwest Virginia (March 1972): 64–70, quoting at 70 from G. W. L. Bickley to John Bickley, October 23, 1846, Bernard Gibson Collection.

2. Ibid., 64, 71–72. Gloria Jahoda, "The Bickleys of Virginia," *Virginia Magazine of History and Biography* 66, no. 4 (October 1958): 463, 477–78, indicates that Bickley went at various times by "George Washington Lafayette Bickley" and "George William Lamb Bickley."

3. Jahoda, "The Bickleys of Virginia," 478; "The History of Phrenology," www.phrenology.org/intro.html.

4. *Abingdon Virginian*, October 4, 1867; Hagy, "George Washington Lafayette Bickley," 72.

5. Harvey Wickes Felter, M.D., *Historical Sketch of the Eclectic Medical Institute, Cincinnati* (Cincinnati: Serial Publication of the Lloyd Library, 1911), 9–10, 12; John S. Haller Jr., *Medical Protestants: The Eclectics in American Medicine, 1825–1949* (Carbondale: Southern Illinois University Press, 1994), 110–22; Crenshaw, "Knights of the Golden Circle,", 24–25; Klement, *Dark Lantern*, 7.

6. George W. L. Bickley, M.D., *History of the Settlement and Indian Wars of Tazewell County, Virginia* (Cincinnati: Morgan, 1852); George W. L. Bickley, *Adalaska, Or The Strange and Mysterious Family of the Cave of Genreva* (Cincinnati: H. M. Rulison, 1853).

7. Geo. W. L. Bickley, M.D., "Introductory Lecture, Delivered before the Eclectic Medical Class, November 6, 1852," *Eclectic Medical Journal* 12 (March 1853): 102–11; Prof. G. W. L. Bickley, "History of the Eclectic Medical Institute of Cincinnati and Its Ethical Peculiarities," *Eclectic Medical Journal* 16 (January 1857): 9–15; ibid. (February 1856): 57–64; ibid. (March 1857): 105–12; ibid. (April 1857) 153–56.

8. George W. L. Bickley, M.D., "Review of 'Report of Eclectic Physicians,'" *Eclectic Medical Journal* 12 (March 1853): 119–21.

9. Klement, *Dark Lanterns*, 7–8; "The Extraordinary Career of an American Adventurer," *Abingdon Virginian*, October 4, 1867.

10. Bickley to John J. Crittenden, July 20, 1856, Library of Congress Archives.

11. *Bickley's West American Review* 1, no. 6 (Cincinnati: Morgan and Overland Printers, 1853): 172, 174.

12. *New York Times*, March 7, 1854; *United States Magazine and Democratic Review*, January 1852; Yonatan Eyal, *The Young America Movement and the Transformation of the Democratic Party, 1828–1861* (New York: Cambridge University Press, 2007), 73–76, 162–63, 209–12; Robert D. Sampson, *John L. O'Sullivan and His Times* (Kent, Ohio: Kent State University Press, 2003), 192–93; Robert E. May, *Manifest Destiny's Underworld: Filibustering in Antebellum America* (Chapel Hill: University of North Carolina Press, 2002), 112–13. In January 1855, Prof. G. W. L. Bickley was at the Broadway Tabernacle in New York City delivering a series of lectures titled "Doomed Cities of Antiquity," which he said was to raise funds for an exploratory visit to Asia Minor that might help establish the truth of Scriptural prophesy ("Doomed Cities of Antiquity," *New York Times*, January 16, 1855).

13. Handwritten address to "Brothers of the Continental Union," Bickley Papers, National Archives; Klement, *Dark Lanterns*, 8 n. 3; Crenshaw, "Knights of the Golden Circle," 25; Lause, *A Secret Society History of the Civil War*, 24–32.

14. W. Darrell Overdyke, *The Know-Nothing Party in the South* (Baton Rouge: Louisiana State University Press, 1950), 34–171; 265–95; Tyler Anbinder, *Nativism and Slavery: The Northern Know Nothings and the Politics of the 1850s* (New York: Oxford University Press, 1992), 162–269; *San Antonio Ledger and Texan*, February 11, 1860, citing the *McKinney Messenger* and *Dallas Herald* and noting that the KGC was "not the KN, for that is dead they say." Bickley's chapter of the Continental Union fizzled out in a year, and his involvement with

the Know-Nothings appears to have been similarly short-lived (Crenshaw, "Knights of the Golden Circle," 25; Klement, *Dark Lanterns*, 8).

15. *Cincinnati Daily Gazette*, August 6, 1863; Klement, *Dark Lanterns*, 8; Lause, *A Secret Society History of the Civil War*, 64; George N. Vourlojianis, *The Cleveland Grays: An Urban Military Company, 1837–1919* (Kent, Ohio: Kent State University Press, 2002), 20–21.

16. Klement, *Dark Lanterns*, 8.

17. *Cincinnati Daily Gazette*, August 6, 1863; Klement, *Dark Lanterns*, 8.

18. "The American Colonization and Steamship Company of "1,"" in *Rules, Regulations and Principles of the K. G. C.*, Bickley Papers, National Archives.

19. *Cincinnati Daily Gazette*, August 6, 1863; Klement, *Dark Lanterns*, 8.

20. Eric H. Walther, *The Shattering of the Union: America in the 1850s* (Wilmington, Del.: Scholarly Resources, 2004), xviii, 18; Eric H. Walther, *The Fire-Eaters* (Baton Rouge: Louisiana State University Press, 1998), 61–63, 88, 98–99, 140, 144. "An Authentic Exposition of the 'K. G. C.," 5, alleges that the KGC arose out of the principles of the "Southern Rights Associations" and that they were devoted to "the re-establishment of the African slave trade and the acquisition of new slave territory."

21. *Charleston (S.C.) Courier Tri-Weekly*, March 14, 1860.

22. Sanford, *Treason Unmasked*, 5, 7.

23. George Fort Milton, *Abraham Lincoln and the Fifth Column* (New York: Vanguard Press, 1942), 66; Greeley, *American Conflict*, 1: 350; Basil Rauch, *American Interest in Cuba: 1848–1855* (New York: Octagon, 1974), 302; W. J. Hughes, *Rebellious Ranger: Rip Ford and the Old Southwest* (Norman: University of Oklahoma Press, 1964), 121–22; "The National Government and Secret Societies," *Zanesville (Ohio) Daily Courier*, April 13, 1861; *New York Times*, August 30, 1861.

24. Rauch, *American Interest in Cuba*, 228–29; "The Order of the Lone Star," *United States Magazine and Democratic Review*, January 1853, 80–83; *Baltimore Sun*, October 28, 1851, and August 26, 1852; Oliver T. Morton, *The Southern Empire and Other Papers* (Boston: Houghton Mifflin, 1892), 48; *New York Times*, March 13, 1855.

25. May, *Manifest Destiny's Underworld*, xi, 3–4, 53–54. One critical U.S. Navy officer described filibusters as "those glorious regenerators who go with the torch of enlightenment to weak countries to commit all kinds of outrages" (Stephen Dando-Collins, *Tycoon's War: How Cornelius Vanderbilt Invaded a Country to Overthrow America's Most Famous Military Adventurer* [Cambridge, Mass.: Da Capo Press, 2008], 321, quoting Frederick K. Chatard to William Seton, July 20, 1857, Chatard Papers).

26. Orville J. Victor, *The Comprehensive History of the Southern Rebellion and the War for the Union* (New York: J. D. Torrey, 1862), 133; Joseph A. Stout Jr.: *Schemers and Dreamers: Filibustering in Mexico, 1848–1921* (Fort Worth: Texas Christian University Press, 2002), 64–65; Robert E. May, *The Southern Dream of a Caribbean Empire: 1854–1861* (Baton Rouge: Louisiana State University Press, 1973), 90–91.

27. *Boston Daily Atlas*, September 6, 1852; *New York Weekly Herald*, October 23, 1862; Charles H. Brown, *Agents of Manifest Destiny: The Lives and Times of the Filibusters* (Chapel Hill: University of North Carolina Press, 1980), 94–95, 101–5, 117–19.

28. C. Brown, *Agents of Manifest Destiny*, 75–88; *Baltimore Sun*, August 23, 1852.

29. Act of April 20, 1818 (3 stat. 447); "The Neutrality Law," *New York Times*, June 8, 1866.

30. Stout, *Schemers and Dreamers*, 41.

31. The *New Orleans Daily Evening Picayune*, December 4, 1861, lists Senator John Henderson as an attendee of Lone Star Division, No. 3. *Zanesville (Ohio) Daily Courier*, April 13, 1861; Milton, *Abraham Lincoln and the Fifth Column*, 66. The OLS constitution pledges to "diffuse throughout the world the principles of liberty and republicanism." On its cover, a warrior is pictured gazing at a city (perhaps Havana) with a large, lone star on the horizon; beneath the image appears the Latin aphorism, "Forti et fideli nil difficile" [fortitude and fidelity are not difficult] (*Constitution of the Order of the Lone Star*, City of Lafayette [New Orleans: printed at the *Daily Delta* Office, 1851], Library of Congress Archives).

32. *New York Daily News*, March 18, 1855; Rausch, *American Interest in Cuba*, 228.

33. "The Order of the Lone Star," *Baltimore Sun*, August 26, 1852. The OLS reportedly played a key role in advancing dark-horse Franklin Pierce as the 1852 Democratic presidential candidate. Once Pierce was elected, OLS leaders such as Pierre Soule, John O'Sullivan, and George Sanders were rewarded with diplomatic posts in Europe, where they could directly rail and plot against the tyrannies of monarchical rule (*Zanesville [Ohio] Daily Courier*, April 13, 1861; *New York Times*, August 30, 1861; Rausch, *American Interest in Cuba*, 270).

34. Stephen B. Oates, ed., *Rip Ford's Texas* (Austin: University of Texas Press, 1963), xviii–xxx; David G. McComb, *Texas: A Modern History* (Austin: University of Texas Press, 1989), 46–56.

35. Oates, ed., *Rip Ford's Texas*, 217; W. J. Hughes, *Rebellious Ranger: Rip Ford and the Old Southwest* (Norman: University of Oklahoma Press, 1989), 121–22.

36. *San Antonio Ledger*, April 6, 1854. The *New York Times* of March 13, 1855, indicates that the OLS ritual was composed by General Henderson during the autumn of 1851 at Lafayette, Louisiana, and that the spectacle incorporated was "a theatrical burlesque upon, the trying ordeal undergone by the companions of LOPEZ."

37. Paul N. Spellman, *Forgotten Texas Leader: Hugh McLeod and the Texan Santa Fe Expedition* (College Station: Texas A&M Press, 1999), 163–67; Eric H. Walther and Charles H. Brown, *Agents of Manifest Destiny: The Lives and Times of the Filibusters* (Chapel Hill: University of North Carolina Press, 1980), 273–313; *William Lowndes Yancey: The Coming of the Civil War* (Chapel Hill: University of North Carolina Press, 2006), 209; Oliver T. Morton, *The Southern Empire, With Other Papers* (Boston: Houghton Mifflin, 1892), 48.

38. Walther, *Fire-Eaters*, 85–97 (quote at 94). Rausch, *American Interest in Cuba*, 228, indicates that Quitman was a leading member of the OLS's Supreme Council.

39. Walther, *Fire-Eaters*, 99,104–7; Robert E. May, *John A. Quitman: Old South Crusader* (Baton Rouge: Louisiana State University Press, 1985), 228.

40. May, *John A. Quitman*, 279; *Baltimore Sun*, August 26, 1852. Quitman's lingering influence was so instrumental that several accounts indicate the KGC was "instituted in Mississippi during the year 1854 . . . to cultivate the martial spirit of [the South]" (*New York Herald*, March 21, 1860; Wallace Putnam Reed, *History of Atlanta Georgia* [Syracuse, N.Y.:

D. Mason, 1889], 92). "The K. G. C.," *Natchez (Miss.) Daily Free Trader,* April 11, 1860, stated that "Gen. Quitman was the founder of the order of the K. G. C."

41. May, *Manifest Destiny's Underworld,* 110; May, *John A. Quitman,* 270–94; May, *Southern Dream of a Caribbean Empire,* 49–51. Diane Neal and Thomas W. Kremm, *The Lion of the South: General Thomas C. Hindman* (Macon, Ga.: Mercer University Press, 1993), 26, indicate that Hindman received the June 1854 circular letter and enrolled ten men from Helena, Arkansas. T. S. Anderson to Quitman, April 24, 1854, MS Am 798, item no. 4, noted that John S. Ford raised a company of Texas Rangers and a corps of mounted riflemen. J. McDonald to Quitman, March 26, 1854; and item nos. 115–120, confirming Hindman's participation, John Anthony Quitman Papers, Houghton Library, Harvard University.

42. Quitman to C. A. L. Lamar, New Orleans, January 5, 1855, MS Am 798, item no. 171, John Anthony Quitman Papers, Houghton Library, Harvard University. This letter labeled "highly confidential" further indicates that to avoid a breach of the U.S. neutrality laws, the arming of the men was to take place outside U.S. territory and that influential men in Mexico had agreed to turn over their ports near Cuba so that Quitman could launch his expedition from Mexican territory.

43. Rauch, *American Interest in Cuba,* 289, citing *Memphis Whig* of June 1854; May, *John A. Quitman,* 290–94. Some supporters urged Quitman to undertake the recruitment privately and integrate obligations as to secrecy before making disclosures regarding the expedition's details (J. R. Dufrocq to John S. Thrasher, January 29, 1855, MS Am 798, item no. 49, Quitman to C. A. L. Lamar, January 5, 1855, MS Am 798, item 171, John Anthony Quitman Papers, Houghton Library, Harvard University).

44. May, *John A. Quitman,* 277; May, *Southern Dream of a Caribbean Empire,* 54–55.

45. May, *John A. Quitman,* 283–87; May, *Southern Dream of a Caribbean Empire,* 59–61; Robert Kagan, *Dangerous Nation* (New York: Knopf, 2006), 241–42.

46. May, *John A. Quitman,* 283–87, 291, 294–95; Kagan, *Dangerous Nation,* 241–42; Walther, *Fire-Eaters,* 108.

47. Walther, *Fire-Eaters,* 109–10.

48. Walther, *Shattering of the Union,* 56–58, 83–84, 109–10, 151.

49. Ibid., 166–69.

50. McComb, *Texas: A Modern History,* 47–56; "Narrative History of Texas Annexation," Texas State Library, www.tsl.state.tx.us/ref/abouttx/annexation/index.html.

51. *K. G. C.: A Full Exposition of the Southern Traitors,* 4, quoting Robert. C. Tyler letter of April 4, 1860, to potential KGC recruits indicating that Tyler had become commander of Maryland's KGC Regiment in early 1859. Bickley later claimed he went to college in Baltimore (*Columbus [Ohio] Crisis,* December 30, 1863).

52. *Texas State Gazette,* April 4, 1854, noted that "the Order of the Lone Star was fast rising into importance" in Washington. Letter from Bickley, President, American Legion, in "K.G. C.," *Norfolk Southern Argus,* April 17, 1861, stating: "In Washington city, within hearing of the President's house, the troops of this Order have been constantly and openly drilled." Bickley later also stated in the *Columbus (Ohio) Crisis,* December 30, 1863: "The emigrants

or troops of the K. G. C. were publicly drilled in Washington, with the full cognizance of the Government."

## CHAPTER TWO: FORMAL ORGANIZATION

1. *Lincoln Assassination Evidence*, 545–46, 1209.

2. Kimmel, *Mad Booths of Maryland*, 158.

3. Robert. C. Tyler to potential KGC recruits, April 6 and 15, 1860, in *K. G. C.: A Full Exposition of the Southern Traitors*, 3–5; Ezra J. Warner, *Generals in Gray: Lives of the Confederate Commanders* (Baton Rouge: Louisiana State University Press, 1959), 312–13, 394–95 n. 482; Stuart W. Sanders, "Robert Charles Tyler: Last American Civil War Confederate General Slain in Combat," *MHQ: The Quarterly Journal of Military History* (June 2006): 1. According to information attributed to W. Ken Tyler, great-great-grandson of General Tyler, Robert Tyler's family had resided in an area between Memphis and Jackson, Tennessee, when he was born in 1833, and Robert moved to Baltimore several years later to reside with his uncle (www.angelfire.com/ga3/confederaterebels/tyler.html).

4. William A. Tidwell with James O. Hall and David Winfred Gaddy, *Come Retribution: The Confederate Secret Service and the Assassination of Lincoln* (Jackson: University Press of Mississippi, 1998), 228–29; copy of Cypriano Ferrandini's KGC captain's commission dated August 6, 1859, in Ferrandini file at James O. Hall Research Center, Surratt Society, Clinton, Md.; "Was Barber at Old Barnum's," *Baltimore Sun*, December 21, 1910.

5. *American Cavalier*, May 28, 1859, Bickley Papers, National Archives. While the *Cavalier* masthead claims that C. P. Curtis is the editor and proprietor, the paper was undoubtedly Bickley's creation.

6. "Letter from Cuba" and "Mexico and Cuba," *American Cavalier*, May 28, 1859, Bickley Papers, National Archives; May, *Southern Dream of a Caribbean Empire*, 163–89.

7. "Letter from Vera Cruz," *American Cavalier*, May 28, 1859, Bickley Papers, National Archives.

8. Howard K. Beale, ed., *The Diary of Edward Bates, 1859–1866* (Washington, D.C.: U.S. Government Printing Office, 1933), 18–19.

9. Samuel Sullivan Cox, *Eight Years in Congress, from 1857 to 1865: Memoirs and Speeches* (New York: D. Appleton, 1865), 134–35; John Bassett Moore, ed., *The Works of James Buchanan: Comprising His Speeches, State Papers, and Private Correspondence*, vol. 9, *1860–1868* (Philadelphia: Lippincott, 1910), 32–33; Walter V. Scholes, *Mexican Politics during the Juarez Regime, 1855–1872* (Columbia: University of Missouri, 1957), 47–55; Jonathon C. Olliff, *Reforma Mexico and the United States: A Search for Alternatives to Annexation, 1854–1861* (Tuscaloosa: University of Alabama Press, 1981), 109.

10. *New Orleans True Delta*, October 10, 1859; Olliff, *Reforma Mexico and the United States*, 98, 139; Brian Hamnett, *Profiles in Power: Juarez* (London: Longman, 1994), 116–30.

11. Frederick Law Olmsted, *A Journey through Texas, or, A Saddle Trip on the Southwestern Frontier* (1857; repr., Austin: University of Texas Press, 1978), 453–57; Morton, *Southern*

*Empire,* 48; Lately Thomas, *Between Two Empires: The Life Story of California's First Sena-tors, William McKendree Gwin* (Boston: Houghton Mifflin, 1969), 292.

12. John Gesick, "The 1855 Callahan Raid into Mexico: Pursuing Indians or Hunting Slaves," *Journal of Big Bend Studies* 19 (2007): 47, 53; Stout, *Schemers and Dreamers,* 40–42.

13. C. A. Bridges, "The Knights of the Golden Circle: A Filibustering Fantasy," *Southwest-ern Historical Quarterly* 44, no. 3 (January 1941): 287, 291 n. 15; Morton, *Southern Empire,* 48; Linda S. Hudson, "The Knights of the Golden Circle in Texas, 1858–1861: An Analysis of the First (Military) Degree Knights," in *The Southern Star of the Confederacy: Texas during the Civil War,* ed. Kenneth W. Howell (Denton: University of North Texas Press, 2009), 54; Olliff, *Reforma Mexico and the United States,* 98, 139.

14. *Degree Book: First, or Company Degree of the 28,* Bickley Papers, National Archives. Mexico's Liberal cabinet did consider (but subsequently rejected) the use of "10,000 Yankee mercenaries" around this time (Bridges, "Knights of the Golden Circle," 291; Oliff, *Reforma Mexico and the United States,* 139).

15. "Letter from New York [From Our Own Correspondent]," dated June 16, 1859, in *San Francisco Daily Evening Bulletin,* July 14, 1859; *Augusta (Ga.) Chronicle,* June 18, 1859, post-ing a similar report based on "the *New York Tribune* of Tuesday."

16. "Letter from New York [From Our Own Correspondent]," dated June 16, 1859, in *San Francisco Daily Evening Bulletin,* July 14, 1859. The *Baltimore Sun* of June 23, 1859, de-scribes the script as "a certificate of the Knights of the Golden Circle for one dollar, issued to the name of Glister, and signed R. C. Tyler, secretary, George Bickley, commander. It is made payable in 1865, with interest at ten percent, in land, at $1 per acre or in specie, at the city of Andalusia. It bears the emblematic circle of the order and some hieroglyphics."

17. *New York Herald Tribune,* June 15, 1859.

18. "Manifest Destiny: The 'Knights of the Golden Circle,'" *New York Times,* August 23, 1859, containing Bickley's letter of July 20, 1859, from White Sulphur Springs, Virginia, origi-nally published in the *Baltimore Daily Exchange.*

19. "The K. G. C. in Action," *Arkansas True Democrat,* September 7, 1859.

20. William Kauffman Scarborough, ed., *The Diary of Edmund Ruffin* (Baton Rouge: Louisiana State University Press, 1972), 1: 330–34.

21. Thomas W. Cutrer, *Ben McCulloch and the Frontier Military Tradition* (Chapel Hill: University of North Carolina Press, 1993), 164; Charles Pinnegar, *Brand of Infamy: A Bi-ography of John Buchanan Floyd* (Westport, Ct.: Greenwood, 2002), 62–63; Douglas Lee Gibbony, ed., *Littleton Washington's Journal: Life in Antebellum Washington, Vigilante San Francisco and Confederate Richmond* (Washington, D.C.: Xibris, 2001), 159, entry for Sep-tember 8, 1859.

22. Scarborough, ed., *Diary of Edmund Ruffin,* 1: 330–34.

23. John Jennings, *The Virginia Springs, and Springs of the South and West* (Philadel-phia: Lippincott, 1859): 119–25: The Greenbrier, www.greenbrier.com/site/about-history .aspx.

24. "The K. G. C. in Action," *Arkansas True Democrat,* September 7, 1859. The initials of the reporter, who claimed to be "a Northern man," were "R. L. A." The *Arkansas True*

*Democrat* notes that it had received the story from "an exchange which appears to have been originally copied from the New York Tribune." The paper indicates that a branch of the "new secret society" was being organized in Little Rock.

25. Ibid.

26. Ibid.

27. W. E. Woodruff, *With the Light Guns in '61-'65: Reminiscences of Eleven Arkansas, Missouri and Texas Light Batteries in the Civil War* (Little Rock, Ark.: Central Printing Co., 1903), 5, www.researchonline.net/arcw/history/00785.pdf; *Macon (Ga.) Telegraph,* August 28, 1862. The *Janesville (Wisc.) Weekly Gazette and Free Press,* indicates that Tolar had a major's commission signed on July 4, 1859, by Bickley and James Waldmeyers, brigadier general and secretary of war of the KGC's American Legion. Copy of Ferrandini commission in "Ferrandini" file at the James O. Hall Research Center, Clinton, Md.; Tidwell, *Come Retribution,* 228-29, 239 n. 6.

28. "The K. G. C. in Action," *Arkansas True Democrat,* September 7, 1859. Writing from prison, Bickley later published the platform that he said resulted from the Greenbrier conference endorsing the continuation of slavery and proposing "to try to acquire a sufficiency of territory South of our present national boundaries to give an equal representation to the Southern as to the Northern States" (*Columbus [Ohio] Crisis,* December 30, 1864).

29. "K. G. C. Proclamation," September 12, 1859, by George Bickley, K. G. C., "Prest. American Legion," in *Rules, Regulations and Principles of the K. G. C.,* issued by Order of the Congress of the K. C. S. and the General President, Head-Quarters, Washington City, D.C. (New York: Benj. Urner, Printer, 1859), 1-7, Bickley Papers, National Archives.

30. *Rules, Regulations and Principles of the K. G. C.,* 8-40, containing General Order 52 at 19-24; *Degree Book,* Bickley Papers, National Archives.

31. "Laws of the American Legion, K. G. C. Military Department," in *Rules, Regulations and Principles of the K. G. C.,* 8-40.

32. "General Order 52," issued from "Headquarters, American Legion, K. G. C., Washington D.C., Sept. 12, 1859," in *Rules, Regulations and Principles of the K. G. C.,* 19-24.

33. "Laws of the American Legion, K. G. C., Military Department," in *Rules, Regulations and Principles of the K. G. C.,* 9-19.

34. This *Degree Book* was found among Bickley's possessions at the time of his July 1863 capture. From its context, this *Degree Book* appears to be nonpublic and drafted in 1859 since it references the social maxims of the "Regulations." While no code has been found to this early *Degree Book,* the bracketed entries are suggested by the context or from the code for later KGC rituals (Bickley Papers, National Archives).

35. *Degree Book,* Bickley Papers, National Archives.

36. David M. Potter, *The Impending Crisis: 1848-1861* (New York: Harper Collins, 1976), 197, indicates that James D. B. DeBow, the editor of *DeBow's Review,* advocated making New Orleans the commercial center of a rich tropical empire. The entry "Knights of the Golden Circle" in William S. Powell, ed., *Encyclopedia of North Carolina* (Chapel Hill: University of North Carolina, 2006), 651-52, notes that Charles Henry Foster's *Murfreesboro (N.C.) Citizen* pushed for territorial acquisition outside federal authority.

37. William C. Davis, *Rhett: The Turbulent Life and Times of a Fire-Eater* (Columbia: University of South Carolina Press, 2001), 377; Walther, *Fire-Eaters*, 48, 148, 150.

38. Emerson David Fife, *The Presidential Election of 1860* (New York: Macmillan, 1922), 148, citing *Congressional Globe*, 36th Cong., 1st sess., vol. 1, 571; Percy Lee Rainwater, *Mississippi: Storm Center of Secession: 1850–1861* (Baton Rouge: Claitor, 1938), 72.

39. Clement Eaton, "Henry A. Wise and the Virginia Fire Eaters of 1856," *Mississippi Valley Historical Review* 21, no. 4 (March 1935): 506.

40. Eric H. Walther, *William Lowndes Yancey: The Coming of the Civil War* (Chapel Hill: University of North Carolina Press, 2006), 209, 219–20; May, *Manifest Destiny's Underworld*, 249; Joseph Hodgson, *The Cradle of the Confederacy; Or, The Times of Troup, Quitman and Yancey* (Mobile: printed at the Register Publishing Office, 1876), 292–94; Scarborough, ed., *Diary of Edmund Ruffin*, 1:188–89, entry for May 14, 1858.

41. Andrew Dickson White, "The Conspiracy to Break up the Union, the Plot and Its Development: Breckinridge and Lane the Candidates of a Disunion Party" (Washington, D.C., August 1860), 85, in *The American Party Battle: Election Campaign Pamphlets, 1828–1876*, ed. Joel H. Sibley, vol. 2, *1854–1876* (Cambridge: Harvard University Press, 1999); Allan Nevins, *The Emergence of Lincoln: Douglas, Buchanan, and Party Chaos, 1857 to 1859* (New York: Scribner's Sons, 1950), 1: 414–18.

42. William Yancey to Louis Wigfall, April 16, 1858, Louis Wigfall Papers, Library of Congress, Washington, D.C.

43. Walther, *William Lowndes Yancey*, 222; Walther, *Fire-Eaters*, 71.

44. *Louisville Democrat*, September 2, 1860, which says Yancey knew more about the Knights than he chose to tell. Ollinger Crenshaw, *The Slave States in the Presidential Election of 1860* (Gloucester, Mass.: Peter Smith, 1969), 110, citing *Athens (Ga.) Southern Watchman*, which states that the KGC was thought to be Yancey's "Southern League" by another name.

45. Chester G. Hearn, *Companions in Conspiracy: John Brown and Gerrit Smith* (Gettysburg, Pa.: Thomas, 1996), 57–67.

46. Titone, *My Thoughts Be Bloody*, 208–14; *Lincoln Assassination Evidence*, 1391–92: statement of Grover Wren; Asia Booth Clarke, *The Unlocked Book: A Memoir of John Wilkes Booth by His Sister* (New York: G. P. Putnam's Sons, 1938), 113–14.

47. "A Baltimore 'K. G. C.,'" *New York Herald*, November 3, 1859, containing "Letter to the Editor" from R. C. Tyler, Col. First Maryland Regiment K.G.C., October 31, 1859.

48. Hearn, *Companions in Conspiracy*, 41–56, 67–80.

49. Henry T. Shanks, *The Secession Movement in Virginia: 1847–1861* (New York: AMS, 1971), 92; William A. Link, *Roots of Secession: Slavery and Politics in Antebellum Virginia* (Chapel Hill: University of North Carolina Press, 2002), 191–92.

50. "A Soldier of Fortune," *New York Times*, April 7, 1860, indicates that at least one KGC castle existed in the Bowery. *New York Herald*, December 9, 1859; "Henry Clay Pate," http://kansasboguslegislature.org/mo/pate_h_c.html.

51. Alvy L. King, *Louis Wigfall: Southern Fire-Eater* (Baton Rouge: Louisiana State University Press, 1970), 79; Dale Somer, "James P. Newcomb: The Making of a Texas Radical," *Southwestern Historical Quarterly* 72, no. 4 (April 1969): 449, 455.

## CHAPTER THREE: THE DRIVE FOR MEXICO

1. "Third Annual Message," December 19, 1859, in *Works of James Buchanan*, ed. J. Moore, 10: 339, 353–59.

2. *K. G. C.: First, or Military Degree*, 7.

3. Jack Thorndyke Greer, *Leaves from a Family Album [Holcombe and Greer]*, ed. Jane Judge Greer (Waco, Texas: Texian Press, printers, 1975), 34. Greer's January 26, 1860 "Appeal" is also reproduced in James O. Hall, "A Magnificent Charlatan: George Washington Lafayette Bickley Made a Career of Deceit," *Civil War Times Illustrated* 18, no. 10 (February 1980): 40–41.

4. Greer, *Leaves from a Family Album*, 33–50; Elizabeth Wittenmeyer Lewis, *Queen of the Confederacy: The Innocent Deceits of Lucy Holcombe Pickens* (Denton: University of North Texas Press, 2002), 36–46, 60–61.

5. Greer, *Leaves from a Family Album*, 33–50; Handbook of Texas Online: "Greer, Elkanah Bracken"; Warner, *Generals in Gray*, 118.

6. At one point, Greer gave a characteristically abbreviated speech to a Texas regiment leaving for the Civil War that consisted of "Fellow Soldiers: Deeds not Words." It brought down the house (Letter [undated] from Colonel Phil Crump of Jefferson, Texas, Greer Family Papers, U.S. Military History Institute, Carlisle, Pa.).

7. Clement A. Evans, ed., *Confederate Military History*. A Library of Confederate States History in Seventeen Volumes Written by Distinguished Men of the South. Wilmington, N.C.: Broadfoot, 1987–89 (1899; repr., Wilmington, N.C.: Broadfoot, 1987), 10: 514–17; "David Searcy Greer" and his father "Captain James Greer," in Jonathan Kennan Thompson Smith, ed., *Death Notices from the Christian Advocate, Nashville, Tennessee, 1880-1882 (Of Those Persons Born up to and Including the Year 1830)* (Jackson, Tenn.: J. K. T. Smith, 2000), 32–35, www.tngenweb.org/records/tn_wide/obits/nca/nca7-04.htm.

8. Lewis, *Queen of the Confederacy*, 36–61; Greer, ed., *Leaves from a Family Album [Holcombe and Greer]*, 33–50; Orville Vernon Burton and Georganne B. Burton, eds. *The Free Flag of Cuba: The Lost Novel of Lucy Holcombe Pickens* (Baton Rouge: Louisiana State University Press, 2002).

9. Vicki Betts, ed., "The Memoirs of Horace Chilton, 1858–1873, Part One," *Chronicles of Smith County Texas* 30, no. 1 (Summer 1991): 4–5; Douglas Hale, *The Third Texas Cavalry in the Civil War* (Norman: University of Oklahoma Press, 1993), 47; Handbook of Texas Online: "Chilton, George Washington."

10. During 1858, the ladies of Tyler presented George Chilton with a large flag containing the KGC's Maltese cross superimposed on Texas's seven-point star with the name "Tyler Guards" in its center and containing ten red stripes and nine white stripes that represented both the Deep South's slave states as well as the slave territories that the KGC planned to acquire (Allan K. Sumrall, *Battle Flags of Texas in the Confederacy* [Austin: Eakin, 1995], 23; Hudson, "Knights of the Golden Circle in Texas," 53).

11. E. Greer to John Theodore Holcombe, February 8, 1860, in Greer, ed. *Leaves from a Family Album*, 35–36.

12. Llerena Friend, *Sam Houston: The Great Designer* (Austin: University of Texas Press, 1954), 298, citing *State Gazette for the Campaign*, July 25, 1857; Walter H. Bell, "Knights of the Golden Circle: Its Organization and Activities in Texas Prior to The Civil War" (master's thesis, Texas College of Arts and Industry, 1965), 76, quoting from Greer to Houston, February 20, 1860, *Governor's Letters*, Texas State Library Archives, Austin.

13. Friend, *Sam Houston*, 298– 308; Jerry D. Thompson, ed., *Fifty Miles and a Fight: Major Samuel Peter Heintzelman's Journal of Texas and the Cortina War* (Austin: Texas State Historical Society, 1998), 184 n. 41; Crenshaw, "Knights of the Golden Circle," 42; Dunn, "The KGC in Texas, 1860–1861," 548. Fife, *Presidential Campaign of 1860*, 145, indicates that in March 1860, several northern newspapers, including the *Chicago Herald*, supported the need for a protectorate and eventually "control and final absorption of Mexico."

14. Houston to Elkanah Greer, February 29, 1860, in *The Writings of Sam Houston: 1813–1863*, ed. Amelia W. Williams and Eugene Barker (Austin: University of Texas Press, 1942), 7: 495.

15. Houston to Ben McCulloch, February 13, 1860, in *Writings of Sam Houston*, ed. Williams and Barker, 7: 473–75; Houston to John Floyd, February 13, 1860, ibid.

16. Marquis James, *The Raven: A Biography of Sam Houston* (Austin: University of Texas Press, 1929), 394–95; Nathan Howard, "The Texas Rangers in the Civil War," *Southern Historian* 23 (Spring 2002): 43–50.

17. Sam Houston, "To the People of Texas," March 23, 1860; Sam Houston, "To John S. Ford," March 24, 1860, in *Writings of Sam Houston*, ed. Williams and Barker, 7:538–41; Bell, "Knights of the Golden Circle," 82; Spellman, *Forgotten Texas Leader*, 164–67.

18. Michael L. Collins, *Texas Devils: Rangers and Regulars on the Lower Rio Grande, 1846–1861* (Norman: University of Oklahoma Press, 2008), 183–220; Hudson, "Military Knights of the Golden Circle in Texas," 173–212; David C. Jones to Editor of the *Telegraph*, November 16, 1860, in Jimmie Hicks, "Some Letters Concerning the Knights of the Golden Circle in Texas, 1860–1861," *Southeastern Historical Quarterly* 65, no. 1 (July 1961): 83–84.

19. James Pike, *The Scout and Ranger: Being the Personal Adventures of Corporal Pike of the Fourth Ohio Cavalry* (Cincinnati: Hawley, 1865), 137–39.

20. *San Antonio Ledger and Texan*, February 11, 1860, citing the *McKinney Messenger* and *Dallas Herald*.

21. Dunn, "KGC in Texas, 1860–1861," 548; Crenshaw, "Knights of the Golden Circle," 42; Bell, "Knights of the Golden Circle," 83–85. Hudson, "Military Knights of the Golden Circle in Texas," 193–94, 178, indicates that Thomas Carothers, a KGC castle leader in Huntsville, Texas, was Sam Houston's cousin and 1859 campaign manager.

22. *New York Herald*, May 3, 1860.

23. Collins, *Texas Devils*, 189, quoting from Robert E. Lee to A. M. Lea, March 1, 1860, Sam Houston Papers, Texas State Library and Archives, Austin.

24. *Louisville Journal*, July 18, 1861.

25. Olliff, *Reforma Mexico and the United States*, 139–49. Back in July 1859, it appears that Bickley was leaning toward Mexico's Conservative, or clerical, Party since he refers to the Liberal Party as "daring demagogues" who drew support from "the Negroes, mulattoes,

peons, 'greasers,' and the very scum of Mexican society" (*New York Times*, August 23, 1859, publishing Bickley's July 20, 1859, letter to the *Baltimore Daily Exchange*).

26. Samuel Sullivan Cox, *Eight Years in Congress, from 1857 to 1865: Memoirs and Speeches* (New York: Appleton, 1865), 140, from Congressman Cox's address of March 19, 1860.

27. Ibid., 151.

28. *Congressional Globe*, 36th Cong., 1st sess., pt. II (April 10, 1861): 1632.

29. "Mexican Affairs—K. G. C.'s," *Norfolk Southern Argus*, April 9, 1860.

30. *Montgomery (Ala.) Daily Confederation*, April 18, 1860, quoting correspondent from *Richmond (Va.) Dispatch*.

31. *Petersburg (Va.) Press*, February 7, 1860; "Gen. V. D. Groner," in Dr. R. A. Brock, *Virginia and Virginians* (Spartanburg, S.C.: Reprint Company, 1973), 2: 553–55; W.E.C., "Gen. V. D. Groner," *Confederate Veteran* 12, no. 4 (1904): 294–95; William H. Steward, ed., *History of Norfolk County Virginia and Representative Citizens* (Chicago: Biographical Publishing, 1902), 610; Thomas C. Parramore, with Peter C. Stewart and Tommy L. Bogger, *Norfolk: The First Four Centuries* (Charlottesville: University Press of Virginia, 1994), 198.

32. *Daily Ohio Statesman*, March 30, 1860, April 7, 1860, quoting report from "a Baltimore paper" and April 2, 1860, report from the *Memphis Avalanche*.

33. *New York Herald*, March 21, 1860.

34. *Yazoo Democrat* (Yazoo City, Miss.), April 7, 1860; *Louisville Courier*, May 30, 1861, citing Congressman Cox's statement in *Congressional Globe*, March 19, 1861.

35. *San Antonio Ledger and Texan*, February 2, 1860, quoting from *Dallas Herald*.

36. Bell, "Knights of the Golden Circle," 78, citing *Dallas Herald*, March 28, 1960.

37. "The K. G.C.'s," *Little Rock Old Line Democrat*, April 5, 1860; "Scott-Yarbrough House," Auburn Heritage Association, www.auburnheritage.org/history-markers.html; Shelby County, Tenn.—Census—1870, Memphis Ward No. 4, http://files/usgwarchives.net/tn/shelby/census/1870/1870-memphis-ward4.txt.

38. *Washington, D.C., Constitution*, March 13, 1860; *New York Herald*, March 19, 1860, from the *New Orleans Courier*, March 6, 1860; Dunn, "KGC in Texas," 552–53.

39. *Macon Daily Telegraph*, March 23, 1860; *New York Herald*, April 5, 1860; Dunn, "KGC in Texas," 553; Henry C. Castellanos, *New Orleans As It Was: Episodes of Louisiana Life* (repr., Baton Rouge: Louisiana State University Press, 2006), ix–xiii; *Montgomery (Ala.) Daily Confederate*, March 23, 1860; Bruce S. Allardice, *Confederate Colonels: A Biographical Register* (Columbia: University of Missouri Press, 2008), 202–3: "Howard, James Ross."

40. "The Knights of the Golden Circle," *Norfolk Southern Argus*, April 7, 1860. The *Montgomery (Ala.) Daily Confederate*, March 25, 1860, indicates that in a subsequent interview, one of these Virginia gentlemen (likely Groner) gave assurance that KGC prospects were never more favorable than at the present time, that their commander [Bickley] had never issued a single order without its first being forwarded to the U.S. secretary of state, and that the KGC was based on the recognition that the North would never allow any more slave states in the Union. The *Natchez (Miss.) Daily Free Trader*, March 30, 1860, indicates that a "distinguished" KGC member will be addressing the citizens of Vicksburg, Mississippi, shortly.

41. "The Knights of the Golden Circle," *Norfolk Southern Argus*, April 7, 1860.

42. *Washington, D.C., Constitution,* March 28, 1860; *New York Herald-Tribune,* March 31, 1860.

43. Crenshaw, "Knights of the Golden Circle," 34 n. 46; Wallace Putnam Reed, ed., *History of Atlanta, Georgia: With Illustrations and Biographical Sketches of Some of Its Prominent Men and Pioneers* (D. Mason, 1889), 90–91.

44. May, *Southern Dream of a Caribbean Empire,* 151 n. 25, citing letter to Alexander Stephens, March 22, 1860, Stephens Papers, Library of Congress; *Augusta Daily Constitutionalist,* March 21, 1860; Reed, *History of Georgia,* 91; *Charleston (S.C.) Courier Tri-Weekly,* March 24, 1860.

45. *Macon (Ga.) Weekly Telegraph,* April 7, 1860.

46. Dunn, "KGC in Texas," 550–51 n. 21; *Macon (Ga.) Telegraph,* April 2, 1860; *New York Herald,* March 21, 1860; *Weekly Raleigh (N.C.) Register,* February 8, 1860, citing the *Petersburg (Va.) Press.*

47. *Petersburg (Va.) Press,* January 28, 1860, citing correspondent of the *Charleston Mercury;* Hudson, "Knights of the Golden Circle in Texas," 54, 65 n. 7.

48. Bridges, "Knights of the Golden Circle," 1, 5 n. 25, quoting *Dallas Herald,* April 4, 1860.

49. *Baton Rouge Daily Gazette & Comet,* April 5, 1860; *New York Times,* April 3, 1860.

50. *New York Herald,* May 3, 1860, containing report from Matamoras of April 19, 1860.

51. Thompson, ed., *Fifty Miles and a Fight,* 230–31; *Petersburg (Va.) Press,* January 28, 1860; *Address to the Citizens of the Southern States by Order of the Convention of K. G. C. held at Raleigh, N. C.,* May 7–11, 1860, http://gunshowonthenet.com/AfterTheFact/KGC/KGC0571860.html (hereafter *KGC Address to the Citizens of the Southern States*).

52. *New York Herald,* March 10, 1860; Olliff, *Reforma Mexico and the United States,* 146–48.

53. Bell, "Knights of the Golden Circle," 80, citing Williams, ed., *The Writings of Sam Houston, 1813-1863,* 7: 534; "Voice of America" *Dallas Morning News,* May 29, 1948, citing Houston's Official Notice; *New York Herald,* May 3, 1860.

54. Card signed by J. D. Howell and W. M. Rainey in *New Orleans True Delta,* April 5, 1860, cited in Bell, "Knights of the Golden Circle," 87, and in Reed, *History of Atlanta, Georgia* (Syracuse, N.Y.: D. Mason, 1889), 91. *New Orleans Times-Picayune,* April 5, 1860; *Daily Columbus (Ga.) Enquirer,* April 7, 1860.

55. Bell, "Knights of the Golden Circle," 88, citing *Washington, D.C., National Intelligencer,* April 11, 1860, quoting *Charleston Mercury.*

56. James T. McIntosh, ed., *The Papers of Jefferson Davis* (Baton Rouge: Louisiana State University Press, 1992), 3: 331–33 n. 6; Ishbel Ross, *First Lady of the South: The Life of Mrs. Jefferson Davis* (New York: Harper and Brothers, 1958), 42; H. Forno to Quitman, January 22, 1855, MS Am 796, item 60–61, John Anthony Quitman Papers; William C. Davis, *Jefferson Davis: The Man and His Hour* (Baton Rouge: Louisiana State University Press, 1991), 135, 263.

57. *Little Rock (Ark.) Old Line Democrat,* April 5, 1860.

58. *New Orleans Evening Picayune,* April 5, 1860; Bell, "Knights of the Golden Circle," 87. In his memoirs, General William Sherman writes of being visited in New Orleans by "a

high officer in the order of 'Knights of the Golden Circle'" sometime before November 1860 (William T. Sherman, *Memoirs of General William T. Sherman* [repr., New York: Library of America, 1990], 171).

59. *Macon (Ga.) Daily Telegraph,* April 10, 1860; Bell, "Knights of the Golden Circle," 88, quoting *Tyler Reporter,* May 16, 1860.

60. Warner, *Generals in Gray,* 289: "William Edwin Starke." Thompson, ed., *Fifty Miles and a Fight,* 237 n. 26, indicates that the mysterious "g" [Greenborough?] was the one who became suspicious and asked for proof regarding the KGC's wherewithal. "Greenborough" is alternatively spelled "Greenhow" and "Greenough" in various newspapers (*New York Herald,* April 8, 1860; *Macon Weekly Telegraph,* April 14, 1961).

61. *Macon (Ga.) Telegraph,* April 14, 1860. A detailed reply to the New Orleans charges was made by Bickley's nephew Charles in a letter to the Raleigh Press (*Norfolk Southern Argus,* May 15, 1861, cited at Crenshaw, "Knights of the Golden Circle," 39 n. 69).

62. *KGC Address to the Citizens of the Southern States,* 23.

63. Ibid., 22, quoting statement by Major Henry C. Castellanos, Marshall, Texas, April 17, 1860.

64. Reed, *History of Atlanta, Georgia,* 92.

65. Bell, "Knights of the Golden Circle," 86–87, quoting from *[S. P.] Heintzelman Journal,* April 25, 1860, Library of Congress; Thompson, ed., *Fifty Miles and a Fight,* 237 n. 26. Stephen Dando-Collins, *Tycoon's War: How Cornelius Vanderbilt Invaded a Country to Overthrow America's Most Famous Military Adventurer* (Cambridge, Mass.: Da Capo Press, 2008), 293, 400, indicates that Lockridge was Walker's recruiter in New Orleans and assumed a substantial command in Nicaragua. Hudson, "Knights of the Golden Circle in Texas," 58, notes that Lockridge was a Knight.

66. *New York Times,* April 20, 1860.

67. *K. G. C.: A Full Exposure of the Southern Traitors and the Knights of the Golden Circle,* citing Tyler's April 15, 1860, letter to a potential recruit in Boston. Lockridge had recently deserted Walker and was contemplating his own colonizing expedition to northern Mexico, which would have given him an incentive to undercut the Knights' efforts (Brown, *Agents of Manifest Destiny,* 445). In late 1861, the "filibusters formerly known as the Knights of the Golden Circle" were reported as virtually controlling New Orleans ("New Orleans and Secession," *Cedar Valley [Iowa] Times,* December 12, 1860, from the *Philadelphia North American*).

68. *Montgomery (Ala.) Daily Confederation,* May 2, 1860.

69. *K. G. C.: A Full Exposure of the Southern Traitors: The Knights of the Golden Circle,* 5–8, containing General Order No. 546 and "Circular Letter" transmitted from "Head-quarters, American Legion, K. G. C., Mobile Alabama, April 6, 1860," by "James Ross Howard, K. G. C." to "Col. R. C. Tyler, First Maryland Regiment, K. G. C.; "Howard, James Ross," in Bruce S. Allardice, *Confederate Colonels: A Biographical Register* (Columbia: University of Missouri Press, 2008), 202–3; Robert J. Driver, *The First and Second Maryland Infantry, C. S. A.* (Bowie, Md.: Heritage, 2004), 5.

70. *KGC Address to the Citizens of the Southern States,* 21–22.

# CHAPTER FOUR: A REGIONAL COALITION

1. "General Order No. 546" and "Circular Letter" from "George Bickley, K. G. C., President American Legion" transmitted from "Head-quarters, American Legion, K. G. C., Mobile Alabama, April 6, 1860, Special Order," by "James Ross Howard, K. G. C." to "Col. R. C. Tyler, First Maryland Regiment, K. G. C.," found in *K. G. C.: A Full Exposure of the Southern Traitors: The Knights of the Golden Circle*, 5–8. A slightly different version of General Order 546, and the "Circular Letter," as sent from Mobile on April 6, 1860, by "Geo. Bickley" to "Col. V. D. Groner," appears in the *Norfolk Southern Argus*, April 17, 1860.

2. "Circular Letter" from Howard to Tyler, April 6, 1860, 6–7. The enumeration that appears in the Bickley "Circular Letter" to Groner in the *Norfolk Southern Argus*, April 17, 1860, also includes "S. J. Richardson of Texas" but excludes "Lieut. Col. Tillery of S. C."

3. "Circular Letter" from Howard to Tyler, April 6, 1860, 7.

4. Ibid.; E. Greer "to the K's. G. C. of Tennessee, Mississippi, Louisiana, and Alabama," January 26, 1860, in *Leaves from a Family Album*, 34. The *Little Rock (Ark.) True Democrat*, May 9, 1861, reports castles of six hundred Knights in Little Rock. "Camden's Golden Knights," *Ouachita Valley Ledger* (1981), 1–2, reports several Knights' castles in Camden, Arkansas.

5. "Circular Letter" from Howard to Tyler, April 6, 1860, 7. The *Petersburg (Va.) Press*, February 7, 1860, describes Groner's KGC coordinating role for Norfolk, Petersburg, Richmond, Virginia. Dr. Thomas C. Parramore, *Trial Separation: Murfreesboro, North Carolina and the Civil War* (Murfreesboro Historical Association, 1998), 14, describes expansion of KGC into North Carolina. R. C. Tillery, who had attended the Knights' August 1859 Greenbrier convention, subsequently served in Col. Ashby's Virginia Cavalry Regiment during the Civil War (*Macon [Ga.] Daily Telegraph*, August 28, 1862).

6. "Circular Letter" from Howard to Tyler, April 6, 1860, 7; *Little Rock (Ark.) Old Line Democrat*, April 5, 1860; "H. C. Young," 1870 Shelby County, Tennessee Census, Memphis Ward No. 4, http://files.usgwarchives.org/tn/shelby/census/1870/1870-memphis-ward4.txt.

7. "Circular Letter" from Howard to Tyler, April 6, 1860, 7. R. A. Crawford fought in Bartow's First Georgia Regulars during the Civil War ("Col. R. A. Crawford," *Courant American*, Cartersville, Georgia, May 19, 1892, 4, www.gabartow.org/obits.CrawfordRA.shtml). Bickley's "Circular Letter" to "Col. R. C. Tyler, First Maryland Regiment, K. G. C.," found in *K. G. C.: A Full Exposure of the Southern Traitors: The Knights of the Golden Circle*, 5–8, also mentions "a regiment forming in South Carolina, by Lt. Col. S. H. Tillery." "Samuel H. Tillery, who had been born in South or North Carolina around 1833 and resided in Washington County, Texas in 1860, is listed as a member of Terry's Texas Rangers" (The Online Archives of Terry's Texas Rangers, www.terrytexasrangers.org/biographical_notes/t/tillery_sh.htm).

8. "Circular Letter" from Howard to Tyler, April 6, 1860, 7–8.

9. White, "The Conspiracy to Break up the Union," in *The American Party Battle: Election Campaign Pamphlets, 1828–1876*, ed. Joel H. Sibley (Cambridge: Harvard University Press, 1999), 88; Davis, *Rhett*, 379–80; Walther, *Fire-Eaters*, 72–73, 140; *Nashville Patriot*, July 11, 1860. *An Authentic Exposition of the K. G. C.*, 15, charges that the Knights used their influence

to advance the Democratic rupture as a way to find out how many northern men sympathized with the South. It says a January 1860 speech in the KGC castle of New Orleans swore, "The next administration shall be purely Southern or we will have no administration at all."

10. John Witherspoon Dubose, *The Life and Time of William Lowndes Yancey: A History of Political Parties in the United States, from 1834 to 1864* (New York: Peter Smith, 1942), 2: 457; Potter, *The Impending Crisis*, 407–10.

11. *KGC Address to the Citizens of the Southern States*, 22, reproducing "Card to the K. G. C. of Texas" from Sam J. Richardson, April 27, 1860.

12. Bell, "Knights of the Golden Circle, 91, citing *New Orleans Daily Crescent*, May 18, 1860; Thompson, ed., *Fifty Miles and a Fight*, April 20, 1860.

13. "K. G. C.—Convention of Knights," *Norfolk Southern Argus*, May 14 and 15, 1860 (from the *Raleigh Press* of May 10 and 11). The July 1860 *KGC Address to the Citizens of the Southern States*, 23–35, also contains an edited version of the KGC convention proceedings for the third and fourth day.

14. "K. G. C. —Convention of Knights," *Norfolk Southern Argus*, May 14 and 15, 1860; "Correspondence of the Baltimore Republican, K. G. C. Raleigh, N. C., May 8th, 1860," *Norfolk Southern Argus*, May 14, 1860.

15. *KGC Address to the Citizens of the Southern States*, 27; *Norfolk Southern Argus*, May 15, 1860; Keith Bohannon, "Paul Jones Semmes," in *The Confederate General*, ed. William C. Davis and Julie Hoffman (Harrisburg, Pa.: National Historical Society, 1991), 5: 138–39; *Yazoo Democrat* (Yazoo City, Miss.), August 11, 1860; Lyman H. Clark, "Brig. Gen. Paul Jones Semmes," term paper for "Civil War History" class at Columbus [Ga.] College, indicates that Semmes had been born at Montford's Plantation, Wilkes County, Georgia, on June 4, 1815, and had previously served as brigadier general for militia in the eastern part of Georgia. Joseph McMurran to Semmes, August 7, 1860, Semmes to Maj. W. H. Chase, January 25, 1861, Box 6, Folder 34: Joseph Mahan Collection, Columbus (Ga.) State University Archives.

16. *Norfolk Southern Argus*, May 15, 1860; Overdyke, *The Know-Nothing Party in the South*, 121, 277; Diffee William Standard, *Columbus, Georgia in the Confederacy: The Social and Industrial Life of the Chattahoochee River Port* (New York: William-Frederick Press, 1954), 36–37.

17. "K. G. C.—CONVENTION OF KNIGHTS, Fourth Day," *Norfolk Southern Argus*, May 15, 1860; *KGC Address to the Citizens of the Southern States*, 25–28.

18. "An Open Letter to the Knights of the Golden Circle," from "Geo. Bickley, K. G. C., President of the American Legion," in *Richmond Whig*, July 17, 1860, Bickley Papers, National Archives.

19. Overdyke, *The Know-Nothing Party in the South*, 121, 277; Standard, *Columbus, Georgia in the Confederacy*, 36–37.

20. *Norfolk Southern Argus*, May 15, 1860; T. Conn Bryan, *Confederate Georgia* (Athens: University of Georgia, 1953), 203; Parramore, *Trial Separation*, 14; *Murfreesboro (N.C.) Citizen*, August 30, 1860; "George Goldthwaite," Encyclopedia of Alabama, http://encyclopediaofalabama.org/face/Article.jsp?id=h-2968.

21. *Raleigh Weekly Reporter*, May 16, 1861.

22. *KGC Address to the Citizens of the Southern States*. Also reproduced in *Louisville Daily Democrat*, September 2, 1860, under the title "Address to the Southern People." In the preface to the address, Bickley states that "it has been prepared at intervals while canvassing the State of Virginia in furtherance of the objects of the K. G. C."

23. Ibid., 17–19.

24. Ibid., 14, 17.

25. Ibid., 7, 16.

26. Ibid., 7, 19–21, 29.

27. Ibid., 28.

28. "An Open Letter to the Knights of the Golden Circle," *Richmond Whig*, July 17, 1860.

29. *Mobile Tribune*, August 10, 1860.

30. *Washington, D.C., Daily National Intelligencer*, August 3, 1860.

31. *Louisville Democrat*, August 12, 1860.

32. *North Carolina Standard* (Raleigh), August 8, 1860.

33. *KGC Address to the Citizens of the Southern States*, 27.

34. Crenshaw, "Knights of the Golden Circle," 39 n. 70, citing the *Lynchburg Virginian* in the *Charleston Mercury* of January 1, 1861, regarding Bickley's Lynchburg, Virginia visit. The *Middleton, N.Y., Banner of Liberty*, August 22, 1860, indicates that Bickley also spoke in Farmington, Virginia.

35. *Atlanta Daily Intelligencer*, June 30, 1860; *Louisville Democrat*, August 12, 1861. At Norfolk, Bickley was again accompanied by Spangler, Clark, as well as KGC Major Phillips.

36. *Norfolk Southern Argus*, May 16, 1860.

37. *Harrison Flag* (Marshall, Tex.), July 20, 1860.

38. *Washington, D.C., Daily National Intelligencer*, August 3, 1861, citing *Boston Journal*.

39. *Corpus Christi (Tex.) Ranchero*, August 4, September 1, 8, 1860; *Harrison Flag* (Marshall, Tex.), September 22, 1860; Donald E. Reynolds, *Texas Terror: The Slave Insurrection Panic of 1860 and the Secession of the Lower South* (Baton Rouge: Louisiana State University Press, 2007), 1–214; Donald E. Reynolds, *Editors Make War: Southern Newspapers in the Secession Crisis* (Nashville: Vanderbilt University Press, 1966), 98–117.

40. *Little Rock (Ark.) True Democrat*, August 11, 1860.

41. Frazier, *Blood and Treasure*, 14, citing *Dallas Herald*, February 29, 1860; Handbook of Texas Online: "Pryor, Charles R."

42. Bell, "Knights of the Golden Circle," 126, citing *Dallas Herald*, March 28, 1860, states that after a "brilliant cotillion" given in Dallas, another company of Knights left Dallas for the "seat of war." Hudson, "Knights of the Golden Circle in Texas," indicates that in February 1861, Lt. Cryll Miller of the Lancaster [Texas] KGC took the U.S. flag from Camp Cooper as a memento to *Dallas Herald* secessionist editor Charles Pryor (58–59), and that KGC member John Good was captain of the Dallas Light Artillery Company (187).

43. Hudson, "Knights of the Golden Circle in Texas," 55, 65 n. 12.

44. Crenshaw, *Slave States in the Presidential Campaign of 1860*, 92–97; Bell, "Knights of the Golden Circle," reproducing "Financial Degree K. G. C., Opening," 207, 213.

45. Collins, *Texas Devils*, 222.

46. *Harrison Flag* (Marshall, Tex.), September 29, 1860, 2; *Marshall (Tex.) Republican,* July 28, 1860; *Corpus Christi (Tex.) Ranchero,* August 4, 1860; William W. White, "The Texas Slave Insurrection of 1860," *Southwestern Historical Journal* 52, no. 8 (January 1949): 281–82, citing *Daily Picayune,* September 8, 1860.

47. Roy Franklin Nichols, *The Disruption of American Democracy* (New York: Macmillan, 1948), 363–64; Crenshaw, *Slave States in the Presidential Campaign of 1860,* 105–6, citing R. S. Holt to Joseph Holt, November 9, 1860; Stephen A. Channing, *Crisis of Fear: Secession in South Carolina* (New York: Norton, 1974), 264–71.

48. Crenshaw, *Slave States in the Presidential Election of 1860,* 102, citing *Montgomery Daily Mail,* October 24, 1860.

49. "Knights of the Golden Circle," *Murfreesboro (N.C.) Citizen,* August 30, 1860; Overdyke, *The Know-Nothing Party in the South,* 121, 277; Standard, *Columbus, Georgia in the Confederacy,* 36–37.

50. Bell, "Knights of the Golden Circle," 94, citing *New Orleans Daily Crescent,* July 2, 1860, and 97–98, citing the *Harrison Flag* (Marshall, Tex.), August 10, 1860, quoting the *Semiweekly Civilian and Gazette.*

51. *Middleton, N.Y., Banner of Liberty,* August 1, 1860; *New York Herald,* July 24, 1861.

52. *Washington, D.C., Constitution,* August 8, 1860; *Floridian and Journal,* August 8, 1860.

53. Charles Allen Smart, *Viva Juarez: The Life of Benito Juarez (1806-1872), President of Mexico* (London: Eyre and Spottiswoode, 1963), 220–30; *Murfreesboro (N.C.) Citizen,* September 6, 1860.

54. *Corpus Christi (Tex.) Ranchero,* September 15, 22, and 29, 1860.

55. *Little Rock (Ark.) Old-Line Democrat,* September 20, 1860; *Washington, D.C., Constitution,* September 8, 1860, citing the *Norfolk Day Book.*

56. *Baltimore Sun,* September 9, 1860.

57. *Alexandria Gazette and Virginia Advertiser,* September 4, 1860; *New York Herald,* September 10, 1860; Reed, ed., *History of Atlanta Georgia,* 92, citing *Brownsville (Tex.) Intelligencer,* October 12, 1860; *Baltimore Sun,* September 5 and October 1, 1860.

58. "Muster of the K.G.C.'s," *Baltimore Sun,* October 1, 1860, referencing the *Memphis Avalanche.*

## CHAPTER FIVE: TRANSFORMING TO SECESSION

1. According to "Bradley," Spangler specifically referenced as KGC members "Gov. [Isham Green] Harris of Tenn., MR. KNOX WALKER" (likely C. Knox Walker of Memphis, a delegate to the 1860 Democratic Convention), and "W. G. [William Ganaway] BROWNLOW," the outspoken editor of the *Knoxville Whig.* In his simultaneously published response, Dr. Brownlow denied he was a KGC member; he said he heard Bickley speak a few nights before in nearby Athens, Tennessee (where the KGC was reported to have forty-five members), but he knew nothing more than what he heard or saw in the papers ("How Is It—Will Gov. Harris Answer?" *Nashville Republican Banner,* September 15, 1860).

2. "How Is It—Will Gov. Harris Answer?" *Nashville Republican Banner,* September 15, 1860.

3. *Corpus Christi (Tex.) Ranchero,* September 22, 1860.

4. Ibid., September 29, 1860.

5. *Washington, D.C., Constitution,* October 23, 1860; Hubert Howe Bancroft, *The Works,* vol. 16, *History of Texas and the North Mexican States, 1884–89* (San Francisco: Historical Company, 1890), 433, indicates that Bickley and his nephew Charles were "employed to organize 'castles' or lodges in Texas, receiving as remuneration for the work the initiation fees paid by incoming members."

6. *Corpus Christi (Tex.) Ranchero,* October 13 and 27, 1860.

7. Ibid., October 27, 1860; *Constitutional Union,* November 16, 1860, citing Bickley's statement to the *Galveston News.* Bridges, "Knights of the Golden Circle," 10, citing *True Issue,* September 13, 1860, note 57, indicates that a Boston paper reported that Bickley had placed an order with a Massachusetts manufacturer for a large quantity of arms to be delivered in Matamoros during October 1860.

8. Dunn, "KGC in Texas, 1860–1861," 555.

9. Hudson, "Military Knights of the Golden Circle in Texas," 176, indicates that Charles was either George Bickley's nephew or son.

10. "Movements of the K. G. C.," *Norfolk Southern Argus,* November 3, 1860, publishing V. D. G. [Groner] letter.

11. "The 'K. G. C.,'" *San Antonio (Tex.) Alamo Express,* November 15, 1860, referencing the *Austin Southern Intelligencer.*

12. Pike, *Scout and Ranger,* 137–38.

13. "The 'K. G. C.,'" *San Antonio (Tex.) Alamo Express,* November 15, 1860, referencing the *Austin Southern Intelligencer.*

14. Handbook of Texas Online: "George Washington Paschal."

15. *K. G. C. First, or Military Degree,* 4.

16. "The 'K. G. C.,'" *San Antonio (Tex.) Alamo Express,* November 15, 1860, referencing the *Austin Southern Intelligencer.*

17. *K.G.C. First, or Military Degree,* 4.

18. *Corpus Christi (Tex.) Ranchero,* August 4, September 1 and 8, 1980; *Harrison Flag* (Marshall, Tex.), September 22, 1860; Reynolds, *Texas Terror,* 54–77.

19. "Haitian Revolution (1791–1804)," An Online Reference Guide to African American History, by Quintard Taylor, www.blackpast.org/.

20. Dunn, "KGC in Texas, 1860–1861," 555–56.

21. Walter, *Fire-Eaters,* 169–72. Wigfall was reported to have boasted about the KGC at Willard Hotel in Washington City (*Congressional Globe,* 36th Cong., 1st sess., pt. II, 1632).

22. Hicks, "Some Letters Concerning the Knights of the Golden Circle in Texas," 82–84; Bickley to Editor of the *Telegraph,* November 12 and 15, 1860; Hudson, "Military Knights of the Golden Circle in Texas," 188, 204; *Marshall (Tex.) Republican,* November 17, 1860; *Indianola (Tex.) Courier,* November 24, 1860.

23. Kevin R. Young, *To the Tyrants Never Yield: A Texas Civil War Sampler* (Plano, Tex.: Wordware, 1992), 32–33.

24. *Petersburg (Va.) Press*, February 7, 1860; Powell, ed., *Encyclopedia of North Carolina*, 651–52: "Knights of the Golden Circle."

25. *Middletown (N.Y.) Banner of Liberty*, December 19, 1860, citing *Norfolk Day Book;* Bridges, "The Knights of the Golden Circle: A Filibustering Fantasy," 10, citing *New Orleans Picayune*, September 12, 1860.

26. Brock, *Virginia and Virginians*, 2: 553–55; "General V. D. Groner by W. E. C.," *Confederate Veteran* 12, no. 4 (1904): 294–95; Steward, ed., *History of Norfolk County*, 610–11; Parramore, *Norfolk*, 198–99; Elliott L. Story Journal, vol. 6, August 1860, Virginia Historical Society Library.

27. "Movements of the K. G. C.," *Norfolk Southern Argus*, November 3, 1860, publishing V. D. G. [Groner] letter.

28. Jerry Thompson, ed., *Texas and New Mexico on the Eve of the Civil War: The Mansfield and Johnston Inspections, 1859–1861* (Albuquerque: University of New Mexico Press, 2001), 1–6.

29. David Donald, ed., *Inside Lincoln's Cabinet: The Civil War Diaries of Salmon P. Chase* (New York: Longmans, Green, 1954), 125–26, entry for September 8, 1862.

30. Ibid., 126.

31. Samuel Wylie Crawford, *The Genesis of the Civil War: The Story of Sumter* (New York: Charles L. Webster, 1887), 162–67; Joseph Holt's confidential report to President James Buchanan subsequently published in *Congressional Globe, Appendix*, August 6, 1861, 457–58.

32. Walter L. Buenger, *Secession and the Union in Texas* (Austin: University of Texas Press, 1984), 155, citing Reagan to Roberts, November 1, 1860.

33. Robert E. May, *Manifest Destiny's Underworld: Filibustering in Antebellum America*, 251, notes that Reagan was antifilibustering. Hudson, "Military Knights of the Golden Circle in Texas, 1854–1861," 202, states that "Reagan is thought to be a Knight [KGC], due to his membership in the Knights of Palestine." Crenshaw, *The Slave States in the Presidential Election of 1860*, 285, notes that Reagan said he would favor resistance if Lincoln was elected.

34. Oates, ed., *Rip Ford's Texas*, xxxvii; James Smallwood, *Born in Dixie: Smith County Origins to 1875*, vol. 1 of *The History of Smith County, Texas* (Austin, Tex.: Eaton, 1999), 159–61, 167.

35. Bickley to editor of the *Telegraph*, November 3, 1860, in Hicks, "Some Letters Concerning the Knights of the Golden Circle in Texas," 82, in which Bickley claims that during the preceding ten days, he had helped establish seven new Texas castles containing a total of 156 new members and "eleven equipped and provided companies have been tendered and accepted."

36. "The K. G. C.'s," *Texas Republican* (Marshall), November 17, 1860.

37. Bickley to editor of *Telegraph*, November 12, 1860, in Hicks, "Some Letters Concerning the Knights of the Golden Circle in Texas," 82–83.

38. "Knights of the Golden Circle," *Harrison Flag* (Marshall, Tex.), November 17, 1860.

39. *Degree Book, First, or Company Degree of the 28*, Bickley Papers, National Archives.

NOTES TO PAGES 72–76

40. The *Louisville Journal*, July 18, 1861, cites portions of the First Degree ritual used in Kentucky (probably around mid-1860). Since the KGC was then operating on a decentralized regional basis, the ritual used in Kentucky may not have been exactly the same as the one used in Texas.

41. *K. G. C. First, or Military Degree*, 6.

42. Ibid., 2–3, 9; Clayton E. Jewett, *Texas in the Confederacy: An Experiment in Nation Building* (Columbia: University of Missouri Press, 2002), 51–52 n. 13.

43. Bell, "Knights of the Golden Circle," containing "Financial Degree, K. G. C.," 207–17.

44. *Louisville Journal*, July 18, 1861; Mayo Fesler, "Secret Political Societies in the North during the Civil War," *Indiana Magazine of History* 14, no. 3 (September 1918): 183, 198–99.

45. "North Texan" of Sherman, Texas, to the editor, *Louisville Journal*, February 2, 1861.

46. R. H. Williams, *With the Border Ruffians: Memories of the Far West, 1852-1868*, book 2 (London: John Murray, 1908), 169.

47. *Texas Republican* (Marshall), November 17, 1860.

48. Hicks, "Some Letters Concerning the Knights of the Golden Circle in Texas," 82–85.

49. David Stroud, *Flames and Vengeance: The East Texas Fires and the Presidential Election of 1860* (Kilgore, Tex.: Pinecrest, 1992), 80.

50. Bickley to editor of *Telegraph*, November 12 and 15, 1860, in Hicks, "Some Letters Concerning the Knights of the Golden Circle in Texas," 82–84.

51. "An Alabama K. G. C." to the editor, *Montgomery (Ala.) Daily Confederate*, March 25, 1860.

52. Francis Richard Lubbock, *Six Decades in Texas* (Austin: Ben C. Jones, Printers, 1900), 303; *New York Herald*, December 18, 1860. In addition to Marshall, the KGC organized a number of similar prosecession rallies in Galveston and San Antonio at this time (Dunn, "KGC in Texas," 559; Young, *To the Tyrants Never Yield*, 38–39).

53. Bell, "Knights of the Golden Circle," 167, citing *McCulloch Papers* (letter of October 5, 1860), Archives, Barker Library, Austin, Texas.

54. Cutrer, *McCulloch and the Frontier Military Tradition*, 174–75; "Our Texas Correspondence," *Charleston Mercury*, October 31, 1860.

55. Rev. James W. Hunnicutt, *The Conspiracy Unveiled, The South Sacrificed; or, The Horror of Secession* (Philadelphia: Lippincott, 1863), 247, citing *Norfolk Day Book* of early December 1860.

56. A. White, "The Conspiracy to Break up the Union, the Plot and Its Development," 5, also reproduced in Joel H. Sibley, ed., *The American Party Battle* (Cambridge: Harvard University Press, 1999), 92–93; Christopher J. Olsen, *Political Culture and Secession in Mississippi: Masculinity, Honor, and the Antiparty Tradition, 1830-1860* (New York: Oxford University Press, 2000), 183.

57. Pettus to Groner, December 8, 1860, in *Correspondence of Governor John Jones Pettus, 1859-1860, Governor's Records, Series E*, vol. 49, Mississippi Department of Archives and History, Jackson; *New York Herald Tribune*, January 5, 1861; Robert W. Dubay, *John Jones Pettus: Mississippi Fire-Eater: His Life and Times, 1813-1867* (Jackson: University Press of Mississippi, 1975), 75–76.

214

58. Steward, ed., *History of Norfolk County Virginia and Representative Citizens*, 610.

59. Charles Anderson, *Texas, before, and on the Eve of the Rebellion: A Paper Read before the Cincinnati Society of Ex-Army and Navy Officers, January 3, 1884* (Cincinnati: Peter G. Thompson, 1884), 72, 81.

## CHAPTER SIX: THE PARAMILITARY'S CORE

1. *Texas Republican* (Marshall), November 17, 1860; *LaGrange (Tex.) States Right Democrat,* May, 1, 1861. Dabney Lewis, a Knight from Houston County, Texas, similarly described the KGC to his father as "a Southern movement & should there be a war then we are bound to go in defense of the south" (Dabney Lewis letter, January 4, 1861, reproduced in *Sword & Saber,* catalogue no. 78 [summer 1995]).

2. According to Sanford, *Treason Unveiled,* 17–18, the Knights engaged in a concerted effort toward the end of the 1860 presidential campaign to expand their own numbers and sent every available man to establish castles, with the Calhoun Castle of Charleston, South Carolina, credited "with rapid growth of the secession snake."

3. "Knights of the Golden Circle," *Murfreesboro (N. C.) Citizen,* August 30, 1860.

4. John R. Galvin, *The Minute Men: The First Fight: Myths and Realities of the American Revolution* (Washington, D.C.: Potomac, 2006), 10–11.

5. *New York Herald,* November 10, 1860.

6. Stephen A. Channing, *Crisis of Fear: Secession in South Carolina* (New York: Norton, 1974), 269–70 nn. 33 and 37. Stephen A. West, "Minute Men, Yeomen, and the Mobilization for Secession in the South Carolina Upcountry," *Journal of Southern History* 71, no. 1 (February 2005): 82, 87, indicates that the Limestone Springs Guards paraded under a flag emblazoned with a lone star.

7. Channing, *Crisis of Fear,* 269–70 nn. 33 and 37; Walter Brian Cisco, *Wade Hampton: Confederate Warrior, Conservative Statesman* (Washington, D.C.: Brassey's, 2004), 51–53; Warner, *Generals in Gray,* 163–64: "David R. Jones"; Scarborough, *Ruffin, Diary,* 1: 483, 486.

8. *Washington, D.C., Constitution,* October 20, 1860; West, "Minute Men, Yeomen and Secession in the South Carolina Upcountry," 51.

9. West, "Minute Men, Yeomen, and Mobilization for Secession in the South Carolina Upcountry": 89; Channing, *Crisis of Fear,* 269 n. 33.

10. West, "Minute Men, Yeomen, and Mobilization for Secession in the South Carolina Upcountry," 76; *Washington, D.C., Constitution,* November 9, 1860; *New York Herald,* November 9, 1860.

11. Greeley, *American Conflict,* 1: 34 n. 12.

12. The *Washington, D.C., Constitution,* December 15, 1860, indicates that Colonel Thomas C. Hindman was one of the formulators of the Minute Men movement in Arkansas. *Macon Weekly Telegraph,* November 13 and 15, 1860; *Raleigh (N.C.) Standard,* October 31, 1860; *Georgia Weekly Telegraph (Macon),* October 25, 1860; *Raleigh (N.C.) Standard,* October 31, 1860; *Philadelphia Inquirer,* November 10, 1860; Jennett Blakeslee Frost, *Rebellion in the United States, or the War of 1861: Being a Complete History of Its Rise and Progress,*

*Commencing with the Presidential Election* . . . (Hartford, Ct.: 1862), 87. Knights participated directly in a grand rally at Jackson organized by the Minute Men (*Daily Mississippian* [Jackson], November 30, 1860).

13. *Daily Ohio Statesman,* December 1, 1860; Craig M. Simpson, *A Good Southerner: The Life of Henry A. Wise of Virginia* (Chapel Hill: University of North Carolina Press, 1985); *Norfolk Southern Argus,* October 26, 1860.

14. Groner to Pettus, December 6, 1860, Mississippi Department of Archives and History; Hunnicott, *Conspiracy Unveiled,* 247, citing *Norfolk Day Book* of early December 1860.

15. Wallace Putnam Reed, ed., *History of Atlanta, Georgia* (Syracuse, N.Y.: D. Mason, 1889), 90, citing *Atlanta Daily Intelligencer,* March 20, 1860; *Atlanta Daily Intelligencer,* March 21 and 22, 1860; Thomas G. Dyer, *Secret Yankees: The Union Circle in Confederate Atlanta* (Baltimore: John Hopkins University Press, 1999), 35.

16. *Atlanta Daily Intelligencer,* November 10, 12, 16, and 23, 1860.

17. John Witherspoon Dubose, *The Life and Time of William Lowndes Yancey: A History of Political Parties in the United States, from 1834 to 1864* (New York: Peter Smith, 1942), 2: 450; John Hope Franklin, *A Southern Odyssey: Travelers in the Antebellum North* (Baton Rouge: Louisiana State University Press, 1976), 250–53.

18. *San Antonio Daily Ledger and Texan,* January 11, 1861, and February 4, 1861; Bell, "Knights of the Golden Circle," 126, 134. The wife of the captain of the San Antonio castle reported that the San Antonio Guards were composed of "the young men of the K. G. C.'s" and that the order included "many of the old Texans and the wealthiest and most influential men of the community" (Terrell Armistead Crow and Mary Moulton Barden, *Live Your Own Life: The Family Papers of Mary Bayard Clarke, 1854–1886* [Columbia: University of South Carolina Press, 2003], 59). Paul N. Spellman, *Forgotten Texas Leader: Hugh McLeod and the Texan Santa Fe Expedition,* 125, 167, 171–72; Handbook of Texas Online: "Texas National Guard."

19. Hudson, "Military Knights of the Golden Circle in Texas," 187, indicates that Good's Artillery Unit subsequently served the Confederacy as the Good-Douglas Battery supporting Greer's Third Texas Cavalry. Douglas Hale, *The Third Texas Cavalry in the Civil War* (Norman: University of Oklahoma Press, 1993), 48.

20. *An Authentic Exposition of the K. G. C.,* 77.

21. Parramore, *Norfolk,* 198, citing *Norfolk Day Book,* August 17, 1860.

22. Hudson, "Knights of the Golden Circle in Texas," 53.

23. *The Biographical Cyclopedia of Representative Men of Maryland and District of Columbia* (Baltimore: National Biographical, 1879), 402: "Archer, Robert Harris"; "Death of Col. Robert H. Archer, " *Bel Air (Md.) Aegis & Intelligencer,* March 15, 1878; Robert H. Archer, K.G.C. Commission, dated December 17, 1859, appointment by the State of Maryland as Captain of the Spesutia Rangers, dated February 16, 1860, notes by James Chrismer, Archer file, Harford County Historical Society, Bel Air, Md.; David R. Craig, "James J. Archer: The Little Gamecock" (master's thesis, Morgan State University, May 1983), 52–57; "A CARD. *To the Young Men of the 2d Congressional District of Maryland, Bel Air (Md.) Aegis,* December 1, 1860.

24. *New York Herald,* July 22, 1860.

25. James M. Rufsell et al. to Semmes, November 15, 1861, Semmes to H. H. Water, Esquire, January 20, 1861, Box 6, Folder 34, Joseph Mahan Collection, Columbus State University Archives.

26. Louise Biles Hill, *Joseph Brown and the Confederacy* (Chapel Hill: University of North Carolina Press, 1939), 38 n. 36; William W. Freehing and Craig M. Simpson, eds., *Secession Debated: Georgia's Showdown in 1860* (New York: Oxford University Press, 1992), xii– xiii.

27. *Macon (Ga.) Weekly,* November 22, 1861; Florence Fleming Corley, *Confederate City: Augusta Georgia: 1860–1865* (Columbia: University of South Carolina Press, 1960), 30; Greeley, *American Conflict,* 1: 337.

28. *New York Herald,* December 5, 1860; Frost, *Rebellion in the United States,* 84; Greeley, *American Conflict,* 1: 337; Chas. I. Williams to Semmes, November 24, 1861, W. J. Hardee to Semmes, November 24, 1861, Box 6, Folder 34, Joseph Mahan Collection, Columbus State University Archives. Following the Milledgeville convention, Pillow urged Tennessee governor Isham Harris to raise and equip twenty thousand to fifty thousand volunteers (Nathaniel Cheairs Hughes Jr. and Roy P. Stonesifer Jr., *The Life and Times of Gideon J. Pillow* [Chapel Hill: University of North Carolina Press, 1993], 155).

29. "From Maj. Ben. McCulloch to the Governor of Texas—An Appeal for Texas." *Texas State Gazette* (Austin), December 29, 1860, containing McCulloch letter of November 18, 1860; Cutrer, *Ben McCulloch and the Frontier Military Tradition,* 174–75.

30. Ben McCulloch to Henry McCulloch, November 25, 1860, Eleanor S. Brockenbrough Library, Museum of the Confederacy, Richmond, Va. McCulloch further stated that if not needed at home, "I have determined to offer my services to this State [South Carolina] should any attempt be made to coerce her into submission."

31. A. White, Democratic National Committee, *The Conspiracy to Break up the Union,* 10–11 (also found at Joel H. Sibley, ed., *The American Party Battle: Election Campaign Pamphlets, 1828–1876,* vol. 2, *1854–1876* [Cambridge: Harvard University Press, 1999], 109–10), citing Breckinridge's December 21, 1859, speech at Frankfort, Ky.; Davis, *Breckinridge: Statesman, Soldier, Symbol,* 208, 238–43; Crenshaw, *Slave States in the Presidential Election of 1860,* 109–10, 160, 163, 174–75. Stephen Douglas said that while not every Breckinridge man was a disunionist, every disunionist was a Breckinridge man (Johanssen, *Stephen A. Douglas,* 790).

32. *New York Herald,* September 6, 1860, reporting Breckinridge's Ashland speech of September 6, 1860, in which he notes at page 6 that "one of the oldest and most eminent of our public men has not [only] said I was a disunionist, but has intimated that I am connected with an organization whose bone and body is disunion. I refer to Mr. Crittenden and to a speech he made in Louisville." Emerson David Fite, *The Presidential Campaign of 1860* (New York: Macmillan, 1911), 175; Davis, *Breckinridge: Statesman, Soldier, Symbol,* 239. *Narrative of Edmund Wright,* 54–55, indicates that there were reports that Breckinridge had received the Knights' backing when he was nominated for the vice presidency in 1856.

33. Walther, *William Lowndes Yancey and the Coming of the Civil War,* 251–54. "The Coming Revolution," *New York Herald,* July 24, 1860, charges Yancey and South Carolina congressman Laurence Keitt with preparing to lead the South into disunion. *An Authentic*

*Exposition of the K. G. C.* by a "Member of the Order" (Indianapolis: C. O. Perrine, 1861), 21–27.

34. Dubose, *Life and Times of William Lowndes Yancey,* 2: 490–97; Walther, *William Lowndes Yancey and the Coming of the Civil War,* 254–57; Noel C. Fisher, *War at Every Door: Partisan Politics and Guerilla Violence in East Tennessee, 1860–1869* (Chapel Hill: University of North Carolina Press, 1977), 12–15.

35. Dubose, *Life and Times of William Lowndes Yancey,* 2: 496–98; Walther, *William Lowndes Yancey and the Coming of the Civil War,* 258–59.

36. Dubose, *Life And Times of William Lowndes Yancey,* 2: 494–507; Walther, *William Lowndes Yancey and the Coming of the Civil War,* 260–67; Fite, *Presidential Campaign of 1860,* 214–17; "Letter from Ex-Governor Lowe of Maryland," *Savannah (Ga.) Daily Morning News,* December 24, 1861; Harold Bell Hancock, *Delaware during the Civil War: A Political History* (Wilmington: Historical Society of Delaware, 1961), 31.

37. *Louisville Journal,* January 6, 1861; Ronald Ray Alexander, "Central Kentucky in the Civil War, 1861–1865" (Ph.D. diss., University of Kentucky, 1976), 44–45.

38. *Louisville Daily Democrat,* August 12, 1860.

39. "Mr. Yancey and the Knights of the Golden Circle—Letter from Mr. Yancey," *Louisville Courier,* January 19, 1861, where Yancey replies: "I have twice been earnestly solicited to join the order, and refused to do so." The KGC's Third Degree oath prohibited disclosing membership, however, and even if not a member, Yancey could have still been generally affiliated with the KGC's political wing, where involvement by prominent politicians was of a less formal, advisory nature (*Louisville Journal,* July 18, 1861; Pike, *Scout and Ranger,* 138).

40. Dubose, *Life and Times of William Lowndes Yancey,* 529–37; Walther, *William Lowndes Yancey and the Coming of the Civil War,* 269–73; Evans, ed., *Confederate Military History,* 13: 8; Allan Nevins, *The Emergence of Lincoln: Douglas, Buchanan, and Party Chaos, 1857 to 1859* (New York: Scribner's Sons, 1950), 2: 308.

41. *Baltimore Sun,* October 23, 1860, and November 3, 1860. The name "National Volunteers" was chosen since the local Bell and Everett supporters in the Baltimore area were already using the name "Minute Men" to refer to their quasi-military organization (Report of Select Committee of Five, House of Representatives, *Alleged Hostile Organization Against the Government within the District of Columbia,* Report No. 79, 36th Cong., 2nd sess. [cited hereafter as "Hostile Organization Testimony"], 137–38: Cypriano Ferrandini).

42. Norma B. Cuthbert, *Lincoln and the Baltimore Plot, 1861: From Pinkerton Records and Related Papers* (San Marino, Calif.: Huntington Library, 1949), 92–93, 136 n. 37; Hostile Organization Testimony, 145–52: Otis K. Hilliard, 158–60: Joseph H. Boyd; Tidwell, *Come Retribution,* 228.

43. Cuthbert, *Lincoln and the Baltimore Plot, 1861,* 141 n. 47; Hostile Organization Testimony, 98–101: Enoch Lowe.

44. Cuthbert, *Lincoln and the Baltimore Plot 1861,* 28–29, 35–38, 46–49, 92–93, 141 nn. 47 and 48; Tidwell, *Come Retribution,* 228–29, 239 n. 6; Hostile Organization Testimony, 116–17, 120. George W. Walling, *Recollections of a New York Chief of Police* (New York: Caxton, 1888), 71, notes that the presiding officer and military instructor of one "Southern [National]

Volunteers" company was "a Texan, Captain Hayes by name . . . with great flashing eyes and long floating hair, topped with a huge white sombrero." This may have been former Texas Ranger Captain (and KGC) Jack Hayes, who maintained ties with the Baltimore area. The headquarters of the Baltimore Knights was reported to have been a house at the corner of Hanover and Lombard Streets (*Baltimore Sun*, July 25, 1884).

45. Cuthbert, *Lincoln and the Baltimore Plot 1861*, 48; Hostile Organization Testimony, 145: O. K. Hilliard, who admitted knowledge of the KGC but denied membership.

46. Hostile Organization Testimony, 120: J. Tyler Powell; 162–63: John H. Boyd. George Washington Howard, *The Monument City* (Baltimore: J. D. Ehlers, 1873), 557–59, states that McMahon had represented Baltimore in the Maryland legislature from 1823 to 1828, but after this he avoided public office, despite the fact that President Tyler had dispatched Virginia governor Henry Wise to try to convince McMahon to become Tyler's attorney general ("An Introduction to the Author," in *Historical View of Maryland Government*, Maryland Heritage Series no. 3, preceding John V. L. McMahon, *An Historical View of the Government of Maryland from Its Colonization to the Present Day* [Baltimore: F. Lucas Jr. 1831], 1: 1–7). John Thomson Mason, *Life of John Van Lear McMahon* (Baltimore: Eugene L. Didier, 1879), 136, indicates that despite his ill-health, McMahon was named as a member of a revolutionary "Board of Public Safety" in a bill the Maryland secessionists tried to pass in April 1861. George R. Debman Jr., "I Remember the Last Days of the Famed Eutaw House," *Sunday Sun Magazine*, June 16, 1963. The *Baltimore Sun*, July 25, 1884, later notes that the headquarters of the Knights of the Golden Circle was at Hanover and Lombard Streets, the same headquarters used by John Hopkins Medical Societies.

47. Hostile Organization Testimony, 11: James G. Berrett, 121: J. Tyler Powell; Arch Fredric Blakey, *General John H. Winder, C.S.A.* (Gainesville: University of Florida Press, 1990), 49; *War of the Rebellion: A Compilation of the Official Records of the Union and Confederate Armies*, 128 vols. (Washington, D.C.: U.S. Government Printing Office, 1880–1901), Series II, vol. 2, 721–748 [hereafter cited as OR II, 2: 721–48].

48. Hostile Organization Testimony, 109: Cornelius Boyle, 146–48; Otis K. Hillard, 158–60: Joseph H. Boyd; James Croggon, "Washington in 1860," *Evening Star*, April 1, 1911 (pt. 2, p. 4), www.bythesofhistory.com/DCHistory/Collections/Croggon/Croggon_19110401.html.

49. Dr. Cornelius Boyle obituary, March 12, 1878 (from Washington newspaper in Surratt library file); Hostile Organization Testimony, 106–8: Cornelius Boyle.

50. Hostile Organization Testimony, 123: J. Tyler Powell, 128; John H. Goddard; John and Charles Lockwood, *The Siege of Washington: The Untold Story of the Twelve Days That Shook the Union* (New York: Oxford University Press, 2011), 109; "Garnett, A. Y. P.," *The GW and Foggy Bottom Historical Encyclopedia*, Columbia College and the American Civil War, 3, http://encyclopedia.gwu.edu/gwencyclopedia/indexphph/Columbian_College_and_the_American_Civil_War.

51. Hostile Organization Testimony, 116–17, 120: J. Tyler Powell, who also said that Boyle had decided to join the secret organization. Tidwell, *Come Retribution*, 10, 69–70, indicates that Major Boyle would later be responsible for Confederate intelligence operations in northern Virginia.

52. Hostile Organization Report, 116–17: J. Tyler Powell; David Scott Turk, *Give My Kind Regards to the Ladies: The Life of Littleton Quinton Washington* (Bowie, Md.: Heritage, 2001), 10–19; John B. Jones, *A Rebel War Clerk's Diary,* ed. Earl Schenck Meirs (Baton Rouge: Louisiana State University Press, 1993), 329. Virginia fire-eater Edmund Ruffin described L. Q. as encouraging the maintenance of "southern principles & urging cooperative action of the people of Washington with Virginia and Maryland when seceding (*Ruffin Diary,* 1: 535–36, entry of January 19, 1861).

53. Hancock, *Delaware during the Civil War,* 35, 49–56, 68–69, 135; John S. Spruance, *Delaware Stays in the Union* (Newark: University of Delaware Press, 1955), 18–19.

54. Hunter to Lincoln, October 20, 1860, in *The Collected Works of Abraham Lincoln, 1860-1861,* ed. Roy P. Basler (New Brunswick, N.J.: Rutgers University Press, 1953), 4: 132 n. 1.

55. Lincoln to Hunter, October 26, 1860, in *Collected Works of Abraham Lincoln, 1860- 1861,* ed. Basler, 4: 132.

56. Speed to Lincoln, November 14, 1860, Joshua Fry Speed Papers, Library of Congress.

57. R. H. Williams, *With the Border Ruffians,* 158.

58. Speed to Lincoln, November 14, 1860, in *Collected Works of Abraham Lincoln,* ed. Basler, 4: 141 n. 1; *Louisville Journal,* June 5, 1861. The *Louisville Daily Democrat,* a Douglas paper, had, on September 2, 1860, published the *KGC Address to the Citizens of the Southern States* under the title "Address to the Southern People" and proceedings from the Raleigh Convention. Lincoln generally held the threats from secret societies in "good natured contempt," although his cabinet officers regarded them as having "the deepest import" (Nicolay and Hay, *Abraham Lincoln,* 8: 8).

59. Speed to Lincoln, May 19, 1860, Joshua Fry Speed Papers, Library of Congress.

60. Allan Nevins, *The Emergence of Lincoln: Prologue to Civil War, 1859-1861* (New York: Scribner's Sons, 1950), 2: 293, citing unpublished diary of Charles Francis Adams; Henry Adams; "The Great Secessionist Winter of 1860–61," in *The Great Secession Winter of 1860-61 and Other Essays,* ed. George Hochfield (New York: Sagamore, 1958), 4, 7; Theodore Calvin Pease and James G. Randall, eds., *The Diary of Orville Hickman Browning,* (Springfield: Trustees of the Illinois Historical Library, 1925), 1: 466. May, *Southern Dream of a Caribbean Empire,* 179, notes that Douglas had backed the Cuba initiatives of 1854 and 1859, defended William Walker in 1856, and suggested a plan to Alexander Stevens as late as December 1860 that would allow Mexico to enter the Union as a slave state if the South agreed not to secede.

61. George Fort Milton, *The Eve of Conflict: Stephen A. Douglas and the Needless War* (Boston: Houghton Mifflin, 1934), 492–99.

## CHAPTER SEVEN: SEIZURE OF FEDERAL FORTS AND ARSENALS

1. Donald, ed., *Inside Lincoln's Cabinet,* 126.

2. Sanford, *Treason Unmasked,* 17. *Narrative of Edmund Wright,* 56, alleges that "FLOYD was the great light of the Washington [KGC] Sanhedrin; and, without doubt, 'J. B.' [John Breckinridge] was his prophet."

3. Crawford, *Genesis of the Civil War*, 141. During November 1860, Howell Cobb was convinced by his Georgia supporters to come home and spearhead Georgia's immediate secession. While there were charges that Cobb aided Floyd directly and indirectly with money and credit, he nevertheless left the Buchanan administration in early December in a fairly cordial and forthright manner (Thomas P. Kettle, *History of the Great Rebellion: The Secession of the Southern States* [Hartford, Ct.: F. A. Howe, 1865], 32; John Eddins Simpson, *Howell Cobb: The Politics of Ambition* [Chicago: Adams, 1973], 142–45).

4. Dayton E. Pryor, *The Beginning and the End: The Civil War Story of Federal Surrenders before Fort Sumter and Confederate Surrenders after Appomattox* (Bowie, Md.: Heritage, 2001), 56–95; "The Capture of Fort Pulaski," http://ourgeorgiahistory.com/wars/Civil_War/ftpulaski.html.

5. Charles Pinnegar, *Brand of Infamy: A Biography of John Buchanan Floyd* (Westport, Ct.: Greenwood, 2002), 41–69; W. A. Swanberg, "Was the Secretary of War a Traitor?" *American Heritage* 14, no. 4 (February 1963): 34. Floyd's chief War Department clerk, Mr. Callahan, subsequently became a prosecession editor for the *Constitutional Union* and a confidant of John Surratt (*Lincoln Assassination Evidence:* 1084–85).

6. Kettle, *History of the Great Rebellion*, 35; Edward S. Cooper, *Traitors: The Secession Period, November 1860–July 1861* (Rutherford, N.J.: Fairleigh Dickinson University Press, 2008), 33–34. OR III, 1: 22, notes that Governor Pettus wrote Floyd on December 31, 1860, seeking Mississippi's full allocation of 1862 arms even though the state would secede in ten days; page 28 shows that the six Cotton States received 18.5 percent of the federal arms after January 1, 1860. The *Janesville (Wisc.) Daily Gazette* of December 31, 1860 alleged: "The secretary of war, Floyd, is equally bold in his treason. . . . We learn that the arsenals of the free states are empty, while those of the south are overflowing. Charleston has been furnished with 70,000 stand of arms during the last four years, while that of Springfield, Ill. has not thirty muskets which are fit for service."

7. During 1860, 115,000 improved muskets were transferred from the northern arsenals at Springfield and Watervliet to five arsenals in the South (OR III, 1: 38–40; David J. Eicher, *Dixie Betrayed: How the South Really Lost the Civil War* [New York: Little, Brown, 2006], 55; *An Authentic Exposition of the K. G. C.:* 35–36).

8. Floyd insisted that South Carolina governor Gist channel his purchases of up to fifty thousand arms through G. B. Lamar, head of the Bank of the Republic in New York, who was a Georgia-born secession sympathizer and was known to have supported the Order of the Lone Star (Cooper, *Traitors*, 33–35; Swanberg, "Was the Secretary of War a Traitor?" 34–35). Federal arms were also channeled to other pro-South individuals and groups, including the Phillips County militia that would lead the insurgent takeover of the Little Rock arsenal in February 1861 (OR III, 1: 29–30).

9. "Arms in the South," *Clarkesville Chronicle*, January 13, 1860. John Hope Franklin, *The Militant South: 1800–1861* (Boston: Beacon, 1964), 245, describes the same report as appearing in the *Memphis Appeal* and *DeBow's Review*.

10. Greeley, *American Conflict*, 2: 19; Warner, *Generals in Gray*, 193–94.

11. Alvin M. Josephy Jr., *The Civil War in the American West* (New York: Vintage, 1993), 234–35; Charles P. Roland, *Albert Sidney Johnston: Soldier of Three Republics* (Lexington: University Press of Kentucky, 2001), 3–4, 54–80, 240–60. The *Philadelphia Inquirer*, on March 22, 1861, reported: "The Cabinet [Lincoln's] had been discussing reports from California and Texas respecting the connection of certain officers with the rumored movements of the Knights of the Golden Circle."

12. Nicolay and Hay, *Abraham Lincoln*, 4: 179–80.

13. Alfred Roman, *The Military Operations of General Beauregard in the War Between the States, 1861–1865* (New York: Harper and Brothers, 1884), 15; Cooper, *Traitors*, 53–54; T. Harry Williams, *P. G. T. Beauregard: Napoleon in Gray* (Baton Rouge: Louisiana State University Press, 1955), 45–46; Philip Shriver Klein, *President James Buchanan: A Biography* (University Park: Pennsylvania State University Press, 1962), 398. *Narrative of Edmund Wright*, 56, alleges that Beauregard established a castle of the Knights at West Point to influence the young cadets to support the southern cause that led to his dismissal in January 1861.

14. H. Williams, *P. G. T. Beauregard*, 45; Gerald A. Patterson, "Arming the South with Guns from the North, *America's Civil War*, October 2007; Hardee to Semmes, November 24, 1860, Semmes Letters of December, 11, 20, 22, 25, and 26, 1860, and related Contracts in Box 6, Folder 34, Joseph Mahan Collection, Columbus State Archives.

15. Nicolay and Hay, *Abraham Lincoln*, 2: 316–17, citing extract from Floyd's Diary of November 8, 1860; *New York Herald*, December 7, 1860.

16. James Buchanan, *Mr. Buchanan's Administration on the Eve of the Rebellion* (New York: D. Appleton, 1866), 103, 289; Crawford, *Genesis of the Civil War*, 162–65; John S. Eisenhower, *Agent of Manifest Destiny: The Life and Times of General Winfield Scott* (New York: Free Press, 1997), 346.

17. Adams, "Great Secessionist Winter of 1860–61, 5; Crawford, *Genesis of the Civil War*, 167–68.

18. Roy Franklin Nichols, *The Disruption of American Democracy* (New York: Macmillan, 1948), 377–84; Pinnegar, *Brand of Infamy*, 90–92.

19. J. Moore, ed., *Works of James Buchanan*, 11: 7, 12, 18; Nichols, *Disruption of American Democracy*, 384–85.

20. Crawford, *Genesis of the Civil War*, 168–69; Buchanan, *Mr. Buchanan's Administration on the Eve of the Rebellion*, 169–70.

21. OR III, 1: 15; Frost, *Rebellion in the United States*, 98–101.

22. *Janesville (Wisc.) Daily Gazette*, December 31, 1860.

23. OR III, 1: 35–36; Nichols, *The Disruption of American Democracy*, 420; Pinnegar, *Brand of Infamy*, 96–97; Crawford, *Genesis of the Civil War*, 216–17.

24. Nichols, *Disruption of American Democracy*, 418–20; Swanberg, "Was the Secretary a Traitor?" 36–37.

25. Crawford, *Genesis of the Civil War*, 142–45.

26. *Richmond Enquirer*, January 1, 1861; Nichols, *Disruption of American Democracy*, 425; Swanberg, "Was the Secretary a Traitor?" 37, 96–97; David Detzer, *Allegiance: Fort Sumter, Charleston, and the Beginning of the Civil War* (New York: Harcourt, 2001), 80–82,

139–41; *Evergreen City Times* (Sheboygan, Wisc.), February 8, 1861, containing the grand jury presentations against Floyd for maladministration in office, complicity in the abstraction of bonds, and conspiracy against the government.

27. Pinnegar, *Brand of Infamy*, 105; Crawford, *Genesis of the Civil War*, 217.

28. Swanberg, "Was the Secretary of War a Traitor?" 97; *Fond Du Lac (Wisc.) Weekly Commonwealth*, January 17, 1861, reproducing *New York Tribune* article.

29. Crawford, *Genesis of the Civil War*, 150.

30. King, *Louis T. Wigfall*, 104–7; *Narrative of Edmund Wright*, 55.

31. Pryor, *Beginning and the End*, 193–94.

32. Hostile Organization Testimony, 169, citing *National Inquirer* of January 31, 1861, and *Richmond Enquirer*, December 17, 1860; Simpson, *A Good Southerner*, 240, citing *Alexandria Gazette and Public Advertiser*, December 28, 1860.

33. "Fighting in the Union—Position of Gov. Wise," *Weekly Raleigh (N.C.) Register*, December 26, 1860; Frost, *Rebellion in the United States*, 84–85.

34. Frost, *Rebellion in the United States*, 93.

35. Detzer, *Allegiance*, 99; Crawford, *Genesis of the Civil War*, 89; David Winfred Gaddy, "William Norris and the Confederate Secret Service," *Maryland Historical Magazine* 70, no. 2 (Summer 1975): 167–88.

36. Brock, *Virginia and Virginians*, 2: 553–54, notes: "[Groner] perfected a secret organization for the capture of Fortress Monroe, which would have been successfully accomplished but for the interference of Governor Letcher." Nicolay and Hay, *Abraham Lincoln: A History*, 3: 421, citing Governor Letcher's Message, December 2, 1861.

37. Steward, ed., *History of Norfolk County, Virginia*, 610; Simpson, *A Good Southerner*, 241.

38. "The Meeting of the Minute Men," *Wilmington (N.C.) Daily Herald*, December 13, 1861.

39. Noble J. Tolbert, ed., *The Papers of John Willis Ellis*, vol. 2, *1860–1861* (Raleigh: State Department of Archives and History, 1964), 476–77.

40. Ibid., 2: 554, 560; OR I, 1: 475–76; Michael D. Hogan, "North Carolina Forts (Part 3): Ft. Johnston in Transition," Historic Southport, www.southportncmagazine.com/forts_3_johnston.html.

41. OR I, 1: 475: Report of January 9, 1861, from U.S. Army Ordinance Sergeant James Reilly to Colonel S. Cooper; John G. Barrett, *The Civil War in North Carolina* (Chapel Hill: University of North Carolina Press, 1963), 6.

42. Tolbert, ed., *Papers of John Willis Ellis*, 2: 554–55, Ellis to Buchanan, January 12, 1861, 560; OR I, 1: 475–76; Michael D. Hogan, "North Carolina Forts (Part 3): Ft. Johnston in Transition," Historic Southport, www.southportncmagazine.com/forts_3_johnston.html.

43. Jacob Thompson to Ellis, December [n.d.] 1860, in *Papers of John Willis Ellis*, ed. Tolbert, 2: 543–46: Dubay, *John Jones Pettus*, 81. Thompson finally resigned from the Buchanan administration on January 8, 1861, after alerting the Charleston secessionists of the approaching *Star of the West* expedition to relieve Fort Sumter (Cooper, *Traitors*, 41–48; *New York Herald*, January 11, 1861).

44. OR I, 53: 111–16; Louis Bile Hill, *Joseph E. Brown and the Confederacy* (Chapel Hill: University of North Carolina Press, 1939), 42.

45. Ellis to Joseph Brown, January 14, 1861, *Papers of John Willis Ellis*, ed. Tolbert, 2: 558–59.

46. *Semi-Weekly (Jackson) Mississippean*, January 17, 1859; Dubay, *John Jones Pettus*, 78–79, 83; Rainwater, *Mississippi*, 215; "Mississippi Secession," http://virtualology.com/us-civilwarhall/mississippisecession.com/; OR I, 53: 120.

47. "The Fort at Ship Island," *New Orleans Daily True Delta*, January 16, 1861; Allardice, *Confederate Colonels*, 202–3: "Howard, James Ross."

48. OR I, 1: 329.

# CHAPTER EIGHT: THE PLOT TO SEIZE THE DISTRICT OF COLUMBIA

1. Donald, ed. *Inside Lincoln's Cabinet: The Civil War Diaries of Salmon P. Chase*, 125–26; Sanford, *Treason Unmasked*, 22, similarly charged: "The inauguration of Mr. Lincoln being near at hand, a plot was laid by the Knights to assassinate him and capture Washington inasmuch such a thrilling movement would strike terror into the hearts of the abolitionists—offer an opportunity to rob the national Treasury and thus secure the entire field in advance."

2. "How Is It?—Will Gov. Harris Answer?" *Nashville Republican Banner*, September 15, 1860; "K. G. C." *Alamo Express*, October 15, 1860.

3. "K. G. C.," *Norfolk Southern Argus*, April 17, 1860.

4. Russel H. Beatie, *Army of the Potomac: Birth of Command, November 1860–September 1861* (Cambridge, Mass.: Da Capo Press, 2002), 16–21; Ernest B. Furguson, *Freedom Rising: Washington in the Civil War* (New York: Vintage, 2005), 12–15, 80; David S. and Jeanne T. Heidler, eds., *Encyclopedia of the American Civil War* (New York: Vintage, 2005), 2068–71: "Washington D.C."

5. Nevins, *Emergence of Lincoln*, 2: 293.

6. Hostile Organization Testimony, 53–57: General Winfield Scott; Charles P. Stone, "Washington on the Eve of the War," *Century Magazine*, July 1883, in Phillip Van Doren Stern, *Secret Missions of the Civil War* (New York: Bonanza, 1959), 48.

7. Joseph Holt's confidential report to President Buchanan, February 11, 1861, subsequently published in *Congressional Globe*, Appendix, August 6, 1861, 457–58. Holt's letter of February 18, 1861, reproduced in John A Logan, *The Great Conspiracy: Its Origin and History* (New York: A. R. Hart, 1886), 122–25, notes: "More than six weeks ago, the impression had already extensively obtained that a Conspiracy for the accomplishment of this guilty purpose [occupation of Washington City] was in process of formation if not fully matured."

8. Hostile Organization Testimony, 53–57: General Winfield Scott.

9. Joseph Medill to Abraham Lincoln, December 26, 1980, Abraham Lincoln Papers at the Library of Congress, http://memory.loc.gov/cgi-bin/query/r?ammen/mal:@filed(DOCID+@lit(d0534200); Heidler, eds., *Encyclopedia of the American Civil War*, 1310–11: Medill, Joseph.

10. Hostile Organization Testimony, 100–101: Enoch Lewis Lowe, 167–73: Thomas Hicks; Michael J. Kline, *The Baltimore Plot: The First Conspiracy to Assassinate Abraham Lincoln* (Yardley, Pa.: Westholme, 2008), 11.

11. Hostile Organization Testimony, 166: Governor Thomas Hicks, quoting from January 3, 1861, "Address to the People of Maryland"; Kline, *Baltimore Plot,* 11 and 95, citing James C. Welling to Thomas H. Hicks, December 21, 1860, Accession No. 47948, MS 1313, Maryland Historical Society, Baltimore.

12. George L. Radcliff, *Governor Thomas H. Hicks of Maryland and the Civil War* (Baltimore: John Hopkins Press, 1901), 27–35; Hostile Organization Testimony, 98–102: Enoch Lowe; Cuthbert, ed., *Lincoln and the Baltimore Plot, 1861,* 141 n. 47. An observer reported witnessing a Baltimore meeting where he saw "eight men kneel on their left knees and swear with uplifted hands that they would assassinate Governor Hicks unless he convened the State Legislature for the purpose of 'reading or taking' Maryland out of the Union" (*Lincoln Assassination Evidence,* 482: Joseph Fell).

13. Paul H. Bergeron, ed., *The Papers of Andrew Johnson,* vol. 8, *May–August 1865* (Knoxville: University of Tennessee Press, 1989), 312: Thomas Ewing Sr. to Johnson, June 29, 1865.

14. Logan, *Great Conspiracy,* 249–51, quoting *Washington, D.C., National Intelligencer,* January 9, 1861; May, *John A. Quitman,* 280; Handbook of Texas Online: "Evans, Lemuel Dale."

15. *Dodge County (Wisc.) Citizen,* Jan. 24, 1861, reproducing "The Disunion Program," *National Intelligencer,* January 11, 1861; Henry Wilson, *History of the Rise and Fall of the Slave Power* (Boston: James R. Osgood, 1877), 3: 133–34, 137, confirming that the byline "Eaton" was Hon. L. D. Evans of Texas and that he similarly told Congressman Henry Wilson that militant associations formed throughout the South had "reached the magnitude and solidarity of an army," and were prepared to move "at a moment's notice" to break up Congress before February 15 and prevent Lincoln's inauguration.

16. Wilson, *History of the Rise and Fall of the Slave Power,* 3: 137; Cutrer, *Ben McCulloch and the Frontier Military Tradition,* 189; McCulloch letter to Sam Houston, December 29, 1860, *Texas State Gazette; Washington, D.C., Daily National Intelligencer,* June 3, 1861, noting that Ogilvie Byron Young said he was authorized by Texas secession leaders to take a company of Texas Rangers and Mississippi troops to Washington to fight against the government.

17. King, *Louis T. Wigfall,* 106–7; D. Girald Wright, *A Southern Girl in '61: The War-time Memories of a Confederate Senator's Daughter* (New York: Doubleday, Page, & Company, 1905), 30; Nichols, *Disruption of American Democracy,* 491, *Texas Republican,* February 23, 1861; OR I, 51 [Pt. 2]: 8; OR I, 52 [Pt. 2]: 27, 53, 133.

18. Hostile Organization Testimony, 118–19: Cornelius Boyle, quoting the *Washington Evening Star,* January 17, 1861; *Washington, D.C., Constitution,* January 11, 1861; "The National Volunteers of Washington: Their Aid Tendered to Secession," *Philadelphia Inquirer,* November 11, 1861.

19. Hostile Organization Testimony, 33–39; James Hicks, 92–96: Benjamin Berry; Beatie, *Army of the Potomac,* 19–20.

20. Hostile Organization Testimony, 88–92: Charles Stone; Anthony S. Pitch, *"They Have Killed Papa Dead": The Road to Ford's Theatre, Abraham Lincoln's Murder, and the Rage for Vengeance* (Hanover, N.H.: Steerforth, 2008), 3, citing Winfield Scott to Joseph Holt, January 28, 1861; Beatie, *Army of the Potomac*, 19, 23–24.

21. Beatie, *Army of the Potomac*, 21–22; Tidwell, *Come Retribution*, 69. Cooper, *Traitors*, 34, indicates that Schaeffer was "an ex-lieutenant in the Third United States Artillery," after which he became an employee of the Interior Department.

22. Kline, *Baltimore Plot*, 38; Fife, *Presidential Election of 1860*, 165, quoting from the *Atlanta (Ga.) Southern Confederacy*.

23. Hostile Organization Testimony, 87: Jacob Thompson, 171: Governor Thomas H. Hicks.

24. Joseph Holt's confidential report to President Buchanan, February 11, 1861, subsequently published in *Congressional Globe*, Appendix, August 6, 1861, 457–58.

25. Kline, *Baltimore Plot*, 17, 42, 68–71, 173; Cuthbert, ed., *Lincoln and the Baltimore Plot*, 23–25; George W. Walling, *Recollections of a New York Chief of Police* (New York: Caxton, 1888), 68–77.

26. *Congressional Globe*, 36th Cong., 2d sess., February 16, 1861, 58; http://bioguide.congress.gov : Howard, Branch, Dawes, Cochrane, Reynolds; *Davenport (Iowa) Daily Gazette*, January 28, 1861.

27. Hostile Organization Testimony, 1–178, Theodore Roscoe, *The Web of Conspiracy: The Complete Story of the Men Who Murdered Abraham Lincoln* (Englewood Cliffs, N.J.: Prentice Hall, 1959), 7.

28. Hostile Organization Testimony, 136–37: Ferrandini; 145–47: O. K. Hilliard.

29. *Congressional Globe*, 36th Cong., 2d sess., February 16, 1861.

30. Basler, ed., *Collected Works of Abraham Lincoln*, 4: 190.

31. Ibid., 4: 151: Lincoln to Elihu Washburne, December 13, 1861, 183: Lincoln to William H. Seward, February 1, 1861; Albert Dennis Kirwin, *John J. Crittenden: The Struggle for the Union* (Lexington: University of Kentucky Press, 1962), 388–89; Benjamin P. Thomas, *Abraham Lincoln: A Biography* (New York: Knopf, 1967), 229–31.

32. Basler, ed., *Collected Works of Abraham Lincoln*, 4: 194–96; Michael Davis, *The Image of Lincoln in the South* (Knoxville: University of Tennessee Press, 1971), 29, citing *Louisville Courier*, February 13, 1861.

33. Cuthbert, ed., *Lincoln and the Baltimore Plot*, 26–27.

34. Basler, ed., *Collected Works of Abraham Lincoln*, 4: 197–200.

35. Kline, *Baltimore Plot*, 92–93. Lincoln's handlers had already been advised by Baltimore Republicans not to organize any public display in the southern-leaning city where he had received fewer than two thousand votes (Cuthbert, ed., *Lincoln and the Baltimore Plot, 1861*, 142 n. 50).

36. Robert S. Harper, *Lincoln and the Press* (New York: McGraw-Hill, 1951), 90–91, citing *Syracuse (N. Y.) Journal*, reprinted by *New York World*, February 27, 1861; *New York Herald*, February 26, 1861. The *Berkshire County Eagle* (Pittsfield, Mass.), February 28, 1861, alleges that an obstruction had been placed on the track at the Indiana-Kentucky line that would have derailed the train if not discovered.

37. Kline, *Baltimore Plot*, 91; *Daily Cleveland Herald*, February 2, 1861.

38. Buchanan, *Administration on the Eve of Rebellion*, 169; Hostile Organization Testimony, 61–62: General Winfield Scott; John D. Eisenhower, *Agent of Destiny: The Life and Times of General Winfield Scott* (New York: Free Press, 1997), 349–50; Kline, *Baltimore Plot*, 90–91.

39. Titone, *My Thoughts Be Bloody*, 240–42; Kline, *Baltimore Plot*, 129–37; Tidwell, *Come Retribution*, 255–57; Kimmel, *Mad Booths of Maryland*, 157–60; Rhodehamel, *Right or Wrong, God Judge Me*, 47–49.

40. Cuthbert, ed., *Lincoln and the Baltimore Plot*, 2, 5, 32–38; Kline, *Baltimore Plot*, 53, 110–14, 342–43.

41. Cuthbert, ed., *Lincoln and the Baltimore Plot*, 6– 7, 36–37, 45, 64–65 ; Roscoe, *Web of Conspiracy*, 7; Kline, *Baltimore Plot*, 59–61, 112–13; Hostile Organization Testimony, 132–34: Cypriano Ferrandini. "Military in Harford," *Baltimore Sun*, February 20, 1860, indicates that "B. H. Keen" was second lieutenant of the sixty-two-member Spesutia Rangers recently organized at Perrymanville [*sic*] that had chosen "R. H. Archer, who was a member of a volunteer company in the Mexican war" as its captain.

42. Cuthbert, ed., *Lincoln and the Baltimore Plot*, 53, 64–65, 93; Kline, *Baltimore Plot*, 182–83. Isaac H. Arnold, "The Baltimore Plot to Assassinate Abraham Lincoln," *Harper's New Monthly Magazine*, June 1868, 126, indicates that "the police of Baltimore, under control of Marshal Kane, would act in concert with the conspirators." Kane later denied this and explained his actions in an article that appeared in the *New York Times*, January 25, 1868.

43. Lockwood, *Siege of Washington*, 130; *Baltimore Sun*, December 12, 1900; J. Thomas Scharf, *History of Maryland: From the Earliest Period to the Present Day* (Hatboro, Pa.: Tradition, 1967), 3: 413.

44. OR II, 1: 563, 619–20, 624–25; "Important Arrest in Baltimore," *Scientific American*, n.s., 5, no. 2 (July 13, 1861): 18; Gordon Samples, *Lust for Fame: The Stage Career of John Wilkes Booth* (Jefferson, N.C.: McFarland, 1982), 170.

45. Bruce Chadwick, *The Two American Presidents: A Dual Biography of Abraham Lincoln and Jefferson Davis* (Secaucus, N.J.: Carol, 1999), 136; Cuthbert, ed., *Lincoln and the Baltimore Plot*, 44–53, 59, 89–91, 138 n. 39; Tidwell, *Come Retribution*, 227–33; Frank Van Der Linden, *Lincoln: The Road to War* (Golden, Colo.: Fulcrum, 1991), 199–201.

46. Cuthbert, ed., *Lincoln and the Baltimore Plot*, 1861, 77–78, 83; Eisenhower, *Agent of Destiny*, 352–53.

47. Robert S. Harper, *Lincoln and the Press* (New York: McGraw-Hill, 1951), 82, 87–91. Pinkerton agents continued their contact with the Baltimore conspirators and confirmed they had indeed intended to carry out the assassination (Cuthbert, ed., *Lincoln and the Baltimore Plot*, 90–94). The *Janesville (Wisc.) Daily Gazette*, March 9, 1861, states that New York Metropolitan Police detectives DeVoe and Sampson had been "fully initiated" into the secret organization planning to assassinate Lincoln. Kline, *Baltimore Plot* , 276–77, notes that after Lincoln's arrival in Washington, Missouri senator Waldo P. Johnson was overheard remarking to Virginia's James Seddon, "How the devil did he [Lincoln] get through Baltimore?"

## CHAPTER NINE: RUSTLING TEXAS OUT OF THE UNION

1. J. J. Bowden, *The Exodus of Federal Forces from Texas, 1861* (Austin, Tex.: Eakin, 1986), 32–33; Oates, ed., *Rip Ford's Texas*, xxxv–xxxvi; James Smallwood, *Born in Dixie: Smith County Origins to 1875: The History of Smith County, Texas* (Austin, Tex.: Eakin, 1999), 1: 159, 161–62, 166–67.

2. Oates, ed., *Rip Ford's Texas*, xxxv; Hughes, *Rebellious Ranger*, 188–89.

3. Odie Faulk, *General Tom Green: Fightin' Texas* (Waco: Texan Press, 1963), 35; E. D. Winkler, ed., *Journal of the Secession Convention of Texas, 1861* (Austin, 1912), reproduced at *Southwestern Historical Quarterly Online*, http://tarlton.law.utexas.edu/constitutions/pdf/pdf1861/index1861.html, 10–13 n. 2.

4. Anderson, *Texas, before, and on the Eve of Rebellion*, 37; Hudson, "Military Knights of the Golden Circle, 75, discusses the KGC's "old buoys [*sic*] network" of local sheriffs and castle and militia captains that was likely involved in the distribution and follow-up for the December 3 call.

5. Bell, "Knights of the Golden Circle," 167.

6. King, *Louis T. Wigfall*, 104–5, citing Wigfall and others: "To Our Constituents," December 14, 1860.

7. Oates, ed., *Rip Ford's Texas*, xxxv; Anderson, *Texas, before, and on the Eve of Rebellion*, 83–86.

8. Smallwood, *Born in Dixie*, 161–62, 167; Hudson, "Knights of the Golden Circle in Texas," 53, indicates that John Robertson was a Knight. Sumrall, *Battle Flags of Texans*, 23, states that Mrs. John Robertson (along with Mrs. George Chilton) helped make the flag for Tyler Guards in 1858 that honored the Knights of the Golden Circle.

9. Earl Wesley Fornell, *The Galveston Era: The Texas Crescent on the Eve of Secession* (Austin: University of Texas Press, 1976), 286–87; Handbook of Texas Online: "Bryan, Guy Morrison"; Smallwood, *Born in Dixie*, 161; Joe T. Timmons, "Texas on the Road to Secession" (Ph.D. diss., University of Chicago, 1973), 1: 723–24 n. 1, citing "Private" correspondence from William P. Rogers to O. M. Roberts, December 26, 1860.

10. Major J. T. Sprague, United States Army, "The Texas Treason," paper read before the New York Historical Society, June 25, 1861, in *Rebellion Record, ed. F. Moore*, 1: 109–10, Document 21.

11. Winkler, ed., *Journals of the Secession Convention of Texas, 1861*, 10–12.

12. At the time of the public meeting, KGC organizers from Texas and Louisiana were recruiting in Galveston (Earl Wesley Fornell, *The Galveston Era: The Texas Crescent on the Eve of Secession* [University of Texas Press, 1976], 285–86).

13. Anna Irene Sandbo, "The First Session of the Secession Convention of Texas," *Southwestern Historical Quarterly* 18, no. 2 (October 1914), reproduced at *Southwestern Historical Quarterly Online*, http://tarlton.law.utexas.edu/constitutions/pdf/pdf1861/index1861.html, 10. James Newcomb, *Sketch of Secession Times in Texas* (San Francisco, 1863), 7, claims that out of the eighty thousand eligible, only ten thousand Texans voted in the delegate election.

14. Marion K. Wisehart, *Sam Houston: American Giant* (Washington: Robert B. Luce, 1962), 593–94.

15. Llerena Friend, *Sam Houston: The Great Designer*, 333–34; Jewett, *Texas in the Confederacy*, 55.

16. Bell, "Knights of the Golden Circle," 169–73; Oates, ed., *Rip Ford's Texas*, xxxvi, 317.

17. Hudson, "Knights of the Golden Circle in Texas," 56, 59. Known KGC members at the convention were George Chilton, John Ford, Alfred Hobby, John Littleton, Thomas and John Lubbock, John C. Robertson, C. A. Russell, John A. Wilcox; suspected KGC include Pryor Lee and Philip Luckett (Hudson, "Military Knights of the Golden Circle in Texas" [master's thesis, Stephen F. Austin University, 1990], 173–239).

18. Dunn, "KGC in Texas," 549; Message to the Legislature of Texas in Extra Session, January 21, 1861, in *Writings of Sam Houston*, ed. Williams and Barker, 8: 236, 249–52; Spellman, *Forgotten Texas Leader Hugh McLeod*, 167; James Farber, *Texas C. S. A.: A Spotlight on Disaster* (New York: Jackson, 1947), 18–19.

19. Buenger, *Secession and the Union in Texas*, 144; Sandbo, "The First Session of the Secession Convention of Texas," *Southwestern Historical Quarterly Online*, 10–11.

20. Mrs. Caroline Baldwin Darrow, "Recollections of the Twiggs Surrender," in *Battles and Leaders of the Civil War* (New York, 1970), 8: 33. Newcomb, *Sketch of Secession Times in Texas* (San Francisco, 1863), 10, describes Baylor as "a bad man with a murderous reputation [who had] raised three or four hundred men in the northern counties." Frazier, *Blood and Treasure*, 27; Friend, *Sam Houston: Great Designer*, 335.

21. For example, in addition to the identified KGC convention delegates, Allison Nelson had been a brigadier general with Lopez's Cuban expedition, and Henry Maltby had been a filibusterer with William Walker in Nicaragua (see the related entries in Handbook of Texas Online).

22. Buenger, *Secession and the Union in Texas*, 144.

23. Oates, ed., *Rip Ford's Texas*, xxxvii.

24. Buenger, *Secession and the Union in Texas*, 145; Sandbo, "The First Session of the Secession Convention of Texas," *Southwestern Historical Quarterly Online*, 12–13.

25. Hudson, "Knights of the Golden Circle in Texas," 56; Sumrall, *Battle Flags of Texans in the Confederacy*, 25; Winkler, ed., *Journal of the Secession Convention 1861*, 28; Handbook of Texas Online: "Luckett, Philip Nolan," and "Wilcox, John Allen."

26. Buenger, *Secession and the Union in Texas*, 146; Sandbo, "The First Session of the Secession Convention of Texas," *Southwestern Historical Quarterly Online*, 13–14.

27. Buenger, *Secession and the Union in Texas*, 147.

28. Sandbo, "The First Session of the Secession Convention of Texas," *Southwestern Historical Quarterly Online*: 14–15; Buenger, *Secession and the Union in Texas*, 147–48.

29. Buenger, *Secession and the Union in Texas*, 147–48; Wisehart, *Sam Houston*, 599–600.

30. Wisehart, *Sam Houston*, 600–601; Buenger, *Secession and the Union in Texas*, 153–54; Winkler, *Journal of the Secession Convention of Texas, 1861;* "The First Session of the

Secession Convention of Texas," *Texas Historical Quarterly Online*, 61–66; Jewett, *Texas in the Confederacy*, 64.

31. Wisehart, *Sam Houston*, 602.

32. Buenger, *Secession and the Union in Texas*, 163–64; Jewett, *Texas in the Confederacy*, 63; Kenneth Wayne Howell, "'When the Rabble Hiss, Well May Patriots Tremble': James Web Throckmorton and the Secession Movement in Texas, 1854–1861," *Southwestern Historical Quarterly* 109, no. 4 (April 2006): 490.

33. Jewett, *Texas in the Confederacy*, 64; Buenger, *Secession and the Union in Texas*, 151.

34. Sprague, "The Texas Treason," in *Rebellion Record*, 1: 111–15; Bowden, *Exodus of Federal Forces from Texas: 1861*, 39–41, quoting Waite to Twiggs, February 12, 1861.

35. Bowden, *Exodus of Federal Forces from Texas: 1861*, 41–42; Young, *To the Tyrants Never Yield*, 42; Farber, *Texas C.S.A.*, 58, quoting from *Alamo Express*, February 6, 1861.

36. Bowden, *Exodus of Federal Forces from Texas: 1861*, 44–45. McCulloch had returned from South Carolina just in time to be appointed colonel of the Texas State Cavalry and receive instructions to secure the surrender of the federal forces and property (Young, *To the Tyrants Never Yield*, 40).

37. Young, *To the Tyrants Never Yield*, 40; Bowden, *Exodus of Federal Forces from Texas: 1861*, 45–48.

38. Bowden, *Exodus of Federal Forces from Texas: 1861*, 49, 134 n. 1; Dunn, "KGC in Texas," 568; Collins, *Texas Devils*, 232.

39. R. Williams, *With the Border Ruffians*, 163; Alvin M. Josephy, *The Civil War in the American West* (New York: Vintage, 1991), 25; Bell, "Knights of the Golden Circle," 178–80.

40. Crow and Barden, eds., *Live Your Own Life: The Family Papers of Mary Bayard Clarke, 1854–1886*, 59–61. Mrs. Clarke, the wife of the KGC San Antonio Castle leader, indicated that the KGC-affiliated militia units had mustered at the armory the night before; John A. Wilcox (who is also listed as the head of one of the San Antonio castles) was known as "John Allen Wilcox" in Texas but is referenced as "John Alexander Wilcox" during his earlier life in Mississippi ("Wilcox, John Allen," Texas State Historical Association, www.tshaonline.org/handbook/online/articles/fwi10). McIntosh, ed., *The Papers of Jefferson Davis*, 2: 203 n. 14; Bowden, *The Exodus of Federal Forces from Texas: 1861*, 49, 134 n. 1; Hudson, "Military Knights of the Golden Circle in Texas," 215–17.

41. Dunn, "KGC in Texas," 568; Hudson, "Knights of the Golden Circle in Texas," 58; Bell, "Knights of the Golden Circle," 178–81; Young, *To the Tyrants Never Yield*, 43; "Letter to Gen. Twiggs," *Tri-Weekly Alamo Express*.

42. Bowden, *The Exodus of Federal Forces from Texas: 1861*, 51–52, 62; Darrow, "Recollections of the Twiggs Surrender," 286.

43. Wisehart, *Sam Houston*, 603–4; Dunn, "KGC in Texas," 568–69; Emory M. Thomas, *The Confederate Nation: 1861–1865* (New York: Harper and Row, 1979), 85.

44. Bowden, *Exodus of Federal Forces from Texas: 1861*, 56, citing *Alamo Express*, February 19, 1861; Young, *To the Tyrants Never Yield*, 53.

45. OR I, 1: 5–6; II, 1: 8.

46. OR II, 1: 9–10, indicates that Twiggs was dismissed from the U.S. Army on March 1 for "treachery to the flag of his country." Dunn, "KGC in Texas," 568, quoting Dallas *Herald*, February 27, 1861.

47. OR I, 1: 609: McCulloch to John Reagan, February 25, 1861; Young, *To the Tyrants Never Yield*, 68.

48. Bell, "Knights of the Golden Circle," 160, 182; Bowden, *Exodus of Federal Forces from Texas: 1861*, 65–79; Dunn, "KGC in Texas," 569–570; Hudson, "Knights of the Golden Circle in Texas," 57–58. Young, *To the Tyrants Never Yield*, 58, states that Knights were also involved in the forced surrender of the evacuating U.S. troops during mid-April 1861.

49. "Castle K. G. C.," *Tri-Weekly Alamo Express*, February 21, 1861, citing *S. A. Herald*. A few months later, Newcomb's press was burned to the ground by a KGC mob amid threats to hang 150 of San Antonio's most prominent Unionists. Newcomb wisely decided to leave town (Dunn, "KGC in Texas," 570; Newcomb, *Sketch of Secession Times in Texas*, 12).The KGC was also accused of driving thousands of Germans out of Texas to Mexico (*New York Times*, March 28, 1861).

50. "Texas K. G. C. State Convention," *La Grange (Tex.) States Right Democrat*, March 7, 1861; *San Antonio Daily Ledger & Texan*, February 25 and March 19, 1861. A Vision of the Past," *San Antonio Daily Light*, September 17, 1903, reported that the KGC convention also elected W. R. Cowan, Esq. of Lockhart and Victor W. Thompson, of La Grange, secretaries; Dr. J. E. Park, of Seguin, sergeant-at-arms, and E. B. Thomas, of Atascosa, inside sentinel.

51. Bell, "Knights of the Golden Circle," 139, citing *Tri-Weekly Alamo Express*, March 22, 1861.

52. Bell, "Knights of the Golden Circle," 184, citing *Daily Ledger and Texan*, May 27, 1861.

53. Bell, "Knights of the Golden Circle," 182; Dunn, "KGC in Texas," 557–67, analyzes the public vote on secession in the twenty-seven Texas counties where the KGC is known to have had castles. Dale Baum, *The Shattering of Texas Unionism: Politics in the Lone Star State during the Civil War* (Baton Rouge: Louisiana State University Press, 1996), 76; Newcomb, *Sketch of Secession Times in Texas*, 7; Jewett, *Texas in the Confederacy*, 56, 64.

54. Bell, "Knights of the Golden Circle," 182; Winkler, ed., *Journal of the Secession Convention*, 74, 208–9.

55. Wisehart, *Sam Houston*, 609–11; Williams and Barker, eds., *The Writings of Sam Houston*, 7:268–71; Hudson, "Knights of the Golden Circle in Texas," 58.

56. Wisehart, *Sam Houston*, 611–13; Bell, "Knights of the Golden Circle," 183–84.

57. Newcomb, *Sketch of Secession Times in Texas*, 6, further states: "After secession was consummated they [the Knights] were suppressed by the very persons who had used them."

# CHAPTER TEN: SPREADING SECESSION

1. "Arkansas in the Civil War," www.lincolnandthecivilwar.com. "The Extraordinary Career of an American Adventurer," *Abingdon Virginian*, October 4, 1867, indicates that while at Napoleon, Bickley proposed a scheme to solve the Arkansas credit problem. "Knights of the Golden Circle," *Arkansas True Democrat* (Little Rock), May 9, 1861.

NOTES TO PAGES 127-128

2. "Knights of the Golden Circle," *Arkansas True Democrat* (Little Rock), May 9, 1861; Tres Williams, "Camden's Golden Knights," *Ouachita Valley Ledger*, 1981, 1–2; "Circular Letter," *Norfolk Southern Argus*, April 14, 1860; Warner, *Generals in Gray*, 188: "Elkanah Bracken Greer."

3. Neal and Kremm, *Lion of the South*, 26–42, 52–53, 70–71; "Augustus Larrentree," January 5, 1860, *Little Rock (Ark.) Old Line Democrat*; "Incendiary Fires in Texas," August 16, 1860, ibid., "Knights of the Golden Circle," September 20, 1860, ibid.; Michael B. Dougan, *Confederate Arkansas: The People and Policies of a Frontier State in Wartime* (Tuscaloosa: University of Alabama Press, 1991), 37, 52; *Washington, D.C., Constitution*, December 15, 1860.

4. Thomas A. DeBlack, *With Fire and Sword: Arkansas, 1861-1874* (Fayetteville: University of Arkansas Press, 2003), 14–16; Dougan, *Confederate Arkansas*, 37–39, 45.

5. Congressman Thomas Hindman and his prosecessionist sidekick Robert Ward Johnson sent a joint message to the insurgents that showed they were in control: "Don't attack arsenal unless success is certain. . . . Pledge might be required not to remove or injure arms without notice. Please telegraph us." ("The War Nearly Started Here . . . Seizing the U.S. Arsenal at Little Rock," 9–14 and 15, containing Hindman-Johnson February 8, 1861, telegram from Washington). Arkansas congressman Albert Rust subsequently charged that Hindman had remotely orchestrated the seizure of the Little Rock arsenal by pressuring Governor Rector from Washington and directing the Helena insurgents who were backed by secessionists from the nine plantation counties (James M. Woods, *Rebellion and Realignment: Arkansas Road to Secession* [Fayetteville: University of Arkansas Press, 1987], 129, citing Albert Rust to David Williams, February 7, 1861).

6. The first unit to respond was Helena's Yell Rifles, commanded by Captain Patrick Cleburne, a young Irish immigrant who was a close friend and legal partner of Hindman. A company of mounted and armed cavalry arrived over land commanded by Captain Gist, brother of South Carolina's governor. The Phillips County Guards, from the surrounding county, soon joined them. Several other impromptu units came up the Arkansas River to join the militia vanguard (Dougan, *Confederate Arkansas*, 41–42; Evans, *Confederate Military History*, 14: 6–9; "The War Nearly Started Here . . . Seizing the U.S. Arsenal at Little Rock," 1–5, www. geocities.com/capitalguards/arsenal.htm, containing *Arkansas State Gazette*, February 9, 1861, which indicates that volunteer companies from different parts of the state had been "informed by telegraph or otherwise that the Arsenal here was to be reinforced").

7. Evans, ed., *Confederate Military History*, 14:8. The southern Arkansas insurgents believed Governor Rector had summoned them (Michael B. Dougan, "'An Eternal Chitter Chatter Kept up in the Galleries': The Arkansas Secession Convention in Action, March–June 1861," in *The Die Is Cast: Arkansas Goes to War, 1861*, ed. Mark Christ [Little Rock, Ark.: Butler Center Books, 2010], 18; "The War Nearly Started Here . . . Seizing the U.S. Arsenal at Little Rock," 9–10; OR I, 1: 638, 641, containing January 29–February 9, 1861, correspondence between Rector, Totten, and others, including Rector communication of February 6, 1861; W. Buck Yearns, *The Confederate Governors* [Athens: University of Georgia Press, 1985], 46).

8. Dougan, *Confederate Arkansas*, 43–45; 18– 21; DeBlack, *With Fire and Sword*, 24, 28.

9. William Gerald McLoughlin, *After the Trail of Tears* (Chapel Hill: University of North Carolina Press, 1993), 155–65; William Gerald McLoughlin, *Champions of the Cherokees: Evan and John B. Jones* (Princeton: Princeton University Press, 1990), 343–45, 349, 364–65, 370–71, 378–81; Kenny A. Franks, *Stand Watie and the Agony of the Cherokee Nation* (Memphis: Memphis State University Press, 1979), 120.

10. Franks, *Stand Watie*, 116–17; McLoughlin, *After the Trail of Tears*, 176–77. Getler and Brewer, *Shadow of the Sentinel*, 53–56, 59–65, 73–74, speculate that Albert Pike, as "Sovereign Grand Commander of the Scottish Rites Free Masons," was connected with the KGC.

11. Franks, *Stand Watie*, 114–15, indicates that "Watie's followers became active in the Knights of the Golden Circle." McLoughlin, *After the Trail of Tears*, 156–59; Woodward, *Cherokees*, 257–59; Theda Perdue, *Slavery and the Evolution of Cherokee Society: 1540–1866* (Knoxville: University of Tennessee Press, 1979), 129–37.

12. Franks, *Stand Watie*, 116–18; Woodward, *Cherokees*, 265–69; "The Keetoowah Society and the Avocation of Religious Nationalism in the Cherokee Nation, 1855–1867," *U.S. Data Repository*, 1–19, www.us-data.org/us/minges/keetood2.html.

13. James W. Parins, *John Rollin Ridge: His Life and Works* (Lincoln: University of Nebraska Press, 2004), 180–82, 195; OR I, 50 (pt. 2): 938, 940; Leonard B. Waitman, "The Knights of the Golden Circle," *San Bernardino County Museum Association Quarterly* 15, no. 4 (summer 1968): 14–16.

14. Waitman, "Knights of the Golden Circle," 13–14; Henry H. Goldman, "Southern Sympathy in Southern California, 1860–1865," *Journal of the West* 4, no. 4 (1965): 578–82, OR I, 50 (pt. 2): 589–91.

15. Izola Forrester, *This One Mad Act: The Unknown Story of John Wilkes Booth and His Family* (Boston: Hale, Cushman and Flint, 1937), 406, notes that "Gwin had been the head of the Knights of the Golden Circle in the State of California during the Civil War." Hubert Howe Bancroft, *The Works*, vol. 24, containing *History of California—1860–1890*, vol. 7 (San Francisco: History Company, 1890), 279–80 n. 7, quotes from the *Stockton Independent* that "Gwin was at the head of this conspiracy." Jeff LaLande, "'Dixie' of the Pacific Northwest: Southern Oregon's Civil War," *Oregon Historical Quarterly* 100, no. 1 (spring 1999): 61–62 and 78 n. 75, which notes that the name "Knights of the Golden Circle" was used by Joseph Lane and Gwin to identify members of the Pacific republic conspiracy.

16. Lately Thomas, *Between Two Empires: The Life Story of California's First Senator, William McKendress Gwin*, 1–49, 109–10, 232–33, 290–91; Charles Mial Dustin, "The Knights of the Golden Circle: The Story of the Pacific Coast Secessionists," *Pacific Monthly* (1911): 495, 501; Joseph Ellison, "Designs for a Pacific Republic, 1843–62," *Oregon Historical Quarterly* 31, no. 4 (December 1930): 319, 331.

17. OR I, 50 (pt. 2): 938–41, in which the membership of the KGC together with the upper-level Knights of the Columbian Star is estimated at fifty thousand. Bancroft, *Works*, vol. 24, containing *History of California, 1860–1890*, vol. 7, 266–67 n. 23, 282, 307–9; Aurora Hunt, *The Army of the Pacific: Its Operations in California, Texas, Arizona, New Mexico, Utah, Nevada, Oregon, Washington, Plains Region, Mexico, etc., 1860–1866* (repr., Mechanicsburg, Pa.: Stackpole, 2004), 179, 342–48.

18. Ellison, "Designs for a Pacific Republic, 1843–62," 319–42; G. Thomas Edwards, "Six Oregon Leaders and the Far-Reaching Impact of America's Civil War," 10, 21–22, and Jeff LaLande, "'Dixie' of the Pacific Northwest: Southern Oregon's Civil War," 33, 41–43, 48–49, 61–62 and note 75 on 78, both found in *Oregon Historical Quarterly* 100, no. 1 (spring 1999). Four hundred Knights were also reported in "Knights of the Golden Circle," *Portland Weekly Oregonian*, April 27, 1861.

19. Asbury Harpending, a Walker filibusterer who had made millions from land acquisitions in Mexico, subsequently disclosed the secret society meeting and related plot (James H. Wilkins, ed., *The Great Diamond Hoax and Other Stirring Stories in the Life of Asbury Harpending* [Norman: University of Oklahoma Press, 1958], 16–21). Bancroft, *The Works*, vol. 24, containing *History of California—1860–1890*, vol. 7, 288–89 n. 13, lists eighteen conspirators (possibly KCS) involved with Harpending in an 1863 privateering operation to harass Union ships off California and intercept federal gold shipments.

20. George H. Tinkham, "California during the Civil War," 1–2, extracted from Panama-Pacific Exposition Edition (1915) of *California Men and Events, 1769–1890*, by the California State Military Museum at www.militarymuseum.org/CAandCW@.html, indicates that the Knights "claimed to have 20,000 men [and] at the opportune moment they intended to revolt and seize the forts and government buildings. Dustin, "The Knights of the Golden Circle: The Story of the Pacific Coast Secessionists," 499, states that "the eight hundred selected to capture the Government property at San Francisco, was headed by [KGC leader] Senator William Gwin of California." Benjamin Franklin Gilbert, "The Confederate Minority in California," *California Historical Society Quarterly* 20 (June 1841): 154–56; OR I, 50 (pt. 2): 938–41.

21. Wilkens, ed., *Great Diamond Hoax*, 20.

22. Gilbert, "The Mythical Johnston Conspiracy,"167–69. Waitman, "The Knights of the Golden Circle," 14, notes that more than one-third of the Sixth Regiment stationed at San Francisco ultimately did leave to join the Confederate army.

23. Charles P. Roland, *Albert Sidney Johnston: Soldier of Three Republics* (Lexington: University Press of Kentucky, 2001), 248–60; Elijah Kennedy, *The Contest for California in 1861* (Boston: Houghton Mifflin, 1912), 72–75, 79–84, Secretary of War Floyd, who had secretly sent fifty thousand stands of arms to San Francisco in late 1860, had appointed Johnston as one of his last official acts, apparently at Senator Gwin's insistence (Gene C. Armistead, "California's Confederate Militia: The Los Angeles Mounted Rifles," in California and the Civil War website, by California State Military Museum, www.militarymuseum.org/LosAngelesMountedRifles2.html, 1–2).

24. Harpending said a majority of the conspirators then voted not to proceed with the seizures and subsequently became distracted by the silver found at Nevada's Comstock lode (Wilkens, ed., *Great Diamond Hoax*, 23–31). Roland, *Albert Sidney Johnston*, 245–46.

25. Gilbert, "Mythical Johnston Conspiracy," 169–71; Bancroft, *The Works*, vol. 24 containing *History of California—1860–1890*, vol. 7, 282–83 n. 8; Dustin, "Knights of the Golden Circle," 495–96.

26. Johnston subsequently resigned and after a stint with his pro-South relatives in Los Angeles, headed on horseback across the desert to Richmond, where he was commissioned in September 1861 by Jefferson Davis as major general, the second-highest officer in the Confederate army (Roland, *Albert Sidney Johnston*, 250–60). Armistead, "California's Confederate Militia: The Los Angeles Mounted Rifles," 4–6.

27. Hunt, *Army of the Pacific*, 342–49; OR I, 50 (pt. 2): 938–41. In 1862, John Rollin Ridge moved from Maryville, California, to Nevada City, where he continued to recruit for the Knights of the Columbian Star, in which he was reportedly an officer (Parins, *John Rollin Ridge: His Life and Works*, 198, 208).

28. *Murfreesboro (N.C.) Citizen*, August 30, 1860; *Baltimore Sun*, September 5, 1860; *Murfreesboro (N.C.) Daily Confederate*, April 18, 1861; "Circular Letter," *Norfolk Southern Argus*, April 17, 1860; Frost, *Rebellion in the United States*, 93.

29. Of the 122 delegates against immediate secession, seventy were moderates or conditional Unionists who opposed coercion and hoped for an accommodation with the federal government on southern grievances (Henry T. Shanks, *The Secession Movement in Virginia, 1847–1861*, 158–60). Andrew Jackson Hamilton, Lorenzo Sherwood, and Henry O'Reilly, Democratic League of New York, *Origin and Objects of the Slaveholders' Conspiracy Against Democratic Principles As Well As Against the National Union* (New York: Baker A. Godwin Printers, 1862), 10–11; "The Plottings of Rebellion," including letter from Muscoe R. H. Garnett of Virginia to Wm. H. Trescott of South Carolina, May 3, 1851.

30. Paul A. Atkins, "Henry Wise and the Virginia Secession Convention: February 13–April 17, 1861" (master's thesis, University of Virginia, May, 1850), 166; Simpson, *A Good Southerner*, 241, 248; John A. Cutchins, *A Famous Command: The Richmond Light Infantry Blues* (Richmond, Va.: Garrett and Massie, 1934), 68.

31. John Morton Callahan, *History of West Virginia: Old and New* (Chicago: American Historical Society, Inc., 1923), 1: 336: statement of John J. Davis in *Clarksburg Guard* at the beginning of 1861.

32. Shanks, *Secession Movement in Virginia*, 161–62; Callahan, *History of West Virginia*, 1: 340–41: account of James C. McGrew, member of convention.

33. Edward P. Crapol, *John Tyler: The Accidental President* (Chapel Hill: University of North Carolina Press, 2006), 264; Shanks, *Secession Movement in Virginia*, 145–46, 160–61, 171–72; Scarborough, *Diary of Edmund Ruffin*, 1: 122–23, entry of November 11, 1857.

34. OR I, 1: 263–64; Shanks, *Secession of Virginia*, 159, 179–80; Turk, *Give My Kind Regards to the Ladies*, 25–26. L. Q. wrote to Harvie on March 24, 1861, asking him to join in a prosecession speaking campaign, noting: "Jeff Davis, Toombs, & Yancey carried their States by work & speaking to the people. This has made them the recognized leaders of the movement." (L. Q. Washington to Lewis Harvie, March 24, 1861, Harvie Family Papers, 1831–1913, Section 1, Correspondence, 1835–1887, of Lewis Edwin Harvie of "Dykeland," Amelia County, Va., Virginia Historical Society).

35. OR, I, 1: 276, 278; 51 [pt. 2]: 9–10; 53: 133–34; Turk, *Give My Kind Regards to the Ladies*, 25–29; King, *Louis T. Wigfall*, 114.

36. Kline, *Baltimore Plot,* 25, 343, citing *Papers of Jefferson Davis,* 7: 51–52 n. 7, and 61 n. 4. In late April, "Mr. Walters of Baltimore" worked with Henry Wise and secession leaders in Richmond "to form camp for Baltimore and point of attack on Washington from the west" (OR, I, 52 [pt. 2]: 32).

37. *Baltimore Sun,* March 16, 1861, which also noted that "the people of Maryland . . . would never be able to get out of the United States, for there were combinations at Washington winding around them, and like the coils of the anaconda, they would crush them into submission and make them slaves of the North."

38. OR I, 1: 276, 278; 53: 134–35.

39. *Bel Air (Md.) Aegis,* December 1, 1860; King, *Louis T. Wigfall,* 114; Daniel D. Hartzler, *A Band of Brothers: Photographic Epilogue to Marylanders in the Confederacy* (New Windsor, Md.: published by author, 1992), 35, *The Civil War Told by Those Who Lived It* (New York: Library of America, 2011), 283, quoting William Howard Russell Diary, entry of April 17, 1861.

40. Cutrer, *Ben McCulloch and the Frontier Military Tradition,* 188–91; *Philadelphia Inquirer,* March 17, 1861. Wright, *A Southern Girl in '61,* 33–35, indicates that on March 29, McCulloch joined Wigfall and former President Tyler at an elegant dinner at the home of James and Henningham Lyons, one of Richmond's most distinguished families. Mrs. Lyons was the sister of Henry Wise, while her husband, James, would later became Virginia's representative to the Confederate Congress.

41. Cutrer, *Ben McCulloch and the Frontier Military Tradition,* 189; Thomas, *Between Two Empires,* 232–45; Forrester, *This One Mad Act,* 406; *New Orleans Daily Picayune,* April 5, 1861, which states: "Major Ben McCulloch, at the head of 2000 Virginians, was at Alexandria on Monday."

42. Shanks, *Secession Movement in Virginia,* 188; Callahan, *History of West Virginia,* 338, citing Marshall M. Dent, writing in the *Morgantown Star.*

43. James C. McGregor, *The Disruption of Virginia* (New York: Macmillan, 1922), 153 n. 1.

44. Shanks, *Secession Movement in Virginia,* 184–88; Callahan, *History of West Virginia,* 338, citing Marshall M. Dent, writing in the *Morgantown Star;* MacGregor, *Disruption of Virginia,* 143–44, 153 n. 1; F. N. Boney, *John Letcher of Virginia: The Story of Virginia's Civil War Governor* (Tuscaloosa: University of Alabama Press, 1966), 110.

45. Shanks, *Secession Movement in Virginia,* 158–60, 188–90.

46. Conrad, "The Break-up of a Nation," 8, Conrad letter of March 28, 1861; Daniel W. Crofts, *Reluctant Confederates: Upper South Unionists in the Secession Crisis* (Chapel Hill: University of North Carolina Press, 1989), 320.

47. *Wellsburg (Va.) Herald,* March 22, 1861, reporting Marshall Dent's letter to the *Morgantown (Va.) Star* of March 9, 1861, www.wvculture.org/history/sequicentennial/18610309 .html.

48. McGregor, *Disruption of Virginia,* 167, quoting the circular letter as published in the *Richmond Whig* of April 6, 1861; Atkins, "Henry A. Wise and the Virginia Secession Convention," 117–18; F. J. Barnes of Williamsburg, Virginia, replied to Dr. G. W. Bagby regarding the circular letter on March 30, 1861: "I have just received a circular letter which I am requested

to answer addressing you. I shall probably be in Richmond about the time mentioned (16 April) and should be delighted to be able to do something toward devising or carrying out a plan for securing Virginia and the whole South their rights." (Barnes to Bagby, March 30, 1861, F. J. Barnes MSS, Virginia Historical Society).

49. William H. Edwards, "A Bit of History," *West Virginia Historical Magazine Quarterly* (July 1902), www.wvculture.org/HISTORY/statehood/abitofhistory.html. Callahan, *History of West Virginia,* 340, describes the arrivals as "hundreds, if not thousands, of desperate characters who were prepared to do the bidding of the cabal whatever it might be."

50. Scarborough, ed., *Diary of Edmund Ruffin,* 2: 568–69, entry of February 1863; Simpson, *A Good Southerner,* 241, 248; Crofts, *Reluctant Confederates,* 318.

51. McGregor, *Disruption of the Union,* 161–62; Shanks, *Secession Movement in Virginia,* 192–95; Callahan, *History of West Virginia,* 340– 41, account of James C. McGrew.

52. Boney, *John Letcher of Virginia,* 111; Ernest B. Furguson, *Ashes of Glory: Richmond at War* (New York: Knopf, 1996), 32–33.

53. Arkins, "Henry Wise and the Virginia Secession Convention," 136, quoting Pickens to Letcher.

54. Basler, *Collected Works of Abraham Lincoln,* 4: 331–32; Boney, *John Letcher of Virginia,* 112, quoting Letcher to Simon Cameron, April 16, 1861.

55. Atkins, "Henry Wise and the Virginia Secession Convention," 137–40.

56. Conrad to his wife, April 15, 1861, in Conrad, "Break-up of a Nation," 19–22; Crofts, *Reluctant Confederates,* 320–21; Shanks, *Secession Movement in Virginia,* 200; Callahan, *History of West Virginia,* 340– 41, account of James C. McGrew.

57. Atkins, "Henry Wise and the Virginia Secession Convention," 138–44; Callahan, *History of West Virginia,* 341: account of James C. McGrew.

58. John B. Jones, *A Rebel War Clerk's Diary* (Baton Rouge: Louisiana State University Press, 1958), 4–5, entry of April 16, 1861; Shanks, *Secession Movement in Virginia,* 202–3.

59. Chester G. Hearn, *Six Years of Hell: Harpers Ferry during the Civil War* (Baton Rouge: Louisiana State University Press, 1996), 45–51. Thomas S. Harman, "The Secession Crisis in the Shenandoah Valley: How Staunch Unionists Became Ardent Confederates" (senior thesis, Duke University, 1979), 60, 63, 72, indicates that Imboden had been defeated as a convention delegate from the Shenandoah Valley due to his strong southern-rights proclivities, and that he planned to lead a mass exodus of large landholders to Florida if Virginia didn't secede.

60. Spenser C. Tucker, *Brigadier General John D. Imboden: Confederate Commander in the Shenandoah* (Lexington: University Press of Kentucky, 2003), 29; Barton H. Wise, *The Life of Henry A. Wise of Virginia* (New York: Macmillan, 1899), 274–77.

61. Jones, *A Rebel War Clerk's Diary,* 5, entry of April 17, 1861; William A. Link, *Roots of Secession: Slavery and Politics in Antebellum Virginia* (Chapel Hill: University of North Carolina Press, 2002), 242.

62. Wise, *Life of Henry Wise of Virginia,* 280.

63. Ibid., 280–81; Harman, "Secession Crisis in the Shenandoah Valley," 70.

64. Jones, *A Rebel War Clerk's Diary,* 6, entry of April 17, 1861; Boney, *John Letcher of Virginia,* 115; McGregor, *Disruption of Virginia,* 171–78.

65. Jones, *A Rebel War Clerk's Diary*, 5–6, entry of April 17, 1861; Atkins, "Henry Wise and the Virginia Secession Convention," 159; Link, *Roots of Secession*, 242. A few days later, Wise from his sickbed told William M. Ambler to urge Richmond authorities to cut off Harpers Ferry from the west, "to form camp for Baltimore and point of attack on Washington from the west," and emplace heavy guns on the Potomac River and at Hampton to prevent the federals at Fort Monroe from taking the heights (OR I, 51 [pt. 2]: 32).

66. Jones, *A Rebel War Clerk's Diary*, 5–6; Wise, *The Life of Henry Wise of Virginia*, 279–80; Atkins, "Henry Wise and the Virginia Secession Convention," 144–48; Link, *Roots of Secession*, 242.

67. OR I, 50 (pt. 1): 589–91. In 1863, A. Sanford wrote: "Virginia was, by acts of the Knights of the Golden Circle, declared out of the union, as was Arkansas and Tennessee, and they fully expected that every remaining Southern State would soon follow." (Sanford, *Treason Unmasked*, 29).

# CHAPTER ELEVEN: CALL TO ARMS

1. OR I, 1: 297: L. P. Walker to Beauregard, April 10, 1861.

2. H. W. Burton, *History of Norfolk, Virginia*, 610; Brock, *Virginia and Virginians*, 553; W. E. C., "Gen. V. D. Groner," *Confederate Veteran* 12, no. 4 (1904): 294; *San Francisco Daily Evening Bulletin*, March 22, 1860; *Daily Atlanta Intelligencer*, April 19, 1861; "Army Appointments," *Macon Daily Telegraph*, March 23, 1861.

3. William C. Davis, *A Government of Our Own: The Making of the Confederacy* (Baton Rouge: Louisiana State University Press, 1994), 26, 114, 157, 181–83, notes that John Reagan from Texas subsequently accepted the postmaster general position (316). James P. Jones and William Warren Rogers, eds., "Montgomery As the Confederate Capital: View of a New Nation," *Alabama Historical Quarterly* 26, no. 1 (Spring 1964): 68; *Dictionary of American Biography* (New York: Scribner, 1928–58), 4: 71–72: "Chilton, William Paris."

4. Albert Burton Moore, *Conscription and Conflict in the Confederacy* (New York: Hillary House, 1963), 6, citing *Richmond Enquirer*, August 8, 1861,"ascertained from official data."

5. William C. Harris, *Leroy Pope Walker: Confederate Secretary of War* (Tuscaloosa: Confederate Publishing, 1962), 35; W. Davis, *A Government of Our Own*, 321; "Montgomery As the Confederate Capital: View of a New Nation," 73–74.

6. "Our Texas Correspondence," *Charleston Mercury*, October 31, 1860.

7. "Knights of the Golden Circle," *Arkansas True Democrat* (Little Rock), May 9, 1861.

8. Ibid.

9. *Philadelphia Inquirer*, April 4, 1861.

10. Bickley to Davis, April 3, 1861, in *Papers of Jefferson Davis*, ed. McIntosh, 7: 87; W. Davis, *A Government of Our Own*, 335; "Montgomery As the Confederate Capital," 62.

11. Benson J. Lossing, "New Orleans Hears That Sumter Has Fallen," in *Prologue to Sumter: The Beginnings of the Civil War from the John Brown Raid to the Surrender of Fort Sumter*, comp. Philip Van Doren Stern (Greenwich, Ct.: Fawcett, 1961), 535.

12. Bayly Ellen Marks and Mark Norton Schatz, eds., *Between North and South: A Maryland Journalist Views the Civil War: The Narrative of William Wilkins Glenn, 1861-1869* (Rutherford, N.J.: Fairleigh Dickinson University Press, 1976), 27–28; George William Brown, *Baltimore and the Nineteenth of April 1861* (Baltimore: John Hopkins University Press, 2001), 36–39; Greeley, *American Conflict*, 1: 462.

13. OR I, 2: 577.

14. Lockwood, *Siege of Washington*, 90; Greeley, *American Conflict*, 1: 462.

15. Festus P. Summers, *The Baltimore and Ohio in the Civil War* (Gettysburg, Pa.: Stan Clark Military Books, 1993), 52; Greeley, *American Conflict*, 1: 462.

16. Lockwood, *Siege of Washington*, 107–11.

17. Scott Sumpter Sheads and Daniel Carrol Toomey, *Baltimore during the Civil War* (Linthicum, Md.: Toomey, 1997), 15–20; G. Brown, *Baltimore and the Nineteenth of April 1861*, 42–55.

18. Nicolay and Hay, *Abraham Lincoln*, 4: 122, quoting George P. Kane to Bradley T. Johnson, April 19, 1861; G. Brown, *Baltimore and the Nineteenth of April 1861*, 70. Harold R. Manakee, *Maryland in the Civil War* (Baltimore: Maryland Historical Society, 1961), 37–40, notes that Bradley Johnson's company of seventy arrived before noon on April 20 and, by the end of the day, were joined by four other units from across Maryland.

19. Greeley, *American Conflict*, 1: 464; G. Brown, *Baltimore and the Nineteenth of April, 1861*, 56–57, 63; Leslie R. Tucker, *Major Isaac Ridgeway Trimble: Biography of a Baltimore Confederate* (Jefferson, N.C.: McFarland, 2005), 91, 108–10.

20. A telegram from Edward G. Parker to Mayor George Wm. Brown, May 11, 1861, Maryland Historical Society Archives, alleges that the KGC was behind the Baltimore mobs (J. Thomas Scharf, *The Chronicles of Baltimore: Being a Complete History of "Baltimore Town" and Baltimore City: From the Earliest Period to the Present Day* [Baltimore: Turnbull Brothers, 1874], 611–12).

21. J. Thomas Scharf, *History of Maryland: From the Earliest Period to the Present Day* (Hatboro, Pa.: Tradition, 1967), 3: 413–14, notes that Marshall Kane not only directed the police in the bridge burning but also the Baltimore City Guard, for which Kane served as a colonel (Sheads and Toomey, *Baltimore during the Civil War*, 23).

22. OR II, 1: 675, states that on April 22, T. Parkin Scott had obtained an authorization from Virginia governor John Letcher for the shipment of five thousand flintlock muskets as a loan to the Maryland troops with consignment to William T. Walters (the Baltimore liquor-store owner through whom Confederate authorities channeled funds to assist in Wigfall's recruiting for the South). Scarborough, ed., *Diary of Edmund Ruffin*, 2: 7, entry of April 23, 1861, notes that "an agent has come on here [Richmond] to ask for cannon & small arms, & they have been furnished & sent on." Harold R. Manakee, *Maryland in the Civil War*, 41–42; Sheads and Toomey, *Baltimore during the Civil War*, 129; Warner, *Generals in Gray*, 290–91: "George Hume 'Maryland' Steuart"; OR I, 2: 29–30.

23. Edward G. Parker to Mayor George Wm. Brown, telegram, May 11, 1861, Maryland Historical Society Archives. "Affairs in Baltimore," *New York Times*, June 1, 1861, reports:

"Fifty Knights of the Golden Circle and a Lieutenant, who have been stationed at Harpers Ferry [where Blanton Duncan's Kentuckians were stationed] were yesterday in Baltimore, and made arrangements for a grand secret plot to again take possession of Baltimore."

24. William A. Howell, "Memories of Wilkes Booth: An Old Associate's Recollection of the Trying Days of '60 and '61," *Baltimore Sun*, November 21, 1899. William A. Howell appears to be the older brother of Gustavus A. Howell, a Confederate courier who was associated with several of the Lincoln assassination conspirators (Joseph E. "Rick" Smith and William L. Richter, "Gus Howell: Smarmy, Arrogant Blockade Runner and Murderer or Effective, Behind-the-Lines, Confederate Operative?" *Surratt Courier* 36, no. 9 [September 2011]: 3–8, Charles County, MD, 1850 U.S. Census, ftp.us-census.org/pub/usgenweb/census/md/charles/1850; Titone, *My Thoughts Be Bloody*, 246–47, 251–53; Kimmel, *Mad Booths of Maryland*, 161–62. The *Bel Air (Md.) Aegis & Intelligencer*, January 22, 1886, in which Col. Herman Stump, the Commander of the Harford county militia, said that "John Wilkes Booth, a member of the company, stole through the picket lines and gave [Stump] notice that the [Union] soldiers were in search of him." *New York Tribune*, May 12, 1865. *Lincoln Assassination Evidence*, 645–46, 1148, indicates that John Harrison, from Harford County, was a member of the KGC.

25. Clarke, *Unlocked Book*, 115–17.

26. OR I, 2: 29–32.

27. Kimmel, *Mad Booths of Maryland*, 168.

28. Kevin Conley Ruffner, *Maryland's Blue and Gray: A Border State's Union and Confederate Junior Officer's Corps* (Baton Rouge: Louisiana State University Press, 1997), 81–84; William Hanchett, *The Lincoln Murder Conspiracies* (Urbana: University of Illinois Press, 1983), 43–44.

29. Driver, *First and Second Maryland Infantry, C. S. A.*, 5; Allardice, *Confederate Colonels*, 202–3: "Howard, James Ross."

30. "Biography of Robert Harris Archer," in Lt. Col. Robert H. Archer, SCV Camp #2013 at http://rharchercamp.org/; Warner, *Generals in Gray*, 11: "James Jay Archer."

31. William C. Davis and Julie Hoffman, *The Confederate General* (Harrisburg, Pa.: National Historical Society, 1991), 5: 66–67; "Col. Robert C. Tyler," *Confederate Veteran* 15, no. 1 (January 1907), 237; Hughes and Stonesifer Jr., *Life and Times of Gideon J. Pillow*, 157–58; "General Robert Charles Tyler," in James Walter Fertig, "Secession and Reconstruction of Tennessee" (Ph.D. diss., University of Chicago, 1898), 24–27. According to his great-grandson, Tyler had been born in 1833 in the area between Memphis and Jackson where he had spent his early childhood (http://civilwarsoldiers.blog.spot.com/2006/02/csa-15th regiment-tennessee-infantry.html).

32. "Col. Robert Charles Tyler," *Confederate Veteran*, 237; Stuart W. Sanders, "Robert Charles Tyler: Last American Civil War General," *MHQ: The Quarterly Journal of Military History* (Spring 2006): 3; Warner, *Generals in Gray*, 312–13, 395 n. 482; Ed Gleeson, *Illinois Rebels: A Civil War Unit History of G Company, 15th Tennessee Regiment Volunteer Infantry* (Carmel: Guild Press of Indiana, 1996), 16–18, 27–28; "CSA 15th Regiment, Tennessee Infantry," from Civil War Soldiers & Regiments, http://civilwarsoldiers.blog.spot.com/2006/02/csa-15th regiment-tennessee-infantry.html.

33. During the Mexican War, James H. R. Taylor served as a captain in the First Mississippi Rifles, commanded by Jefferson Davis. In November 1861, he was the subject of a court-martial and resigned from Confederate service; he died and was buried in Memphis in October 1867 (John P. Cothern, *Confederates of Elmwood: A Compilation of Information Concerning Confederate Soldiers and Veterans Buried at Elmwood Cemetery Memphis, Tennessee* [Winchester, Md.: Heritage, 2007], 164; Dunbar Rowland, *Encyclopedia of Mississippi History* [Madison, Wisc.: Selwyn A. Brant, 1907], 2: 259; *Daily Memphis Avalanche,* October 31, 1867).

34. OR I, 7: 777–79; 32 (pt. 2): 673–74; II, 1: 854–60; Oliver P. Temple, *East Tennessee and the Civil War* (repr., Johnson City, Tenn.: Overmountain, 1995), 416–18.

35. *Columbus (Ga.) Daily Sun,* November 22, 1860; *Scioto (Ohio) Gazette,* March 26, 1861; *Daily Atlanta Intelligencer,* April 11, 12, 14, 15, and 18; Warner, *Generals in Gray,* 272–73: "Col. William Shepherd." *Confederate Veteran* 32, no. 1 (January 1924), notes that Colonel Semmes organized his regiment at Tybee Island, Georgia.

36. "Col. Gaulding," *Daily Atlanta Intelligencer,* April 19, 1861; "Arrival and Departure of Georgia Troops for Virginia," ibid., April 27, 1861.

37. Warner, *Generals in Gray,* 61–62: "Douglas Hancock Cooper."

38. Standard, *Columbus, Georgia, in the Confederacy,* 36–37; *Macon Daily Telegraph,* April 2, 1860, and July 31, 1861.

39. Cooper, *Traitors,* 165–66.

40. OR I, 51 (pt. 2): 37–38; Norma Dix Winston, "George D. Prentice and Secession in Kentucky" (master's thesis, Department of History, University of Chicago, 1939), 26– 27; *Clarksville Chronicle,* July 31, 1861.

41. J. Stoddard Johnston, *Confederate Military History of Kentucky: Kentucky during the Civil War* (Pensacola, Fla., 2006), 33–34; "Card from Col. Blanton Duncan," *Louisville Daily Courier,* April 18, 1861; OR I, 52 (pt. 2): 43–44, 49–50; J. Stoddard Johnston, *Memorial History of Louisville* (Chicago: American Biographical Publishing, 1896), 1: 162; Merton E. Coulter, *The Civil War and Readjustment in Kentucky* (New York: Oxford University Press, 1926), 48–49.

42. *Daily Atlanta Intelligencer,* April 16, 20, and 23, 1861.

43. W. Davis, *A Government of Our Own,* 353.

44. "Knights of the Golden Circle," *Memphis Daily Appeal,* May 7, 1861.

45. Handbook of Texas Online: "Wilcox, John Allen"; La Grange (Tex.) *States Right Democrat,* March 7, 1861; Odie Faulk, *General Tom Green: Fightin' Texan* (Waco: Texian Press, 1963), 33–37; Dando-Collins, *Tycoon's War,* 203–4, 333; Warner, *Generals in Gray,* 117–18: "Thomas Green"; Handbook of Texas Online: "Green, Thomas"; Hudson, "Knights of the Golden Circle in Texas," 61.

46. "Knights of the Golden Circle," *Memphis Daily Appeal,* May 7, 1861.

47. Vicki Betts, "'Private and Amateur Hangings': The Lynching of W. W. Montgomery, March 15, 1863," *Southwestern Historical Quarterly 98,* no. 2 (October 1984): 145–46; Hudson, "Military Knights of the Golden Circle in Texas," 204–5: "Charles Arden Russell"; Hudson, "Knights of the Golden Circle in Texas," 61.

48. Evans, ed., 15: 42–47; Hale, *Third Texas Cavalry in the Civil War*, 26–29; Cutrer, *Ben McCulloch and the Frontier Military Tradition*, 188; Frazier, *Blood and Treasure*, 37; Ben Irwin Wiley, ed., *Fourteen Hundred and 91 Days in the Confederate Army: A Journal Kept by W. W. Heartsill for Four Years, One Month and One Day* (Wilmington, N.C.: Broadfoot, 1987), xxiii, 2–3; Young, *To the Tyrants Never Yield*, 58–67.

49. Hale, *Third Texas Cavalry in the Civil War*, 26–30 and 61–69, notes that Greer's Third Texas Cavalry played an important role in the victory achieved by Ben McCulloch's Confederate Army of the West at the Battle of Wilson's Creek on August 10, 1861. Hudson, "Military Knights of the Golden Circle in Texas," 173–212, 222, 236–37; S. B. Barron, *The Lone Star Defenders: A Chronicle of the Third Texas Cavalry, Ross' Brigade* (New York: Neal, 1908), 27–28; Cutrer, *Ben McCulloch and the Frontier Military Tradition*, 134–35, 192–98. A Colt revolver held at the Wilson's Creek Battlefield National Park bears the engraving: "Presented to Col. E. B. Greer 3rd Texas Cav. by Knights of the Golden Circle, 1861" (Wilson's Creek National Battlefield website).

50. Tres Williams, "Camden's Golden Knights," *Ouachita Valley Ledger*, 1981; "Knights of the Golden Circle: Memories of One Who Wore Gray," *Ouachita County Historical Society*, 15, no. 3 (March 1985), 66–70; Gregory J. W. Urwin, "Notes on the First Confederate Volunteers from Ouachita County, Arkansas, 1861," *Military Collector & Historian*, 49, no. 2 (summer 1997): 83–84. Ron Field, *The Confederate Army 1861–65*, vol. 4, *Virginia and Arkansas* (Oxford: Osprey, 2006), 41, shows Camden Knights with red hunting shirts that had been worn by Ben McCulloch's KGC storming the Alamo. The *Columbus (Ga.) Daily Sun*, November 22, 1860, reported that the Columbus Guards also wore a red jacket and black pants.

51. Craig L. Symonds, *Stonewall of the West: Patrick Cleburne and the Civil War* (Lawrence: University Press of Kansas, 1997), 48–49; Neal and Kremm, *Lion of the South*, 88–90.

52. *La Grange (Tex.) State Rights Democrat*, March 7, 1861. One observer indicated that while Masonic meetings continued in Confederate army camps, he witnessed no KGC or conclaves of other secret societies (*Lincoln Assassination Evidence*, 367: statement of David H. Cockerill, lieutenant in Stonewall Brigade of Second Virginia Infantry; cf. the findings of the Indianapolis grand jury investigation; the *Jamestown [N.Y.] Journal*, August 22, 1862, alleged that the KGC extends "through every department of the rebel army").

53. "An Address to the Knights of the Golden Circle in Texas, by C. A. Russel," *La Grange (Tex.) State Rights Democrat*, May 16, 1861; Bell, "Knights of the Golden Circle," 141. C. A. Russell was a lawyer and land speculator in Helena who had been appointed governor of Arizona by James Buchanan in 1857 and replaced KGC John Littleton in the Second Texas Secession Convention (Hudson, "Military Knights of the Golden Circle in Texas," 204–5).

54. Wright, *A Southern Girl in '61*, 36–45. King, *Louis A. Wigfall*, 118–23, notes that the Texas secession convention had recently offered Wigfall the state's governorship, but he declined since he wanted a military command that could be more easily achieved if he resided at the Confederate capital.

55. W. Davis, *A Government of Our Own*, 211; King, *Louis A. Wigfall*, 128–29.

56. Crow and Barden, eds., *Live Your Own Life*, 67; Allardice, *Confederate Colonels*, 102.

57. *San Francisco Daily Evening Bulletin,* April 30, 1861; King, *Louis A. Wigfall,* 125; Cutrer, *Ben McCulloch and the Frontier Military Tradition,* 193.

58. W. Davis, *A Government of Our Own,* 215. A career officer disdainfully described non–West Pointers as "parlor Knights" and "scarred veterans from Nicaragua" who seemed to spring up "as if by magic" (Victor M. Rose, *Ross' Texas Brigade: Being a Narrative of Events Connected With Its Service in the Late War Between the States* [Louisville, Ky.: printed at Courier-Journal, 1881], 15).

59. McCulloch to Wigfall, April 2, 1861, in Cutrer, *Ben McCulloch and the Frontier Military Tradition,* 194–98.

60. "Montgomery As the Confederate Capital: View of a New Nation," 9; King, *Louis A. Wigfall,* 126.

61. William Howard Russell, *My Diary North and South* (repr., New York: Harper and Brothers, 1954), 88, entry for May 5, 1861; May, *Manifest Destiny's Underworld,* 283–84.

62. Brown, *Agents of Manifest Destiny,* 366–67, 445–46; Dando-Collins, *Tycoon's War,* 267–68; May, *Manifest Destiny's Underworld,* 274, 353 n. 99; W. Davis, *A Government of Our Own,* 215–16.

63. "Gen. John Thomas Pickett, Find a Grave Memorial, www.findagrave.com/; W. Davis, *A Government of Our Own,* 305, 320; OR II, 3: 1520. May, *Manifest Destiny's Underworld,* 276, 285, notes that the hot-headed Pickett would do more harm than good by telling Mexico's foreign minister that if Mexico didn't stop allowing Union troops to cross its territory, "30,000 Confederate diplomats' might cross the Rio Grande".

64. McIntosh, ed., *Papers of Jefferson Davis,* 7: 144, 179; Terry Jones, *"Lee's Tigers": The Louisiana Infantry in the Army of Northern Virginia* (Baton Rouge: Louisiana State University Press, 1987), 6–7.

65. *Cincinnati Daily Enquirer,* October 9, 1861, noted that Wheat was "leader of K. G. C.'s." The *San Francisco Daily Evening Bulletin,* September 14, 1861, reported that Wheat was mortally wounded at Battle of Bull Run at thirty-five years of age. Terry Jones, *"Lee's Tigers,"* 4–5; Charles L. Dufour, *Gentle Tiger: The Gallant Life Of Roberdeau Wheat* (Baton Rouge: Louisiana State University Press, 1957), 1–4, 120–25.

66. Simpson, *A Good Southerner,* 253, 255–63; OR I, 2: 908–9; Ella Lonn, *Foreigners in the Confederacy* (Gloucester, Mass.: P. Smith, 1965), 189; E. Kidd Lockard, "The Unfortunate Military Career of Henry A. Wise in Western Virginia," *West Virginia History* 31, no. 1 (October 1969): 42–54; OR I, 2: 838, 908–9; I, 5: 150–65.

67. King, *Louis A. Wigfall,* 126–27, 131; Warner, *Generals in Gray,* 336–37; Hudson, "Military Knights of the Golden Circle in Texas," 192–93, 203, 234; Dunn, "KGC in Texas," 556; Stewart Sifakis, *Compendium of the Confederate Armies: Texas* (New York: Facts on File, 1995), 106–12.

68. Rose, *Ross' Texas Brigade,* 15–16; May, *Manifest Destiny's Underworld,* 283; Handbook of Texas Online: "Ross's Brigade, C. S. A."

69. Hudson, "Military Knights of the Golden Circle in Texas," 183–84, 208–9, 216; Hudson, "Knights of the Golden Circle in Texas," 61.

70. Hudson, "Knights of the Golden Circle in Texas," 61–62.

71. Gasper Tochman to Davis, May 25, 1861, in McIntosh, ed., *Papers of Jefferson Davis*, 7: 179; May, *Manifest Destiny's Underworld*, 233–34. John Smith Dye, *History of the Plots and Crimes of the Great Conspiracy to Overthrow Liberty in America* (repr., New York: self-published, 1866), 114, states: "The Golden Circle, and other secret military organizations, gave [the Confederacy] a great advantage in getting an organized army early into the field."

## CHAPTER TWELVE: THE STRUGGLE FOR KENTUCKY

1. Kent Masterson Brown, *The Civil War in Kentucky: Battle for the Bluegrass State* (Mason City, Iowa: Savas, 2000), i–ii, 23, notes that Lincoln was reported to have said, "I hope to have God on my side but I must have Kentucky." Lincoln to Orville H. Browning, September 22, 1861, in Basler, ed., *Collected Works of Abraham Lincoln*, 4: 532, in which Lincoln wrote, "I think to lose Kentucky is nearly the same as to lose the whole game."

2. "Knights of the Golden Circle," *Memphis Daily Appeal*, May 7, 1861, containing Bickley's "Order to the Army of K. G. C.," which further states: "Two regiments are now being formed in the State [Kentucky] to be held subject to the orders of the Governor. The order now has 16,343 men in the field and the president has no hesitation in saying that the number can be duplicated if necessity requires." Bickley had earlier claimed that "he had 4000 acres of land in Virginia—had spent $90,000 of his private fortune in practicalizing his favorite schemes—had collected some $400,000 or $500,000 more . . . [and] had 150,000 men enrolled in the United States, and 35,000 more in Mexico" ("Knights of the Golden Circle," *Philadelphia Inquirer*, April 5, 1861).

3. Beriah Magoffin, a gentleman farmer and lawyer from central Harrodsburg, had been elected in 1859 on a states'-rights platform that endorsed the proslavery *Dred Scott* decision, encouraged the acquisition of Cuba, and denounced the sectional agitators of the North (Arndt Stickles, *Simon Bolivar Buckner: Borderland Knight* (Chapel Hill: University of North Carolina Press, 1940), 45–46; *Madison [Wisc.] Daily Argus Democrat*, January 10, 1859). Magoffin's brothers in Arizona and Missouri were ardent secessionists (Frasier, *Blood and Treasure*, 34–35; William B. Claycomb, "President Lincoln and the Magoffin Brothers" [Dayton, Ohio: Morningside Bookshop, 1984]: www.morningsidebooks.com). The purported KGC author of *An Authentic Exposition of the "K. G. C."* charged: "Governor Magoffin, is said to be himself a Knight of the first magnitude" (58). Union General George B. McClellan said: "From reliable information, I am sure that the Governor of Kentucky is a traitor" (OR I, 51 [pt. 1]: 375: McClellan to Townsend, May 10, 1861).

4. Merton E. Coulter, *The Civil War and Readjustment in Kentucky* (New York: Oxford University Press, 1926), 48–51, 83–85.

5. Gary Lee Williams, "James and Joshua Speed: Lincoln's Kentucky Friends" (Ph.D. diss., Duke University, 1971), 83, citing *Louisville Weekly Journal*, May 28, 1861; "The Conspiracy," *Louisville Journal*, May 16, 1861; "Something Requiring Explanation," *Louisville Journal*, May 23, 1861. Luke Blackburn would later become involved with the Confederate secret service in Canada and an ineffectual 1864 plot to distribute yellow-fever-infested clothing

and bedding to several northern locations (including to President Lincoln in Washington) (Tidwell, *Come Retribution*, 185–86).

6. *Louisville Journal*, May 8 and June 4, 1861; *An Authentic Exposition of the "K. G. C,"* 41.

7. "State Rights Convention in Russellville," *Louisville Journal*, May 30, 1861, quoting a letter "from a gentleman of reliability and respectability" who was at the Russellville meeting; Coulter, *The Civil War and Readjustment in Kentucky*, 36–37. While Bickley's letter has not surfaced, Governor Isham T. Harris had led Tennessee into secession during January–June 1861 (Sam Davis Elliott, *Confederate Governor and United States Senator: Isham G. Harris of Tennessee* [Baton Rouge: Louisiana State University Press, 2010], 60–72).

8. *Louisville Journal*, May 30, 1861.

9. Roger Bartman, "The Contributions of Joseph Holt to the Political Life of the United States (Ph.D. diss., Department of History, Fordham University, 1958), 210, citing Mary Stevens to Holt, May 28, 1861; "A Castle of the Knights of the Golden Circle Discovered in Marion County," *Cleveland Plain Dealer*, October 10, 1861.

10. *Philadelphia Inquirer*, May 15, 1861.

11. *Louisville Journal*, June 4, 1861, alleging that ten thousand KGC were summoned; ibid., June 5, 1861, publishing text of secret circular; and ibid., August 12, 1861, publishing names of KGC Third Degree members; *Cincinnati Daily Enquirer*, June 5, 1861.

12. *Louisville Journal*, May 23, 1861, text of Wolfe resolutions; ibid., May 24, 1861; "Investigating Committees," *Louisville Courier*, May 25, 1861; "K. G. C.—An Open Letter to the Kentucky Legislature," ibid., May 30, 1861.

13. "K. G. C.—An Open Letter to the Kentucky Legislature," *Louisville Courier*, May 30, 1861.

14. *Louisville Journal*, June 5, 1861.

15. "The Treasonable Plot Confessed," *Frankfort (Ky.) Commonwealth*, June 4, 1861.

16. "Canvass in the Second District—Bickley's Knights at Work," letter to the editors of *Louisville Journal* from "C," dated June 6, 1861, found in Bickley Papers, National Archives.

17. "Paducah Correspondence," *New York Herald*, September 29, 1861.

18. "Armed Neutrality," *Louisville Journal*, May 28, 1861; "Bickley Recruiting in Simpson County," ibid., June 4, 1861, "Major Tilghman's Secret Plan to Hurry Kentucky out of Union," ibid., June 6, 1861; Berry F. Craig, "The Jackson Purchase of Kentucky in the Secession Crisis of 1860–1861" (master's thesis, Murray State University, 1973), 48–56, 77–78.

19. Daniel Stevenson, "General Nelson, Kentucky, and Lincoln Guns," *Magazine of American History* 10 (July–December 1883): 115–27; Coulter, *The Civil War and Readjustment in Kentucky*, 53–56, 67, 82–85; Craig, "Jackson Purchase Region of Kentucky," 44.

20. "Hon. Jos. Holt to J. F. Speed," dated May 31, 1861, in *Letters of the Hon. Joseph Holt, the Hon. Edward Everett and Commodore Charles Stewart, on the Present Crisis* (Philadelphia: William S. Martien and Alfred Martien, 1861), 5–34 (quote at 24); Harry A. Volz III, "Party, State, and Nation: Kentucky and the Coming of the American Civil War" (Ph.D. diss., Ann Arbor, Mich. 1982), 435–55.

21. Captain Thomas Speed, *The Union Cause in Kentucky: 1860–1865* (New York: Putnam and Sons, 1907), 88; Roger J. Bartman, "The Contribution of Joseph Holt to the Political

Life of the United States" (Ph.D. diss., Fordham University, 1958), 215, quoting Nelson to Holt, July 2, 1861.

22. Stickles, *Simon Bolivar Bucker*, 71–72; Robert Emmett McDowell, *City of Conflict: Louisville in the Civil War, 1861-1865* (Louisville Civil War Roundtable, 1962), 36–42.

23. Geoff Walden, "Camps Boone and Burnett, Tennessee," First Kentucky "Orphan Brigade," www.rootsweb.com/~orphanhm/campboone.htm; Ed Porter Thompson, *History of the Orphan Brigade* (Louisville, Ky.: Lewis N. Thompson, 1898), 43–44; *Louisville Journal*, June 6, 1861; Craig, "Jackson Purchase Region of Kentucky," 50–56, 75; *Kentucky Statesman* (Louisville), July 9, 1861.

24. J. H. L. of Elkton, Ky., letter to the editor, *Louisville Journal*, July 16, 1861.

25. *Louisville Journal*, July 18, 1861; James Row to Bickley, July 26, 1861, Bickley Papers, National Archives, Washington, D.C.

26. *Clarksville (Tenn.) Chronicle*, August 2, 1861.

27. Ibid., July 31, 1861. John D. Morris was a Kentuckian from Christian County who, as a young man, had migrated to Texas and participated in the Texas Revolution against Mexico. In April 1861, he was sent to New Orleans to oversee the confiscation of northern funds deposited in its banks and in late 1861 was appointed by the Confederate government to sequester the deposits of Kentucky banks. He later attached himself to the First Kentucky Cavalry (Confederate) commanded by Ben Hardin Helm (www.kentuckygenealogy.org/christian/biography_of_john_d_morris.htm; "Morris, John Dabney," in Allardice, *Confederate Colonels*, 283: OR IV, 1:799, 904–5). In July 1861, Tennessee governor Isham Harris was raising Tennessee troops for the Confederacy (Elliott, *Confederate Governor and United States Senator*, 86–87).

28. William Nelson to Joseph Holt, August 1, 1861, Joseph Holt Papers, Library of Congress.

29. "Encampment at Muldraugh's Hill," *Louisville Journal*, July 8, 1861; "The K. G. C.—The State Guard," *Louisville Journal*, August 21, 1861; Ronald Ray Alexander, "Central Kentucky in the Civil War: 1861–1865 (Ph.D. diss., University of Kentucky, 1976), 72, 74–76.

30. "The Order of the Knights of the Golden Circle—Important Revelation," *Louisville Journal*, July 18, 1861. From its context, it appears that the KGC ritual that Prentice published (including it numbered code) was the one used by the KGC before September 15, 1860.

31. Ibid.

32. Ibid.

33. "Knights of the Golden Circle," *Louisville Journal*, August 12, 1861. The other KGC Third Degree members listed were "G. Glavis, Wm. E. Jones, H. C. McCortle, W. B. Hoke, J. Bast, A. A. Urban, . . . E. D. Ricketts, . . . P. A. Malone."

34. "An Open Letter to the Knights of the Golden Circle," *Richmond Whig*, July 17, 1861; Benjamin M. Harney to Grant, Jan. 19, 1876, in *The Papers of Ulysses S. Grant*, ed. John Y. Simon, vol. 27, *January 1-October 31, 1876* (Carbondale: Southern Illinois University Press, 1967), 353–54.

35. Alexander, "Central Kentucky in the Civil War," 87–88; "Lincolnism in Kentucky," *Louisville Courier*, July 29, 1861.

36. Joseph Holt, "Address," Delivered at Louisville, July 13, 1861, in *Rebellion Record*, ed. F. Moore, 2: 297–303, Document 90; Roger J. Bartman, "The Contribution of Joseph Holt to the Political Life of the United States" (Ph.D. diss., Fordham University, New York), 216–20.

37. Craig, "Jackson Purchase Region of Kentucky in the Secession Crisis of 1860–1861," 84–87; Speed, *Union Cause in Kentucky*, 88–89, 348 (Wickliffe quote at para. 8), citing *Congressional Globe*, August 6, 1861.

38. "The Duty of Good Citizens," *Louisville Journal*, August 8, 1861; Alexander, "Central Kentucky in the Civil War," 90.

39. Coulter, *Civil War and Readjustment in Kentucky*, 113; "The [Louisville] Peace Meeting," *Louisville Journal*, August 20 and 24, 1861.

40. *Louisville Journal*, October 6, 1861. Dye, *History of the Plots and Crimes of the Great Conspiracy*, 114, alleges that Breckinridge remained in Kentucky until September 21 "to use his influence to unite that State with Jeff. Davis." Breckinridge confidant James Clay was arrested as a traitor in southern Kentucky trying to escape. *Lowell (Mass.) Daily Citizen and News*, October 1, 1861.

41. *Louisville Courier*, August 27, 1861, describing various peace meetings; Davis, *Breckinridge: Statesman, Soldier, Symbol*, 281–89, 296–97; Warner, *Generals in Gray*, 34–35: "John Cabal Breckinridge"; ibid., 38–39: "Simon Bolivar Buckner."

42. Hughes, *Life and Wars of Gideon J. Pillow*, 194–95; Craig, "Jackson Purchase Region of Kentucky in the Secession Crisis of 1860–1861," 92–93.

43. "Paducah Correspondence," *New York Herald*, September 29, 1861. These "secret" KGC castle documents were supposedly sent to Washington but have never resurfaced. Grant's September 6, 1861, report referenced "letters and dispatches" that were seized, but these have never been found (Grant to Freemont, Sept. 6, 1861, in *Papers of Ulysses S. Grant*, ed. Simon, 2: 196–98 n. 6).

44. Jennie Angell Mengell, "The Neutrality of Kentucky in 1861" (master's thesis, University of Louisville, 1925), 65–67; "The Kentucky Resolutions" adopted September 12, 1861, in *Rebellion Record*, ed. F. Moore, 3: 129, Document 45; Steven E. Woodworth, *Jefferson Davis and His Generals: The Failure of the Confederate Command in the West* (Lawrence: University Press of Kansas, 1990), 40–45.

45. *Clarkesville (Tenn.) Courier*, August 2, 1861. In September 1861, Bickley further offered to provide a regiment of mounted Kentuckians to Confederate secretary of war Walker, but it was declined due to the inability of the Confederates to arm them (Bickley letter dated September 3, 1861, Bickley Papers, National Archives).

46. Crenshaw, "Knights of the Golden Circle," 45, citing Bickley to Letcher, February 3, 1862.

47. Ibid.; "29th North Carolina Regiment," http://thomaslegion.net/29th.html.

48. Dunn, "KGC in Texas, 1860–1861," 573, citing Bickley Papers, National Archives; see *Boston Daily Advertiser*, August 2, 1861, for a humorous tongue-in-cheek article regarding Bickley's claimed exploits.

49. Hudson, "Knights of the Golden Circle in Texas," 59–62. The *Corpus Christi (Tex.) Ranchero*, July 20, 1861, reported that the Corpus Christi Knights who had not done so were being urged to take the oath of allegiance to the Confederate States of America.

50. *San Antonio Daily Ledger and Texan,* May 27, 1861.

51. Newcomb, *Sketch of Secession Times in Texas,* 6.

52. With respect to the northeastern states, a flourishing castle was reported in Philadelphia in early 1861 (*Milwaukee Sentinel,* April 18, 1861). Parker French, a Texas KGC and former Walker filibuster, was arrested at Bradford, Connecticut, in November 1861 (after visiting Boston and Philadelphia), where a plot was alleged to seize the arsenal, navy yard, and public property. French had papers that were a counterpart to the KGC Constitution and Bylaws (but titled "Knights of the Golden Square") (La Fayette Baker, *Spies, Traitors and Conspirators of the Late Civil War* [Philadelphia: John E. Potter, 1894], 99–107; OR II, 2: 1275–78). The KGC was also alleged to be operating in Berks County, Pennsylvania, but arrests and exposure generally ended KGC activity in the East (Mayo Fesler, "Secret Political Societies in the North during the Civil War," *Indiana Magazine of History* 14, no. 3 [September 1918]: 222–23).

53. Fesler, "Secret Political Societies in the North during the Civil War," 214–22. The wife of Union General John Logan writes of harassment by a KGC member over her hiring a Negro in southern Illinois (Mrs. John A. Logan, *Reminiscences of a Soldier's Wife: An Autobiography* [Carbondale: Southern Illinois University Press, 1997], 149–51). "The K. G. C.s in Trouble," *Jamestown (N.Y.) Journal,* August 22, 1862, reported that the grand jury alleged during late 1861/early 1862 that the KGC had extended itself from every part of the South into Indiana, where it had an estimated fifteen thousand members, as well as in other northern states. Cf. George Bickley's December 1863 "Address" from prison denying that there were KGC in the northern states (*Columbus [Ohio] Crisis,* December 30, 1863).

54. Jennifer L. Weber, *Copperheads: The Rise and Fall of Lincoln's Opponents in the North* (New York: Oxford University Press, 2006), 54, 80, 92; *Scioto (Ohio) Gazette,* July 30, 1861; "A Castle of the Knights of the Golden Circle Discovered in Marion County [Ohio]," *Cleveland (Ohio) Plain Dealer,* October 8, 1861; *Sandusky (Ohio) Register,* October 15, 1861; "Arrest of KGC Leader Alleging That More Than Three Thousand in Southern Ohio Counties," *Cleveland (Ohio) Plain Dealer,* November 11, 1861; OR III, 3: 69–71.

55. "Important Developments: The Knights of the Golden Circle Again: The United States Grand Jury of the Indiana District Present the Organization as Treasonable," *New York Times,* August 7, 1862; "The K. G. C. in Trouble," *Jamestown (N.Y.) Journal,* August 22, 1862; "Some Facts about the Order in Indiana," *Wooster (Ohio) Republican;* "Knights of the Golden Circle Arrests by the Government," *New York Times,* September 1, 1862.

56. *New Jersey State Gazette and Republican,* April 21, 1863; Fesler, "Secret Political Societies in the North during the Civil War," 207, 224; OR III, 3: 62–72.

57. James A. Ramage, *The Life of General John Hunt Morgan* (Lexington: University of Press of Kentucky, 1986), 158–82; Cathryn J. Prince, *Burn the Town and Sack the Banks: Confederates Attack Vermont* (New York: Carroll and Graf, 2006), 67–68; *New York Herald,* July 31, 1864. At the time, Colonel Robert C. Tyler, was serving as provost-general for Bragg's Army of Tennessee with responsibility for secret service activities, John W. Headley, *Confederate Operations in Canada and New York* (New York: The Neale Publishing Company, 1906), 67–68.

58. "Memorandum of condition of public affairs in Indiana to be submitted to the President and honorable Secretary of War," by Henry B. Carrington, Colonel, Eighteenth, U.S. Infantry, Comdg. At Indianapolis, in Tidwell, *Come Retribution*, 195; OR II, 5: 108, 364–65: March 19, 1863. General Lewis Wallace would subsequently note that "Morgan . . . was lured into Indiana by promises that the display of his flag there would be the signal of rebellion by a secret organization known as "Knights of the Golden Circle" (Lewis Wallace, *Lew Wallace: An Autobiography* [New York: Harper and Brothers, 1906], 656). Morgan's second-in-command, General Basil Duke, later said the Knights provided no assistance during the raid and that they only met two or three members of the order in Indiana (Fesler, "Secret Political Societies in the North during the Civil War," 214, citing Statement of Gen. Basil Duke, March 28, 1903).

59. "Pogue's Run Battle Was Slapstick Fight," *Indianapolis News*, May 20, 1963; *Indianapolis in the War of the Rebellion, Report of the Adjutant General: A Reprint of Volume 1 of the Eight-Volume Report Prepared by W. H. H. Terrell and Published in 1868* (Indiana Historical Society, 1960), 372.

60. See Klement, *Dark Lanterns*, 27–28, which contends that alleged KGC support to Morgan was a myth developed to cover up General Carrington's incompetence.

61. Ramage, *Life of General John Hunt Morgan*, 177–83.

62. Crenshaw, "Knights of the Golden Circle," 45–46.

63. George L. Gibbs memo, July 23, 1863, "Identification of Bickley and Articles found among the effects of George W. L. Bickley," Bickley Papers, National Archives. At the time of his capture, Bickley was described as five feet eleven inches, and having a fair complexion, light hair, and blue eyes.

64. An attorney filed an application for Bickley's release after he was brought to Fort Lafayette in New York, but the federal government avoided a hearing by moving him to Fort Warren in Boston's harbor during March 1865 ("Denial of the Application of George W. L. Bickley to Be Discharged," *New York Times*, May 11, 1865; Klement, *Dark Lanterns*, 29–33).

## CHAPTER THIRTEEN: A REJUVENATED KGC?

1. OR II, 7: 232; "The Great Northwest Conspiracy," *Philadelphia Inquirer*, July 29, 1864; Albert Castel, *General Sterling Price and the Civil War in the West* (Baton Rouge: Louisiana State University Press, 1968), 195–96. Phineas Wright had lived in New Orleans from 1850 to 1857, where he admired the filibusterers and laid the plans for his new secret society (Klement, *Dark Lanterns*, 64–65).

2. Klement, *Dark Lanterns*, 66–72; Fesler, "Secret Political Societies in the North during the Civil War," 224–35. The OAK grand commanders in early 1864 included William A. Bowles (Illinois), Judge J. F. Bullitt (Kentucky), Harrison H. Dodd (Indiana), Charles L. Hunt (Missouri) and James A. McMaster (New York). The four military district commanders (major generals) in Indiana were Lambdin P. Milligan of Hunington County, John C. Walker of LaPorte, Andrew Humphreys of Greene, and William Bowles of Orange (William Henry Harrison Terrell, *Indiana in the War of the Rebellion: Report of the Adjutant General* [repr., Indiana Historical Society, 1960]: 1: 379).

3. Felix Stiger, ed., *Treason History of the Order of Sons of Liberty* (Hemphill, Tex.: Dogwood, 1903), 39.

4. OR II, 7: 231, 247.

5. Peter F. Stevens, "The Saga of Lambdin P. Milligan," *Indiana Horizons*, Summer 1988, 26–27; Fesler, "Secret Political Societies in the North during the Civil War," 224, 232; Ben Pittman, ed., *The Trials for Treason at Indianapolis, Disclosing the Plans For Establishing a Northwestern Confederacy* . . . (Cincinnati: Moore, Wilstach, and Baldwin, 1865), 107 (Felix G. Stiger testimony); and 119–20 (Elliott Robertson testimony), indicating that the lodge in Randolph County, Indiana, changed from the KGC to the OAK between the spring and fall of 1863.

6. *Philadelphia Inquirer*, July 29, 1864; *New York Herald*, July 31, 1864.

7. "Arrest of Four Knights of the Golden Circle—Excitement at Reading," *New York Herald*, April 10, 1863. "The Reading Sensation," *New York Herald*, April 11, 1863, alleges that the KGC oath asked: "Are you in favor of the abduction of Abraham Lincoln?" Report of Jno. S. Richards, March 17, 1863, from Reading, Berks County, Pa., OR III, 3: 75; Mayo Fesler, "Secret Political Societies in the North during the Civil War," 222–23. Chapters of the KGC were alleged to exist at Mohrsville in Berks County and at Lynnville in Lehigh County, Pennsylvania ("Political Arrests," *Reading [Pa.] Daily Times*, April 13, 1863; Richard E. Matthews, *Lehigh County Pennsylvania in the Civil War: An Account* [Lehighton, Pa.: Times News Printing, 1989], 57–58 n. 14).

8. Frank L. Klement, *Dark Lanterns* 73–90, 105–35, 234–44, contends that the arrests of some of the OAK/SOL members were the result of entrapment and that the size and effectiveness of these societies were greatly exaggerated. A letter was also circulated in April 1862 purporting to show that former President Franklin Pierce was a member of the Knights, but Pierce vehemently denied it and the letter was shown to be a hoax ("Franklin Pierce and the K. G. C.'s," *New York Herald Tribune*, April 4, 1862; Larry Gara, *The Presidency of Franklin Pierce* [Lawrence: University Press of Kansas, 1991], 179–80).

9. Weber, *Copperheads*, 25–26.

10. "Knights of the Golden Circle," in Scott L. Mingus, *Flames beyond Gettysburg: The Gordon Expedition, June 1863: A History and Tour Guide* (Columbus, Ohio: Ironclad, 2009), 555 n. 2, citing Cassandra Morris Small letters, York County (Pa.) Heritage Trust files; Tidwell, *Come Retribution*, 184; Jubal Anderson Early, *War Memoirs: Autographical Sketch and Narrative of the War Between the States* (Bloomington: Indiana University Press, 1960), 265.

11. *Official Report of the Judge Advocate General of the United States Army on the "Order of American Knights" Alias, Order of Sons of Liberty: A Western Conspiracy in Aid of the Southern Rebellion* (Washington, D.C.: Bureau of Military Justice, War Department, October 8, 1864), OR II, 7: 930–53.

12. *Wisconsin Patriot*, August 8, 1863. A Republican election broadside titled "Copperhead Conspiracy in the North-West: An Exposé of the Treasonable Order . . ." begins: "In 1863, this order [O. A. K.] existed in the state of Indiana, under the name of 'Knights of the Golden Circle' . . ."; "Copperhead Conspiracy in the North-West: An Exposé of the Treasonable Order of the 'Sons Of Liberty,' Vallandigham, Supreme Commander," printed by the Union

NOTES TO PAGES 173–175

Congressional Committee (New York: Gray, 1864). Klement, *Dark Lanterns*, 90, notes that the linkage with the KGC helped the Republicans win the 1864 elections.

13. Klement, *Dark Lanterns*, 72–74; Stiger, ed., *Treason History of the Order of Sons of Liberty*, 49.

14. Confederate Lieutenant General Leonidas Polk asserted that these "formidable associations" if "properly used . . . could be of great value to our cause" (*Lincoln Assassination Evidence*, 904–5: Endorsement of Lt. Gen. L. Polk, Feb. 27, 1864). J. B. Jones, *A Rebel War Clerk's Diary at the Confederate States Capital*, ed. Howard Swigett (New York: Old Hickory Bookshop, 1935), 2: 155, contains a report from one of General Morgan's secret agents in a February 1864 letter from Lieutenant Colonel R. A. Alston.

15. Larry E. Nelson, *Bullets, Ballots, and Rhetoric: Confederate Policy for the United States Presidential Contest of 1864* (Tuscaloosa: University of Alabama Press, 1980), 19–22; "Prison Camps of the American Civil War," http://delawarepublicrecordsearch.org/71/prison-camps-of-the-american-civil-war/, 4.

16. In his report, Tucker also said the OAK had more than 100,000 members in Illinois and Indiana, around 40,000 in New York and Ohio, and more than 15,000 in Iowa, New Jersey, and Missouri (G. E. Rule, *Tucker's War: Missouri and the Northwest Conspiracy* [2002], 17–18, Appendix C: Confidential Statement J. W. Tucker to Jefferson Davis, March 14, 1861, www.civilwarstlouis.com/history2/tuckerswar.htm).

17. Nelson, *Bullets, Ballots, and Rhetoric*, 22–24; Judah Benjamin to John Slidell, April 30, 1864, in *Official Records, Navies*, Series II, vol. 3: 1105–6; William A. Tidwell, *April '65: Confederate Covert Action in the American Civil War* (Kent, Ohio: Kent State University Press, 1995), 129–31; John W. Headley, *Confederate Operations in Canada and New York* (New York: Neale, 1906), 218–23.

18. OR I, 50 (pt. 2): 930–31 and 938–41. Beriah Brown, a San Francisco newspaper editor, served as the KCS's "Governor General" and former California governor John Bigler was reportedly a member. Bancroft, *The Works*, vol. 24, containing *History of California—1860-1890*, vol. 7, 282, 308–9, indicates that Weller, after losing the election for San Francisco sheriff, advocated resistance to the draft and was imprisoned from July through August 1863. Laurence Fletcher Talbot, "California Secession Support of the Southern Confederacy: The Struggle, 1861–1865" (Ph.D. diss., Union Institute, 1995), 124.

19. OR I, 43 (pt. 2): 930–38: Report of Thompson to Judah Benjamin; Oscar A. Kinchen, *Confederate Operations in Canada and the North: A Little Known Phase of the Civil War* (North Quincy, Mass.: Christopher, 1970), 44–45; Nelson, *Bullets, Ballots, and Rhetoric*, 86–87.

20. Headley, *Confederate Operations In Canada And New York*, 224–30; Terrell, *Indiana in the War of the Rebellion*: 377–78; Kinchen, *Confederate Operations Canada and the North*, 61, 224–25, reproducing letter from T. E. Lacy (Clay) to Mr. W. P. Carson (Thompson), August 3, 1864. Ben Wood and his brother Fernando were alleged to be tied in with the KGC (Milton, *Abraham Lincoln and the Fifth Column*, 154; Menahem Blondheim, ed., *Copperhead Gore: Benjamin Wood's Fort Lafayette and Civil War America* [Bloomington: Indiana University Press, 2006], 61).

21. Kinchen, *Confederate Operations in Canada and New York*, 67–70; Headley, *Confederate Operations in Canada and New York*, 227–30; Tidwell, *Come Retribution*, 198–99; OR II, 8: 234, 244–45; Klement, *Dark Lanterns*, 202–17. The Indianapolis treason trials were held before a military commission in December 1864, at which eight of the alleged Chicago ringleaders were convicted. The KGC was still active in Missouri and some Knights did journey to Chicago for the planned uprising (OR II, 7: 257; Mason Emerson, *Missouri's Secret Confederate Agents: The Knights of the Golden Circle* [Blue and Grey Book Shoppe, 2002], 2–3 reproducing letter from T. B. Webb).

22. Nat Brandt, *The Man Who Tried to Burn New York* (San Jose: toExcel, 2000), 100–102; "Definition of Civil War Terms," www.civilwarhome.com/terms.htm.

23. Headley, *Confederate Operations in Canada and New York*, 274–81; OR I, 43 (pt. 2): 930, 934.

24. Tidwell, *April '65*, 142–45; Hall, *Come Retribution*, 328–34; Asia Booth Clarke, *The Untold Book: A Memoir of John Wilkes Booth by His Sister* (New York: Putnam's Sons, 1931), 115–17; Kimmel, *Mad Booths of Maryland*, 179, 349 n. 24; *Lincoln Assassination Evidence*, 691: Henry Higginson. Sam Arnold later said that Booth had a pass signed by General Grant that allowed him to travel to the South during the war, also that Booth told Michael O'Laughlen's brother that he held a commission in the Confederate army (ibid., Samuel Bland Arnold, "Lincoln Conspiracy and the Conspirators," *Baltimore American*, 1902, 3, 6). *Assassination of Lincoln*, Report No. 104, July 1866, House of Representatives, 39th Cong., 1st sess., Washington, D.C., notes that "Doctor J. W. Booth" had been referenced in Confederate Department of War records.

25. *Lincoln Assassination Evidence*, 1400–1401: H. C. Young to Stanton, April 20, 1865; *Right or Wrong*, 101–2 n. 2; Ernest C. Miller, *John Wilkes Booth in the Pennsylvania Oil Region: Including the Complete Interviews of Louis J. Mackey Done in 1894 at Franklin, Pennsylvania, with People Who Had Known Booth during his 1864 sojourn here* (Meadville, Pa.: Crawford County Historical Society, 1987), 61, interview with Frank L. Mears citing letters between Booth and Thomas Y. Mears; OR I, 32 (pt. 2): 671. After the Canadian meeting, Booth journeyed via Cairo, Illinois, and Memphis to New Orleans for a month of performances, where he spent much time with Hiram Martin, a Confederate blockade-runner (John S. Kendall, *The Golden Age of New Orleans Theatre* [Baton Rouge: Louisiana State University Press, 1952], 497–98).

26. Hall, *Come Retribution*, 263–65; Kimmel, *Mad Booths of Maryland*, 186; Tidwell, *April '65*, 142–45. Alfred E. Penn alleged that the scheme to assassinate Lincoln and his cabinet was discussed around the time of the August 1864 Chicago Convention (*Lincoln Assassination Evidence*, 1039–40). Driver, *First & Second Maryland Infantry, C. S. A.*, 366, writes that Arnold returned to Baltimore in February 1864 due to the illness of his mother.

27. Hall, *Come Retribution*, 332–33, references a report from Union spy Colonel Ambrose Stevens that one of the Confederate peace commissioners (likely Sanders) was urging a plan to assassinate Lincoln before the November election to cause chaos in the North and on the night of Lincoln's assassination received a suspicious telegram from Washington, which he immediately answered (*Lincoln Assassination Evidence*, 136–37: D. R. P. Bigley of Montreal,

April 20, 1865). Edward Valentine, a Richmond sculptor who knew John Wilkes Booth during 1858–59, later said that Booth's April 1865 assassination did not represent the South but rather the followers of Mazzini (letter from Valentine Museum, April 26, 1941, in David Rankin Barbee Papers, Georgetown University; Giuseppe Mazzini—biography, "Young Italy Risorgimento": www.age-of-the-sage.org/historical/biography/giuseppe_mazzini.html).

28. Tidwell, *April '65*, 126, 135, 142–45; *Lincoln Assassination Evidence*, 621 n. 1; "Patrick Charles Martin" file, Surratt Society Library, Clinton, Md. Entries #344 at RG 393, Register 121, 8th Army Corps, Military Prison, Baltimore, National Archives, indicates that Patrick Martin was arrested on May 22, 1863, the same day as "Louis Powell" (entry 325) and three weeks after "Henry Ferrandini" (entry 180) (April 29, 1863).

29. Samuel Bland Arnold and Michael W. Kauffman, eds., *Memoirs of a Lincoln Conspirator*, ed. Michael W. Kauffman (Bowie, Md.: Heritage, 2008), 122–23; *Lincoln Assassination Evidence*, 343: Samuel K. Chester. Tidwell, *Come Retribution*, 264, notes that at the time of his August 1864 meeting with Arnold and Chester, Booth was already aware of precise information as to Lincoln's habits and movements. "Prison Camps of the American Civil War," 4, http://delawarepublicrecordsearch.org/71/prison-camps-of-the-american-civil-war/.

30. Virgil Carrington Jones, *Ranger Mosby* (Chapel Hill: University of North Carolina Press, 1944), 118–19, 183; Ramage, *Rebel Raider*, 66–74, 118–19, 241–42. There had also been a February 1864 attempt to kidnap Vice President-elect Andrew Johnson at Louisville (Headley, *Confederate Operations in Canada and New York*, 402–10). In August 1864, Confederate secretary of war James Seddon also provided Captain Thomas Nelson Conrad of Virginia's Third Cavalry Regiment with authority to organize a secret mission to kidnap Lincoln and release the Confederates held at Washington's Old Capitol Prison (Tidwell, *Come Retribution*, 281–85, citing Thomas Nelson Conrad, *A Confederate Spy* [New York: J. S. Ogilvie, 1892], 68–74; Tidwell, *April '65*, 70–75).

31. "Plots to Assassinate or Kidnap President Lincoln," *New York Daily Tribune*, March 19, 1864. "A Rebel Conspiracy Thwarted—Plot to Seize Mr. Lincoln," *Zanesville (Ohio) Daily Courier*, September 24, 1864, references a Washington letter in the *New York Commercial* of several months before.

32. Thomas A. Jones, *J. Wilkes Booth: An Account of His Sojourn in Southern Maryland after the Assassination of Abraham Lincoln, His Passage across the Potomac, and His Death in Virginia* (Chicago: Laird and Lee, 1893), 32–43. In late 1864, Booth also met with Thomas Harbin, a resourceful agent of the Confederate Secret Service in Virginia, to seek help in moving the abducted Lincoln across the Potomac. Harbin gave Booth the name of John Surratt and others eventually involved in the abduction plot (Hall, *Come Retribution*, 6, 337; *The Surratt Family & John Wilkes Booth*, compiled from the research of James O. Hall, The Surratt Society, Clinton, Maryland, 11; *Lincoln Assassination Evidence*, 216, 696, 842, 868).

33. *Lincoln Assassination Evidence*, 340, 343: Samuel K. Chester; 665, 674, 677: David Herold. Booth had originally met Herold in April 1863 when Herold was serving as an apothecary clerk at Thompson's drugstore, which supplied the White House. The two may have been involved in a subsequent plot to poison Lincoln (*The Mad Booths of Maryland*, 173; Louis J. Weichmann, Floyd E. Risvold, ed., *A True History of Abraham Lincoln and of the*

*Conspiracy of 1865* [New York: Knopf, 1975], 43–44, 63–64). When separately questioned after his arrest, conspirator Louis Powell cryptically said: "You have not got the half of them" (Pitch, *"They Killed Papa Dead!"* 310).

34. Tidwell, *Come Retribution*, 414; Rhodehamel, ed., *"Right or Wrong: God Judge Me,"* 140–42; Klement, *Dark Lanterns*, 70–75. An anonymous correspondent reported to Stanton that Booth had been at a supper at August Belmont's house in November 1864 and that Belmont, Fernando Wood, and other New York City Democratic leaders were aware of the conspiracy to murder President Lincoln (*Lincoln Assassination Evidence*, 29–30).

35. Pitch, "They Have Killed Papa Dead!," 114–15, 121–27.

36. Klement, *Dark Lanterns*, 33 n. 98, references James R. Gilmore to Holt, April 22, 1865, in Holt Papers, Library of Congress. Maj. Harvey A. Allen, notations and enclosures, May 18, 1865, in Bickley Papers, Library of Congress. Neither source indicates what Bickley actually said, but it is assumed he denied involvement in Lincoln's assassination since his contemporaneous writings try to project the KGC as a mere Mexican colonization society.

37. *Lincoln Assassination Evidence*, 392: memorandum from Chas. Cowland, April 21, 1865; see also 727–28, where U.S. State Department emissary "B" reports on May 10, 1865, from Paris that rebel agent "Johnson," who left Washington the day after the assassination, said he knew of the timing of the planned attack on Lincoln, that he had been watching Grant for two days, that the plot to assassinate included "some 15 of the Yankee leaders," and that a secret expedition was still afoot emanating from the "Pacific Coast."

38. *Lincoln Assassination Evidence*, 235–37; OR II, 8:523–25: H. L. Burnett to Stanton, May 2, 1865.

39. *Lincoln Assassination Evidence*, 332: statement of Thomas H. Carmichael that Michael O'Laughlen "confessed to having belonged to the Knights of the Golden Circle," 1206, 1210; ibid., statement of Samuel K. J. Street indicating: "[Michael O'Laughlen's] brother and I joined the Knights of the Golden Circle about eight years ago and I think he did also"; 1294–95: Mary Ann Van Tyne [Tine].

40. *Lincoln Assassination Evidence*, 545–548, 1206–1210: Samuel K. J. Street, 332: Thomas H. Carmichael, 550: Arrest of Street, 1003: Colonel Henry Steel Olcott, 1349: William H. Wells.

41. Samuel Bland Arnold, "Lincoln Conspiracy and the Conspirators," *Baltimore American*, 1902, 6, indicates that the Arnolds had grown up in Booth's old Baltimore neighborhood where their father operated a Bakery-Confectionery. Driver, *First & Second Maryland Infantry, C.S.A.*, 366, notes that Sam Arnold had a younger brother serving as a postmaster's clerk with the Army of Tennessee. Percy E. Martin, "Sam Arnold and Hooktown," *History Trails* 16, no. 4 (Summer 1992): 13–16.

42. Michael W. Kauffman, "Edman Spangler: A Life Rediscovered," *Surratt Courier* (November 1986); *Lincoln Assassination Evidence*, 546–47: case of Edmund Spangler.

43. *The Assassination of President Lincoln and Trial of the Conspirators*, U.S. Army Military Commission, 1865, compiled and arranged by Ben Pittman (Cincinnati: Moore, Wilstach and Baldwin, 1865), 313–14; Betty J. Ownsbey, *Alias "Paine": Lewis Thornton Powell, the Mystery Man of the Lincoln Conspiracy* (Jefferson, N.C.: McFarland, 1993), 28–30, 35–46,

regarding the Branson boardinghouse as well as David Preston Parr's china shop, where Powell linked up with John Surratt.

44. Ownsbey, *Alias "Paine,"* 17, 28–30, 35–46, quoting *Baltimore Sun* of March 15, 1864, which indicates that Powell was arrested under the name of "Louis Payne" and charged with being a spy, but released after taking the oath of allegiance. Pittman, *The Assassination of President Lincoln and Trial of the Conspirators*, 313–14; Pitch, *"They Have Killed Papa Dead!"* 353; Hanchett, *The Lincoln Murder Conspiracies*, 49, notes that Lewis Powell referred to Booth as "Captain" and would follow him anywhere.

45. *Lincoln Assassination Evidence*, 19. The anonymous correspondent relates the KGC to the Maryland Know-Nothing Party (of which Booth was a member) and further names "Geddes," "Surratt," "the late chief clerk of the Sixth auditors who published the Know-Nothing organ in Baltimore" as well as Atley, John Ford, and Marshal Kane.

46. Michael W. Kauffman, "David Edgar Herold: The Forgotten Conspirator," *Surratt Society News* (November 1981): 23; *Washington Star*, October 7, 1864, which indicates that Adam Herold was a native of Baltimore and a member of a number of benevolent societies.

47. Elizabeth Steger Trindal, *Mary Surratt: An American Tragedy* (Gretna, La.: Pelican, 1996), 45–46, 54, 63–66, 231–32; Andrew C. Jampoler, *The Last Lincoln Conspirator: John Surratt's Flight from the Gallows* (Annapolis, Md.: Naval Institute Press, 2008), 23–24; "The Surratt Family & John Wilkes Booth," compiled from the research of James O. Hall (Clinton, Md.: Surratt Society, 1990), 5–7. "Internment Today of Remains of Isaac D. Surratt," *Washington Star*, November 5, 1907, notes that Isaac had been educated as a civil engineer. *The Private Journal and Diary of John H. Surratt, the Conspirator* links John Surratt to the KGC, but it is a fabrication written in 1866 by dime-store novelist Dion Haco.

48. Paul H. Bergen, ed., *The Papers of Andrew Johnson*, vol. 9, September 1865– January 1866 (Knoxville: University of Tennessee Press, 1991), 228: Frederick Steel to O. H. Howard, October 11, 1865; Jampoler, *Last Lincoln Conspirator*, 277 n. 17.

49. *Lincoln Assassination Evidence*, 328–31: Louis J. Carland, 346–47: Samuel Knapp Chester, James P. Ferguson, 489, and 1013 n. 2.

50. *Lincoln Assassination Evidence*, 486–88: James P. Ferguson, see also 546–47 and 1109: statement furnished by W. P. Wood re Jacob Ritterspaugh; Weichman, *True History of the Assassination*, 154–55; Kauffman, "Edman Spangler: A Life Rediscovered," *Surratt Society News* 11 (November 1986): 33–34.

51. *Lincoln Assassination Evidence*, 448–49: J. S. Drake relaying assertions of boys who worked at Ford's.

52. *Lincoln Assassination Evidence*, 108, 329, 591–92, 922–23, 1383 (re: Gifford); 251, 638, 831–34, 1003–04, 1120–21 (re: Maddox); 329, 383–384, 448–49, 1007 (re: Lamb); 73, 516–24, 556, 1375, 1392 (re: Henry Clay Ford). In his statement at 522, Harry Clay Ford said Mr. Wright and Mr. Gifford, as well as the carpenters and the property man could have been the most useful in assisting in Booth's escape through the back of the theater. At *Lincoln Assassination Evidence*, 19–20, an anonymous correspondent from Baltimore also urged that attention be given to the ticket seller, the carpenter (likely Spangler), the lamp cleaner, and the ushers.

53. *Lincoln Assassination Evidence*, 845–48: John Matthews, 1308: letter from R. W. Walker, 344–46: Samuel Knapp Chester.

54. *Lincoln Assassination Evidence*, 1077–78: Wm. J. Rainnie; Clarke, *Unlocked Book*, 111 n. 1. In December 1864, Booth had also offered to disclose "something of great importance" to his longtime agent, Matthew Canning, who had owned the theaters in Columbus, Georgia, and Montgomery, Alabama, where Booth appeared in late 1860 (*Lincoln Assassination Evidence*, 1128–29: E. D. Sanders). Booth also kidded with his longtime actor friend Edwin Hunter that he intended to shoot the president (Weichmann, *True History of the Assassination*, 94–95).

55. *Lincoln Assassination Evidence*, 677: David Herold.

56. Tidwell, *Come Retribution*, 463–64; *Norfolk Southern Argus*, April 18, 1860: Bickley's Circular Letter referencing KGC "Major R. H. Archer of Md." Archer had served as a lieutenant colonel with the 55th VA CSA but in 1862 became the assistant adjutant general for the command of his brother, Confederate General James J. Archer ("Biography of Robert Harris Archer," *Sons of Confederate Veterans*, http://rharchercamp.org). John Tayloe VI, a son of a wealthy Virginia plantation owner, had served in the Ninth Virginia Cavalry and asserted at the time of his arrest that he was a member of Mosby's partisan rangers (Tidwell, *Come Retribution*, 463).

57. William A. Tidwell, *April '65: Confederate Covert Action in the American Civil War* (Kent, Ohio: Kent State University Press, 1995): 179, 189–90, writes that on April 15, a mounted cavalry force of Mosby's partisans was in St. Mary's County, Maryland, fewer than five miles from where the escaping Booth was located. Mosby was a Confederate colonel and his unit was designated the 43rd Virginia Battalion (Allardice, *Confederate Colonels*, 284).

58. *Lincoln Assassination Evidence*, 1201: Richard H. Stewart [Stuart]. Booth's ultimate destination was reported to be Mexico, where he hoped to find sanctuary (Jampoler, *Last Lincoln Conspirator*, 26–27). Jones, *Ranger Mosby*, 262, notes that at the time Mosby and his men were contemplating leaving for Mexico.

59. Tidwell, *Come Retribution*, 68–70, 75; Daniel Carroll Toomey, *The Civil War in Maryland* (Baltimore: Toomey, 1983), 149–50. Tidwell, *April '65*, 164, 185, notes that General Robert E. Lee felt that Boyle's undercover work and contacts were so significant that he disapproved of Boyle's proposed transfer in 1863 noting: "Major Boyle was commissioned specially for the special service on which he is now engaged. I know of no one who can take his place."

60. *Lincoln Assassination Evidence*, 1223. Boyle's first wife, Fanny, was related to Confederate spy Thomas Greene, who operated out of Washington (*Washington Post*, March 12, 1878; Tidwell, *Come Retribution*, 72–73). Thomas Green had two sons in Mosby's Rangers. At the time of Fanny Green's arrest, she was found with a large packet of mail to be sent south (*Lincoln Assassination Evidence*, 474).

61. OR II, 7: 251–252: statements of William Taylor, 309: statement of Edward F. Hoffman.

62. Owensby, *Alias Payne*, 54.

63. Rhodehamel, *Right or Wrong, God Judge Me*, 121–22; Tidwell, *Come Retribution*, 418, citing portion of Atzerodt's confession. An anonymous correspondent reported that Ben Wood and former Oregon congressman George Knox Shiel (a reputed Knight) were part of

"a large conspiracy" that resulted in Lincoln's assassination (*Lincoln Assassination Evidence,* 51). Scrap Books—"Colonel George K. Shiel" newspaper articles, SB276, 89–91, Oregon Historical Society Research Library, note that Shiel was an "out-and-out secessionist." Several reports also indicate that the Order of American Knights spearheaded a plot against Lincoln and his cabinet beginning in August 1864 (*Lincoln Assassination Evidence,* 102).

64. Cuthbert, ed., *Lincoln and the Baltimore Plot,* 93; Gordon Samples, *Lust for Fame: The Stage Career of John Wilkes Booth* (McFarland, 1982), 170.

65. OR II, 1:563; Hall, *Come Retribution,* 180–81, 187–88, 330.

66. OR IV, 3: 717: Geo. P. Kane to Jefferson Davis, Oct. 8, 1864, in which Kane notes that "my knowledge of things up to the Canada line would very materially facilitate" a secret service role. Lee to Seddon, June 26, 1864, in *The Wartime Papers of R. E. Lee,* ed. Clifford Dowdey (Boston: Little, Brown, 1961), 808: which notes the secret Marshall Kane project. "Colonel George P. Kane," *Daily Richmond Examiner,* February 22, 1864, notes that Kane was involved in "illegitimate warfare."

67. In late 1864, Jacob Thompson was heralding the formation of a new more militant society called "the Order of the Star" (which may have been referring to the Order of the Columbian Star), OR I, 43 (Pt. 2), 934, 935: Thompson to J. P. Benjamin, December 3, 1864.

# EPILOGUE

1. Warner, *Generals in Gray,* 200–201, 272–73. OR I, 8: 297–99, notes that after McCulloch's death at the Battle of Pea Ridge/Elkhorn Tavern, Colonel Elkanah Greer assumed command of the remaining forces on the field.

2. Sanders, "Robert Charles Tyler," 6–7.

3. Cothern, *Confederates of Elmwood,* 164, indicates that Taylor died of yellow fever in Memphis in October 1867.

4. Groner had assumed a cavalry command in southeast Virginia during the spring of 1862, and on October 1, 1862, he became colonel of the Sixty-First Virginia Infantry that was later incorporated into Mahone's Virginia Brigade (Allardice, *Confederate Colonels,* 176). The Sixty-First Virginia Regiment, www.nkclifton.com/61streg2,htm. After the war, Groner became a shipping agent, married the daughter of former U.S. Supreme Court justice John Campbell, and purchased land along the Norfolk waterfront, where he built several oyster houses and a wharf with private docks. He became quite wealthy and renewed his friendship with President Ulysses Grant that had begun shortly after the South's surrender at Appomattox, when Grant intervened at Groner's request to stop ill-treatment of Confederate officers (Burton, *History of Norfolk,* 613–14). "Groner, Virginius Despeaux," Biog./Hist. Note, Library of Virginia Online Reference Services. Groner remained involved in Democratic politics and is listed as a district delegate from Virginia at the National Democratic Convention of 1872. He died on November 25, 1903, and is buried at Cedar Grove Cemetery in Norfolk (Hunnicutt, *Conspiracy Unveiled,* 35).

5. Greer, ed., *Leaves from a Family Album,* 37–44; Warner, *Generals in Gray,* 118; Handbook of Texas Online: "Elkanah Greer" and "Marshall, Texas." Marshall had become the capi-

tal for the Missouri state government-in-exile so it is possible that Greer may have had some contact with Major General Sterling Price, the OAK southern commander (William R. Geise, "Missouri's Confederate Capital in Marshall, Texas," *Southwestern Historical Quarterly* 46, no. 8 [October 1962]: 200–202). Following the war, Greer lived in semi-retirement at Marshall. He died on March 25, 1877, at his sister's home at De Valls Bluff, Arkansas, and is buried at Elmwood Cemetery in Memphis.

6. Duff's Partisan Rangers were part of the Thirty-Third Regiment, Texas Cavalry. In January 1866, Chilton was arrested by Union authorities in Texas and indicted, along with others, for the 1863 lynching of W. W. Montgomery, a Unionist commander in Mexico (Chilton maintained his innocence). Later that fall, Chilton was elected to the U.S. Congress (from the Smith County area), but was denied his seat by congressional authorities because of the Texas indictment. Chilton returned to Texas for a short time but soon fled to Kentucky, where his sister resided. By March 1869, he had established a law practice in Louisville. He returned to Tyler in 1874 and led a troubled life until he passed away in 1885 (Betts, "Private and Amateur Hangings," 145–66.

7. *Lincoln Assassination Evidence*, 1400–1401; *Railroad Age Gazette* 40 (October 29, 1905), 498.

8. After the war, Howard wrote for the London *Times* (London), served as a soldier-of-fortune fighting in the Carlist Wars in Spain, and became an Indian agent, passing away in November 1892. His epitaph says: "Few men possessed, or deserve, a wider circle of friends" ("Howard, James Ross," Allardice, *Confederate Colonels*, 202–3).

9. Arthur W. Bergeson Jr., *Guide to Louisiana Confederate Military Units, 1861–1865* (Baton Rouge: Louisiana State University Press, 1996), 11; Henry C. Castellanos, *New Orleans As It Was: Episodes in Louisiana Life* (1978; repr., Baton Rouge: Louisiana State University Press, 2006), ix–xix, which indicates Castellanos died impoverished in 1895; *Columbus (Ga.) Daily Enquirer*, August 8, 1896, which indicates that Castellanos died on August 7, 1896.

10. Klement, *Dark Lanterns*, 33; Milton, *Abraham Lincoln and The Fifth Column*, 86; Crenshaw, "Knights of the Golden Circle," 46–47; *Baltimore Sun*, August 17, 1867.

11. *New York Times*, March 21, 1865, reproducing Bickley's letter. Bickley had begun recasting the KGC as solely a colonization society in his "Appeal" published in the *Columbus (Ohio) Crisis* on December 12, 1863, while he was being held prisoner at Columbus.

12. "Circular" and "General Order from Its President," *New York Times*, July 11, 1865. The Charles Templeton referred to was likely the same "C. Templeton" referenced in the captured Bickley papers as having visited the Mexican consul in July of 1859: Entry 33, Disc 1, Folder 2.8, Records of the Office of the Judge Advocate General (ARMY), Record Group 153, Bickley Papers, National Archives.

13. Klement, *Dark Lanterns*, 29–33; Crenshaw, "Knights of the Golden Circle," 46–47; Milton, *Abraham Lincoln and the Fifth Column*, 86; "Death of General Bickley," *Baltimore Sun*, August 17, 1865; Michael W. Kauffman, *American Brutus: John Wilkes Booth and the Lincoln Conspiracies* (New York: Random House, 2004), 391; Ethel W. Felber, Assistant Secretary-Treasurer, Green Mount Cemetery to James O. Hall, July 12, 1976, in Surratt Soci-

ety Library and e-mail from Dan Monahan, Green Mount Cemetery Superintendent to Laurie Verge, Surratt Society Director, September 1, 2011.

14. See Alan Axelrod, *The International Encyclopedia of Secret Societies and Fraternal Orders*, 37, 91–97, 156, 241–42, 278; Lause, *A Secret Society History of the Civil War*, 11–14, 52–66, 92–118. Axelrod, *International Encyclopedia*, x–xii, categorizes the types of secret societies as social, benevolent, ethnic, trade, mystical, political, and criminal. Some societies span a number of these such as the Brotherhood of the Union, which incorporated social betterment and superpatriotic mystical elements, or the Freemasons, which incorporates social, trade, and mystical elements. In formulating the KGC, Bickley attempted to incorporate appealing elements from existing secret societies, such as clandestine codes and rituals, and then added the popular motif of the chivalric knight.

15. Axelrod, *The International Encyclopedia of Secret Societies and Fraternal Orders*, 135–36; 270; Lause, *A Secret Society History of the Civil War*, 11–14; Mitchell Snay, *Fenians, Freedman, and Southern Whites* (Baton Rouge: Louisiana State University Press, 2007), 54–80.

16. Lossing, "New Orleans Hears That Sumter Has Fallen," in *Prologue to Sumter: The Beginnings of the Civil War from the John Brown Raid to the Surrender of Fort Sumter*, 535; Russell, *My Diary North and South*, 88, entry for May 5, 1861; May, *Manifest Destiny's Underworld*, 283–84.

17. W. Davis, "A Government of Our Own," 351; OR I, 50 (Pt. 2): 1038–39: Placido Vega to Maj. Gen. Irvin McDowell, November 2, 1861, in which Vega pleads for military assistance from the U.S. federal government for Juárez's beleaguered government in Mexico. Heidler, eds., *Encyclopedia of the American Civil War*, 1268–69: "Maximilian, Ferdinand, 1326–27: "Mexico," 1384–85, "Napoleon III." At the end of the Civil War, many Confederate officers and politicians went to live in Mexico after Maximilian offered to supply them with land in northern Mexico (on which he later reneged) (Andrew Rolle, *The Lost Cause: The Confederate Exodus to Mexico* [Norman: University of Oklahoma Press, 1965], 37–124).

18. The Knights' strong-arm measures help explain why the countervailing opposition to secession by southern Unionists that was expected by Lincoln, Seward, and the Republicans did not take place (Nevins, *Emergence of Lincoln*, 2: 305–6; Crofts, *Reluctant Confederates*, 221–22).

19. The original Ku Klux Klan founded at Pulaski, Tennessee, in early 1866 by six prominent ex-Confederate soldiers, practiced threats and violence to intimidate Negroes and Northern schoolteachers and politicians. By 1867, the Klan was operating on a multistate basis and involved a number of ex-Confederate generals including Nathan Bedford Forrest, who had been elected grand wizard of the Invisible Empire (Jack Hurst, *Nathan Bedford Forrest, A Biography* [New York: Vintage, 1994], 278–79, 284–87; David M. Chalmers, *Hooded Americanism: The First Century of the Ku Klux Klan, 1865–1965* [Garden City, N.Y.: Doubleday, 1965], 8–11, 14–21). Getler and Brewer, in *Shadow of the Sentinel*, 67–77, note that the "KGC spawned the original KKK."

20. As claimed by Bickley in his April 1860 "Circular Letter," it is likely that the KGC did reach fifty thousand members based on the separately estimated membership in California

(16,000), Kentucky (8,000), and Texas (8,000), as well as the multiple castles reported in Alabama, Arkansas, Georgia, Indian Territory, Maryland, Missouri, North Carolina, Tennessee, and Virginia. With an estimated fifteen thousand men from the merged Order of the Lone Star, the KGC spread rapidly in 1860 through the tireless recruiting of Bickley, Greer, Groner, Tyler and other state leaders with support from affiliated editors and politicians.

21. Getler and Brewer, *Shadow of the Sentinel*, 77–80, 96–114.

# BIBLIOGRAPHY

## PRIMARY SOURCES

### MANUSCRIPTS

*Columbus (Ga.) State University Archives*
Joseph Mahan Collection.

*Museum of the Confederacy, Richmond, Virginia*
**Eleanor S. Brockenbrough Library**
Ben McCulloch to Henry McCulloch, November 25, 1860.

*Emory University, Atlanta, Georgia*
**Manuscript Archives and Rare Book Library**
Letters between Alexander McGhee and Frances Garland Singleton Wallace, 1854–
1861. Collection Description: Biographical Note for Alexander McGhee Wallace.
http://marbl.library.emory.edu.

*Georgetown University, Washington, D.C.*
**Lautenberg Library, Special Collections and Archives**
David Rankin Barbie Files.

*Harford County Historical Society, Belair, Maryland*
Robert H. Archer, K.G.C. commission dated December 17, 1859.
Robert H. Archer appointment as captain of the Spesutia Rangers by the State of
Maryland.

*Harvard University, Cambridge, Massachusetts*

**Houghton Library**

John Anthony Quitman Papers.

*Library of Congress, Washington, D.C.*

Constitution of the Order of the Lone Star. City of Lafayette: Printed at the Daily Delta Office, New Orleans, 1851.

Robert Anderson Papers.

John J. Crittenden Papers.

Joseph Holt Papers.

Abraham Lincoln Papers.

Joshua Fry Speed Papers.

Louis Wigfall Papers.

*Maryland Historical Society Archives, Baltimore*

Telegram from Edward G. Parker to Mayor George Wm. Brown, May 11, 1861.

*Mississippi Department of Archives and History, Jackson*

Governor's [John J. Pettus] Correspondence.

*Oregon Historical Society Library, Portland*

**Scrap Books**

"Colonel George K. Shiel" newspaper articles, SB276, 89–91.

*Surratt Society, Clinton, Maryland*

**James O. Hall Research Center**

Cypriano Ferrandini File—KGC captain's commission and interview with daughter.

Dr. Cornelius Boyle obituary, March 12, 1878 (from unidentified Washington newspaper).

Ethel W. Felber, Assistant Secretary-Treasurer, Green Mount Cemetery, to James O. Hall, July 12, 1976; and e-mail from Dan Monahan, Green Mount Cemetery Superintendent to Laurie Verge, Surratt Society Director, September 1, 2011.

Knights of the Golden Circle File.

Patrick Charles Martin File.

*Sword & Saber Catalogue*

Dabney Lewis correspondence, reproduced in *Sword & Saber*, catalogue no. 78 (summer 1995).

*Texas Library and Historical Commission, Austin*

Journals of the Secession Convention, 1861.

*Texas State Historical Association, Selected Texas Primary Source Documents, www.tshalonline.org/lone-star-history-links.1054*

Louis Wigfall, December 6, 1860, Senate speech.

*University of Texas, Austin*

*Constitution and By-Laws of the Order of the Lone Star,* Division No. Two, City of New Orleans. Printed at the *Daily Delta* Office, New Orleans, 1851.

*K. G. C. First, or Military Degree.* San Antonio: Herald Steam Press, 1860.

*K. G. C. Ritual.* Castroville Castle, 1861.

*U.S. Military History Institute, Carlisle, Pa.*

Greer Family Papers.

*Virginia Historical Society, Richmond*

F. J. Barnes, MSS.

Harvie Family Papers.

Elliott L. Story Journal.

NEWSPAPERS

*Abingdon Virginian*
*Alamo Express* (San Antonio, Tex.)
*Alexandria Gazette and Virginia Advertiser*
*American Cavalier* (May 28, 1859, found in Bickley Papers, National Archives)
*Arkansas (Little Rock) True Democrat*
*Atlanta (Ga.) Daily Intelligencer*
*Augusta (Ga.) Chronicle*
*Baltimore Sun*
*Banner of Liberty* (Middleton, N.Y.)
*Berkshire County Eagle* (Pittsfield, Mass.)
*Boston Daily Advertiser*
*Boston Daily Atlas*
*Cedar Valley (Iowa) Times*
*Charleston Courier Tri-Weekly*
*Charleston Mercury*
*Cincinnati Daily Enquirer*
*Cincinnati Daily Gazette*

*Citizen* (Murfreesboro, N.C.)

*Clarkesville (Va.) Chronicle*

*Cleveland (Ohio) Plain Dealer*

*Columbus (Ga.) Daily Sun*

*Constitution* (Washington, D.C.)

*Constitutional Union* (Des Arc, Ark.)

*Crisis* (Columbus, Ohio)

*Current American* (Cartersville, Ga.)

*Daily Argus Democrat* (Madison, Wisc.)

*Daily Atlanta Intelligencer*

*Daily Cleveland (Ohio) Herald*

*Daily Columbus (Ga.) Enquirer*

*Daily Confederation* (Montgomery, Ala.)

*Daily Constitutionalist* (Augusta, Ga.)

*Daily Evening Bulletin* (San Francisco)

*Daily Gazette & Comet* (Baton Rouge, La.)

*Daily Herald* (Wilmington, N.C.)

*Daily Ledger and Texan* (San Antonio)

*Daily Memphis Avalanche*

*Daily Mississippian* (Jackson, Miss.)

*Daily Morning News* (Savannah, Ga.)

*Daily National Intelligencer* (Washington, D.C.)

*Daily Ohio Statesman* (Columbus, Ohio)

*Daily Times* (Leavenworth, Kans.)

*Dallas Morning News*

*Danville (Ky.) Review*

*Davenport (Iowa) Daily Gazette*

*Dodge County (Wisc.) Citizen*

*Evening Bulletin* (San Francisco)

*Floridian and Journal* (Tallahassee)

*Fond du Lac (Wisc.) Weekly Commonwealth*

*Frankfort (Ky.) Commonwealth*

*Fresno (Ca.) Bee Republican*

*Galesville (Wisc.) Transcript*

*Georgia Weekly Telegraph* (Macon)

*Harrison (Tex.) Flag*

*Hellsburg Herald* (western Va.)

*Indianola (Tex.) Courier*

*Janesville (Wisc.) Daily Gazette*

*Kentucky Statesman* (Lexington)

*Louisville Courier*
*Louisville Democrat*
*Louisville Journal*
*Lowell (Mass.) Daily Citizen and News*
*Macon (Ga.) Telegraph*
*Memphis Daily Appeal*
*Milwaukee Sentinel*
*Mobile Register*
*Mobile Tribune*
*Nashville Patriot*
*Nashville Republican Banner*
*Natchez (Miss.) Daily Free Trader*
*New Orleans Times-Picayune*
*New Orleans True Delta*
*New York Daily News*
*New York Daily Tribune*
*New York Herald*
*New York Times*
*Norfolk (Va.) Southern Argus*
*North Carolina Standard* (Raleigh)
*Ohio Repository* (Canton)
*Old Line Democrat* (Little Rock, Ark.)
*Ouachita Valley Ledger* (Camden, Ark.)
*Philadelphia Inquirer*
*Press* (Petersburg, Va.)
*Raleigh (N.C.) Standard*
*Raleigh (N.C.) Weekly Register*
*Ranchero* (Corpus Christi, Tex.)
*Reading (Pa.) Daily Times*
*Republican* (Marshall, Tex.)
*Richmond Enquirer*
*Richmond Whig*
*San Antonio Daily Light*
*San Antonio Ledger and Texan*
*Sandusky (Ohio) Register*
*Scioto (Ohio) Gazette*
*Semi-Weekly Mississippean* (Jackson)
*Sentinel* (Monroe, Wisc.)
*Southern Intelligencer* (Charleston, S.C.)
*State Gazette and Republican* (Trenton, N.J.)

*State Rights Democrat* (La Grange, Tex.)

*Texas State Gazette* (Austin)

*True Democrat* (Little Rock, Ark.)

*Weekly Gazette and Free Press* (Janesville, Wisc.)

*Weekly Oregonian* (Portland)

*Weekly Raleigh (N.C.) Register*

*Weekly Union and American* (Nashville, Tenn.)

*Wisconsin Patriot* (Madison)

*Wooster (Ohio) Republican*

*Yazoo Democrat* (Yazoo City, Miss.)

*Zanesville (Ohio) Daily Courier*


## GOVERNMENT PUBLICATIONS AND RECORDS

### Local and State Records

Charles County, Maryland 1850 U.S. Census. ftp.us-census.org/pub/usgenweb/censusu/ md/charles/1850.

Governor's Records, Series E, vol. 49, Pettus to Groner, December 8, 1860, in Correspondence of Governor John Jones Pettus, 1859–1860.

*Indianapolis in the War of the Rebellion, Report of the Adjutant General, A Reprint of Volume 1 of the Eight Volume Report Prepared by W. H. H. Terrell and Published in 1868.* Indiana Historical Society, 1960.

Shelby County, TN—Census—1870, Memphis Ward No. 4.

### U.S. Government

Act of April 20, 1818 (3 stat. 447) [Neutrality Act].

*Congressional Globe*, 36 Cong., 1st sess. (1861). Washington, D.C.

House of Representatives, 36th Cong., 2d sess., Report No. 79: *Alleged Hostile Organization Against the Government within the District of Columbia.* Select Committee of Five, Washington, D.C., February 14, 1861.

House of Representatives, 39th Cong., 1st sess., Report No. 104: *Assassination of Lincoln.* Committee on the Assassination of Lincoln. Washington, D.C., July 1866.

### National Archives and Records Administration, Washington, D.C.

Judge Advocate General Office, Record Group 153

George W. Bickley Papers

*American Cavalier: A Military Journal devoted to the Extension of American Civilization,* May 28, 1859.

*Degree Book: First, or Company Degree of the 28.*

Handwritten Address to "Brothers of the Continental Union."
Bickley to Gen. Ambrose Burnside, dated August 1, 1863.
*Rules, Regulations and Principles of the K. G. C.*, issued by Order of the Congress of the K.C.S. and the General President, Headquarters. Washington D.C.: Benj. Urner, Printer, September 1859.

**U.S. Military History Institute, Carlisle, Pa.**
Greer Family Papers.

### *U.S. War Department*

*Official Records of the Union and Confederate Navies in the War of the Rebellion.* Washington, D.C.: U.S. Government Printing Office, 1894–1922.
*Official Report of the Judge Advocate General of the United States Army on the "Order of American Knights" Alias, Order of Sons of Liberty: A Western Conspiracy in Aid of the Southern Rebellion.* Washington, D.C.: War Department, Bureau of Military Justice, October 8, 1864.
U.S. Army Military Commission. *The Assassination of President Lincoln and Trial of the Conspirators*, 1865. Compiled and arranged by Ben Pittman. Cincinnati: Moore, Wilstach and Baldwin, 1865.
*War of the Rebellion: A Compilation of the Official Records of the Union and Confederate Armies*, Series I–IV. 128 vols. Washington D.C.: U.S. Government Printing Office 1880.

## COLLECTED WORKS WRITTEN BY CONTEMPORARIES AND PARTICIPANTS, PUBLISHED PRIMARY SOURCES, MEMOIRS, AND UNIT HISTORIES

Adams, Henry. *The Great Secession Winter of 1860–61*. In *The Great Secession Winter of 1860–61 and Other Essays*, edited by George Hochfield. New York: Sagamore, 1958.
"Address to the Citizens of the Southern States by Order of the Convention of K. G. C. Held at Raleigh, N.C., May 7–11, 1860." http://gunshowonthenet.com/AfterThe-Fact/KGC/KGC0571860.html.
Anderson, Charles. *Texas, before, and on the Eve of the Rebellion. Paper read before the Cincinnati Society of Ex-Army and Navy Officers, January 3, 1884.* Cincinnati: Peter G. Thompson, 1884.
Arnold, Samuel Bland. "Lincoln Conspiracy and the Conspirators." *Baltimore American*, 1902.
Arnold, Samuel Bland, and Michael W. Kauffman, eds. *Memoirs of a Lincoln Conspirator.* Bowie, Md.: Heritage, 2008.

*An Authentic Exposition of the "K. G. C." "Knights of the Golden Circle": or, A History of Secession from 1834 to 1861 by a Member of the Order.* Indianapolis: Perrine, 1861.

Baker, La Fayette. *Spies, Traitors and Conspirators of the Late Civil War.* Philadelphia: John E. Potter, 1894.

Barron, S. B. *The Lone Star Defenders: A Chronicle of the Third Texas Cavalry, Ross' Brigade.* New York: Neal, 1908.

Basler, Roy P., ed. *The Collected Works of Abraham Lincoln.* Vol. 4, *1860–1861.* New Brunswick, N.J.: Rutgers University Press, 1953.

Beale, Howard K., ed. *The Diary of Edward Bates, 1859–1866.* Washington, D.C.: U.S. Government Printing Office, 1933.

Bergeron, Paul H., ed. *The Papers of Andrew Johnson.* Vol. 8, *May–August 1865.* Knoxville: University of Tennessee Press, 1989.

Betts, Vicki, ed. "The Memoirs of Horace Chilton, 1858–1873, Part One." *Chronicles of Smith County Texas* 30, no. 1 (Summer 1991): 1.

Bickley, George W. L. *Adalaska, Or, The Strange and Mysterious Family of the Cave of Genreva.* Cincinnati: H. M. Rullison, 1853.

———. *History of the Settlement and Indian Wars of Tazewell County, Virginia.* Cincinnati: Morgan, 1852.

———. "History of the Eclectic Medical Institute of Cincinnati and Its Ethical Peculiarities." *Eclectic Medical Journal* 16 (February 1856): 57; (January 1857): 9; (March 1857): 105; (April 1857): 153.

———. "Introductory Lecture, Delivered before the Eclectic Medical Class, November 6, 1852." *Eclectic Medical Journal* 12 (March 1853): 102.

———. "Review of 'Report of Eclectic Physicians.'" *Eclectic Medical Journal* 12 (March 1853): 119.

*Bickley's West American Review* 1, no. 6. Cincinnati: Morgan & Overland Printers, 1853.

*The Biographical Cyclopedia of Representative Men of Maryland and District of Columbia.* Baltimore: National Biographical Publishing, 1879.

Blondheim, Menahem, ed. *Copperhead Gore: Benjamin Wood's Fort Lafayette and Civil War America.* Bloomington: Indiana University Press, 2006.

Brown, George William. *Baltimore and the Nineteenth of April 1861: A Study of the War.* Baltimore: John Hopkins University Press, 2001.

Buchanan, James. *Mr. Buchanan's Administration on the Eve of the Rebellion.* New York: D. Appleton, 1866.

Burton, Orville Vernon, and Georganne B. Burton, eds. *The Free Flag of Cuba: The Lost Novel of Lucy Holcombe Pickens.* Baton Rouge: Louisiana State University Press, 2002.

Castellanos, Henry C. *New Orleans As It Was: Episodes of Louisiana Life.* 1978. Reprint, Baton Rouge: Louisiana State University Press, 2006.

Clairbourne, J. F. H., ed. *Life and Correspondence of John Quitman.* Vol. 2. New York: Harper and Brothers, 1860.

Clarke, Asia Booth. *The Unlocked Book: A Memoir of John Wilkes Booth by His Sister.* New York: Putnam's Sons, 1931.

"Col. Robert C. Tyler." *Confederate Veteran* 15 (January 1907): 237.

"Col. William S. Sheperd." *Confederate Veteran* 32, no. 1 (January 1924): 351.

Conrad, Robert Y. "The Break-up of a Nation: Robert Y. Conrad Letters at the Virginia Secession Convention." *Winchester-Frederick County Historical Society Journal* 8 (1994–95).

*Copperhead Conspiracy in the North-West: An Exposé of the Treasonable Order of the "Sons of Liberty, Vallandigham, Supreme Commander."* Printed by the Union Congressional Committee. New York: Gray, 1864.

Cox, Samuel Sullivan. *Eight Years in Congress, from 1857 to 1865: Memoirs and Speeches.* New York: Appleton, 1865.

Crow, Terrell Armistead, and Mary Moulton Barden, eds. *Live Your Own Life: The Family Papers of Mary Bayard Clarke, 1854–1886.* Columbia: University of South Carolina Press, 2003.

Cuthbert, Norma B., ed. *Lincoln and the Baltimore Plot, 1861: From Pinkerton Records and Related Papers.* San Marino, Calif.: Huntington Library, 1949.

Darrow, Caroline Baldwin. "Recollections of the Twiggs Surrender." In *The Opening Battles,* vol. 1 of *Battles and Leaders of the Civil War,* by Robert Underwood Johnson and Clarence Clough Buel (New York: Century, 1887–88), 33–38.

Donald, David, ed. *Inside Lincoln's Cabinet: The Civil War Diaries of Salmon P. Chase.* New York: Longmans, Green, 1954.

Dowdey, Clifford, ed. *The Wartime Papers of R. E. Lee.* Boston: Little Brown, 1961.

Dye, John Smith. *History of the Plots and Crimes of the Great Conspiracy to Overthrow Liberty in America.* Reprint: New York: self-published, 1866.

Early, Jubal Anderson. *War Memoirs: Autographical Sketch and Narrative of the War Between the States.* Bloomington: Indiana University Press, 1960.

Edwards, William C., and Edward Steers Jr., eds. *The Lincoln Assassination: The Evidence.* Urbana: University of Illinois Press, 2009.

Edwards, William H. "A Bit of History." *West Virginia Historical Magazine Quarterly,* July 1902. www.wvculture,org/HISTORY/statehood/abitofhistory.html.

Evans, Clement A., ed. *Confederate Military History.* A Library of Confederate States History in Seventeen Volumes Written by Distinguished Men of the South. Wilmington, N.C.: Broadfoot, 1987–89.

Frost, Jennett Blakeslee. *Rebellion in the United States or the War of 1861: Being a Complete History of Its Rise and Progress Commencing with the Presidential Election . . .* Hartford, 1862–64.

"Gen. V. D. Groner." by W. E. C., *Confederate Veteran* (Nashville, Tenn.) 12, no. 4 (1904): 294.

Gibbony, Douglas Lee, ed. *Littleton Washington's Journal: Life in Antebellum Washington, Vigilante San Francisco & Confederate Richmond.* Washington, D.C.: Xibris, 2001.

Graf, Leroy P., ed. *The Papers of Andrew Johnson.* Vols. 6–9 (1862–January 1866). Knoxville: University of Tennessee Press, 1989.

Greeley, Horace. *The American Conflict: A History of the Great Rebellion.* Vols. 1 and 2. Hartford: O. D. Case, 1865.

Greer, Jack Thorndyke. *Leaves from a Family Album [Holcombe and Greer].* Edited by Jane Judge Green. Waco, Tex., 1975.

Hamilton, Andrew Jackson, Lorenzo Sherwood, and Henry O'Reilly, Democratic League of New York. *Origin and Objects of the Slaveholders' Conspiracy against Democratic Principles As Well As against the National Union.* New York: Baker A. Godwin Printers, 1862.

Headley, John W. *Confederate Operations in Canada and New York.* New York: Neale, 1906.

Hicks, Jimmy. "Some Letters Concerning the Knights of the Golden Circle in Texas, 1860–1861." *Southeastern Historical Quarterly* 65, no. 1 (July 1961): 80–86.

Holt, Joseph. "Address." Delivered at Louisville, July 13, 1861. In *The Rebellion Record: A Diary of American Events,* edited by Frank Moore, vol. 2. New York: Arno, 1977. Document 90: 297–303.

Howell, William A. "Memories of Wilkes Booth: An Old Associate's Recollection of the Trying Days of '60 and '61." *Baltimore Sun,* November 21, 1899, reproduced in *Pathways,* November 1985.

Hunnicutt, Rev. James W. *The Conspiracy Unveiled, The South Sacrificed; or, The Horror of Secession.* Philadelphia: Lippincott, 1863.

"Important Arrest in Baltimore." *Scientific American,* n.s., 5, no. 2 (July 13, 1861): 18.

Jennings, John. *The Virginia Springs, and Springs of the South and West.* Philadelphia: Lippincott, 1859.

Johnston, William Preston. *The Life of Gen. Albert Sidney Johnston.* New York: D. Appleton, 1878.

Jones, John B. *A Rebel War Clerk's Diary.* Edited by Earl Schenck Meirs. Baton Rouge: Louisiana State University Press, 1993.

Jones, J. B. *A Rebel War Clerk's Diary at the Confederate States Capital.* 2 vols. Edited by Howard Swigett. New York: Old Hickory Bookshop, 1935.

Jones, Thomas A. *J. Wilkes Booth: An Account of His Sojourn in Southern Maryland after the Assassination of Abraham Lincoln, His Passage across the Potomac, and His Death in Virginia.* Chicago: Laird and Lee, 1893.

"The Kentucky Resolutions." Adopted Sept. 12, 1861. In *The Rebellion Record: A Diary of American Events*, edited by Frank Moore, vol. 3. New York: Arno, 1977. Document 45: 129.

Kettle, Thomas P. *History of the Great Rebellion: The Secession of the Southern States . . . from Official Sources*. Hartford, Ct.: F. A. Howe, 1865.

K. G. C., *A Full Exposition of the Southern Traitors; The Knights of the Golden Circle: Their Startling Schemes Frustrated*. Boston: E. H. Bullard, 1861[?].

"Knights of the Golden Circle: Memories of One Who Wore Gray." *Ouachita County Historical Quarterly* 15, no. 3 (March 1985): 66.

*Letters of the Hon. Joseph Holt, the Hon. Edward Everett and Commodore Charles Stewart, on the Present Crisis*. Philadelphia: William S. Martien and Alfred Martien, 1861.

Logan, John A. *The Great Conspiracy*. Freeport, N.Y.: Books for Libraries Press, 1971.

Logan, Mrs. John A. *Reminiscences of a Soldier's Wife: An Autobiography*. Carbondale: Southern Illinois University Press, 1997.

Lossing, Benson J. "New Orleans Hears That Sumter Has Fallen." In *Prologue To Sumter: The Beginnings of the Civil War from the John Brown Raid to the Surrender of Fort Sumter*, compiled by Philip Van Doren Stern. Greenwich, Ct.: Fawcett, 1961.

Lubbock, Francis Richard. *Six Decades in Texas*. Austin: Ben C. Jones & Co. Printers, 1900.

Marks, Bayly Ellen, and Mark Norton Schatz , eds. *Between North and South: A Maryland Journalist Views the Civil War: The Narrative of William Wilkins Glenn, 1861–1869*. Rutherford, N. J.: Fairleigh Dickinson University Press, 1976.

McIntosh, James T., ed. *The Papers of Jefferson Davis*, Vols. 1, 3, and 7. Baton Rouge: Louisiana State University Press, 1992.

McMahon, John V. L. *An Historical View of the Government of Maryland from Its Colonization to the Present Day*. Vol. 1. Baltimore: F. Lucas, Jr. 1831. Includes "An Introduction to the Author." *Maryland Heritage Series*, no. 3.

Moore, Frank, ed. *The Rebellion Record: A Diary of American Events*. New York: Arno, 1977.

Moore, John Bassett, ed. *The Works of James Buchanan: Comprising His Speeches, State Papers, and Private Correspondence*. Vols. 9–11: 1860–1868. Philadelphia: Lippincott, 1910; New York: Antiquarian Press, 1960.

Morton, Oliver T. *The Southern Empire, With Other Papers*. Boston: Houghton Mifflin, 1892.

*Narrative of Edmund Wright: His Adventures and Escape from the Knights of the Golden Circle*. Cincinnati: J. R. Hawley, 1864.

Newcomb, James. P. *Sketch of Secession Times in Texas and Journal of Travel from Texas through Mexico Including a History of the "Box Colony."* San Francisco, 1863.

Nicolay, John G., and John Hay. *Abraham Lincoln: A History,* Vols. 2 and 8. New York: Century, 1890.

Oates, Stephen B., ed. *Rip Ford's Texas.* Austin: University of Texas Press, 1963.

Olmsted, Frederick Law. *A Journey through Texas or a Saddle Trip on the Southwestern Frontier.* 1857. Reprint, Lincoln: University of Nebraska Press, 2004.

"The Order of the Lone Star." *United States Magazine and Democratic Review,* January 1853, 80.

Pease, Calvin Theodore, and James G. Randall, eds. *The Diary of Orville Hickman Browning,* Vol. 1. Springfield Trustees of the Illinois Historical Library, 1925.

Pickett, John Thomas. "Gen. John Thomas Pickett, Find a Grave Memorial: www .findagrave.com.

Pike, James. *The Scout and Ranger: Being the Personal Adventures of Corporal Pike of the Fourth Ohio cavalry.* Cincinnati: J. R. Hawley, 1865.

Pittman, Ben, ed. *The Trials for Treason at Indianapolis Disclosing the Plan for Establishing a Northwestern Confederacy...* Cincinnati: Moore, Wilstach and Baldwin, 1865.

Pomfrey, J. W. *A True Disclosure and Exposition of the Knights of the Golden Circle Including The Secret Signs, Grips, and Charges, of the Three Degrees, As Practiced by the Order.* Cincinnati: Printed for the author, 1861.

"Reward, National Park Service, Wilson's Creek National Battlefield." Stolen Artifacts website: www.civilwar.org/pdfs/wilsoncreekreward.pdf.

Rhodehamel, John, and Louis Taper, eds. *"Right or Wrong, God Judge Me": The Writings of John Wilkes Booth.* Urbana: University of Illinois Press, 1997.

Russell, William Howard. *My Diary North and South.* Reprint: New York: Harper, 1954.

Sanford, A. *Treason Unmasked: An Exposition of the Origins, Objects and Principles of the Knights of the Golden Circle.* Albion, N.Y.: John Marsh, 1863.

Scarborough, William Kauffman, ed., *The Diary of Edmund Ruffin.* Vols. 1 and 2. Baton Rouge: Louisiana State University Press, 1972.

"Scott-Yarbrough House." Auburn Heritage Association website: www.auburnheri tage.org/histoirc-markers.html.

Sherman, William T. *Memoirs of General William T. Sherman.* Vol. 1. Reprint, New York: Library of America, 1990.

Simon, John Y., ed. *The Papers of Ulysses S. Grant.* Vol. 2 (April–September 1861), and Vol. 27 (January 1–October 31, 1876). Carbondale: Southern Illinois University Press, 1967.

Smith, Jonathan K. T., ed. *Death Notices from the* Christian Advocate, *Nashville, Tennessee, 1880–1882 (Of Those Persons Born up to and Including the Year 1830).* Jackson, Tenn.: J. K. T. Smith, 2000. www.tngenweb.org/records/tn_wide/obits/ nca/nca7-04.htm.

Sprague, J. T., Major, United States Army. "The Texas Treason." Paper read before the New York Historical Society, June 25, 1861. In *The Rebellion Record: A Diary of American Events*, edited by Frank Moore, vol. 1. New York: Arno, 1977. Document 21: 109–10.

Stone, Charles P. "Washington on the Eve of the War." *Century*, July 1883. In *Secret Missions of the Civil War*, edited by Phillip Van Doren Stern. New York: Bonanza, 1959.

Stiger, Felix, ed. *Treason History of the Order of Sons of Liberty, 1903*. Reprint, Hemphill, Tex.: Dogwood, 1994.

Thompson, Jerry D., ed. *Fifty Miles and a Fight: Major Samuel Peter Heintzelman's Journal of Texas and the Cortina War*. Austin: Texas State Historical Society, 1998.

Tolbert, Noble J., ed. *The Papers of John Willis Ellis*. Vol. 2, *1860–1861*. Raleigh: State Department of Archives and History, 1964.

Wallace, Lewis. *Lew Wallace: An Autobiography*. New York: Harper and Brothers, 1906.

Walling, George W. *Recollections of a New York Chief of Police*. New York: Caxton, 1888.

Weichman, Louis. *A True History of Abraham Lincoln and of the Conspiracy of 1865*. Edited by Floyd Risvold. New York: Knopf, 1975.

White, Andrew Dickson (Democratic National Committee). "The Conspiracy to Break up the Union, the Plot and Its Development: Breckinridge and Lane the Candidates of a Disunion Party." Washington, D.C., August 1860, 85. In *The American Party Battle: Election Campaign Pamphlets, 1828–1876*, edited by Joel Sibley, vol. 2, *1854–1876*. Cambridge: Harvard University Press, 1999.

Wiley, Ben Irwin. *Fourteen Hundred and 91 Days in the Confederate Army: A Journal Kept by W. W. Heartsill for Four Years, One Month and One Day*. Wilmington, N.C.: Broadfoot, 1987.

Wilkins, James H., ed. *The Great Diamond Hoax and Other Stirring Stories in the Life of Asbury Harpending*. Norman: University of Oklahoma Press, 1958.

Williams, Amelia W., and Eugene C. Barker, eds. *The Writings of Sam Houston: 1813–1863*. Vol. 7. Austin: University of Texas Press, 1942.

Williams, R. H. *With the Border Ruffians: Memories of the Far West, 1852–1868*. Book 2. Lincoln: University of Nebraska Press, 1982.

Wilson, Henry. *Rise and Fall of the Slave Power in America*. Vol. 3. Boston: James R. Osgood, 1877.

Winkler, E. D., ed. *Journal of the Secession Convention of Texas, 1861*. Austin: 1912. Texas Library and Historical Commission: http://tarlton.law.utexas.edu/constitutions/pdf/pdf1861/index1861.html.

Woodruff, W. E. *"With the Light Guns in '61–'65": Reminiscences of Eleven Arkansas, Missouri and Texas Light Batteries in the Civil War*. Little Rock: Central Printing, 1903. www.researchonline.net/arcw/history/00785.pdfl.

Wright, D. Girald. *A Southern Girl in '61: The War-time Memories of a Confederate Senator's Daughter.* New York: Doubleday, Page, 1905.

## SECONDARY SOURCES

Allardice, Bruce S. *Confederate Colonels: A Biographical Register.* Columbia: University of Missouri Press, 2008.

Anbinder, Tyler. *Nativism and Slavery: The Northern Know Nothings and the Politics of the 1850s.* New York: Oxford University Press, 1992.

"Arkansas in the Civil War." www.lincolnandthecivilwar.com/.

Armistead, Gene C. "California's Confederate Militia: The Los Angeles Mounted Rifles." California State Military Museum. www.militarymuseum.org/LosAngelesMounted Rifles2.html.

Arnold, Isaac H. "The Baltimore Plot to Assassinate Abraham Lincoln." *Harper's New Monthly Magazine,* June 1868, 123.

Axelrod, Alan. *The International Encyclopedia of Secret Societies and Fraternal Orders.* New York: Facts on File, 1997.

Bancroft, Hubert Howe. *The Works.* Vol. 24 containing *History of California—1860–1890,* vol. 7. San Francisco: History Company, 1890.

Barrett, John G. *The Civil War in North Carolina.* Chapel Hill: University of North Carolina Press, 1963.

Baum, Dale. *The Shattering of Texas Unionism: Politics in the Lone Star State during the Civil War.* Baton Rouge: Louisiana State University Press, 1996.

Beatie, Russel H. *Army of the Potomac: Birth of Command: November 1860–September 1861.* Cambridge, Mass.: Da Capo Press, 2002.

Bergeson, Arthur W., Jr. *Guide to Louisiana Confederate Military Units, 1861–1865.* Baton Rouge: Louisiana State University Press, 1996.

Betts, Vickie. "Private and Amateur Hangings": The Lynching of W. W. Montgomery, March 15, 1863." *Southwestern Historical Quarterly* 98, no. 2 (October 1984): 145.

"Biography of Robert Harris Archer" in Lt. Col. Robert H. Archer, SCV Camp #2013. http://rharchercamp.org/.

Boney, F. N. *John Letcher of Virginia: The Story of Virginia's Civil War Governor.* Tuscaloosa: University of Alabama Press, 1966.

Bowden, J. J. *The Exodus of Federal Forces from Texas, 1861.* Austin, Tex.: Eakin, 1986.

Brandt, Nat. *The Man Who Tried to Burn New York.* San Jose: toExcel, 2000.

Bridges, C. A. "The Knights of the Golden Circle: A Filibustering Fantasy." *Southwestern Historical Quarterly* 44, no. 3 (January 1941): 287.

Brock, R. A. *Virginia and Virginians.* Vol. 2. Spartanburg, S.C.: Reprint Company, 1973.

Brown, Charles H. *Agents of Manifest Destiny: The Lives and Times of the Filibusters.* Chapel Hill: University of North Carolina Press, 1980.

Brown, Kent Masterson. *The Civil War in Kentucky: Battle for the Bluegrass State.* Mason City, Iowa: Savas, 2000.

Bryan, T. Conn, *Confederate Georgia.* Athens: University of Georgia Press, 1953.

Buenger, Walter L. *Secession and the Union in Texas.* Austin: University of Texas Press, 1984.

Burton, H. W. *The History of Norfolk, Virginia.* Norfolk Virginian job print, 1877.

Callahan, John Morton. *History of West Virginia: Old and New.* Vol. 1. Chicago: American Historical Society, 1923.

"The Capture of Fort Pulaski." http://ourgeorgiahistory.com/wars/Civil_War/ftpu laski.html.

Castel, Albert. *General Sterling Price and the Civil War in the West.* Baton Rouge: Louisiana State University Press, 1968.

Chadwick, Bruce. *The Two American Presidents: A Dual Biography of Abraham Lincoln and Jefferson Davis.* Secaucus, N.J.: Carol, 1999.

Chalmers, David M. *Hooded Americanism: The First Century of the Ku Klux Klan, 1865–1965.* Garden City, N.Y.: Doubleday, 1965.

Channing, Stephen A. *Crisis of Fear: Secession in South Carolina.* New York: Norton, 1974.

Cisco, Walter Brian. *Wade Hampton: Confederate Warrior, Conservative Statesman.* Washington, D.C.: Brassey's, 2004.

Clark, Lyman H., "Brig. Gen. Paul Jones Semmes." Term paper prepared for "Civil War History" class at Columbus [Ga.] College [now Columbus State University].

Claycomb, William B. "President Lincoln and the Magoffin Brothers." Dayton, Ohio: Morningside Bookshop, 1984. www.morningsidebooks.com.

Collins, Michael L. *Texas Devils: Rangers and Regulars on the Lower Rio Grande, 1846–1861.* Norman: University of Oklahoma Press, 2008.

Cooper, Edward S. *Traitors: The Secession Period, November 1860–July 1861.* Madison-Teaneck, N.J.: Fairleigh Dickinson University Press, 2008.

Corley, Florence Fleming. *Confederate City: Augusta Georgia: 1860–1865.* Columbia: University of South Carolina Press, 1960.

Cothern John P. *Confederates of Elmwood: A Compilation of Information Concerning Confederate Soldiers and Veterans Buried at Elmwood Cemetery Memphis, Tennessee.* Winchester, Md.: Heritage, 2007.

Coulter, Merton E. *The Civil War and Readjustment in Kentucky.* New York: Oxford University Press, 1926.

Crapol, Edward P. *John Tyler: The Accidental President.* Chapel Hill: University of North Carolina Press, 2006.

Crawford, Samuel Wylie. *The Genesis of the Civil War: The Story of Sumter.* New York: Charles L. Webster, 1887.

Crenshaw, Ollinger. "The Knights of the Golden Circle: The Career of George Bickley." *American Historical Review* 47, no. 1 (Oct. 1941): 23.

——. *The Slave States in the Presidential Election of 1860.* Gloucester, Mass.: Peter Smith, 1969.

Crofts, Daniel W. *Reluctant Confederates: Upper South Unionists in the Secession Crisis.* Chapel Hill: University of North Carolina Press, 1989.

Croggon, James, "Washington in 1860." *Evening Star,* April 1, 1911, pt. 2, p. 4. www .bythesofhistory.com/DCHistory/Collections/Croggon/Croggon_19110401.html.

"CSA 15th Regiment, Tennessee Infantry." Civil War Soldiers & Regiments. http:// civilwarsoldiers.blog.spot.com/2006/02/csa-15th regiment-tennessee-infantry. html.

Cutchins, John A. *A Famous Command: The Richmond Light Infantry Blues.* Richmond: Garrett and Massie, 1934.

Cutrer, Thomas W. *Ben McCulloch and the Frontier Military Tradition.* Chapel Hill: University of North Carolina Press, 1993.

Dando-Collins, Stephen. *Tycoon's War: How Cornelius Vanderbilt Invaded a County to Overthrow America's Most Famous Military Adventurer.* Cambridge, Mass.: Da Capo Press, 2008.

Davis, Michael. *The Image of Lincoln in the South.* Knoxville: University of Tennessee Press, 1971.

Davis, William C. *Breckinridge: Statesman, Soldier, Symbol.* Baton Rouge: Louisiana State University Press, 1974.

——. *A Government of Our Own: The Making of the Confederacy.* Baton Rouge: Louisiana State University Press, 1994.

——. *Jefferson Davis: The Man and His Hour.* Baton Rouge: Louisiana State University Press, 1991.

——. *Rhett: The Turbulent Life and Times of a Fire-Eater.* Columbia: University of South Carolina Press, 2001.

Davis, William C., and Julie Hoffman. *The Confederate General.* Harrisburg, Pa.: National Historical Society, 1991.

DeBlack, Thomas A. *With Fire and Sword: Arkansas, 1861–1874.* Fayetteville: University of Arkansas Press, 2003.

Debman, George R., Jr. "I Remember the Last Days of the Famed Eutaw House." *Sunday Sun Magazine,* June 16, 1963.

"Definition of Civil War Terms." www.civilwarhome.com/terms.htm.

Detzer, David. *Allegiance: Fort Sumter, Charleston, and the Beginning of the Civil War.* New York: Harcourt, 2001.

*Dictionary of American Biography.* Vol. 4. New York: Scribner, 1928–58.

Dougan, Michael B. *Confederate Arkansas: The People and Policies of a Frontier State in Wartime.* Tuscaloosa: University of Alabama Press, 1991.

———. "'An Eternal Chitter Chatter Kept up in the Galleries': The Arkansas Secession Convention in Action. March—June, 1861." In *The Die Is Cast: Arkansas Goes to War, 1861,* edited by Mark K. Christ. Little Rock, Ark.: Butler Center Books, 2010.

Driver, Robert J. *The First and Second Maryland Infantry, C.S.A.* Bowie, Md.: Heritage, 2003.

Dubay, Robert W. *John Jones Pettus: Mississippi Fire-Eater: His Life and Times, 1813–1867.* Jackson: University Press of Mississippi, 1975.

Dubose, John Witherspoon. *The Life and Time of William Lowndes Yancey: A History of Political Parties in the United States, from 1834 to 1864.* Vol. 2. New York: Peter Smith, 1942.

Dufour, Charles L. *Gentle Tiger: The Gallant Life of Roberdeau Wheat.* Baton Rouge: Louisiana State University Press, 1957.

Dunn, Roy Sylvan. "The KGC in Texas, 1860–1861." *Southwest Historical Quarterly* 70, no. 4 (April 1967): 543.

Dustin, Charles Mial. "The Knights of the Golden Circle: The Story of the Pacific Coast Secessionists." *Pacific Monthly* (1911): 501.

Dyer, Thomas G. *Secret Yankees: The Union Circle in Confederate Atlanta.* Baltimore: John Hopkins University Press, 1999.

Eaton, Clement. "Henry A. Wise and the Virginia Fire Eaters of 1856." *Mississippi Valley Historical Review* 21, no. 4 (March 1935): 506.

Edwards, G. Thomas. "Six Oregon Leaders and the Far-Reaching Impact of America's Civil War." *Oregon Historical Quarterly* 100, no. 1 (Spring 1999): 4.

Eicher, David J. *Dixie Betrayed: How the South Really Lost the Civil War.* New York: Little, Brown, 2006.

Eisenhower, John S. *Agent of Manifest Destiny: The Life and Times of General Winfield Scott.* New York: Free Press, 1997.

Elliott, Sam Davis. *Confederate Governor and United States Senator: Isham G. Harris of Tennessee.* Baton Rouge: Louisiana State University Press, 2010.

Ellison, Joseph. "Designs for a Pacific Republic, 1843–62." *Oregon Historical Quarterly* 31, no. 4 (December 1930): 319.

Emerson, Mason. *Missouri's Secret Confederate Agents: The Knights of the Golden Circle.* St. Louis: Blue and Grey Book Shoppe, 2002.

Eyal, Yonatan. *The Young America Movement and the Transformation of the Democratic Party, 1828–1861.* New York: Cambridge University Press, 2007.

Farber, James. *Texas C.S.A.: A Spotlight on Disaster.* New York: Jackson 1947.

Faulk, Odie. *General Tom Green: Fighting Texan.* Waco, Tex.: Texian Press, 1963.

Felter, Harvey Wickes, M.D. *Historical Sketch of the Eclectic Medical Institute, Cincinnati.* Cincinnati, Ohio: Serial Publication of the Lloyd Library, 1911.

Fesler, Mayo. "Secret Political Societies in the North during the Civil War." *Indiana Magazine of History* 14, no. 3 (September 1918): 198.

Field, Ron. *Virginia and Arkansas.* Vol. 4 of *The Confederate Army 1861–65.* Oxford: Osprey, 2006.

Fife, Emerson David. *The Presidential Campaign of 1860.* New York: Macmillan, 1911.

Fisher, Noel C. *War at Every Door: Partisan Politics and Guerilla Violence in East Tennessee, 1860–1869.* Chapel Hill: University of North Carolina Press, 1977.

Fornell, Earl Wesley. *The Galveston Era: The Texas Crescent on the Eve of Secession.* Austin: University of Texas Press, 1976.

Forrester, Izola. *This One Mad Act: The Unknown Story Of John Wilkes Booth and His Family.* Boston: Hale, Cushman and Flint, 1937.

Franklin, John Hope. *The Militant South: 1800–1861.* Boston: Beacon, 1964.

——. *A Southern Odyssey: Travelers in the Antebellum North.* Baton Rouge: Louisiana State University Press, 1976.

Franks, Kenny A. *Stand Watie and the Agony of the Cherokee Nation.* Memphis: Memphis State University Press, 1979.

Frazier, Donald S. *Blood and Treasure: Confederate Empire in the Southwest.* College Station: Texas A&M University Press, 1995.

Freehing, William W., and Craig M. Simpson, eds. *Secession Debated: Georgia's Showdown in 1860.* New York: Oxford University Press, 1992.

Friend, Llerena. *Sam Houston: The Great Designer.* Austin: University of Texas Press, 1954.

Furguson, Ernest B. *Ashes of Glory: Richmond at War.* New York: Vintage, 1996.

——. *Freedom Rising: Washington in the Civil War.* New York: Knopf, 2004.

Gaddy, David Winfred. "William Norris and the Confederate Secret Service." *Maryland Historical Magazine* 70, no. 2 (Summer 1975): 167.

Galvin, John R. *The Minute Men: The First Fight: Myths and Realities of the American Revolution.* Washington, D.C.: Potomac, 2006.

Gara, Larry. *The Presidency of Franklin Pierce.* Lawrence: University Press of Kansas, 1991.

Geise, William R. "Missouri's Confederate Capital in Marshall, Texas." *Southwestern Historical Quarterly* 46, no. 8 (October 1962): 193.

"Gen. John Thomas Pickett, Find a Grave Memorial." www.findagrave.com.

"George Goldthwaite, Encyclopedia of Alabama." http://encyclopediaofalabama.org/face/Article.jsp?id=h-2968.

Gesick, John. "The 1855 Callahan Raid into Mexico: Pursuing Indians or Hunting Slaves." *Journal of Big Bend Studies* 19 (2007): 47.

Getler, Warren and Bob Brewer. *Shadow of the Sentinel: One Man's Quest to Find the Hidden Treasure of the Confederacy.* New York: Simon and Schuster, 1993.

Gilbert, Benjamin Franklin. "The Confederate Minority in California." *California Historical Society Quarterly* 20 (June 1941): 154.

——."The Mythical Johnston Conspiracy." *California Historical Society Quarterly* 28 (June 1949): 165.

Gleeson, Ed. *Illinois Rebels: A Civil War Unit History of G Company 15th Tennessee Regiment Volunteer Infantry.* Carmel: Guild Press of Indiana, 1996.

Goldman, Henry H. "Southern Sympathy in Southern California, 1860–1865." *Journal of the West* 4, no. 4 (1965): 578.

The Greenbrier. www.greenbrier.com/site/about-history.aspx.

Giuseppe Mazzini—biography. "Young Italy Risorgimento." www.age-of-the-sage.org/historical/biography/giuseppe_mazzini.html.

"Groner, Virginius Despeaux." Biog./Hist. Note. Library of Virginia Online Reference Services.

*The GW and Foggy Bottom Historical Encyclopedia,* Columbia College and the American Civil War, p. 3, "Gannett, A. Y. P." http://encyclopedia.gwu.edu/gwencyclopedia/indexphph/Columbian_Colllege_and_the_American_Civil_War.

Haco, Dion. *The Private Journal and Diary of John H. Surratt, the Conspirator.* New York: F. A. Brady, 1866.

Hagy, James. "George Washington Lafayette Bickley: The Early Years." *Historical and Biographical Sketches of Southwest Virginia.* Publication 6 of Historical Society of Southwest Virginia (March 1972): 64.

"Haitian Revolution (1791–1804)." An Online Reference Guide to African American History by Quintard Taylor. www.blackpast.org/.

Hale, Douglas. *The Third Texas Cavalry in the Civil War.* Norman: University of Oklahoma Press, 1993.

Hall, James O. "A Magnificent Charlatan: George Washington Lafayette Bickley Made a Career of Deceit." *Civil War Times Illustrated* 18, no. 10 (February 1980): 40.

Haller, John S. *Medical Protestants: The Eclectics in American Medicine, 1825–1949.* Carbondale: Southern Illinois University Press, 1994.

Hamnett, Brian. *Profiles in Power: Juarez.* London: Longman, 1994.

Hanchett, William. *The Lincoln Murder Conspiracies.* Urbana: University of Illinois Press, 1983.

Hancock, Harold Bell. *Delaware during the Civil War: A Political History.* Wilmington: Historical Society of Delaware, 1961.

The Handbook of Texas Online: A Multidisciplinary Encyclopedia of Texas History, Geography, and Culture Sponsored by the Texas State Historical Association. www.tshaonline.org/handbook/online.

Harper, Robert S. *Lincoln and the Press*. New York: McGraw-Hill, 1951.

Harris, William C. *Leroy Pope Walker: Confederate Secretary of War*. Tuscaloosa: Confederate Publishing, 1962.

Hartzler, Daniel D. *A Band of Brothers: Photographic Epilogue to Marylanders in the Confederacy*. New Windsor, Md.: published by author, 1992.

Hearn, Chester G. *Companions in Conspiracy: John Brown and Gerrit Smith*. Gettysburg, Pa.: Thomas, 1996.

———. *Six Years of Hell: Harpers Ferry during the Civil War*. Baton Rouge: Louisiana State University Press, 1996.

Heidler, David S., and Jeanne T. Heidler, eds. *Encyclopedia of the American Civil War: A Political, Social, and Military History*. New York: Norton, 2000.

"Henry Clay Pate." http://kansasboguslegislature.org/mo/pate_h_c.html.

Hill, Louise Biles. *Joseph Brown and the Confederacy*. Chapel Hill: University of North Carolina Press, 1939.

"The History of Phrenology." http://www.phrenology.org/intro.html.

Hodgson, Joseph. *The Cradle of the Confederacy; Or, The Times of Troup, Quitman and Yancey*. Mobile: printed at the Register Publishing Office, 1876.

Hogan, Michael D. "North Carolina Forts (Part 3) Ft. Johnston in Transition." In *Historic Southport*. www.southportncmagazine.com/forts_3_johnston.html.

Howard, Nathan. "The Texas Rangers in the Civil War." *Southern Historian* 13 (Spring 2002): 42.

Howard, George Washington. *The Monument City*. Baltimore: J. D. Ehlers, 1873.

Howell, Kenneth Wayne. "'When the Rabble Hiss, Well May Patriots Tremble': James Web Throckmorton and the Secession Movement In Texas, 1854–1861." *Southwestern Historical Quarterly* 59, no. 4 (April 2006): 465.

Hudson, Linda S. "The Knights of the Golden Circle in Texas, 1858–1861: An Analysis of the First (Military) Degree Knights." In *The Southern Star of the Confederacy: Texas during the Civil War*, edited by Kenneth W. Howell. Denton: University of North Texas Press, 2009.

Hughes, Nathaniel Cheairs, Jr., and Roy P. Stonesifer Jr. *The Life and Times of Gideon J. Pillow*. Chapel Hill: University of North Carolina Press, 1993.

Hughes, W. J. *Rebellious Ranger: Rip Ford and the Old Southwest*. Norman: University of Oklahoma Press, 1964.

Hunt, Aurora. *The Army of the Pacific: Its Operations in California, Texas, Arizona, New Mexico, Utah, Nevada, Oregon, Washington, Plains Region, Mexico, etc., 1860–1866*. Reprint, Mechanicsburg, Pa.: Stackpole, 2004.

Hurst, Jack. *Nathan Bedford Forrest: A Biography*. New York: Vintage, 1994.

Jahoda, Gloria. "The Bickleys of Virginia." *Virginia Magazine of History and Biography* 66, no. 4 (October 1958): 463.

James, Marquis. *The Raven: A Biography of Sam Houston.* Austin: University of Texas Press, 1929.

Jampoler, Andrew C. *The Last Lincoln Conspirator: John Surratt's Flight from the Gallows.* Annapolis, Md.: Naval Institute Press, 2008.

Jewett, Clayton E. *Texas in the Confederacy: An Experiment in Nation Building.* Columbia: University of Missouri Press, 2002.

Johanssen, Robert W. *Stephen A. Douglas.* New York: Oxford University Press, 1973.

Johnston, J. Stoddard. *Confederate Military History of Kentucky: Kentucky during the Civil War.* Pensacola, Fla.: EBooksOnDisc.com, 2006.

———. *Memorial History of Louisville from Its First Settlement to the Year 1896.* Chicago: American Biographical Publishing, [1896].

Jones, James P., and William Warren Rogers, eds. "Montgomery As the Confederate Capital: View of a New Nation." *Alabama Historical Quarterly* 26, no. 1 (spring 1964): 1.

Jones, Terry. *"Lee's Tigers": The Louisiana Infantry in the Army of Northern Virginia.* Baton Rouge: Louisiana State University Press, 1987.

Jones, Virgil Carrington. *Ranger Mosby.* Chapel Hill: University of North Carolina Press, 1944.

Josephy, Alvin M., Jr. *The Civil War in the American West.* New York: Vintage, 1993.

Kagan, Robert. *Dangerous Nation.* New York: Knopf, 2006.

Kauffman, Michael W. *American Brutus: John Wilkes Booth and the Lincoln Conspiracies.* New York: Random House, 2004.

———. "David Edgar Herold: The Forgotten Conspirator." *Surratt Society News* (November 1981): 23.

———. "Edman Spangler: A Life Rediscovered." *Surratt Society News* (November 1986): 33.

Keehn, David C. "Strong Arm of Secession: The Knights of the Golden Circle in the Crisis of 1861." *North & South* 10, no. 6 (June 2008): 42–57.

"The Keetoowah Society and the Avocation of Religious Nationalism in the Cherokee Nation, 1855–1867." U.S. Data Repository, 1–19. www.us-data.org/us/minges/keetood2.html.

Kendall, John S. *The Golden Age of New Orleans Theatre.* Baton Rouge: Louisiana State University Press, 1952.

Kennedy, Elijah. *The Contest for California in 1861.* Boston: Houghton Mifflin, 1912.

Kimmel, Stanley. *The Mad Booths of Maryland.* Indianapolis: Bobbs-Merrill, 1940.

Kincade, Robert L. "Joshua Fry Speed: Lincoln's Confidential Agent in Kentucky." *Registry of the Kentucky Historical Society* 52, no. 170 (April 1954): 99.

Kinchen, Oscar A. *Confederate Operations in Canada and the North: A Little Known Phase of the American Civil War.* North Quincy, Mass.: Christopher, 1970.

King, Alvy L. *Louis Wigfall: Southern Fire-eater.* Baton Rouge: Louisiana State University Press, 1970.

Kirwin, Albert Dennis. *John J. Crittenden: The Struggle for the Union.* Lexington: University of Kentucky Press, 1962.

Klein, Philip Shriver. *President James Buchanan: A Biography.* University Park: Pennsylvania State University Press, 1962.

Klement, Frank L. *Dark Lanterns: Secret Political Societies, Conspiracies, and Treason Trials in the Civil War.* Baton Rouge: Louisiana State University Press, 1984.

Kline, Michael J. *The Baltimore Plot: The First Conspiracy to Assassinate Abraham Lincoln.* Yardley, Pa.: Westholme, 2008.

LaLande, Jeff. "'Dixie' of the Pacific Northwest: Southern Oregon's Civil War." *Oregon Historical Quarterly* 100, no. 1 (Spring 1999): 32.

Lause, Mark A. *A Secret Society History of the Civil War.* Urbana: University of Illinois Press, 2011.

Lewis, Elizabeth Wittenmyer. *Queen of the Confederacy: The Innocent Deceits of Lucy Holcombe Pickens.* Denton: University of North Texas Press, 2002.

Link, William A. *Roots of Secession: Slavery and Politics in Antebellum Virginia.* Chapel Hill: University of North Carolina Press, 2002.

Lockard, E. Kidd. "The Unfortunate Military Career of Henry A. Wise in Western Virginia." *West Virginia History* 31, no. 1 (October 1969): 42.

Lockwood, John, and Charles Lockwood. *The Siege of Washington: The Untold Story of the Twelve Days That Shook the Union.* New York: Oxford University Press, 2011.

Lonn, Ella. *Foreigners in the Confederacy.* Gloucester, Mass.: P. Smith, 1965.

Manakee, Harold R. *Maryland in the Civil War.* Baltimore: Maryland Historical Society, 1961.

Martin, Percy E. "Sam Arnold and Hooktown." *History Trails* 16, no. 4 (Summer 1992): 13.

Mason, John Thomson. *Life of John Van Lear McMahon.* Baltimore: Eugene L. Didier, 1879.

Matthews, Richard E. *Lehigh County Pennsylvania in the Civil War: An Account.* Lehighton, Pa.: Times News Printing, 1989.

May, Robert E. *John A. Quitman: Old South Crusader.* Baton Rouge: Louisiana State University Press, 1985.

——. *Manifest Destiny's Underworld: Filibustering in Antebellum America.* Chapel Hill: University of North Carolina Press, 2002.

——. *The Southern Dream of a Caribbean Empire: 1854–1861.* Baton Rouge: Louisiana State University Press, 1973.

McComb, David G. *Texas: A Modern History.* Austin: University of Texas Press, 1989.

McDowell, Robert Emmett. *City of Conflict: Louisville in the Civil War, 1861–1865.* Louisville Civil War Roundtable: 1962.

McGregor, James C. *The Disruption of Virginia*. New York: Macmillan, 1922.

McLoughlin, William Gerald. *After the Trail of Tears*. Chapel Hill: University of North Carolina Press, 1993.

———. *Champions of Cherokees: Evan and John B. Jones*. Princeton, N.J., Princeton University Press, 1990.

Miller, Ernest C. *John Wilkes Booth in the Pennsylvania Oil Region: Including the Complete Interviews of Louis J. Mackey Done in 1894 at Franklin, Pennsylvania, With People Who Had Known Booth during His 1864 Sojourn Here*. Meadville, Pa.: Crawford County Historical Society, 1987.

Milton, George Fort. *Abraham Lincoln and the Fifth Column*. New York: Vanguard, 1942.

———. *The Eve of Conflict: Stephen A. Douglas and the Needless War*. Boston: Houghton Mifflin, 1934.

Mingus, Scott L. *Flames Beyond Gettysburg: The Gordon Expedition, June 1863: A History and Tour Guide*. Columbus, Ohio: Ironclad, 2009.

"Mississippi Secession." http://virtualology.com/uscivilwarhall/mississippisecession .com/.

Moore, Albert Burton. *Conscription and Conflict in the Confederacy*. New York: Hillary House, 1963.

"Napoleon (Desha County)." The Encyclopedia of Arkansas History & Culture. www .encyclopediaofarkansas.net/encyclopedia/entry-detail.aspx?entryID=356.

"Narrative History of Texas Annexation." Texas State Library. www.tsl.state.tx.us/ref/ abouttx/annexation/index.html

Neal, Diane, and Thomas W. Kremm. *The Lion of the South: General Thomas C. Hindman*. Macon, Ga.: Mercer University Press, 1993.

Nelson, Larry E. *Bullets, Ballots, and Rhetoric: Confederate Policy for the United States Presidential Contest of 1864*. Tuscaloosa: University of Alabama Press, 1980.

Nevins, Allan. *Douglas, Buchanan, and Party Chaos, 1857 to 1859*. Vol. 1 of *The Emergence of Lincoln*. New York: Scribner's Sons, 1950.

———. *Prologue to Civil War, 1859–1861*. Vol. 2 of *The Emergence of Lincoln*. New York: Scribner's Sons, 1950.

Nichols, Roy Franklin. *The Disruption of American Democracy*. New York: Macmillan, 1948.

Olliff, Jonathon C. *Reforma Mexico and the United States: A Search for Alternatives to Annexation, 1854–1861*. Tuscaloosa: University of Alabama Press, 1981.

Olsen, Christopher J. *Political Culture and Secession in Mississippi: Masculinity, Honor, and the Antiparty Tradition, 1830–1860*. New York: Oxford University Press, 2000.

Overdyke, W. Darrell. *The Know-Nothing Party in the South*. Baton Rouge: Louisiana State University Press, 1950.

Ownsbey, Betty, J. *Alias "Paine": Lewis Thornton Powell, the Mystery Man of the Lincoln Conspiracy.* Jefferson, N.C.: McFarland, 1993.

Parins, James W. *John Rollin Ridge: His Life and Works.* Lincoln: University of Nebraska Press, 2004.

Parramore, Thomas C., with Peter G. Stewart and Tommy L. Bogger. *Norfolk: The First Four Centuries.* Charlottesville: University Press of Virginia, 1994.

——. *Trial Separation: Murfreesboro, North Carolina and the Civil War.* Murfreesboro, N.C.: Murfreesboro Historical Association, 1998.

Patterson, Gerald A. "Arming the South with Guns from the North. *America's Civil War.* October 2007. Published online September 5, 2007. www.historynet.com-americas-civil-war-arming-the-south-with-guns-from-the-north.htm.

Perdue, Theda. *Slavery and the Evolution of Cherokee Society: 1540–1866.* Knoxville: University of Tennessee Press, 1979.

Pinnegar, Charles. *Brand of Infamy: A Biography of John Buchanan Floyd.* Westport, Ct.: Greenwood Press, 2002.

Pitch, Anthony S. *"They Have Killed Papa Dead!" The Road to Ford's Theatre, Abraham Lincoln's Murder, and the Rage for Vengeance.* Hanover, N.H.: Steerforth, 2008.

Potter, David M. *The Impending Crisis: 1848–1861.* New York: Harper Collins, 1976.

Powell, William S., ed. *Encyclopedia of North Carolina.* Chapel Hill: University of North Carolina Press, 2006.

Prince, Cathryn J. *Burn the Town and Sack the Banks: Confederates Attack Vermont.* New York: Carroll and Graf, 2006.

"Prison Camps of the American Civil War." http://delawarepublicrecordsearch.org/71/prison-camps-of-the-american-civil-war/.

Proctor, Ben H. *Not Without Honor: The Life of John H. Reagan.* Austin: University of Texas Press, 1962.

Pryor, Dayton E. *The Beginning and the End: The Civil War Story of Federal Surrenders before Fort Sumter and Confederate Surrenders after Appomattox.* Bowie, Md.: Heritage, 2001.

Radcliff, George L. *Governor Thomas H. Hicks of Maryland and the Civil War.* Baltimore: John Hopkins University Press, 1901.

Rainwater, Percy Lee. *Mississippi: Storm Center of Secession: 1850–1861.* Baton Rouge, La.: Claitor, 1938.

Ramage, James A. *Rebel Raider: The Life of General John Hunt Morgan.* Lexington: University Press of Kentucky, 1986.

Rauch, Basil. *American Interest in Cuba: 1848–1855.* New York: Octagon, 1974.

Reed, Wallace Putnam, ed. *History of Atlanta, Georgia: With Illustrations and Biographical Sketches of Some of Its Prominent Men and Pioneers.* Syracuse, N.Y.: D. Mason, 1889.

Reynolds, Donald E. *Editors Make War: Southern Newspapers in the Secession Crisis.* Nashville: Vanderbilt University Press, 1966.

———. *Texas Terror: The Slave Insurrection Panic of 1860 and the Secession of the Lower South.* Baton Rouge: Louisiana State University Press, 2007.

Richard, Leonard L. *The California Gold Rush and the Coming of the Civil War.* New York: Vintage, 2007.

Roland, Charles P. *Albert Sidney Johnston: Soldier of Three Republics.* Lexington: University Press of Kentucky, 2001.

Rolle, Andrew. *The Lost Cause: The Confederate Exodus to Mexico.* Norman: University of Oklahoma Press, 1965.

Roman, Alfred. *The Military Operations of General Beauregard in the War Between the States, 1861–1865.* New York: Harper and Brothers, 1884.

Roscoe, Theodore. *The Web of Conspiracy: The Complete Story of the Men Who Murdered Abraham Lincoln.* Englewood Cliffs, N.J.: Prentice Hall, 1959.

Rose, Victor M. *Ross' Texas Brigade: Being a Narrative of Events Connected With Its Service in the Late War Between the States.* Louisville, Ky.: Printed at Courier-Journal, 1881.

Ross, Ishbel. *First Lady of the South: The Life of Mrs. Jefferson Davis.* New York: Harper and Brothers, 1958.

Rowland, Dunbar. *Encyclopedia of Mississippi History.* Vol. 2. Madison, Wisc.: Selwyn A. Brant, 1907.

Ruffner, Kevin Conley. *Maryland's Blue and Gray: A Border State's Union and Confederate Junior Officers Corps.* Baton Rouge: Louisiana State University Press, 1997.

Rule, G. E. "Tucker's War: Missouri and the Northwest Conspiracy." 2002. Civil War St. Louis. wwwcivilwarstlouis.com/history2/tuckerswar.htm.

Samples, Gordon. *Lust for Fame: The Stage Career of John Wilkes Booth.* Jefferson, N.C.: McFarland, 1982.

Sampson, Robert D. *John L. O'Sullivan and His Times.* Kent, Ohio: Kent State University Press, 2003.

Sandbo, Anna Irene. "The First Session of the Secession Convention of Texas." *Southwestern Historical Quarterly* 18, no. 6. www.tsha.utexas.edu/publications/journals/shq/online/v018/n2/article_2_print.html.

Sanders, Stuart. "Robert Charles Tyler: Last American Civil War General." *MHQ: The Quarterly Journal of Military History* (Spring 2006): 1.

Scarborough, William Kaufman. *Master of the Big House: Elite Slaveholders of the Mid-Nineteenth-Century South.* Baton Rouge: Louisiana State University Press, 2003.

Scharf, J. Thomas. *The Chronicles of Baltimore: Being a Complete History of "Baltimore Town" and Baltimore City: From the Earliest Period to the Present Day.* Baltimore: Turnbull Brothers, 1874.

——. *History of Maryland: From the Earliest Period to the Present Day*, Vol. 3. Hatboro, Pa.: Tradition, 1967.

Scholes, Walter V. *Mexican Politics during the Juarez Regime, 1855–1872*. Columbia: University of Missouri Press, 1957.

"Scott-Yarbrough House." Auburn Heritage Association website: www.auburnheritage.org/history-markers.html.

Shanks, Henry T. *The Secession Movement in Virginia: 1847–1861*. New York: AMS, 1971.

Sheads, Scott Sumpter, and Daniel Carrol Toomey. *Baltimore during the Civil War*. Linthicum, Md.: Toomey, 1997.

Sifakis, Stewart. *Compendium of the Confederate Armies: Texas*. New York: Facts on File, 1995.

Simpson, Craig M. *A Good Southerner: The Life of Henry A. Wise of Virginia*. Chapel Hill: University of North Carolina Press, 1985.

Simpson, John Eddins. *Howell Cobb: The Politics of Ambition*. Chicago: Adams, 1973.

"The Sixty-First Virginia Regiment." www.nkclifton.com/amer-civ-war/Virginia/61st_Virginia/61streg2.htm.

Smallwood, James. *Born in Dixie: Smith County Origins to 1875: The History of Smith County, Texas*. Vol. 1. Austin, Tex.: Eaton, 1999.

Smart, Charles Allen. *Viva Juarez: The Life of Benito Juarez (1806–1872), President of Mexico*. London: Eyre and Spottiswoode, 1963.

Smith, Joseph E., and William L. Richter. "Gus Howell: Smarmy, Arrogant Blockade Runner and Murderer or Effective, Behind-the-Lines, Confederate Operative?" *Surratt Courier* 36, no. 9 (September 2011): 3.

Smythe, Angela. "Has He Been Hiding in Plain Sight? John Wilkes Booth and the Richmond Grays." May 10, 2010. www.morningfourstars.com/JWB/Hiding_In_Plain_Sight/.

Somer, Dale. "James P. Newcomb: The Making of a Texas Radical." *Southwestern Historical Quarterly* 72, no. 4 (April 1969): 449.

Speed, Thomas. *The Union Cause in Kentucky: 1860–1865*. New York: Knickerbocker, 1907.

Spellman, Paul N. *Forgotten Texas Leader: Hugh McLeod and the Texan Santa Fe Expedition*. College Station: Texas A&M Press, 1999.

Standard, Diffee William. *Columbus, Georgia in the Confederacy: The Social and Industrial Life of the Chattahoochee River Port*. New York: William-Frederick, 1954.

Stevens, Peter F. "The Saga of Lambdin P. Milligan." *Indiana Horizons*, Summer 1988, 25.

Stevenson, Daniel. "General Nelson, Kentucky, and Lincoln Guns." *Magazine of American History* 10 (July–December 1883): 115.

Stevenson, William G. *Thirteen Months in the Rebel army.* New York: A. S. Barnes, 1959.

Steward, William H., ed. *History of Norfolk County Virginia and Representative Citizens.* Chicago: Biographical Publishing, 1902.

Stickles, Arndt. *Simon Bolivar Buckner: Borderland Knight.* Chapel Hill: University of North Carolina Press, 1940.

Stout, Joseph A., Jr. *Schemers and Dreamers: Filibustering in Mexico, 1848–1921.* Fort Worth: Texas Christian University Press, 2002.

Stroud, David. *Flames and Vengeance: The East Texas Fires and the Presidential Election of 1860.* Kilgore, Tex.: Pinecrest, 1992.

Summers, Festus P. *The Baltimore and Ohio in the Civil War.* Gettysburg, Pa.: Stan Clark Military Books, 1993.

Sumrall, Allan K. *Battle Flags of Texas in the Confederacy.* Austin, Tex.: Eakin, 1995.

*The Surratt Family and John Wilkes Booth.* Compiled from the research of James O. Hall. Surratt Society, Clinton, Md.

Swanberg, W. A. "Was the Secretary of War a Traitor?" *American Heritage* 14, no. 4 (February 1963): 34.

Symonds, Craig L. *Stonewall of the West: Patrick Cleburne and the Civil War.* Lawrence: University Press of Kansas, 1997.

Temple, Oliver P. *East Tennessee and the Civil War.* Reprint, Johnson City, Tenn.: Overmountain, 1995.

Thomas, Benjamin P. *Abraham Lincoln: A Biography.* New York: Knopf, 1967.

Thomas, Emory M. *The Confederate Nation: 1861–1865.* New York: Harper and Row, 1979.

Thomas, Lately. *Between Two Empires: The Life Story of California's First Senator, William McKendree Gwin.* Boston: Houghton Mifflin, 1969.

Thompson, Ed Porter. *History of the Orphan Brigade.* Louisville, Ky.: Lewis N. Thompson, 1898.

Thompson, Jerry, ed. *Texas and New Mexico on the Eve of the Civil War: The Mansfield and Johnston Inspections, 1859–1861.* Albuquerque: University of New Mexico Press, 2001.

Tidwell, William A. *April '65: Confederate Covert Action in the American Civil War.* Kent, Ohio: Kent State University Press, 1995.

Tidwell, William A, with James O. Hall and David Winfred Gaddy. *Come Retribution: The Confederate Secret Service and the Assassination of Abraham Lincoln.* Jackson: University of Mississippi Press, 1988.

Tinkham, George H. "California during the Civil War." Extracted from Panama-Pacific Exposition Edition (1915) of *California Men and Events, 1769–1890* by California State Military Museum, at www.militarymuseum.org/CaandCW@.html.

Titone, Nora. *My Thoughts Be Bloody: The Bitter Rivalry between Edwin and John Wilkes Booth That Led to an American Tragedy.* New York: Free Press, 2010.

Toomey, Daniel Carroll. *The Civil War in Maryland.* Baltimore: Toomey, 1983.

Townsend, William H. *Lincoln and the Bluegrass: Slavery and Civil War in Kentucky.* Lexington: University of Kentucky Press, 1975.

Trindal, Elizabeth Steger. *Mary Surratt: An American Tragedy.* Gretna, La.: Pelican, 1996.

Tucker, Leslie R. *Major Isaac Ridgeway Trimble: Biography of a Baltimore Confederate.* Jefferson, N.C.: McFarland, 2005.

Tucker, Spencer C. *Brigadier General John D. Imboden: Confederate Commander in the Shenandoah.* Lexington: University Press of Kentucky, 2003.

Turk, David Scott. *Give My Kind Regards to the Ladies: The Life of Littleton Quinton Washington.* Bowie, Md.: Heritage, 2001.

"29th North Carolina Regiment": http://thomaslegion.net/29th.html.

Urwin, Gregory J. W. "Notes on the First Confederate Volunteers from Ouachita County, Arkansas, 1861." *Military Collector & Historian* 49, no. 2 (Summer 1997): 83.

Van Der Linden, Frank. *The Road to War.* Golden, Colo.: Fulcrum, 1998.

Victor, Orville J. *The Comprehensive History of the Southern Rebellion and the War for the Union.* New York: J. D. Torrey, 1862.

Vourlojianis, George N. *The Cleveland Grays: An Urban Military Company, 1837–1919.* Kent, Ohio: Kent State University Press, 2002.

Waitman, Leonard B. "The Knights of the Golden Circle." *San Bernardino County Museum Association Quarterly* 15, no. 4 (Summer 1968): 1.

Walden, Geoff. "Camps Boone and Burnett, Tennessee." www.rootsweb.com/~orphan hm/campboone.htm.

Walther, Eric H. *The Fire-Eaters.* Baton Rouge: Louisiana State University Press, 1992.

———. *The Shattering of the Union: America in the 1850s.* Wilmington, Del.: Scholarly Resources, 2004.

———. *William Lowndes Yancey: The Coming of the Civil War.* Chapel Hill: University of North Carolina Press, 2006.

"The War Nearly Started Here . . . Seizing the U.S. Arsenal at Little Rock." www.geo cities.com/capitalguards/arsenal.htm.

Warner, Ezra J. *Generals in Gray: Lives of the Confederate Commanders.* Baton Rouge: Louisiana State University Press, 1959.

Weber, Jennifer L. *Copperheads: The Rise and Fall of Lincoln's Opponents in the North.* New York: Oxford University Press, 2006.

West, Stephen A. "Minute Men, Yeomen and Mobilization for Secession in South Carolina." *Journal of Southern History* 71, no. 1 (February 2005): 75.

White, William W. "The Texas Slave Insurrection of 1860." *Southwestern Historical Journal* 52, no. 8 (January 1949): 259.

Williams, T. Harry. *P. G. T. Beauregard: Napoleon in Gray.* Baton Rouge: Louisiana State University Press, 1981.

Williams, Tres. "Camden's Golden Knights." *Ouachita Valley Ledger,* 1981.

Wise, Barton H. *The Life of Henry A. Wise of Virginia.* New York: Macmillan, 1899.

Wisehart, Marion K. *Sam Houston: American Giant.* Washington D.C.: Robert B. Luce, 1962.

Woods, James M. *Rebellion and Realignment: Arkansas Road to Secession.* Fayetteville: University of Arkansas Press, 1987.

Woodward, Grace Steel. *The Cherokees.* Norman: University of Oklahoma Press, 1963.

Woodworth, Steven E. *Jefferson Davis and His Generals: The Failure of the Confederate Command in the West.* Lawrence: University Press of Kansas, 1990.

Yearns, W. Buck. *The Confederate Governors.* Athens: University of Georgia Press, 1985.

Young, Kevin R. *To the Tyrants Never Yield: A Texas Civil War Sampler.* Plano, Tex.: Wordware, 1992.

# UNPUBLISHED WORKS

Alexander, Ronald Ray. "Central Kentucky in the Civil War: 1861–1865." Ph.D. diss., University of Kentucky, 1976.

Atkins, Paul A. "Henry A. Wise and the Virginia Secession Convention: February 13–April 17, 1861." Master's thesis, University of Virginia, 1950.

Bartman, Roger J. "The Contributions of Joseph Holt to the Political Life of the United States." Ph.D. diss., Fordham University, 1958.

Bell, Walter H. "Knights of the Golden Circle: Its Organization and Activities in Texas Prior to the Civil War." Master's thesis, Texas College of Arts and Industry, 1965.

Craig, Berry, "The Jackson Purchase of Kentucky in the Secession Crisis of 1860–1861." Master's thesis, Murray State University, 1973.

Craig, David R. "James J. Archer: The Little Gamecock." Master's thesis, Morgan State University, May 1983.

Fertig, James Walter. "Secession and Reconstruction of Tennessee." Ph.D. diss., University of Chicago, 1898.

Harman, Thomas S. "The Secession Crisis in the Shenandoah Valley: How Staunch Unionists Became Ardent Confederates." Senior thesis, Duke University, spring 1979.

Hudson, Linda Sybert. "Military Knights of the Golden Circle in Texas." Master's thesis, Stephen F. Austin University, 1990.

Mengel, Jennie Angell. "The Neutrality of Kentucky in 1861." Master's thesis, University of Louisville, 1925.

Simpson, Craig Michael. "Henry Wise in Antebellum Politics—1850–1861." Ph.D. diss., Stanford University, 1972.

Talbot, Laurence Fletcher. "California Secession Support of the Southern Confederacy: The Struggle, 1861–1865." Ph.D. diss., Union Institute, 1995.

Timmons, Joe T. "Texas on the Road to Secession. Vol. 1. Ph.D. diss., University of Chicago, 1973.

Volz, Harry A., III. "Party, State, and Nation: Kentucky and the Coming of the American Civil War." Ph.D. diss., University of Virginia, 1982.

Williams, Gary Lee. "James and Joshua Speed: Lincoln's Kentucky Friends." Ph.D. diss., Duke University, 1971.

Winston, Norma Dix. "George D. Prentice and Secession in Kentucky." Master's thesis. University of Chicago, 1939.

# INDEX

Abdington, Va., 83

Abolitionists, 4, 54, 58–59, 64, 73, 78, 83, 110, 114

*Adalaska,* 7

Adams, James, 78

Address to the Citizens of the Southern States, 53–57, 83

Address to the People of Maryland, 102

African slave trade, 15, 39, 54, 68, 79, 103, 127, 128, 196n20

Agitators, 31, 59–60, 83–84

Alabama, 10, 33, 35, 41, 43, 45, 48, 49, 52, 59, 79, 103, 127, 128, 174, 186

*Alamo Express,* 115, 120, 124

Alamo Guards, 80, 121

Alamo Rifles, 121, 124

Alexander, J. K., 79

Ambler, Marshall, 136

Ambler, William, 238n65

*American Cavalier,* 18–19, 199nn5–7

American Colonization and Steamship Company of "1," 9–10, 27

American Knights, Order of. *See* Order of American Knights

American Party, 8, 13. *See also* Know-Nothings

American Patent Company, 9

Ampudia, Pedro de, 142, 144

Anderson, Charles, 76, 113

Anderson, Robert, 94–95, 113, 151, 161

Annapolis, Md., 83

Appomattox Courthouse, Va., 185

Archer, James J., 256n56

Archer, Robert H., 47, 80, 111, 134, 145, 183, 227n41, 256n56

Arkansas, 35, 41, 47, 59, 69, 79, 126–28, 146–47, 149–50, 154, 215n12, 232n6; secession convention, 161

*Arkansas True Democrat,* 23, 200–201n24

Arms, purchase of for South, 90–91

Army, Confederate, 91, 123, 141, 145, 147–49, 154, 156, 159, 172, 184, 186, 190, 252n24

—Alabama: Eleventh Cavalry, 182; Third Cavalry, 145, 186

—Arkansas: First Volunteer Infantry, 149–50; Second Volunteer Infantry, 150

—Army of the West, 331n49; Conscription Bureau, 186

—Georgia: First Infantry Regiment Regulars (Barlow's), 147; Second Infantry Regiment, 146, 241n35

—Indian Territory: First Choctaw and Chickawa Mounted Regiment, 147

—Kentucky, 166; First Cavalry, 246n27; Ninth Cavalry, 164; Recruiting Camps, 161–62; Third Infantry Regiment, 149

—North Carolina: Fourteenth Regiment, Volunteers, 151; Twenty-Ninth Infantry Regiment, 167

—Recruiting for, 133–34, 144–45, 147–48, 161–62

—Regular: Third Cavalry, 145; Twelfth Battalion, Heavy Artillery, 186

—Tennessee: First Infantry Regiment, 158, Fifteenth Infantry Regiment, 145–46; Second Cav. Regiment, 24; Sixth (Wheeler's) Cavalry Regiment, 186

—Texas: Dallas Light Artillery Company, 210n42; Eighth Infantry Regiment, 154; Fifth Cavalry, 186; First Infantry Regiment, 154; First Light Artillery, 193–94; Reserve Corps, 232; Ross' Brigade, 154; Terry's Rangers, 208n7; Third Cavalry (Greer's), 145, 216n19, 242n49; Thirty-Third Cavalry (Duff's Partisan Rangers), 181, 185, 258n6

—Virginia: Fifty-Fifth Infantry Regiment, 145; Malone's Brigade, 257n4; Sixty-First Infantry Regiment, 185, 257n4; Wise's Legion, 153–54

Army, United States, 12, 87, 90–91, 104, 110, 122, 143; Department of New Mexico, 90; Department of the Pacific (including Sixth Regiment), 90–91, 131, 234n22; Department of Texas, 37, 91, 116, 120, 123, 143; Newport, Ky., Barracks, 158; Sixth Massachusetts Volunteer Regiment, 143; Third Artillery, 226n41

Arnold, Samuel B., 145, 176–77, 180, 252n24, 254n41

Ash, William S., 97

Ashby, Turner, 24, 137, 208n5

Ashland, Ky., 217n31

Ashville, Tenn., 167

*Atlanta Daily Intelligencer,* 41, 53, 79

Atlanta, Ga., 41, 47, 51, 79, 106, 146, 147

Atlanta Grays, 79, 80

Atley, 255n45

Atzerodt, George A., 178, 183–84

Auburn, Ala., 40, 52, 57

Augusta, Ga., 41

*Austin Southern Intelligencer,* 65

*Austin State Gazette,* 113

Austin, Tex., 41, 64, 75, 113–14, 119, 125

Avery, William W., 49

"B" (U.S. State Department emissary), 254n37

Bagby, G. W., 236–37n38

Bahia Hondo, Cuba, 11

Bailey, Godard, 94

Baldwin, William, 138

Baltimore, 10–15, 40–41, 47, 49, 53, 83–85, 101, 181, 184, 187, 199n1, 226n35; assassination conspiracy in, 107, 112, 176–77, 180–81, 227n42, 227n47; disunion activities, 102, 142–45, 177, 225n12, 238n65, 239n20; Exeter Street neighborhood, 17; KGC establishment, 17–18, 21, 40 198n51; Recruiting in, 133–34, 144–45; St. Vincent's Church, 17

Baltimore City Guard, 111, 239n21

*Baltimore Daily Exchange,* 22

Baltimore & Ohio Railroad, 142

Barbour, Alfred, 138

Barnes, F. J., 236–37n48

Barnum's Hotel, 84, 111

Barrett, James, 175

Bast, J., 246n33

Bates, Edward, 19

Baton Rouge, La., 41–42

Battle of Gettysburg, 172, 185

Battle of Pea Ridge, Arkansas (aka Elkhorn Tavern), 185, 257n1

Battle of Stones River, 186

Battle of Wilson's Creek, 129, 242n49

Bayard, Thomas F., 86

Baylor, John R., 36, 69, 113, 229n20

Beauregard, Pierre G. T., 91, 123–24, 140, 151–52, 222n13

Bell, John, 65

Belmont, Augustus, 254*n*34

Belnap, Tex., 37

Benjamin, Judah, 152, 174

Berks County, Pa., 250*n*7

Bexar County, Tex., 124

Bickley, Charles, 21, 44, 53, 57–58, 64, 75, 121, 207*n*61, 212n5, 212*n*9

Bickley, Charles Simmons, 6

Bickley, George W. L., 3, 5, 33, 35, 40, 41, 55–56, 62–64, 75, 141–42, 167–68, 194*n*12, 247*n*48; Civil War surgeon, 209–10; early life, 6–9, 198*n*51; establishing KGC, 5, 18, 20–24, 31, 109, 199*n*3, 200*n*16, 201*n*27; KGC propagation, 54–58, 61, 64–67, 205*n*40, 212n5, 212*n*7, 213*n*35, 231n1; open letters, 55–57, 159–60; in prison, 171, 179, 186, 187, 201*n*28, 249*nn*63–64, 254*n*36, 258*nn*11–12; recruiting in Kentucky, 142, 148, 162, 166–67, 242*n*2, 247*n*45; removal as commander-in-chief, 43–45, 50, 54

Bickley Mills (Russel County), Va., 6

*Bickley's West American Review*, 8

Bigler, John, 130, 251*n*18

Billings, E. L., 142

Black Horse Cavalry, 138

Black, M. M., 47, 48

Black Republicans, 2, 71, 78, 111, 177; as derogatory reference to President, 4, 76, 82, 84, 88. *See also* Republican Party

Blackburn, Luke, 156–57, 244–45*n*5

Bonham, Millard, 22, 95

Booth, Edwin, 1

Booth, John Wilkes, 9, 17–18, 30–31, 80; escape, 182–84, 186, 229–31, 252*n*58; kidnapping plot, 177–79, 253*nn*29–30; as KGC, 1–2; Lincoln's assassination, 179–82; in militia, 144–45, 240*n*24; supports South, 110, 252*nn*24–25, 253*n*30, 253*n*33

Border States, 82, 84, 87, 88, 90, 104, 133, 136, 141, 147, 167, 168, 171, 173, 176, 187

Boston, Mass., 83

Bowles, William A., 249*n*3

Bowling Green, Ky., 166

Boyle, Cornelius, 85–86, 105–6, 256*nn*59–60

Bradford, Augustus, 177

Bradford, Conn., 248*n*52

Bradley (by-line), 62–63, 211n1

Bragg, Braxton, 167–68, 248*n*57

Branch, Lawrence O'Bryan, 107–8

Branson, Joseph, 180–81, 254*n*43

Brazil, 29, 54

Brazoria County, Tex., 117

Breckinridge, John, 4, 59, 63, 74, 82, 83, 86, 87, 89, 94, 100–101, 109, 165, 166, 217*n*31, 217*n*32, 247*n*40

Breckinridge and Lane Clubs, 82, 84–85, 104

Bristoe (KGC Captain), 162

Bristol, Tenn., 167

Britain. *See* England

Brotherhood of the Union, 8. *See also* Continental Union

Brown, Albert Gallatin, 29

Brown, Beriah, 130, 251*n*18

Brown, George William, 143

Brown, John, 2, 30–31, 80, 84

Brown, Joseph, 81, 91

Brownlow, William Ganaway, 83, 211n1

Brownsville, Tex., 42, 50, 61, 115

Bryan, Guy, 114

Buchanan administration, 18, 38, 42, 44, 59, 62, 82, 90–95, 157, 166, 174, 223*n*43

Buchanan, James, 4, 19, 21, 32–33, 36, 44, 62, 67, 86, 90–93, 98, 101, 108, 242*n*53

Buckner, Simon, 166

Bullitt, Joshua Fry, 175, 249*n*3

Burn, Tom, 182. *See also* Byrne, William

Burnett, Henry, 179

Burnside, Ambrose Everett, 169

Butler, Benjamin Franklin, 144–45, 176

Byrne, William, 84–85, 103, 110, 142

Cairo, Ill., 166, 252*n*25

California, 21, 43, 48, 87, 126, 129–31, 174, 184

Callahan, James, 36

Callahan (Floyd's clerk), 221*n*5. *See also* Callahan, James

Camden, Ark., 127, 149–50

Camden Knights of the Golden Circle, 149–50, 242*n*50

Cameron County, Tex., 115

Cameron, Simon, 115, 139

Camp Boone, Tenn., 161–62

Camp Clay, Ohio, 161

Camp Douglas, Ill., 175

Camp Holt, Ind., 161

Camp Morton, Ind., 169

Camp Verde, Tex., 120

Campbell, A., 63

Campbell, John, 103

Campbell's Hospital, 178

Canada, 173–77, 184

Canning, Matthew, 256*n*54

Cape Fear Minute Men, 97–98

Cape Fear River, 97–98

Caribbean Islands, 1, 49, 108, 133

Carland, Louis, 181–82

Carlisle, John S., 132, 134–35, 138

Carrington, Henry Beebee, 168

Carroll, William Henry, 146

Castellanos, Henry C., 41, 44, 47, 52, 53, 186, 258*n*9

Castroville, Tex., 167, 210

Catholic Church, 19

Central America, 1, 4, 28–29, 39, 49, 68, 72, 87, 108, 127

Chalmers, David, 136–37

Chambers, Thomas Jefferson, 117

Charles City Courthouse, Va., 52

*Charleston Mercury*, 51, 75, 141

Charleston, S.C., 47, 49, 92–95, 102, 134, 140, 151, 221*n*6, 223*n*43

Charlestown, Va., 142

Chase, Salmon, 70, 183

Cherokee Indians, 128–29

Chester, Samuel, 178, 181

Chicago, Ill., 101, 175, 252*n*21, 252*n*26

*Chicago Tribune*, 102

Chihuahua Province, Mexico, 20, 32, 33, 38, 142

Chilton, George Washington, 33, 229*n*17, 258*n*6; background, 35, 203*n*10; as Confederate officer, 148–49, 154, 181, 186; as KGC leader, 35, 41, 51, 68, 71, 80, 113–15, 126, 140–41

Chilton, William Parrish, 35

Christian County, Ky., 160

Cincinnati, Ohio, 7, 9, 39, 101, 109, 141, 161, 169, 172, 176, 186

Civil War, 2, 5, 89, 109, 131, 136, 140, 190

Clark, Ed, 125

Clark, J. S., 58, 62

Clarke, Mary Bayard, 131, 136, 140, 216*n*18, 230*n*40

Clarke, William J., 121, 151

*Clarkesville Chronicle*, 162

Clarkesville, Tenn., 162

Clay, Clement, 174

Clay, Henry, 161

Clay, James, 164–66, 247*n*40

Cleburne, Patrick, 150, 232*n*6

Cleveland, Tenn., 62–63

Coahuila Province, Mexico, 20, 34, 37

Cobb, Howell, 70, 89, 221*n*3

Cockeysville, Md., 144

Columbia College, 86

Columbia, S.C., 75, 78, 82, 91, 93–94, 98

Columbus, Ga., 51–52, 53, 147, 256*n*54

Columbus Guards, 52, 81, 242*n*50

Columbus, Ohio, 69–70

Comanche Indians, 69

Committees of Public Safety, 77, 104, 116, 119–20, 123

Comstock lode, 234*n*24

Confederate army. *See* Army, Confederate

Confederate blockade runner, 177, 252*n*25

Confederate Commissioners (in Canada), 98, 174–77

Confederate Government, 95, 104, 129, 140–41, 147, 150–51, 156, 158–59, 184, 247*n*49; Bureau of Indian Affairs, 128; Commissioners, 103; Congress of, 35, 119, 125, 140–41, 150–51, 189, 236*n*40; Postmaster General, 71, 140–41, 238*n*3; secret service of, 175–76, 181, 183–84, 240*n*24, 253*n*32, 257*n*66; Torpedo bureau, 184; War Department, 140–41, 177

*Confederate Journal,* 186

Confederate Recruiting Camps (Kentucky), 202–3

Conrad, Charles, 22

Conrad, Robert Y., 132, 135–36

Conrad, Thomas Nelson, 13, 253*n*30

Conspiracy: to capture forts and arsenals, 4, 85–99; seizure of Washington, 87–88, 100, 107–8, 179, 224*n*7, 115*n*15; southern slaveholder's, 15, 62–63, 87–88

Continental Union, 195–96*n*14. *See also* Brotherhood of the Union

Continental Union Party, 65

Cook, John J., 75

Cook, Thomas, 125

Cooper, Douglas, 127, 146–47

Copperheads, 168, 173–74

Corpus Christi, Tex., 61, 247*n*49

*Corpus Christie Ranchero,* 63

Cortinas, 37, 60

Costa Rico, 62

Cotton States (Deep South), 65, 82, 84, 87, 90–91, 102

Covington, Ky., 142

Cowan, W. R., 231*n*50

Cowart, Robert J., 125, 146

Cowlen, Charles, 179

Cox, Samuel Sullivan, 39

Crabb, Henry, 20

Crawford, R. A., 41, 47, 147, 208*n*7

Creek Indians, 129

Crenshaw, William L., 149

Crittenden, John, 8, 11, 82, 217*n*31

Crittenden, William, 11, 35, 108

Cuba, 1, 4, 11, 13–14, 18, 21, 35, 39, 41, 43, 49, 62, 70, 71, 87, 103, 133, 153

Cuban junta, 13

Cuban slaves, 13–14

Cureton, E., 52

Curtis, C. P., 199*n*3

*Daily Evening Bulletin,* (San Francisco), 20–21

*Daily Ledger and Texan* (Dallas), 124, 167

*Dallas Herald,* 40, 58–59, 67, 123

Dallas, Tex., 58–59, 80, 124, 149

Darrow, Caroline, 122

Davis, Garrett, 158

Davis, Jefferson, 29, 34, 43, 78, 101, 131, 133, 140–41, 144, 151–53, 158, 161–62, 166, 173, 184, 241*n*33, 247*n*40

Davis, Varina, 43

De Janette, Daniel, 110

Debow, James D. B., 201*n*36

Delaware, 86–87

Delaware Guards, 87

Democratic Party, 12, 65, 83, 86, 107, 127, 130, 173; Charleston convention (1860), 49–50; Chicago convention (1864), 175; platform plank of 1856, 62; splintering (1860), 4, 29, 208–9*n*9. *See also* States'-rights Democrats

*Democratic Review,* 8

Denton, Tex., 58

DeValls Bluff, Ark., 127, 257–58*n*5

Devoe (metropolitan police detective), 227*n*42

Dillard, Frank W., 51–52, 147

District of Columbia, 15–16, 19, 22, 71, 83, 85, 86, 95, 100–108, 138–39. *See also* Washington, City of

Disunion. *See* Secession (southern)

Doblado, Manuel, 19, 20, 38, 60
Dodd, Harrison H., 175, 249n3
Dodson, Rachel, 8
Dominican Republic, 8
Doolittle, James Rood, 39
Douglas, Stephen Arnold, 19, 49, 65, 76, 86, 87, 88, 100, 217n31, 220n60
Dramatic Star Company (Richmond), 1
Duff, James, 154
Duke, Basil, 249n58
Dunbar, Jno. B., 66
Duncan, Blanton, 147, 156, 159
Duvall (KGC Captain), 162

East India Company, 64
Eaton (by-line), 103–4, 225n15
Eclectic Medical Institute, 7–9
Ed Clark Invincibles, 149
Edgar, William M., 121, 154
Edwards, William H., 135
El Monte, Cal., 129
Electoral College, 106, 109
Ellis, John Willis, 97–98, 147
Elkhorn Tavern. See Battle of Pea Ridge, Arkansas (aka Elkhorn Tavern)
Emigrant aid societies, 63
Empire Club, 10
Encinal County, Tex., 57, 63
England, 19, 37, 54, 124, 152, 187
Eutaw House, 83
Evans, Lemuel D., 103, 225n15
Ewing, Thomas, 103

Fairfax Courthouse, Va., 177
Fauquier County, Va., 137–38
Felton, Samuel M., 106–7, 111–12, 142
Fenian brotherhood, 188
Fernandini, Cypriano (Henry), 17, 24, 107, 110, 184, 199n2, 252n28
Filibustering, 10–11, 13–14, 18, 20, 35, 37, 38, 42–44, 63, 68, 83, 108, 187, 196n25
Fillmore, Millard, 9

Fire-eaters (southern), 28–30, 58–60, 76–79, 97–98, 101–2, 109–10, 127–28
Florida, 48, 237n59
Flournoy, George, 113, 117
Flournoy, T. B., 147
Floyd, John, 4, 22, 36, 83, 89–95, 98, 103, 220n2, 221n6, 221n8, 234n22, 255n45
Ford, Henry Clay, 182, 255n52
Ford, John Salmon, 12, 13, 36, 42, 60, 113–15, 117, 124, 148–49, 154, 198n41, 229n17
Ford, John T., 1
Ford's Theatre, 179
Foree, J. M., 158, 164
Forrest, Nathan Bedford, 146, 176, 259n19
Fort Caswell, 97–98
Fort Ewen, 56
Fort Johnson, 97–98
Fort Lafayette, 170, 249n64
Fort McHenry, 96
Fort Monroe, 92, 96–97, 131, 223n36
Fort Moultrie, 92, 94
Fort Pitt Foundry, 91, 93
Fort Pulaski, 98
Fort Sumter, 92–94, 136, 140, 151, 161, 223n43
Fort Warren, 186–87, 249n64
Forts and Arsenals (federal), 89–90, 136; Charleston harbor, 92–94, 136; Navy yards, 96, 136, 138; Pittsburgh's Allegheny arsenal, 93–94, 98; seizure of, 4, 70, 82, 89–99, 104, 120–23, 136, 138, 143, 149
Foster, Charles Henry, 53, 60, 77, 201n36
Fowler, White, 160
Fox (doctor in San. Fran.), 174
France, 40, 45, 60, 67, 124, 186, 188
Frankfurt Commonwealth, 159–60
Frankfurt, Ky., 159–60
Frederick, Md., 143
The Free Flag of Cuba, 35
Freemasons, 233n10, 242n52
French, Parker, 248n52
Fulton County, Ga., 79

Galveston Artillery Company, 80

Galveston City Guards, 80

Galveston, Tex., 63, 64, 80, 93, 114–15, 148–49, 154

Gammage, Thomas Troop, 37, 40

Garnett, Alexander Y. P., 86, 105, 138

Gaulding, Alexander Archibald, 41, 44, 79, 146

Geddes, 255n45

Geneva, Ala., 6

Georgia, 41, 52, 59, 79, 81–82, 91, 116–17, 120, 128, 146, 150

Georgia Military Convention, 81

Gifford, James, 182, 255n52

Gist (S.C. Governor), 221n6

Gist, S. R., 232n6

Glavis, G., 246n33

Gold, 4, 189

Golden Circle (region), 1, 14

Goldthwart, George, 53

Gonzales County, Tex., 114

*Gonzales Telegraph*, 41

Gonzales, Tex., 41–42

Good, John, 80, 149, 210n42, 216n19

Gordon, J. (Esquire), 53

Gordonsville, Va., 183

Gosport Naval Yard, 96, 136–38

Grant, Ulysses, 247n43, 252n24, 254n37

Great Britain, 21, 64

Greek Fire, 176

Greeley, Horace, 4

Green, John, 96, 113, 148, 154

Green Mount cemetery, 187

Green, Thomas, 256n60

Greenborough (Colonel), 43, 207n60

Greenbrier Resort, 22–23, 90, 201n28. *See also* White Sulphur Springs, Va.

Greencastle, Ind., 6

Greer, Elkanah Bracken, 5, 33–36, 40, 43, 45, 47, 49, 51, 53, 61, 63, 73; as Confederate officer, 5, 140–41, 154–55, 186, 203n6, 242n49, 257n1, 257–58n5; early

life, 33–36; Texas as KGC commander, 33–36, 47, 68, 124, 127

Greer, James, 34

Groner, Virginius Despeaux, 40–41, 47, 51–53, 57–58, 60–61, 64, 79–80, 96–97, 131–32, 223n36, 257n4; as Confederate officer, 5, 140–41, 185; early life, 40–41, 68; as KGC commander, 69, 75, 205n40, 208n5

Guadalupe River, 41

Guanajuato Province, Mexico, 19, 20, 38

Gwin, William, 129–30, 134, 233n15, 234n23


Haco, Dion, 255n47

Halifax, Nova Scotia, 187

Hamlin (Vice President), 106

Hampton, Va., 61, 238n65

Handy (Judge), 106

Harbin, Thomas, 184, 252n30

Hardee, William J., 91

Harford County, Md., 80, 111, 134, 138, 144; militia of, 111, 240n24

Harmony Hall (D.C.), 105

Harney, Ben John, 164

Harney, Ben M., 53, 164

Harney, Thomas E., 184

Harpending, Asbury, 233n19, 234n24

Harpers Ferry, Va., 2, 30, 80, 96, 123, 136–38, 143, 147, 238n65, 239–40n23

Harris, Isham, 147, 157, 162, 166, 211n1, 217n28, 245n7, 246n27

Harrisburg, Pa., 112, 144

Harrison County, Tex., 68, 114, 149

*Harrison Flag*, 71

Harrison, John, 240n24

Harvie, Lewis E., 133, 235n34

Hayes, Jack, 36, 218–19n44

Hedrick, John J., 97–98

Heintzelman, Samuel, 42

Helena, Ark., 127, 198n40, 232n5, 242n53

Henderson, John, 11, 197n31, 197n36

Henderson, Tex., 41

Henningsen, Charles F., 12, 152–54

Henry, Patrick, 96

Herold, Adam, 181, 255n46

Herold, David Edgar, 178, 181, 253–54n33

Hicks, Thomas, 85, 102–3, 106–7, 143, 225n12

Hillard, Otis K., 85, 107–8

Hindman, Thomas, 13, 127–28, 150, 198n40, 215n12, 232n5

Hines, Thomas H., 173, 175

*History of the Settlement and Indian Wars of Tazewell County, Virginia*, 7

Hobby, Alfred, 154, 229n17

Hobby, Edwin, 154

Hoke, W. B., 246n33

Holcombe, Anne, 35

Holcombe, James, 174

Holcombe, Lucy, 35

Holly Springs, Miss., 34, 53, 146

Holt, Joseph, 59, 94–95, 101, 106, 157, 160–62, 164–65, 189, 224n7

Homestead Bills, 72

Hood, John Bell, 154

Houston County, Tex., 215n1

Houston, Sam, 35–37, 39, 42, 64, 66, 69, 81, 114–16, 118–20, 124, 125

*Houston Telegraph*, 74

Houston, Tex., 64, 113

Howard (Captain), 99

Howard, J. Ross, 41, 45, 51, 57–58, 99, 145, 186, 258n8

Howard, William, 107, 240n24

Howell, Gustavus A., 240n24

Howell, Joseph Davis, 43–44

Howell, William A., 144, 240n24

Hudson's Bay Company, 64

Hughes, Thomas, 118

Humphreys, Andrew, 249n3

Hunt, Charles L., 249n2

Hunt, R. A., 106

Hunter, David, 87

Hunter, Edwin, 255n54

Hunter, Robert M. T., 86

Huntsville, Tex., 64

Illinois, 49, 63, 145, 168, 171, 175, 248n53

Imboden, John, 137–38, 237n59

Immortals, 12

Indian Territory, 126–28, 146–47, 149, 152

Indian Trust Fund, 94

Indiana, 168, 171–72, 175, 248nn53–58, 250n12

Indianapolis, Ind., 108, 168, 252n21

Italy, 2, 153, 176

Jackson, Tenn., 145, 199n1

Jaeger (also Iaeger), William G., 47, 53

Jamaican Emancipation, 64

Jefferson (now Tazewell), Va., 6

Johnson, Andrew, 181, 253n30

Johnson, Bradley, 143, 239n18

Johnson ("rebel agent"), 254n37

Johnson, Robert Ward, 232n5

Johnson, Waldo P., 227n42

Johnston, Albert Sidney, 90–1, 131, 234n23, 235n26

Jones, David R., 78

Jones, John B., 154

Jones, Thomas A., 178, 180

Jones, William E., 246n33

Juárez, Benito, 18–20, 24, 32, 38–42, 47, 60, 64, 70, 188, 259n17

Judah, William H., 53

Judd, Norman, 109

Kane, George Marshal, 111, 142–44, 184, 227n42, 239n21, 255n45, 257n66

Kansas, 15, 41

Kansas-Nebraska Act, 14–15

Keen, B. H., 111, 227n41

Keetowahs, 128–29

Keitt, Lawrence, 217n33

Kennedy, John, 107, 112

Kentucky, 48, 83, 109, 142, 145, 147–48, 155, 156–68, 175–76, 244*n*1, 247*n*40; Home Guards, 160; Jackson Purchase region, 160–61; KGC convention in, 158, 189; legislature, 158–59, 161, 164–65; Military Board, 160, 163; neutrality, 156, 161, 164; recruiting in, 161–63; secession (attempted), 157; South-central region, 157; Southern Rights Party, 156–58, 164–66; special congressional elections, 157, 161; State Guard, 156, 162–63, 166; Unionists, 160, 163–65; Union Democratic Party, 161, 165

K. G. C. (or KGC). *See* Knights of the Golden Circle

Kinney (KGC Major from Ky.), 47

Klement, Frank, 194*n*11

Knights of the Golden Circle, 1–2, 6, 14, 32, 39, 152, 196*n*20; addresses to, 53, 57, 83–84; in Alabama, 48, 75; American Colonization and Steamship Co., 9–10; American Legion, 3, 25–26, 46, 48, 51, 54, 65; in Arkansas, 47, 48, 51, 127–28, 141, 147–48, 151, 162, 238*n*67; Army of, 3, 34, 68; in California, 48, 129–31, 233*n*15, 233*n*17, 234*n*20, 251*n*18; Captains of, 3, 32, 37, 73, 77, 154; castles of, 3, 15, 17, 64, 80, 87, 91, 149–50, 157, 160, 162, 166–68; Circular Letter to, 46–49; core of paramilitary groups, 77–88; Council of Thirteen, 3; Degree Works, 20, 27–28, 159, 201*n*34; in Delaware, 86, 87; domestic police force (vigilantism), 55, 59, 62, 66–67, 77, 189; drill, 3, 47, 77, 80, 154, 198*n*52; emblem, 9, 82, 200*n*16; emissaries 37, 53, 57–58, 76, 142, 187, 208*n*5; establishment of, 8, 22–28; exposes about, 4, 163–64; financial, 23 , 46, 48–50, 52–53, 55, 70, 146, 166, 200*n*16; flag, 73; in Georgia, 47, 48, 79, 142; goals of, 1–2, 32–33, 54; gold of, 4–5, 189; at Greenbrier Conference, 22–24, 201*n*28,

208*n*5; in Indian Territory, 128–29; in Kentucky, 83–84, 87, 141, 156–64, 244*n*2, 247*n*43; leaders of (including alleged), 1, 4, 46–48, 53–54, 63, 82, 84–85, 102, 127–28, 250*n*8; Lincoln abduction/assassination, involvement in, 4, 179–84, 224*n*1; in Louisiana, 43, 45, 267*n*67; in Maryland, 17, 47–48, 53–54, 63, 100–102, 144, 198*n*51, 239*n*20; Membership of, 2, 41, 47–48, 54, 61, 62, 76, 114, 129–30, 140, 156–57, 159, 164, 233*n*17, 259–60*n*20; Mexican colonization drive, 18, 21, 26–27, 37–43, 47, 54, 55–56, 60, 61, 62, 69, 73, 142, 163, 165, 187; in Mexico, 3, 21, 25, 54; in Midwest, 163, 168, 172–74, 248*n*53, 249*n*58, 250*n*12; in Mississippi, 146; in Missouri, 48,142, 252*n*21; in North Carolina, 47–48; oaths, 3, 27, 65, 157–58; open letter to, 55–57, 159–160; orders to, 26, 46, 57, 141, 184, 244*n*2, 258n12; organization of, 3, 25, 47–49, 56; in Oregon, 129, 256–57*n*63; origins of, 8–11, 54, 196*n*20, 197*n*40; in Pennsylvania, 215–16, 248*n*5; plots of, 69–71, 88, 100–6, 109–10, 112, 157–58, 172, 234*n*20, 248*n*52; Raleigh convention, 24–26, 45, 46, 49–53, 57, 83, 188; recruiting for, 17, 37, 41, 51, 64–67, 83, 148–49, 157, 212*n*5, 213*n*35; regimental commanders of , 3, 5, 32–35, 43, 46–48, 57, 63–64, 131, 176, 185–86; rituals of, 3, 21–22, 32, 53–54, 65, 72–73, 163, 214*n*40; rules and regulations of, 24–27, 72–73; rumors about, 215–16; secession promotion, 4, 54–55, 84, 113–26, 151, 157, 163–64, 167, 215*n*2, 238*n*67; secrecy of, 3–4, 30, 67, 74, 77, 83, 184; Southern army, nucleus of, 55, 62, 65, 71, 75, 77, 140, 147–48, 150, 166–67, 215*n*1; staff officers of, 51–52, 80; Southern Rights promotion, 41, 62, 70–71, 113–15, 159, 187, 196*n*20; state conventions, 124, 158, 189;

Knights of the Golden Circle (*continued*)
   in Tennessee, 48, 142, 176, 186, 238*n*67;
   terror tactics of , 4, 58–60, 259*n*18; in
   Texas, 15, 32, 34, 44, 47–48, 50–51, 54,
   59, 67–73, 113–26, 141, 148, 150, 186,
   212*n*5, 213*n*35, 215*n*1, 231*n*49; treason,
   alleged by, 4, 5, 74, 157, 163–64, 184; in
   Virginia, 46–48, 63–64, 100, 131, 135,
   139, 141, 208*n*5, 238*n*67; in Washington
   D.C., 86, 100, 103, 183–84, 198*n*52
—Degrees: First—Company (Order of the
   Iron Hand), 2, 26, 53, 65, 66, 71, 73, 159,
   214*n*40; Second—Commercial (Order
   of the True Faith), 2, 28, 65, 73, 159;
   Third—Division (Knights of the Colum-
   bian Star), 2–4, 22, 24, 28, 53, 54, 65, 73,
   130, 158, 163–64, 173–74, 184
Knights of the Golden Square, 248*n*52
Know-Nothings, 1, 8, 13 196–97*n*14,
   255*n*45. *See also* American Party
Knoxville, Tenn., 53, 83
Ku Klux Klan, 189, 259*n*19
Kunkel George, 1

*La Grange States Right Democrat*, 124
La Grange, Tex., 77
Lafayette, La., 197*n*36
*Lafayette True Delta*, 11
Lamar, C. A. L., 13
Lamar, G. B., 221*n*8
Lamb, James, 182
Lamon, Ward Hall, 112
Lancaster Court House, S.C., 52
Lane, Joseph, 233*n*15
Larrantree, Augustus, 47, 127, 141
League of United Southerners, 29–30, 57, 62
Lebanon (Marion County, Ky.), 83
Lee, Albert Miller, 37
Lee, Pryor, 37, 229*n*17
Lee, Robert E., 30, 37–38, 122, 172, 256*n*59
Lehigh County, Pa., 250*n*7
León faction, 12

Letcher, John, 96–97, 132, 135–38, 167,
   223*n*36, 239*n*22
Lewis, Dabney, 215*n*1
Lexington, Ky., 54, 83
Limestone Springs Guards, 215*n*6
Lincoln, Abraham, 15, 108–9, 123, 163,
   220*n*58; attempted abduction/assas-
   sination of, 4, 87, 101, 106–12, 157–58,
   176–79, 183–84, 224*n*1, 226*n*36, 227*n*42,
   227*n*43, 252*n*26, 252–53*n*27, 254*n*37,
   256–57*n*63; election (1860), 65, 67, 69,
   74, 75, 78, 92, 106, 127, 226*n*35, 226*n*36;
   as President, 82–84, 98, 104, 125, 131,
   136, 141, 159, 170, 173, 177, 222*n*11, 244*n*1
Lincoln guns, 158, 160–61
Lindsey, Ben F., 53
Little Rock, Ark., 127–28
Little Rock Arsenal, 127, 232*n*5
Little Rock Guards, 24
*Little Rock True Democrat*, 58
Littleton, John, 36, 229*n*17
Lockridge, Samuel A., 12, 44–45, 51, 124,
   154, 207*n*65, 207*n*67
Logan, John L., 150
*London Times*, 152, 258*n*8
Lone Star, 9, 97, 197*n*33, 215*n*6
Lone Star Rifles, 80, 154
López, Narcisco, 11, 12, 35, 153, 164, 197*n*36
Loring, William W., 90
Los Angeles, Calif., 129, 131, 235*n*26
Louisa County, Va., 136
Louisiana, 10, 34, 43, 45, 48, 52, 57, 93, 99,
   147, 153–54, 157, 186
*Louisville Courier*, 109, 158, 164
*Louisville Daily Democrat*, 83–84, 220*n*58
*Louisville Journal*, 73, 83, 157, 159, 161–65
Louisville, Ky., 47, 53, 83, 87, 142, 147,
   156–58, 163–64, 169, 258*n*6
Lowe, Enoch Louis, 83, 85, 107
Lubboch, John, 229*n*17
Lubboch, Thomas, 154, 229*n*17
Luckett, James, 110

Luckett, Philip Nolan, 117, 120, 229*n*17

Lynchburg, Va., 47, 58, 106, 134

Lynnville (Lehigh County), Pa., 250*n*7, 250*n*7

Lyon, Hennington, 234*n*40

Lyons, James, 234*n*40

Macon, Ga., 41

Maddox, James, 182

Magoffin, Beriah, 147, 156–59, 162, 165–66, 244*n*3

Maltby, Henry, 229*n*21

Maltese cross, 9

Malone, P. A., 246*n*33

Manifest Destiny, 8, 18, 39, 188

Manning (ex-Gov. S.C.), 22

Mansfield, Joseph K., 70

Marion, Ohio, 158

Marshall, Ed, 48

Marshall, Humphrey, 164

Marshall, Tex., 34–35, 45, 50, 53, 58, 59, 68, 71, 74, 75, 77, 148, 186, 258*n*5

Marshall Theatre (Richmond), 30

Martin, Hiram, 252*n*25

Martin, Patrick Charles, 177, 252*n*28

Maryland, 1, 45, 47, 80, 83, 84, 86, 95, 100–103, 177–78, 198*n*51, 239*n*22; attempted secession of, 102–6, 133–34, 142–45, 236*n*37; First Light Division of Volunteers, 144; Maryland militia, 80, 143–45, 239*n*22; Perryville militia, 111; Spesutia Rangers, 80, 111

Maryland Second Congressional District, 80

Marysville, Calif., 129

Mason, John Murray, 14

Mason-Dixon Line, 83

Masons. *See* Freemasons

Matamoros, Mexico, 212*n*7

Mathews, John, 182

Maximilian, Ferdinand, 189, 259*n*17

Mazzini, Guiseppe, 2, 176–77, 188, 252*n*27

McAlpin, A. J., 52

McClellan, George B., 173, 244*n*3

McCortle, H. C., 246*n*33

McCulloch, Ben, 22, 36, 42, 128–29, 134, 217*n*30, 230*n*40; as Confederate officer, 149, 151–52, 154–55, 185, 242*n*49, 257*n*1; as KGC army leader, 120–24, 230*n*36, 242*n*50; as KGC emissary, 53, 57–58, 75, 81–82, 114; threatens Washington, 104, 109, 134, 236*n*40, 236*n*41

McCulloch, Henry, 82, 123, 149

McCullough, John, 182

McGibbony, Augustus, 52

McLeod, Hugh, 12, 13, 167

McMahon, John V. L., 85, 109, 133, 142, 219*n*46

McMaster, James, 249*n*3

McQueen, John, 117

Medill, Joseph, 102

*Memphis Avalanche*, 61

*Memphis Daily Appeal*, 148

Memphis, Tenn., 40, 47, 48, 52, 61, 82, 176, 199*n*1, 240*n*31

Mexican War, 34, 43, 45, 80, 117, 127, 162

Mexico, 4, 11, 16, 18, 20–21, 23, 29, 32–33, 36, 80, 153, 186–88, 198*n*42, 256*n*58, 259*n*17; Conservative Party of, 19–20, 32, 60, 188, 204–5*n*25; Expansionist target, 1, 12–15, 18, 32–28, 41–42, 49, 54, 64, 71, 73, 87, 108, 124, 127, 130, 142, 152, 188, 204*n*13, 207*n*67, 258*n*12, 243*n*63; KGC's planned intervention in, 23, 26, 36–41, 47, 49, 54–55, 60–61, 63–64, 71, 163, 165, 187; Liberal Party of, 18, 19, 38–40, 60, 64, 153, 188, 200*n*14

Mexico City, 12, 19, 32, 40, 60, 142

Military clubs, 79–81

Milledgeville, Ga., convention, 81, 217*n*28

Miller, Cryll, 201*n*42

Milligan, Lambdin P., 172, 249*n*3

Minute Men, 4, 60, 77–79, 87, 96–98, 101, 127, 189, 215*n*12, 218*n*41

Miramón, Miguel, 18, 32, 38, 60

Mississippi, 10–14, 33, 34, 35, 48, 51, 59, 66, 69, 76, 79, 93, 98–99, 106, 128, 140, 146, 186, 197*n*40

Mississippi militia, 34, 140; First Mississippi Rifles, 34, 43; Second Mississippi Rifles, 127

Missouri, 19, 37, 48, 129, 171, 173, 175, 252*n*21

Missouri Compromise, 15, 108

Mobile, Ala., 45, 46, 50, 51, 134

*Mobile Tribune*, 57

Mohrsville (Berks County), Pa., 250*n*7

Montague, Robert, 136, 139

Montgomery, Ala., 29, 51, 53, 60, 75, 104, 119, 125, 134, 140, 142, 150–53

*Montgomery Advertiser*, 94, 110

Montgomery County, Va., 137

Montgomery, W. W., 125

Montreal, Canada, 176

Moore, Thomas Overton, 153

Morehead, James, 164

Morgan, John Hunt, 168–69, 173, 249*n*58

Morris, John D., 162, 246*n*27

Morton, Oliver, 108

Mosby, John Singleton, 177, 183, 256*nn*57–58

Mosby's Rangers, 177–78, 183, 256*nn*57–58

Mudd, Samuel, 177

*Murfreesboro Citizen*, 53, 50, 77, 201*n*36

Napoleon, Ark., 127, 150, 213*n*1

*Nashville Intelligencer*, 103

*Nashville Republican Banner*, 62

Nashville, Tenn., 101, 166

National Rifles, 105–6

National Volunteers, 84, 189, 218*nn*41–44; in Baltimore, 84–85, 102, 107–9, 133, 142; in New York, 108; in Washington, 85–86, 105–7

Nebraska, 41

Nelson, Allison, 229*n*21

Nelson, William, 160–62, 166, 229*n*21

Neutrality laws, 4, 14, 23, 30, 56 198*n*42

New Albany, Ind., 169

New Mexico, 154

*New Orleans As It Was*, 258*n*9

*New Orleans Evening Picayune*, 43

New Orleans, La., 6, 11, 33–34, 40, 42–45, 47–50, 52, 60, 84, 123, 129, 153, 157, 186, 207*n*65, 207*n*67, 208–9*n*9

*New Orleans True Delta*, 43, 99

New York (city), N.Y., 8, 10, 31, 41, 76, 80, 81, 83, 91, 101, 107, 172–73, 175–76, 178, 183, 194*n*12, 254*n*34

New York (state), 110, 142

*New York Daily News*, 175

*New York Herald*, 42, 61, 160, 166

*New York Times*, 186–87

*New York Tribune*, 4, 95, 177, 200–201*n*24

Newcomb, James, 115, 120, 122–26, 167, 189, 231*n*49

Newport, Ky., Barracks, 158

Nicaragua, 12–14, 17

*Norfolk Day Book*, 61, 76

Norfolk Grays, 68, 80

Norfolk Military Academy, 68

Norfolk Minute Men, 96

Norfolk Navy Yard. *See* Gosport Naval Yard

*Norfolk Southern Argus*, 39–40, 69

Norfolk, Va., 40, 41, 45, 47, 52, 61, 69, 131, 138, 257*n*4

Norris, Charles, 96

North Carolina, 6, 10, 47, 49, 60, 69, 90, 97–99, 107, 147, 208*n*5

*North Carolina Standard* (Raleigh), 57

North Texan, 73

Northern prison camps, 173–75, 177

Northwest Confederacy, 175–76, 179

Nuevo León Province, Mexico, 19–20, 34,

Ohio, 37, 103, 168–69, 175

Ohio State Penitentiary, 169

O'Laughlen, Michael, 17, 145, 176–77, 180, 254*n*39

O'Laughlen, William, 17, 180, 252*n*24, 254*n*39
Old Soldier Home (Washington, D.C.), 177–78
Orange County Courthouse, Va., 183
Order of American Knights, 171–74, 179, 183, 249*n*3, 251*n*16, 256–57*n*63. *See also* Sons of Liberty
Order of the Lone Star, 4, 10–15, 28, 35, 36, 97, 188, 197*n*33, 197*n*34, 197*n*36, 197*n*38, 212*n*8
Oregon, 87, 126, 130, 184
O'Sullivan John, 8, 197*n*34
Owens County, Ky., 166

Pacific Republic, 129–31, 233*n*15
Paducah, Ky., 160–61, 166, 247*n*43
Paramilitary organizations, 84, 87, 95–99, 104–6, 111, 127–28, 137–38, 168–69
Paris (France), 45, 254*n*37
Paris, Tenn., 34
Park, J. E. (Dr.), 231*n*50
Parker, Edward G., 239*n*20
Parker, William, 137–38
Parr, David Preston, 180, 255*n*43
Paschal, George Washington, 65–67, 104, 119, 125, 189
Paschal, Isaiah A., 119
Pate, Henry Clay, 31,
Payne, Louis (alias for Lewis Powell), 255*n*44
Penn, Alfred, E., 252*n*26
Pensacola, Fla., 53
Perrymansville, Md., 111, 227*n*41
Personal Liberty Laws, 15, 92–93
Petersburg, Va., 6, 41, 134
Pettus, John, 66, 76, 98, 140, 221*n*6
Philadelphia, Pa., 101, 110, 112
Philadelphia, Wilmington and Baltimore Railroad, 106–7, 111–12, 142
Phillips, Ark., County Guards, 150, 221*n*8, 232*n*6

Phrenology, 7
Pickens, Francis, 35, 75, 78, 91, 96, 136
Pickett, John T., 152–53, 188, 243*n*63
Pierce, Franklin, 14, 197*n*34, 250*n*8
Pike, Albert, 128–39, 233*n*10
Pike, James, 37, 128–29
Pillow, Gideon, 81, 145–47, 166, 217*n*28
Pinkerton agents, 107, 109–12, 227*n*47
Pinkerton, Allan, 107, 109–12
Pittsburgh, Pa., 93–94, 113, 117
Polk, Leonidas, 251*n*14
Port Tobacco, Md., 178
Portsmouth (Scioto County), Ohio, 8
Potomac River, 102, 143, 178, 183, 238*n*67
Potosi, Mexico, 29
Powell, Lewis, 177, 179, 180–81, 252*n*28, 255*nn*43–44
Prentice, George, 83, 158–59, 163–64, 189
Preston, William Ballard, 137
Price, Sterling, 171–72, 257–58*n*5
Pryor, Charles, 58–59, 67, 201*n*42
Pryor, Roger, 30
Pulaski, Tenn., 259*n*19

Queen, William, 177
Quitman expedition (to Cuba), 13–14, 103, 127, 153, 189, 198*nn*41–43
Quitman, John, 12–14, 35, 43, 103, 153, 97–198 *n*40, 198*nn*41–43

Rainey, W. H., 43
Raleigh KGC Convention, 43, 46, 49–53, 83, 188
Raleigh, N.C., 45, 46, 49–53, 102
*Raleigh Press*, 51, 207*n*61
Reading (Berks County), Pa., 172
Reagan, John, 70–71, 213*n*33, 238*n*3
Rector, Henry, 127, 147, 232*n*6
Redwood, William, 154
Refugio County, Tex., 154
Relay, Md., 144
Republic of the Rio Grande, 20

Republican Party, 15, 18–19, 28, 55, 65, 67, 82, 83, 102, 107, 108, 109, 259*n*18. *See also* Black Republicans

Rhett, Robert Barnwell, 29, 47, 49, 75, 78, 82

Richardson (Va. Adj. Gen.), 96

Richardson, Samuel J., 45, 49, 53, 58, 68, 149, 208*n*2

Richmond Blues, 1

*Richmond Enquirer,* 95, 96, 132, 134

Richmond Grays, 30

Richmond Light Infantry Blues, 132–35

Richmond, Va., 1, 3, 12, 17, 30, 61, 83, 95, 102, 134–35, 144, 145, 151, 166, 177–80, 183–85, 236*n*40

Richmond Whig, 55

Richmond's Dramatic Star Company, 1

Ricketts, E. D., 246*n*33

Ridge, John Rollins, 129, 235*n*27

Rio Grande River, 37, 41, 42, 61, 63

Rio Nueces River, 56

Robbins, W. D., 47, 48

Roberts, Oran Milo, 70–71, 113–14, 117–19, 124

Robertson, Capt., 162

Robertson, G. W., 164–65

Robertson, John C., 114, 117, 228*n*8, 229*n*17

Robertson, John C. (Mrs.), 228*n*8

Robespierre, 67

Rock Island, Ill. (prison camp), 175

Rome (Italy), 21

Rosencrans, William, 169

Ross, John, 128–29

Ross, Lawrence Sullivan, 36

Rosseau, Lovell, 161

Ruffin, Edmund, 22, 30, 220*n*52

Rusk (Rusk County), Tex., 40, 41

Russell, Charles A., 147–48, 150, 229*n*17, 242*n*53

Russell County, Va., 6, 7

Russell, William, 152–53

Russellville, Ky., 157, 245*n*7

Russia, 8

Rust, Albert, 232*n*5

Saint-Domingue, 67

Sampson (New York police detective), 227*n*42

San Antonio Guards, 80, 121, 216*n*16

*San Antonio Herald,* 124

San Antonio, Tex., 41, 57, 64, 74, 75, 80, 114, 120–24, 149, 151, 214*n*52, 230*n*40, 231*n*49

San Francisco, Calif., 11, 129, 174; plot to seize military installation, 130–31, 139, 234*n*20

*San Francisco Daily Evening Bulletin,* 20–21

*San Francisco Press,* 130

Sanders, George, 8, 176, 197*n*34, 252*n*27

Sanford, A., 117, 238*n*67

Sanford, John, 117

Savannah, Ga., 98

Schaeffer, Francis, 105–6, 226*n*21

*Scientific Artisan,* 9–10

Scioto County, Ohio, 8, 9

Scott, John, 137

Scott, Nathaniel J., 40, 41, 47, 48, 53, 55

Scott, T. Parkin, 239*n*22

Scott, Walter (Sir), 1

Scott, Winfield, 12, 70, 91–93, 101, 103, 107, 111–12, 120, 122

Secession (southern), 4, 28–29, 54–55, 74, 75, 80–82, 84–85, 89, 91–93, 98, 102–4, 109–28, 131–39, 142–45, 157–62, 167, 187–90

Secret Societies (general), 8–9, 101–2, 107–8, 110, 220*n*58, 257*n*66, 259*n*14

Seddon, James, 227*n*42, 252*n*30

Selma, Ala., 41

Semmes, Paul Jones, 5, 51–52, 81, 146, 155, 209*n*15

Semmes, Raphael, 52

Semple (KGC Surgeon), 40

Seward, Frederick, 111

Seward, William, 24, 107, 108, 111–12, 179, 183

Shenandoah Valley, Va., 237n59

Sheridan, Phillip, 177

Sherman, Tex., 73

Sherman, William, 206–7n58

Shiel, George Knox, 256–57n63

Shinglee, J. A., 53

Ship Island, Miss., 93, 98–99

Silver War (ship), 93

Simms, William Gilmore, 78

Simpson County, Ky., 157

Sims, Bart, 36

Slaughter, James S., 30, 62

Slave code, 29, 49–50

Slave insurrections, 13, 14, 54, 64, 67, 73, 78

Slave trade. See African slave trade

Slaveholder's Conspiracy. See Conspiracy, southern slaveholder's

Slavery, 4, 12, 24, 41, 49, 54–55, 64, 65, 72–73, 83, 84, 108, 117, 127–28, 163, 187, 201n28, 205n40

Slidell, John, 14

Sloan (Capt.), 162

Smith County, Tex., 35, 41, 115, 149, 258n6

Smithville Guards, 97–98

Smithville, N.C., 97

Sonora Province, Mexico, 20, 32, 38, 40, 142

Sons of Liberty, 174–76

Soule, Pierre, 11, 197n34

South America, 29

South Carolina, 35, 48, 59, 75, 78–79, 80–82, 90–94, 96, 104, 108–9, 117, 136, 150, 217n30

Southern Commercial Convention, 29

Southern fire-eaters, 28–30, 90

Southern governors, 3, 41, 55, 62, 66, 69, 71, 74, 188–89

Southern Guard, 81

Southern Manifesto, 95

Southern rights, 1, 4, 14, 54–55, 71, 72, 74, 79, 83, 116, 135, 137–39

Southern Rights Associations, 10, 13, 28, 29, 196n20

Southern Rights Party, 13

Spain, 13–14, 18, 21, 64, 69

Spangler, Edman, 180, 182

Spangler, Isaac, 52, 54, 59, 65

Sparta, Tenn., 168

Speed, Joshua, 87, 160–61

Spesutia Rangers, 80, 111, 224n41

Sprague, John, 114

Springfield, Ill., 106, 175, 221n6

Springfield, Mass., 76

St. Louis, Mo., 47, 101, 171, 175

St. Mary's County, Md., 256n57

St. Vincent's Church (Baltimore), 17

Stanton, Edward, 134, 186, 254n34

Star of the West, 96, 223n43

Starke, W. W., 43–44

States'-rights Democrats, 59, 83, 86, 107, 130. See also Southern rights

Staunton, Va., 83, 137–38

Steel, Jno. H., 53

Steel, Samuel, 254n39

Steuart (Stewart), George, 144

Stevens, Ambrose, 252n27

Stewart, Richard, 183

Stidger, Felix, 172

Stinson, William, 172

Stone, Charles, 105–6

Stones River, Battle of. See Battle of Stones River

Stoughton, Edwin Henry, 177

Street, Samuel K. J., 17, 180, 254n39

Stump, Herman, 144, 240n24

Sulphur Springs, Tex., 41

Sumner, Edwin, 131

Surratt, George, 183

Suratt, Isaac, 181, 255n47

Surratt, John Harrison, 177–78, 180–81, 183, 253n32

Tammany Hall, 10

Tamaulipas Province, Mexico, 32, 38

Tayloe, John VI, 183, 256n56

Taylor, James H. R., 53, 146, 185, 241n33

Taylor, Marion Dekalb, 116

Teel, Trevarian, 121, 154

Tehuantepec, Mexico, 29

Temperance Hall, Washington, D.C., 86

Temple, W. B., 40, 47

Templeton, Charles, 187, 258n12

Tennessee, 12, 33, 35, 48, 62–63, 65, 129, 145–47, 160, 164, 217n28, 238n65

Texas, 1, 12, 15, 21, 31, 33–34, 36, 39, 42, 47, 50, 55, 58–61, 63–75, 82, 90, 93, 103–4, 113, 116–17, 113–26, 142, 148, 150, 159, 181, 189–90; addresses to, 119–20; capitulation of U. S. Army in, 120–23, 242n50; East Texas, 64, 67–68, 120–21, 149; fires in, 58–59; KGC Council of War in, 69–71; KGC State Convention, 124; legislature, 115–16, 125, 134; secession of, 141–42, 157; secession convention, 113–19, 125, 242n54

Texas Hunters, 149

Texas Rangers, 23, 36–37, 42, 69, 134, 151, 198n41, 225n16

Texas Republican, 74

Texas State Cavalry, 230n36; First Texas Mounted Rifles, 149; Second Texas Mounted Rifles, 149; W. P. Lane Rangers, 149

Thomas, E. B., 231n50

Thompson, Jacob, 22, 98, 106, 174–75, 223n43, 257n67

Thompson, Victor W., 124, 231n50

Thompson's Drugstore, Washington, D.C., 253n30

Throckmorton, James, 118–19, 125

Thurston, Stephen Decatur, 97–98

Tiger Guards, 183

Tilghman, Lloyd, 161

Tillery, R. C., 23–24, 47, 208n5

Tillery, Samuel H., 47, 48, 208n2, 208n7

Tolar (Toler), William H., 23–24, 47, 201n27

Toombs, Robert, 188, 235n34

Touchman, Gasper, 152–53

Traboe, Robert, 161

Travis County, Tex., 113

Trimble, Isaac R., 143

Tucker, Joseph Randolph, 136, 173–74, 251n16

Tulane, Calif., 129

Tullahoma, Tenn., 169

Turner, William H., 85, 110

Twiggs, David, 91, 116, 120–23, 231n46

Tyler Guards, 35, 80, 203n10, 228n8

Tyler, John, 15, 86, 96, 131, 139, 219n46, 236n40

Tyler, John, Jr., 96

Tyler, Robert Charles, 5, 17, 21, 44, 47, 51–53, 133, 145–46, 155, 185, 187, 198n51, 199n1, 200n16, 240n32

Tyler, Tex., 35, 59, 68, 71, 113–14, 186, 203n10

Union Army. See Army, United States

Union Hotel (Jefferson, now Tazewell, Va.), 6

Union Leagues, 164, 189

Unionists, 78, 79, 95, 114, 116, 119, 132, 135–37, 146, 168, 259n18. See also Kentucky, Unionists

United States: Congress, 18, 32, 38, 39, 41, 42, 87, 100–102, 104, 107–8, 117, 127, 129, 157; Government of, 33–34, 87, 156, 178–79, 198n52; House Select Committee of Five, 107–9; Interior Department, 94; laws of, 83–84; neutrality laws of, 11, 14, 23, 30, 56, 198n42; Postmaster General, 95; State Department, 205n40; War Department, 22, 90–93, 95, 100, 151, 181

United States Army. See Army, United States